T0215832

Lecture Notes in Computer Science   9930

Commenced Publication in 1973
Founding and Former Series Editors:
Gerhard Goos, Juris Hartmanis, and Jan van Leeuwen

More information about this series at http://www.springer.com/series/8379

Maciej Koutny · Jörg Desel
Jetty Kleijn (Eds.)

Transactions on Petri Nets and Other Models of Concurrency XI

 Springer

Editor-in-Chief

Maciej Koutny
Newcastle University
Newcastle upon Tyne
UK

Guest Editors

Jörg Desel
FernUniversität in Hagen
Hagen
Germany

Jetty Kleijn
Leiden University
Leiden
The Netherlands

ISSN 0302-9743   ISSN 1611-3349   (electronic)
Lecture Notes in Computer Science
ISBN 978-3-662-53400-7   ISBN 978-3-662-53401-4   (eBook)
DOI 10.1007/978-3-662-53401-4

Library of Congress Control Number: 2016950374

Printed on acid-free paper

This Springer imprint is published by Springer Nature
The registered company is Springer-Verlag GmbH Berlin Heidelberg

Preface by Editor-in-Chief

The 11th Issue of LNCS *Transactions on Petri Nets and Other Models of Concurrency* (ToPNoC) contains revised and extended versions of a selection of the best papers from the workshops held at the 36th International Conference on Application and Theory of Petri Nets and Concurrency (Petri Nets 2015, Brussels, Belgium, June 22–26, 2015) and the 15th International Conference on Application of Concurrency to System Design (ACSD 2015, Brussels, Belgium, June 22–26, 2015). It also contains one paper submitted directly to ToPNoC.

I would like to thank the two guest editors of this special issue: Jörg Desel and Jetty Kleijn. Moreover, I would like to thank all the authors, reviewers, and organizers of the Petri Nets 2015 and ACSD 2015 satellite workshops, without whom this issue of ToPNoC would not have been possible.

July 2016   Maciej Koutny

LNCS Transactions on Petri Nets and Other Models of Concurrency: Aims and Scope

ToPNoC aims to publish papers from all areas of Petri nets and other models of concurrency ranging from theoretical work to tool support and industrial applications. The foundations of Petri nets were laid by the pioneering work of Carl Adam Petri and his colleagues in the early 1960s. Since then, a huge volume of material has been developed and published in journals and books as well as presented at workshops and conferences.

The annual International Conference on Application and Theory of Petri Nets and Concurrency started in 1980. The International Petri Net Bibliography maintained by the Petri Net Newsletter contains over 10,000 entries, and the International Petri Net Mailing List has close to 2,000 subscribers. For more information on the International Petri Net community, see: http://www.informatik.uni-hamburg.de/TGI/PetriNets/

All issues of ToPNoC are LNCS volumes. Hence they appear in all main libraries and are also accessible on SpringerLink (electronically). It is possible to subscribe to ToPNoC without subscribing to the rest of the LNCS series.

ToPNoC contains:

- Revised versions of a selection of the best papers from workshops and tutorials concerned with Petri nets and concurrency
- Special issues related to particular subareas (similar to those published in the *Advances in Petri Nets* series)
- Other papers invited for publication in ToPNoC
- Papers submitted directly to ToPNoC by their authors

Like all other journals, ToPNoC has an Editorial Board, which is responsible for the quality of the journal. The members of the board assist in the reviewing of papers submitted or invited for publication in ToPNoC. Moreover, they may make recommendations concerning collections of papers for special issues. The Editorial Board consists of prominent researchers within the Petri net community and in related fields.

Topics

The topics covered include system design and verification using nets; analysis and synthesis, structure and behavior of nets; relationships between net theory and other approaches; causality/partial order theory of concurrency; net-based semantical, logical, and algebraic calculi; symbolic net representation (graphical or textual); computer tools for nets; experience with using nets, case studies; educational issues related to nets; higher-level net models; timed and stochastic nets; and standardization of nets.

Applications of nets to: biological systems; defence systems; e-commerce and trading; embedded systems; environmental systems; flexible manufacturing systems;

hardware structures; health and medical systems; office automation; operations research; performance evaluation; programming languages; protocols and networks; railway networks; real-time systems; supervisory control; telecommunications; cyber physical systems; and workflow.

For more information about ToPNoC see: http://www.springer.com/lncs/topnoc

Submission of Manuscripts

Manuscripts should follow LNCS formatting guidelines, and should be submitted as PDF or zipped PostScript files to ToPNoC@ncl.ac.uk. All queries should be addressed to the same e-mail address.

LNCS Transactions on Petri Nets and Other Models of Concurrency: Editorial Board

Preface by Guest Editors

This volume of ToPNoC contains revised versions of a selection of the best workshop papers presented at the 36th International Conference on Application and Theory of Petri Nets and Other Models of Concurrency (Petri Nets 2015) and the 15th International Conference on Application of Concurrency to System Design (ACSD 2015), and papers describing winning contributions from the model checking contest.

We, Jörg Desel and Jetty Kleijn, are indebted to the Program Committees of the workshops and the model checking contest and in particular to their chairs. Without their enthusiastic work, this volume would not have been possible. Many members of the Program Committees participated in reviewing the new versions of the papers selected for this issue. We asked for the strongest contributions to the following satellite events:

- ATAED 2015: Workshop on Algorithms & Theories for the Analysis of Event Data (chairs: Wil van der Aalst, Robin Bergenthum, Josep Carmona)
- PNSE 2015: International Workshop on Petri Nets and Software Engineering (chairs: Daniel Moldt, Heiko Rölke, Harald Störrle)
- Model Checking Contest @ Petri Nets 2015 (chairs: Fabrice Kordon, Didier Buchs)

The best papers of the workshops were selected in close cooperation with their chairs. The authors were invited to improve and extend their results where possible, based on the comments received before and during the workshops. The resulting revised submissions were reviewed by two referees. We followed the principle of asking for fresh reviews of the revised papers, also from referees not involved initially in the reviewing of the original workshop contributions. All papers went through the standard two-stage journal reviewing process, and eventually nine were accepted after rigorous reviewing and revising. In addition to these first nine papers, two papers were submitted directly to the editor-in-chief of the ToPNoC series and handled by him as is usual for journal submissions. The papers describing the best tools of the model checking contest were evaluated and revised based on remarks and suggestions from several reviewers. They are summarized by the introductory contribution of Fabrice Kordon et al.

The paper "Pragmatics Annotated Coloured Petri Nets for Protocol Software Generation and Verification" by Kent Inge Fagerland Simonsen, Lars M. Kristensen, and Ekkart Kindler provides a formal definition of Pragmatics Annotated Coloured Petri Nets (PA-CPN), a class of Petri nets that can automatically be transformed into protocol software. The paper, moreover, demonstrates how to exploit the structure of PA-CPNs for verification.

The paper "A Petri Net-Based Approach to Model and Analyze the Management of Cloud Applications" by Antonio Brogi, Andrea Canciani, Jacopo Soldani, and PengWei Wang extends the TOSCA standard for specifying the topology and orchestration of cloud applications to behavioral aspects of management operations and their relations with states, requirements, and capabilities. This behavior is modelled by Open Petri Nets, thus supporting automated analysis of deployment plans.

The paper "Non-Interference Notions Based on Reveals and Excludes Relations for Petri Nets" by Luca Bernardinello, Görkem Kılınç, and Lucia Pomello introduces a variety of non-interference notions for Petri nets that indicate that some internal behavior of a Petri net component cannot be inferred from its interface behavior. The notions are based on the previously known *reveals* relation (whenever a certain event occurs in a maximal occurrence net, the related one occurs, too) and a newly introduced, converse *excludes* relation.

The paper "Validating DCCP Simultaneous Feature Negotiation Procedure" by Somsak Vanit-Anunchai investigates the feature negotiation procedure of the Datagram Congestion Control Protocol in RFC 4340 using Coloured Petri Nets and state space analysis. The analysis result shows that the protocol can fail to an undesired state, which has the property that the feature values of both sides do not match and both sides are not aware of the mismatch. Simultaneous negotiation could be broken on even a simple lossless FIFO channel.

The paper "Integrating Petri Net Semantics in a Model-Driven Approach: The Renew Meta-Modeling and Transformation Framework" by David Mosteller, Lawrence Cabac, and Michael Haustermann deals with the development of modeling languages and automated generation of according tools for model-driven development on the basis of ontology-based meta-models. The approach is based on Petri nets; high-level Petri nets and low-level Petri nets in various forms can be used as target models. The RMT framework provides the generation of modeling tools and the transformation into executable and analyzable models, based on the respective Petri net semantics.

The paper "Mining Conditional Partial Order Graphs from Event Logs" by Andrey Mokhov, Josep Carmona, and Jonathan Beaumont uses Conditional Partial Order Graphs (CPOGs) for compact representation of families of partial orders for process mining. In particular, the representation problem of event logs with data is addressed. The paper provides algorithms for extracting both the control flow and the relevant data parameters from a given event log. Moreover, it shows how CPOGs can be used for efficient and effective visualization of the obtained results, which also can be used to reveal the hidden interplay between the control and data flows of a process.

The paper "Conditions for Petri Net Solvable Binary Words" by Kamila Barylska, Eike Best, Evgeny Erofeev, Łukasz Mikulski, and Marcin Piątkowski studies finite words with two letters that can be viewed as behavioral descriptions of place/transition Petri nets, which necessarily neither exhibit concurrency nor choices and possess only two transitions. Two conjectures providing different characterizations of this class of words are motivated and proposed. Several results are described, which amount to a partial proof of these conjectures.

The paper "Self-Tracking Reloaded: Applying Process Mining to Personalized Health Care from Labeled Sensor Data" by Timo Sztyler, Josep Carmona, Johanna Völker, and Heiner Stuckenschmidt provides ideas on how process-mining techniques can be used as a fine-grained evolution of traditional self-tracking, applied for personalized health care and based on daily live data recorded on smart devices. These ideas are applied to data of a set of people, yielding interesting conclusions and challenges.

The paper "A Method for Assessing Parameter Impact on Control-Flow Discovery Algorithms" by Joel Ribeiro and Josep Carmona tackles the problem of identifying parameters in control-flow discovery algorithms that are important for the applicability of the algorithm to a given log, according to a given quality metric. The suggested solution is based on sensitivity analysis. The paper also presents a first, promising evaluation of this approach.

The paper "Negotiations and Petri Nets" by Jörg Desel and Javier Esparza was originally a contribution to the PNSE 2015 workshop and suggested for this issue by the workshop chairs. Since one of the authors, Jörg Desel, is involved as a guest editor of this issue, it was submitted directly to the editor-in-chief and handled by him independently. This paper studies the relation between negotiations, a previously introduced model of concurrency with multi-party negotiation atoms as primitive, and Petri nets. In particular, translations in either directions are considered as well as the resulting relative size of the respective models. The paper shows that sound and deterministic negotiations are closely related to live and safe free-choice Petri nets.

The paper "A Formal Framework for Diagnostic Analysis for Errors of Business Processes" by Suman Roy and A.S.M. Sajeev was submitted directly to ToPNoC through the regular submission track. This article develops a formal framework of diagnosing errors by locating their occurrence nodes in business process models at the level of sub-processes and swim-lanes. Graph-theoretic techniques and Petri net-based analyses are used to detect syntactic and control flow-related errors, respectively. The authors discover how error frequencies change with error depth, how they correlate with the size of the sub-processes and swim-lane interactions in the models, and how they can be predicted in terms of process metrics.

The book ends with contributions from the model checking contest, held at the 2015 Petri Net conference. In the article "MCC 2015 — The Fifth Model Checking Contest," the authors introduce the event itself, but also the algorithms and tools that were successful at the contest. Therefore, this paper can be viewed as an introduction to the remaining four papers, in which the authors of successful tools describe their respective approaches and experiences.

As guest editors, we would like to thank all authors and referees who contributed to this issue. The quality of this volume is the result of the high scientific value of their work. Moreover, we would like to acknowledge the excellent cooperation throughout the whole process that has made our work a pleasant task. We are also grateful to the Springer/ToPNoC team for the final production of this issue.

June 2016   Jörg Desel
                                                                            Jetty Kleijn

Organization of This Issue

Guest Editors

Jörg Desel   FernUniversität in Hagen, Germany
Jetty Kleijn   Leiden University, The Netherlands

Workshop Co-chairs

Wil van der Aalst   Eindhoven University of Technology, The Netherlands
Robin Bergenthum   FernUniversität in Hagen, Germany
Didier Buchs   University of Geneva, Switzerland
Josep Carmona   Universitat Politecnica de Catalunya, Spain
Fabrice Kordon   University of Paris 6, France
Daniel Moldt   University of Hamburg, Germany
Heiko Rölke   DIPF, Germany
Harald Störrle   Technical University of Denmark, Denmark

Reviewers

Wil van der Aalst
Robin Bergenthum
Luca Bernardinello
Seppe vanden Broucke
Lawrence Cabac
Piotr Chrząstowski-Wachtel
José Manuel Colom
Dirk Fahland
Jorge Figueiredo
Luciano García-Bañuelos
Wolfgang Halang
Hendrik Jan Hoogeboom
Fabrice Kordon
Agnes Koschmider

Lars Michael Kristensen
Robert Lorenz
Daniel Moldt
Andrey Mokhov
Laure Petrucci
Marta Pietkiewicz-Koutny
Pascal Poizat
Astrid Rakow
Stefan Schwoon
Natalia Sidorova
Jan Martijn van der Werf
Harro Wimmel
Karsten Wolf
Sebastian van Zelst

Contents

Pragmatics Annotated Coloured Petri Nets for Protocol Software Generation and Verification

Kent Inge Fagerland Simonsen[1,2]([✉]), Lars M. Kristensen[1], and Ekkart Kindler[2]

[1] Department of Computing, Bergen University College, Bergen, Norway
{kifs,lmkr}@hib.no
[2] DTU Compute, Technical University of Denmark, Kgs. Lyngby, Denmark
{kisi,ekki}@dtu.dk

Abstract. Pragmatics Annotated Coloured Petri Nets (PA-CPNs) are a restricted class of Coloured Petri Nets (CPNs) developed to support automated generation of protocol software. The practical application of PA-CPNs and the supporting PetriCode software tool have been discussed and evaluated in earlier papers already. The contribution of this paper is to give a formal definition of PA-CPNs, motivate the definitions, and demonstrate how the structure of PA-CPNs can be exploited for more efficient verification.

1 Introduction

Coloured Petri Nets (CPNs) [1] have been widely used for modelling and verifying protocols. Examples include application layer protocols such as IOTP and SIP, transport layer protocols such as DCCP and SCTP, and network layer protocols such as DYMO and ERDP [2,3]. Formal modelling and verification have been useful in gaining insight into the operation of the protocols and have resulted in improved protocol specifications. However, this work did not fully leverage the investment in making CPN models: the models were used for better understanding and verifying protocols, but not for actually creating implementations of these protocols from the constructed models. There exist only very limited approaches that support the automatic generation of protocol implementations from CPN models that were made for verification purposes. Existing approaches have either restricted the target platform for code generation to the Standard ML language used by the CPN Tools simulator or have considered a specific target language based on platform-specific additions to the CPN models.

This has motivated us to develop an approach and an accompanying tool called *PetriCode* that supports the automated generation of protocol software from CPN models, which was presented [3–7] and evaluated [8] in earlier work. At the core of the PetriCode approach is a slightly restricted subclass of CPNs called *Pragmatic Annotated CPNs* (*PA-CPNs*). The restrictions of PA-CPNs make the structure of the protocol system, its principals, channels, and services explicit. A key feature of PA-CPNs are *code generation pragmatics*, which are syntactical

© Springer-Verlag Berlin Heidelberg 2016
M. Koutny et al. (Eds.): ToPNoC XI, LNCS 9930, pp. 1–27, 2016.
DOI: 10.1007/978-3-662-53401-4_1

annotations to certain elements of the PA-CPNs. These pragmatics represent concepts from the domain of communication protocols and protocol software, and are used to indicate the purpose of the respective modelling element. The role of the pragmatics is to extend the CPN modelling language with domain-specific elements and make implicit knowledge of the modeller explicit in the CPN model such that it can be exploited for code generation. Even though we have used PA-CPNs in our earlier work, a precise formal definition of PA-CPNs was still missing[1].

The contribution of this paper compared to our earlier work is threefold. Firstly, motivated by the practical relevance of the net class demonstrated in earlier work, we give a formal definition of PA-CPNs here. Secondly, we discuss the concepts of PA-CPNs and how they are used for modelling and developing protocol software. Thirdly, we show that PA-CPNs are amenable to verification. Specifically, we show how the structural restrictions allow us to add *service testers* to the model of the protocol, which reduce the state space of the model. Furthermore, we discuss how the structural restrictions of PA-CPNs can be used to automatically compute a progress measure for the *sweep-line method* [10].

For the rest of the paper, we assume that the reader is familiar with the basic concepts of Petri nets and high-level Petri nets. The paper is organised as follows: Sect. 2 introduces the protocol example used throughout this paper and provides the definitions of CPNs needed for defining PA-CPNs. Section 3 gives the formal definition of PA-CPNs. Section 4 discusses the modelling concepts and process of PA-CPNs from an application perspective. Section 5 formalises control flow decomposability, which is central in generating code for the protocol services. Section 6 introduces and formalises service testers. Section 7 shows how to define progress measures for the sweep-line method based on service level and service tester modules of PA-CPNs, and presents results from an experimental evaluation. Finally, in Sect. 8, we discuss related work and, in Sect. 9, we draw the overall conclusions concerning the PetriCode approach.

2   Protocol Example and Coloured Petri Nets

The definition of PA-CPNs is based on the standard definition of hierarchical CPNs [1]. Therefore, we include the definitions and notations for hierarchical CPNs here as far as they are needed for the definition of PA-CPNs. For better understandability, we discuss an example of a hierarchical CPN first before presenting the definitions of CPNs. Note that, in this paper, we give the formal definitions for the syntax of hierarchical CPNs only; we do not give a definition of their semantics. The reason is that PA-CPNs constitute a syntactical restriction of CPNs, so that we do not need to change the semantics of CPNs at all. PA-CPNs have exactly the same semantics as ordinary hierarchical CPNs [1].

Protocol Example. As a running example, we use a protocol consisting of a *sender* and a *receiver* communicating over an unreliable channel which may both

---

[1] Note, that this paper is a revised and extended version of the workshop paper [9].

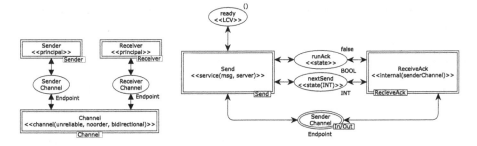

Fig. 1. The system level CPN module (left) and sender principal level module (right).

re-order and loose messages. The sender sends messages tagged with sequence numbers to the receiver and waits for an acknowledgement for each message to be returned from the receiver before sending the next message. Hence, the protocol operates according to the stop-and-wait principle.

The CPN model of this protocol consists of eight hierarchically organised *modules*. Below, we present selected modules of the CPN model[2] in order to illustrate the concepts, the definitions, and the verification techniques in this paper. Figure 1 (left) shows the top-level module consisting of three *substitution transitions* (drawn as double-bordered rectangles) representing the Sender, the Receiver, and the Channel connecting them. The two *places* SenderChannel and ReceiverChannel represent buffering communication endpoints connecting the sender and the receiver to the communication channel. The definition of the *colour set* (type) Endpoint, which determines the kind of tokens that can reside on these two places, is provided in Fig. 2. Each of the three substitution transitions has an associated *submodule* indicated by the rectangular tag positioned next to the substitution transition. These submodules define the behaviour associated with the substitution transitions. The annotations written in ⟨⟨⟩⟩ are *pragmatic* annotations, which are formally introduced in the next section when defining PA-CPNs. These pragmatics indicate the role of certain CPN model elements in the protocol; for now, they can be ignored or considered to be comments.

Figure 1 (right) shows the Sender module, which is the submodule associated with the Sender substitution transition in Fig. 1 (left). It defines the protocol for the Sender principal. The module has two substitution transitions modelling the main operations of the sender which are sending messages (substitution transition Send) and receiving acknowledgements (substitution transition receiveAck). The places ready, runAck, and nextSend are used to model the internal state of the sender. The place ready has an *initial marking* consisting of a token with the colour () (unit), which is the single value contained in the predefined colour set UNIT; this is the CPN equivalent of a "black token" in classical low-level Petri nets. This token indicates that initially the sender is ready to perform a send operation. For a place with colour set UNIT, we omit (by convention) the

---

[2] The complete model is available at http://www.petricode.org/examples/.

specification of the colour set in the graphical representation. The place runAck, which has a boolean colour set, initially contains a token with the value false indicating that the sender initially cannot receive acknowledgements. The place nextSend is used to keep track of the sequence number of the message that the sender is currently sending. The place SenderChannel is a *port place* (indicated by the double border) and is used by the module to exchange tokens with its upper level module in Fig. 1 (left). In this case, SenderChannel is an *input-output port place* as specified by the In/Out tag positioned next to the place. The place is associated with the SenderChannel *socket place* in Fig. 1 (left), which means that any token removed from (added to) this place in the Sender module will also be removed from (added to) the place SenderChannel of the Protocol module.

Figure 3 shows the Send module, which is the submodule associated with the Send substitution transition in Fig. 1 (right). This submodule models the sending of a list of messages from the sender to the receiver. The port places ready, SenderChannel, nextSend, and runAck are associated with the accordingly named socket places in the module shown in Fig. 1 (right). The list of messages to be sent is provided via the place message (at the top of the module) annotated with the driver pragmatic. This place is a *fusion place* as indicated by the rectangular tag positioned next to the place. The name inside the tag specifies the *fusion set* that the place belongs to. A fusion set is a set of places with the property that when tokens are removed from (added to) one place in the set, then the token will be removed from (added to) all members. Conceptually, all the places of a fusion set are merged into a single compound place. The place endSend (at the bottom) annotated with a driver pragmatic is also a member of a fusion set. These fusion sets are used to connect PA-CPNs to service tester modules, which we introduce later; these places are, formally, not part of the service level module or the complete protocol. The places annotated by the driver pragmatic are used by the service tester module to control the order and the parameters of the invocation of the services of the protocol during the verification of the protocol (see Sects. 6 and 7). The code generator ignores these places since, in the actual

---

```
colset Packet   = union DATA : Data + ACK : Ack;
colset EndpointId = INT;

colset ChannelPacket = record src : EndpointId *
                    dest : EndpointId * packet : Packet;

colset ChannelPackets = list ChannelPacket;

colset Endpoint = record name : EndpointId *
                inb  : ChannelPackets * outb : ChannelPackets;
```

Fig. 2. Colour set (type) declarations used in Fig. 1

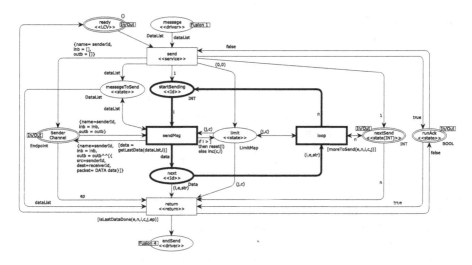

Fig. 3. The send module (service level)

```
colset LimitMap = product INT * INT;
colset Data     = product  INT * INT * STRING;
colset DataList = list Data;

val maxResend = 2;
var i, j, k, l, c, e, n :INT;      var str : STRING;
var data : Data;                    var dataList : DataList;
```

Fig. 4. Colour set (type) declarations used in Fig. 3

protocol software, the services of the protocol are invoked externally; the order in which the services are invoked and the concrete parameters are determined by the protocol's environment.

Sending a list of messages starts with the occurrence of the transition send, which places the messages to be sent on place messageToSend, puts a token on nextSend corresponding to the first sequence number, and a token on runAck to indicate that acknowledgements can now be received. The place limit is used to bound the number of retransmissions of a message. After an occurrence of transition send, transition sendMsg may occur sending a message by putting it in the output buffer modelled by the place SenderChannel. The *guard* on the transition sendMsg (by convention written in square brackets next to the transition) ensures that the data being sent matches the sequence number of the message currently being sent. If the retransmission limit is reached, the sender will stop as modelled by the transition return putting a token on place endSend. If the retransmission limit is not reached for the current message, the transition loop will put a token back on startSending such that the next message can be sent. The colour set definitions and *variables* used in Fig. 3 are provided in Fig. 4.

Formal Definitions of Hierarchical CPNs. Above, we have presented the example CPN model that will be used as a running example throughout this paper, and we have informally introduced the constructs of hierarchical CPNs in the form of modules, substitution transitions, port and socket places, and fusion places.

Next, we formally define hierarchical CPNs. These definitions are later extended when formally defining PA-CPNs. As usual, we use $N = (P, T, A)$ to denote the net structure of a Petri net, where P denotes the set of places, T the set of transitions, and A the set of arcs, respectively. Definition 1 provides the formal definition of CPN modules. In this definition, we use $Type[v]$ to denote the type of a variable v, and we use $EXPR_V$ to denote the set of expressions with free variables contained in a set of variables V. For an expression e containing a set of free variables V, we denote by $e\langle b \rangle$ the result of evaluating e in a binding b that assigns a value to each variable in V. Moreover, $Type[e]$ denotes the type of an expression e. For a non-empty set S, we use S_{MS} to denote the type corresponding to the set of all multi-sets over S.

Definition 1. *A **Coloured Petri Net Module** (Definition 6.1 in [1]) is a tuple $CPN_M = (CPN, T_{sub}, P_{port}, PT)$, such that:*

1. *$CPN = (P, T, A, \Sigma, V, C, G, E, I)$ is a CPN (Definition 4.2 in [1]) where:*
   (a) *P is a finite set of **places** and T is a finite set of **transitions** such that $P \cap T = \emptyset$.*
   (b) *$A \subseteq (P \times T) \cup (T \times P)$ is a set of directed **arcs**.*
   (c) *Σ is a finite set of non-empty **colour sets** and V is a finite set of **typed variables** such that $Type[v] \in \Sigma$ for all variables $v \in V$.*
   (d) *$C : P \to \Sigma$ is a **colour set function** assigning a colour set to each place.*
   (e) *$E : A \to EXPR_V$ is an **arc expression function** that assigns an arc expression to each arc a such that $Type[E(a)] = C(p)_{MS}$, where p is the place connected to the arc a.*
   (f) *$G : T \to EXPR_V$ is a **guard function** that assigns a guard to each transition t such that $Type[G(t)] = Bool$.*
   (g) *$I : P \to EXPR_\emptyset$ is an **initialisation function** that assigns an initialisation expression to each place p such that $Type[I(p)] = C(p)_{MS}$.*
2. *$T_{sub} \subseteq T$ is a set of **substitution transitions**.*
3. *$P_{port} \subseteq P$ is a set of **port places**.*
4. *$PT : P_{port} \to \{IN, OUT, I/O\}$ is a **port type function** that assigns a port type to each port place.*

Socket places of a CPN are not defined explicitly in the above definition, since that information can be derived from the information available in a CPN: if a place has an arc connecting it with a substitution transition, it is a socket place of this transition. For a substitution transition t, the set of its socket places is denoted by $P_{sock}(t)$. Furthermore, $ST(t)$ denotes a mapping that maps each socket place p into its type, i.e., $ST(t)(p) = \mathsf{IN}$ if p is an input socket, $ST(t)(p) = \mathsf{OUT}$ if p is an output socket, and $ST(t)(p) = \mathsf{I/O}$ if p is an input/output socket.

Technically, the arc expression function $E(a)$ is defined for arcs $a \in A$ of the CPN only. For convenience, however, we assume that $E(a) = empty$, whenever $a \notin A$, where the expression $empty$ evaluates to the empty multiset of tokens.

A hierarchical CPN consists of a set of disjoint CPN modules, a submodule function assigning a (sub)module to each substitution transition, and a port-socket relation that associates port places in a submodule to the socket places of its upper layer module. Furthermore, port and socket places can only be associated with each other, if they have the same colour set and the same initial marking. Definition 2 formalises these requirements where T_{sub} denotes the union of all substitution transitions in the modules of the hierarchical CPN.

Definition 2. *A **hierarchical Coloured Petri Net** (Definition 6.2 in [1]) is a four-tuple $CPN_H = (S, SM, PS, FS)$ where:*

1. *S is a finite set of **modules**. Each module is a **Coloured Petri Net Module** $s = ((P^s, T^s, A^s, \Sigma^s, V^s, C^s, G^s, E^s, I^s), T^s_{sub}, P^s_{port}, PT^s)$. It is required that $(P^{s_1} \cup T^{s_1}) \cap (P^{s_2} \cup T^{s_2}) = \emptyset$ for all $s_1, s_2 \in S$ with $s_1 \neq s_2$.*
2. *$SM : T_{sub} \to S$ is a **submodule function** that assigns a **submodule** to each substitution transition. It is required that the module hierarchy (see below) is acyclic.*
3. *PS is a **port–socket relation function** that assigns a **port–socket relation** $PS(t) \subseteq P_{sock}(t) \times P^{SM(t)}_{port}$ to each substitution transition t. It is required that $ST(t)(p) = PT(p')$, $C(p) = C(p')$, and $I(p)\langle\rangle = I(p')\langle\rangle$ for all $(p, p') \in PS(t)$ and all $t \in T_{sub}$.*
4. *$FS \subseteq 2^P$ is a set of non-empty and disjoint **fusion sets** such that $C(p) = C(p')$ and $I(p)\langle\rangle = I(p')\langle\rangle$ for all $p, p' \in fs$ and all $fs \in FS$.*

The module hierarchy of a hierarchical CPN model is a directed graph with a node for each module and an arc leading from one module to another module if the latter module is a submodule of one of the substitution transitions of the former module. The module hierarchy is required to be acyclic and the root nodes of the module hierarchy are referred to as *prime modules*.

3 Pragmatic Annotated CPNs

PA-CPNs mandate a particular structure of the CPN models and allow the CPN elements to be annotated with additional *pragmatics*. In a PA-CPN, the modules of the CPN model are required to be organised into three levels referred to as the *protocol system level*, the *principal level*, and the *service level*. We have seen examples for modules on each of these levels in Sect. 2 already.

In a PA-CPN, it is required that there exists exactly one prime module. This prime module represents the protocol system level. The Protocol module shown in Fig. 1 (left) comprises the protocol system level of the PA-CPN model of our example protocol; it specifies the protocol principals in the system and the channels connecting them. The substitution transitions representing principals are specified using the principal pragmatic, and the substitution transitions representing channels are specified using the channel pragmatic. As mentioned already, all pragmatics annotations of a CPN are included between guillemets: ⟨⟨⟩⟩. Some of the pragmatics can have additional attributes or parameters, which give more detailed information. In our example of Fig. 1 (left), the channel pragmatic has attributes, which specify that the communication channel is bidirectional, unreliable, and does not preserve the order of messages.

On the principal level, there is one module for each principal of the protocol as defined on the protocol system level. Our example protocol has two modules at the principal level: one for the sender and one for the receiver. Figure 1 (right) shows the principal level module for the sender. A principal level module models the services that the principal is providing, and the internal states and life-cycle of the respective principal. For the sender in our example, there are two services: send and receiveAck. Substitution transitions representing services that can be externally invoked are specified using the service pragmatic, whereas services that are to be invoked only internally are specified using the internal pragmatic. The service level modules model the behaviour of the individual services of the principals. The module shown in Fig. 3 is an example of a module at the service level modelling the send service provided by the sender.

We formally define PA-CPNs as a tuple consisting of a hierarchical CPN, a protocol system module (PSM), a set of principal level modules (PLMs), a set of service level modules (SLMs), a set of channel modules (CHMs), and a structural pragmatics mapping (SP) that maps substitution transitions into structural pragmatics and capturing the annotation of the substitution transitions.

Definition 3. *A **Pragmatics Annotated Coloured Petri Net** (PA-CPN) is a tuple $CPN_{PA} = (CPN_H, PSM, PLM, SLM, CHM, SP)$, where:*

1. $CPN_H = (S, SM, PS, FS)$ *is a hierarchical CPN with $PSM \in S$ being a **protocol system module** (Definition 4) and the only prime module of CPN_H.*
2. $PLM \subseteq S$ *is a set of **principal level modules** (Definition 5); $SLM \subseteq S$ is a set of **service level modules** (Definition 6) and $CHM \subseteq S$ is a set of **channel modules** s.t $\{\{PSM\}, PLM, SLM, CHM\}$ constitute a partitioning of S.*
3. $SP : T_{sub} \rightarrow \{\texttt{principal}, \texttt{service}, \texttt{internal}, \texttt{channel}\}$ *is a **structural pragmatics mapping** such that:*
   (a) Substitution transitions with ⟨⟨principal⟩⟩ have an associated principal level module: $\forall t \in T_{sub} : SP(t) = \texttt{principal} \Rightarrow SM(t) \in PLM$.
   (b) Substitution transitions with ⟨⟨service⟩⟩ or ⟨⟨internal⟩⟩ are associated with a service level module:
   $\forall t \in T_{sub} : SP(t) \in \{\texttt{service}, \texttt{internal}\} \Rightarrow SM(t) \in SLM$.
   (c) Substitution transitions with ⟨⟨channel⟩⟩ are associated with a channel module: $\forall t \in T_{sub} : SP(t) = \texttt{channel} \Rightarrow SM(t) \in CHM$.

It should be noted that channel modules do not play a role in the code generation; they constitute a CPN model artifact used to connect the principals for verification purposes. Therefore, we do not impose any specific requirements on the internal structure of channel modules. The behaviour of the channel module must match the characteristics specified by the attributes of the `channel` pragmatics, though. But this is not part of the formal definition of PA-CPNs.

Protocol System Module (PSM). The module shown in Fig. 1 (left) comprises the protocol system level of the example PA-CPN model. It specifies the two protocol principals in the system and the channels connecting them. The substitution transitions representing principals are specified using the `principal` pragmatic, and the substitution transitions representing channels are specified using the `channel` pragmatic. The PSM module is defined as a tuple consisting of a CPN module and a pragmatic mapping *PM* that associates a pragmatic with each substitution transition. The requirement on a protocol system module is that all substitution transitions are annotated with either a `principal` or a `channel` pragmatic. Furthermore, two substitution transitions representing principals cannot be directly connected via a place: there must be a substitution transition representing a channel in between reflecting that principals can communicate via channels only.

Definition 4. *A* **Protocol System Module** *of a PA-CPN with a structural pragmatics mapping SP is a tuple* $CPN_{PSM} = (CPN^{PSM}, PM)$, *where:*

1. $CPN^{PSM} = ((P^{PSM}, T^{PSM}, A^{PSM}, \Sigma^{PSM}, V^{PSM}, C^{PSM}, G^{PSM}, E^{PSM}, I^{PSM}), T^{PSM}_{sub}, P^{PSM}_{port}, PT^{PSM})$ *is a CPN module such that all transitions are substitution transitions:* $T^{PSM} = T^{PSM}_{sub}$.
2. $PM : T^{PSM}_{sub} \to \{\texttt{principal}, \texttt{channel}\}$ *is a* **pragmatics mapping** *s.t.:*
   (a) *All substitution transitions are annotated with either a* `principal` *or* `channel` *pragmatic:* $\forall t \in T^{PSM}_{sub} : PM(t) \in \{\texttt{principal}, \texttt{channel}\}$.
   (b) *The pragmatics mapping PM must coincide with the structural pragmatic mapping SP of PA-CPN:* $\forall t \in T^{PSM}_{sub} : PM(t) = SP(t)$.
   (c) *All places are connected to at most one substitution transition with* $\langle\!\langle\texttt{principal}\rangle\!\rangle$ *and at most one substitution transition with* $\langle\!\langle\texttt{channel}\rangle\!\rangle$: $\forall p \in P^{PSM} : \forall t_1, t_2 \in X(p) : PM(t_1) = PM(t_2) \Rightarrow t_1 = t_2.$

Principal Level Module (PLM). On the principal level, there is one module for each principal of the protocol as defined by the `principal` pragmatic on the protocol system level. Our example protocol has two modules at the principal level corresponding to the sender and the receiver. Figure 1 (right) shows the principal level module for the sender. The principal level module represents the *services* that the principal is providing, and the *internal state* and *life-cycle* of the principal. For the sender, there are two services as indicated by the `service` and `internal` pragmatics on send and receiveAck. The non-port places of a principal level module (places drawn without a double border) can be annotated with either a `state` or an LCV (*life-cycle variable*) pragmatic. Places annotated with a state pragmatic represent internal states of the principal. In Fig. 1 (right), there are two places with ⟨⟨state⟩⟩ used to enforce the stop-and-wait pattern when sending data messages and receiving acknowledgements. Places annotated with an LCV pragmatic represent the life-cycle of the principal and restrict the order in which services can be invoked. As an example, the place ready in Fig. 1 (right) ensures that only one message at a time is sent using the send service.

A principal level module is defined as a tuple consisting of a CPN module and a principal level pragmatic mapping. Each service is represented by a substitution transition which can be annotated with either a service or an internal pragmatic depending on whether the service is visible externally or not.

Definition 5. *A **Principal Level Module** of a PA-CPN is a tuple* $CPN_{PLM} = (CPN_{PLM}, T_{sub}^{PLM}, P_{port}^{PLM}, PT^{PLM}, PLP)$ *where:*

1. $CPN_{PLM} = ((P^{PLM}, T^{PLM}, A^{PLM}, \Sigma^{PLM}, V^{PLM}, C^{PLM}, G^{PLM}, E^{PLM},$ $I^{PLM}), T_{sub}^{PLM}, P_{port}^{PLM}, PT^{PLM})$ *is a CPN module with only substitution tran-sitions:* $T^{PLM} = T_{sub}^{PLM}$.
2. $PLP : T_{sub}^{PLM} \cup P^{PLM} \backslash P_{port}^{PLM} \rightarrow \{\text{service}, \text{internal}, \text{state}, \text{LCV}\}$ *is a **principal level pragmatics mapping** satisfying:*
   (a) *All non-port places are annotated with either a* state *or a* LCV *prag-matic:* $\forall p \in P^{PLM} \backslash P_{port}^{PLM} \Rightarrow PLP(p) \in \{\text{state}, \text{LCV}\}$
   (b) *All substitution transitions are annotated with a* service *or* internal *pragmatic:* $\forall t \in T_{sub}^{PSM} : PLP(t) \in \{\text{service}, \text{internal}\}$.

It should be noted that we do not associate pragmatics with the port places as it follows from the definition of the protocol system module that a port place in a principal level module can only be associated with a socket place connected to a substitution transition with a channel pragmatic.

Service Level Module (SLM). The service level modules specify the behaviour of the respective services of the principals. They constitute the lowest level mod-ules in a PA-CPN model. In particular, there are no substitution transitions in modules at this level. The module in Fig. 3 is an example of a module at the service level. It models the behaviour of the send service in a control flow oriented manner. The control flow path, which defines the control flow of the service, is made explicit via the use of the Id pragmatics. The entry point of the service is indicated by annotating a single transition with a service prag-matic, and the exit (termination) point of the service is indicated by annotating a single transition with a return pragmatic. In addition, non-port places can be annotated with a state pragmatic to indicate that this place models a local state of the service. The driver pragmatic is used by service tester modules (see Sect. 6) to facilitate verification. The places associated with Id pragmatic determine a subnet of the module, which we call the *underlying control flow net*: it is obtained by removing all CPN annotations and considering only places with Id pragmatic and transitions connected to these places, which in Fig. 3, are indicated by places, transitions, and arcs with thick border. This control flow net must follow a certain structure so that there is a one-to-one correspondence to control flow constructs of typical programming languages. This requirement is called *control flow decomposability* and is formally defined in Sect. 5.

A service level module is defined as consisting of a CPN module without substitution transitions and with service level pragmatics as described above. In the definition, we use the notation $\exists!x \in X : p(x)$ to denote that there exists exactly one element x in a set X satisfying a predicate p.

Definition 6. *A **Service Level Module** of a PA-CPN is a tuple $CPN_{SLM} = (CPN_{SLM}, T_{sub}^{SLM}, P_{port}^{SLM}, PT^{SLM}, SLP)$ where:*

1. $CPN_{SLM} = ((P^{SLM}, T^{SLM}, A^{SLM}, \Sigma^{SLM}, V^{SLM}, C^{SLM}, G^{SLM}, E^{SLM}, I^{SLM}), T_{sub}^{SLM}, P_{port}^{SLM}, PT^{SLM})$ *is a CPN module without substitution transitions: $T_{sub}^{SLM} = \emptyset$.*

2. $SLP : T^{SLM} \cup P^{SLM} \backslash P_{port}^{SLM} \rightarrow \{\texttt{Id}, \texttt{state}, \texttt{service}, \texttt{return}, \texttt{driver}\}$ *is a **service level pragmatic mapping** satisfying:*

   (a) *Each place is either annotated with* $\texttt{Id}$, $\texttt{state}$, $\texttt{driver}$ *or is a port place:* $\forall p \in P^{SLM} \backslash P_{port}^{SLM} : SLP(p) \in \{\texttt{Id}, \texttt{state}, \texttt{driver}\}$.

   (b) *There is exactly one* $\langle\!\langle \texttt{service} \rangle\!\rangle$ *transition and one* $\langle\!\langle \texttt{return} \rangle\!\rangle$ *transition:* $\exists!t \in T^{SLM} : SLP(t) = \texttt{service}$ *and* $\exists!t \in T^{SLM} : SLP(t) = \texttt{return}$.

   (c) *All non* $\langle\!\langle \texttt{service} \rangle\!\rangle$ *transitions have exactly one* $\langle\!\langle \texttt{Id} \rangle\!\rangle$ *input place:* $\forall t \in T^{SLM}$ *such that* $SLP(t) \neq \texttt{service} : \exists!p \in P^{SLM} : (p,t) \in A^{SLM} \wedge SLP(p) = \texttt{Id}$.

   (d) *All non* $\langle\!\langle \texttt{return} \rangle\!\rangle$ *transitions have exactly one* $\langle\!\langle \texttt{Id} \rangle\!\rangle$ *output place:* $\forall t \in T^{SLM}$ *such that* $SLP(t) \neq \texttt{return} : \exists!p \in P^{SLM} : (t,p) \in A^{SLM} \wedge SLP(p) = \texttt{Id}$.

3. *For all* $t \in T^{SLM}$ *and* $p \in P^{SLM}$ *we have:*

   (a) *Transitions consume one token from their* $\langle\!\langle \texttt{Id} \rangle\!\rangle$ *input place (if any):* $(p,t) \in A^{SLM} \wedge SLP(p) = \texttt{Id} \Rightarrow |E(p,t)\langle b \rangle| = 1$ *for all bindings b of t.*

   (b) *Transitions produce one token on their* $\langle\!\langle \texttt{Id} \rangle\!\rangle$ *output place (if any):* $(t,p) \in A^{SLM} \wedge SLP(p) = \texttt{Id} \Rightarrow |E(t,p)\langle b \rangle| = 1$ *for all bindings b of t.*

   (c) *The* $\langle\!\langle \texttt{service} \rangle\!\rangle$ *and* $\langle\!\langle \texttt{return} \rangle\!\rangle$ *transitions are connected to exactly one* $\langle\!\langle \texttt{driver} \rangle\!\rangle$ *place:* $\forall t \in T^{SLM}$ *with* $SLP(t) \in \{\texttt{service}, \texttt{return}\}$ $\exists!p \in P^{SLM} : SLP(p) = \texttt{driver} \wedge ((p,t) \in A^{SLM} \vee (t,p) \in A^{SLM})$.

   (d) *A* $\langle\!\langle \texttt{driver} \rangle\!\rangle$ *place can be connected as an input place only to the* $\langle\!\langle \texttt{service} \rangle\!\rangle$ *transition and as an output place only to the* $\langle\!\langle \texttt{return} \rangle\!\rangle$ *transition:* $\forall p \in P^{SLM}, \forall t \in T^{SLM}$ *with* $SLP(p) = \texttt{driver} : ((p,t) \in A^{SLM} \Rightarrow SLP(t) = \texttt{service}) \wedge ((t,p) \in A^{SLM} \Rightarrow SLP(t) = \texttt{return})$.

   (e) *Exactly one token is produced on/consumed from* $\langle\!\langle \texttt{driver} \rangle\!\rangle$ *places:* $\forall p \in P^{SLM}, \forall t \in T^{SLM}$ *with* $SLP(p) = \texttt{driver} : ((p,t) \in A^{SLM} \Rightarrow |E(p,t)\langle b \rangle| = 1) \wedge ((t,p) \in A^{SLM} \Rightarrow |E(t,p)\langle b \rangle| = 1)$ *for all bindings b.*

4. *The underlying control flow net of CPN_{SLM} is control flow decomposable (Definitions 8 and 10).*

4   Protocol Modelling Process

In the previous sections, we have formalised the structural restrictions of CPNs and the pragmatics extensions that make them *Pragmatic Annotated CPNs* (*PA-CPNs*), where some of the restrictions on the control flow structure and the service testers will be formalized only later in Sects. 5 and 6. In order to help modellers coming up with a model meeting these requirements, we briefly discuss the choices underlying the definition of PA-CPNs and how to use the pragmatics in the modelling process.

The structural requirements of PA-CPNs have been distilled from the experience with earlier CPN models of protocols. The structure and annotations of PA-CPNs are designed to help the modeller come up with a clear model and to give clear guidelines for creating a model that – at the same time – can be used for both code generation and verification. As such, the structure of PA-CPNs should be driven by the protocol and its purpose rather than by the artifacts of Petri nets. This is, in particular, reflected by structuring the model in three layers: *protocol system module*, *principal level modules*, and *service layer modules*.

The top layer, the *protocol system module* (PSM), identifies the overall structure of the protocol, which are the *principals* of the protocol and how the principals are connected by *channels* (see Fig. 1 (left) for an example). Each principal and each channel is represented by a substitution transition with a respective annotation, and places connecting the respective principals with channels. The behaviour of each principal is represented by a *principal level module* (PLM), which identifies the *services* of the respective principal (see Fig. 1 (right) for an example) along with the states of the protocol and its life-cycle. The services are represented by substitution transitions annotated with the `service` pragmatics, the state and the life-cycle of the principal are represented by places with `state` and `LCV` pragmatics. The behaviour of each service is then modelled by a *service level module* (SLM), which is associated with the service substitution transitions on the *principal level module* (see Fig. 3 for an example). The service level module has access to the channels that the principal is connected to and the principal's state and life-cycle variables. The most prominent structure (indicated by thick arcs and thick bordered places and transitions) of the service module is the control flow structure, which is identified by the `Id` pragmatics and which needs to follow very specific rules (Sect. 5) so that it can be transformed to control flow constructs of typical programming languages in order to generate human-readable code.

Below, we give an overview of the pragmatics that are at the core of PA-CPNs, as well as their purpose and role in PA-CPNs. Note, however, that the PetriCode approach and the tool [5,6] allow adding new pragmatics. In the top-level module, the *protocol system*, there are `principal` and `channel` pragmatics which are used to annotate substitution transitions, which represent the principals and the channels of a communication protocol (see Fig. 1 (left)). The channel pragmatics can have some attributes or parameters, which define the characteristics of the channel (in our example the channels are unreliable, do not preserve the order of messages, and are bidirectional). Actually, the modules associated with the channel pragmatics are not used for code generation. Instead, the generated code will use implementations of channels from the underlying platform based on the characteristics defined by the attributes. But, for verifying the protocol with standard CPN mechanisms, we need a CPN module for each channel, which however does not have any further structural restrictions, in PA-CPNs.

For *principal level modules* there are mainly three pragmatics: service, state, and LCV. The service pragmatics indicates all services of a principal that are externally visible (i. e. part of the protocols API in the code). It annotates substitution transitions; a module associated with such a substitution transition defines the service in detail. The state pragmatics attached to places of principal level modules define the state of the protocol; these might be used and changed inside services. The LCV pragmatic (for *life-cycle variable*) annotates places that define the life-cycle of the protocol (indicating when which services can be invoked). The LCV pragmatic is similar to the state pragmatic; the main difference is that the value of places with an LCV pragmatic are typically not changed inside the service, but only when a service is started or finished (but this condition is not mandated and formalised in our definition). There is one other pragmatic called internal; it indicates a service of a principal, which is not externally visible and used only by the principal itself. Except for that, the internal pragmatic and the service pragmatic are the same.

For *service level modules*, there are three main pragmatics: service, return, and Id. The service pragmatic indicates the start transition of a service, when the service is invoked. The return pragmatic indicates the transition terminating the service. The control flow from the service transition to the Id transition is indicated by places annotated with Id pragmatics. Actually, the structure defined by these places needs to correspond to control flow constructs, which we define in Sect. 5. Note that the Id pragmatics and the return pragmatics can have expressions as parameters; indicating which value should be returned, or which alternative path in the control flow should be taken. This expression could, in principle, be derived from the CPN and its Standard ML expressions; but for easing code generation, PetriCode comes with a very simple language for that purpose, which make it easier to generate code for different target languages. At last, places in a *service level module* can have state and LCV pragmatics some of which will be port places with the same annotation on the associated socket places in the *principal level modules*. PA-CPNs and PetriCode have some additional pragmatics, which, in principle, could be derived from the net structure. But, for easing code generation for different target language, they can be explicitly added to the model. But, we do not discuss these *derived* pragmatics here. Note also that service and return transitions are attached to places with driver pragmatics. These are not part of the protocol model at all, but indicate how the services are driven by tests (discussed in Sect. 6).

Any model that meets the requirements of PA-CPNs can be used for code generation as well as for verification – irrespective of the way it was produced. The typical modelling process of protocols with PA-CPN starts at the top-level by identifying the principals of the protocol and how they are connected by channels. Then, the services of each principal are identified on the principal level, and then each service is modelled. So the general modelling direction is top-down. Of course, additional services and even additional principals could be added later, when need should be. We believe that for most protocols, the respective modules would fit on a single page and would not need any substructure. For some more complex services, additional submodule structure might be needed. In that case, the requirement would be that the flattened substructure of such a service level module meets the requirements of our formal definition. We therefore do not formalise this possibility here, as it can be considered syntactic sugar.

5   Control Flow Nets and Control Flow Decomposability

As discussed earlier, the control flow structure of a service level module, called the underlying control flow net, must correspond one-to-one to control flow constructs of programming languages. The main purpose of this requirement is to generate readable code.

In this section, we formally define the *underlying control flow net* of a service level module and its one-to-one correspondence to control flow constructs. This is achieved by inductively decomposing the control flow net into a tree of sub-blocks, each of which corresponds to a control flow construct: atomic step, sequence, choice and loop.

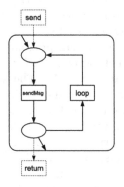

Figure 5 shows the *underlying control flow net* of the service level module from Fig. 3. All places and transitions in the rounded rectangle (representing the block border) are part of the block; an arrow from the block border to a place indicates the entry place of the block; an arrow from a place to the block border indicates the exit place of the block. The control flow net in Fig. 5 can be decomposed in a loop block, which in turn consists of an atomic block.

Fig. 5. Decomposition of the service level module in Fig. 3

First, we define *blocks*: these are Petri nets with a fixed entry and exit place.

Definition 7. *Let* $N = (P, T, A)$ *be a Petri net*, $s, e \in P$. *Then* $B = (P, T, A, s, e)$ *is called a* **block** *with* **entry** s *and* **exit** e. *The block is* **atomic**, *if* $P = \{s, e\}$, $s \neq e$, $|T| = 1$ *and for* $t \in T$, *we have* $^\bullet t = \{s\}$ *and* $t^\bullet = \{e\}$. *The block has a* **safe entry**, *if* $s \neq e$ *and* $^\bullet s = \emptyset$. *The block has a* **safe exit**, *if* $s \neq e$ *and* $e^\bullet = \emptyset$.

An atomic block consists of a single transition (see Fig. 6). For visualising blocks with safe entry and safe exit, we introduce an additional graphical notation, which is also shown in Fig. 6. A crossed out arc from within the block to the start place of that block indicates that the block itself does not return a token to the entry place (safe entry); a crossed out arc from the end place to the interior of the block indicates that the block itself does not remove a token from its exit place (safe exit).

For easing the following definitions, we introduce an additional notation: For a block B_i, we refer to its constituents by $B_i = (P_i, T_i, A_i, s_i, e_i)$ without explicitly naming them every time. The block that is underlying a service level module is determined by all the places with Id pragmatics and the transitions in their pre- and postsets. The unique transition with ⟨⟨service⟩⟩ defines the entry place, and the unique transition with ⟨⟨return⟩⟩ defines the exit place of this block; note that for technical reasons, these two transitions are not part of the block. Therefore, these transitions are shown by dashed lines in Fig. 5. Formally, the control flow net underlying a service level module is defined as:

Definition 8. *Let CPN_{SLM} be a service level module (Definition 6). The* **underlying control flow net** *of CPN_{SLM} is the block $N = (P, T, A, s, e)$ where:*

- $P = \{p \in P^{SLM} \backslash P_{port}^{SLM} \mid SLP(p) = Id\}$.
- $T = T^{SLM} \cap {}^\bullet P \cap P^\bullet$.
- $A = A^{SLM} \cap ((T \times P) \cup (P \times T))\}$.
- $s \in P$ *is the unique place such that there exists a transition $t \in T^{SLM}$ with* $(t, s) \in A^{SLM}$ *and $SLP(t) = $ service.*
- $e \in P$ *is the unique place e such that there exists a transition $t \in T^{SLM}$ with* $(e, t) \in A^{SLM}$ *and $SLP(t) = $ return.*

The control flow of the code that is being generated is obtained by decomposing the underlying control flow net of a service level module into sub-blocks representing the control flow constructs. We define the decomposition in a very general way at first, which does not yet restrict the possible control flow constructs. The decomposition into blocks, just makes sure that all parts of the block are covered by sub-blocks (item 2) and that they overlap on entry and exit places only (item 3). In a second step, the decomposition is restricted in such a way that the decomposition captures certain control flow constructs (Definition 10).

Definition 9. *Let $B = (P, T, A, s, e)$ be a block. A set of blocks $B_1, \dots, B_n$ is a* **decomposition** *of B if the following conditions hold:*

1. *The sub-blocks contain only elements from B, i. e. for each $i \in \{1, \dots, n\}$, we have $P_i \subseteq P$, $T_i \subseteq T$, and $F_i \subseteq F \cap ((P_i \times T_i) \cup (T_i \times P_i))$.*
2. *The sub-blocks contain all elements of B, i. e. $P = \bigcup_{i=1}^{n} P_i$, $T = \bigcup_{i=1}^{n} T_i$, and $F = \bigcup_{i=1}^{n} F_i$.*
3. *The inner structure of all sub-blocks are disjoint, i. e. for each $i, j \in \{1, \dots, n\}$ with $i \neq j$, we have $T_i \cap T_j = \emptyset$ and $P_i \cap P_j = \{s_i, e_i\} \cap \{s_j, e_j\}$.*

As the final step, we define when a decomposition of a block reflects some control flow construct. The definition does not only define decomposability into control flow constructs; it also defines a tree structure which reflects the control flow structure of the block; the type of each node reflects the construct. The

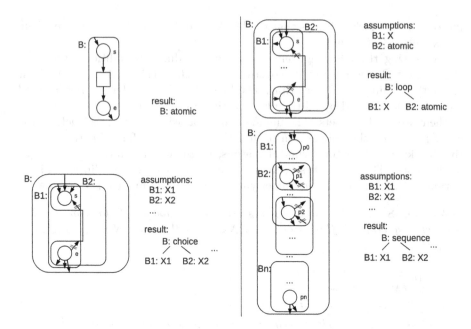

Fig. 6. Inductive definition of block trees

definition is illustrated in Fig. 6. The top right part of Fig. 6 shows the inductive definition of a loop construct: the assumptions are that two blocks $B1$ and $B2$ are identified already. $B1$ is any kind of block (represented by X) with a safe entry place s and a safe exit place e; $B2$ is an atomic block with entry place e and exit place s. Thus, block $B1$ represents the loop body, and block $B2$ the iteration. Then, the union of both blocks and entry place s and exit place e, form a block B, which is a loop consisting of the loop body $B1$ and the atomic block $B2$ for the iteration. The definitions of choices and sequences are similar. Definition 10 below formally defines the block tree as illustrated in Fig. 6.

Definition 10. *A **block tree** associated with a block is inductively defined as:*

Atomic *If B is an atomic block, then the tree with the single node **B:atomic** is a **block tree** associated with B.*

Loop *If B is a block and B_1 and B_2 is a decomposition of B, and for some X, $B_1 : X$ is a block tree associated with B_1, and $B_2 : atomic$ is a block tree associated with B_2, and if B_1 has a safe entry and a safe exit such that $s_1 = s$, $e_1 = e$, $s_2 = e$, $e_2 = s$, then the tree with root **B:loop** and the sequence of subtrees $B_1 : X$ and $B_2 : atomic$ is a **block tree** associated with B.*

Choice *If B is a block and for some n with $n \geq 2$ the set of blocks $B_1, \ldots, B_n$ is a decomposition of B, and have a safe entry and a safe exit, and $B_1 : X_1, \ldots, B_n : X_n$ for some $X_1, \ldots, X_n$ are block trees associated with $B_1, \ldots, B_n$, and if for all $i \in \{1, \ldots, n\}$: $s_i = s$ and $e_i = e$, then the tree* with top node **B:choice** with the sequence of subtrees $B_i : X_i$ is a **block tree** associated with B.

Sequence *If B is a block and for some $n \geq 2$ the set of blocks $B_1, \ldots, B_n$ is a decomposition of B, and, for some $X_1, \ldots, X_n$, the trees $B_1 : X_1, \ldots, B_n : X_n$ are block trees associated with $B_1, \ldots, B_n$, and if there exist different places $p_0, \ldots, p_n \in P$ such that $s = p_0$, $e = p_n$, and for each $i \in \{0, \ldots, n-1\}$ we have $s_i = p_i$, $e_i = p_{i+1}$, and B_i has a safe exit or B_{i+1} has a safe entry, then the tree with root **B:sequence** and the sequence of subtrees $B_i : X_i$ is a **block tree** associated with B.*

*A block for which a block tree exists is said to be **control flow decomposable**.*

Note that in order to simplify the definition of control flow decomposability, the block tree of a block is not necessarily unique according to our definition. For example, a longer sequence of atomic blocks could be decomposed in different ways. In the PetriCode tool, such ambiguities are resolved by making sequences as large as possible. Note also that for two consecutive constructs in a sequence, it should not be possible to go back from the second to the first; therefore, the above definition requires that consecutive blocks have a safe entry or a safe exit. And there are some similar requirements for loops and choices.

6   Service Testers

The service level modules constitute the active part of a PA-CPN model. The execution of a service provided by a principal starts at the transition with a `service` pragmatic. The transitions annotated with a service pragmatic typically have a number of parameters which need to be bound to values in order for the transition to occur. An example of this is the Send service transition in Fig. 3, which has the variable dataList as a parameter. This means that there often is an infinite number of bindings for a service transition. To control the execution of a PA-CPN model, we introduce the concept of *service tester modules* which represent a user invoking the services. Service testers are also exploited for verification (Sect. 7): by invoking the services in a specific order and with some fixed parameters only, they can be used to guarantee that the overall model has a finite state space. The service tester modules are connected to the rest of the PA-CPN model via driver *fusion places* belonging to *fusion sets*. Fusion sets and fusion places are standard constructs of hierarchical CPNs (see Defintion 2). A fusion set consists of a set of fusion places such that removing (adding) tokens from (to) a fusion place is reflected on the markings of all members of the fusion set.

A service tester module can invoke a service provided by the principal by adding tokens to the driver place in the preset of the service's `service` transition; and obtain the result of the service by accessing the driver place in the postset of the service's `return` transition. In addition to driver fusion places, the service testers have places with Id pragmatics, which make the control flow of the service tester explicit in a similar manner as for service level modules.

Figure 7 shows an example of a service tester module for the PA-CPN model from Sect. 2. A service tester module can have many places with Id pragmatics; but only one of them may contain a token initially (place d0 in Fig. 7).

In our example, the service tester first invokes the send service by putting a token to the driver place message of the send service (see Fig. 3). Next, the service tester invokes the receive service in the receiver principal (which has a driver place callReceive not shown in this paper). In the end, the service tester waits for both services to terminate, indicated by tokens on the driver places endReceive and endSend.

Service tester modules are formalised below. Note that we allow service testers to connect to LCV places of the principals of the protocol, so that the services can be called dependent on the state of the life-cycle of the protocol. But, the service testers are not allowed to change the marking of LCV places.

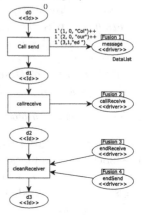

Fig. 7. Service tester module

Definition 11. *A **Service Tester Module** is a tuple* $CPN_{STM} = (CPN_{STM}, T^{STM}_{sub}, P^{STM}_{port}, PT^{STM}, TPM)$ *where:*

1. $CPN_{STM} = ((P^{STM}, T^{STM}, A^{STM}, \Sigma^{STM}, V^{STM}, C^{STM}, G^{STM}, E^{STM}, I^{STM}), T^{STM}_{sub}, P^{STM}_{port}, PT^{STM})$ *is a CPN module with no substitution transitions:* $T^{STM}_{sub} = \emptyset$.
2. $TPM : P^{STM} \rightarrow \{\texttt{Id}, \texttt{driver}, \texttt{LCV}\}$ *is a **tester pragmatic mapping**.*
3. *All transitions have exactly one* $\langle\!\langle \texttt{Id} \rangle\!\rangle$ *input place and exactly one* $\langle\!\langle \texttt{Id} \rangle\!\rangle$ *ouput place:*
   (a) $\forall t \in T^{STM} \exists! p \in P^{STM} : (p, t) \in A^{STM} \land TPM(p) = \texttt{Id}.$
   (b) $\forall t \in T^{STM} \exists! p \in P^{SLM} : (t, p) \in A^{STM} \land TPM(p) = \texttt{Id}.$
4. *In the initial marking there is a single token present on the* $\langle\!\langle \texttt{Id} \rangle\!\rangle$ *places:*
   $\sum_{\{p \in P^{STM} | TPM(p) = Id\}} |I^{STM}(p)\langle\rangle| = 1$
5. *Transitions consume one token from* $\langle\!\langle \texttt{Id} \rangle\!\rangle$ *input places and produces one token on* $\langle\!\langle \texttt{Id} \rangle\!\rangle$ *output places:*
   (a) $\forall t \in T^{STM}$ *and* $p \in P^{STM} : (p, t) \in A^{STM} \land TPM(p) = \texttt{Id} \Rightarrow |E(p, t)\langle b \rangle| = 1$ *for all bindings b of t.*
   (b) $\forall t \in T^{STM}$ *and* $p \in P^{STM} : (t, p) \in A^{STM} \land TPM(p) = \texttt{Id} \Rightarrow |E(t, p)\langle b \rangle| = 1$ *for all bindings b of t.*
6. *Places annotated with* $\langle\!\langle \texttt{LCV} \rangle\!\rangle$ *can only be connected to transitions via double arcs with identical arc expressions:*
   $\forall p \in P^{STM}, t \in T^{STM}$ *such that* $TPM(p) = \texttt{LCV} : E(t, p) = E(p, t).$
7. *The underlying control flow net of* CPN_{STM} *is control flow decomposable (Definitions 8, and 10).*

The modeller must construct the service tester modules such that they satisfy the formal requirements. Service tester modules are connected to a PA-CPN by driver places (fused to the driver places of the services) in order to control the execution of the services. We therefore define a PA-CPN equipped with service tester modules as a hierarchical CPN consisting of a set of modules that constitute a PA-CPN (Definition 3) and a set of service tester modules which are all prime modules. We require that all places belonging to the same fusion set are annotated with identical pragmatics. Furthermore, we require that fusion places are connecting the service level and service tester modules so that they correspond to the invocation of services and collecting results of service execution.

7 Verification and Experimental Results

In this section, we discuss how the sweep-line method can be applied to exhaustively explore the state space of a PA-CPN model equipped with service testers. Exhaustive state space exploration can be used to check that the protocol satisfies certain invariants, to detect unexpected deadlocks, and to check whether the states upon termination are correct, which could for example be that the sent message is identical to the received one. Here, we do not go into specific properties to be verified, but we discuss how to apply the sweep-line method to exhaustively explore the state space. In particular, we show that in addition to restricting the state space of the model and making it finite, the structure of the service testers and the structural requirements imposed by PA-CPNs can be exploited by the sweep-line method [10] to further reduce the peak memory usage during verification by automatically deriving a progress measure.

The Sweep-Line Method and Progress Expressions. The sweep-line method addresses the state explosion problem by exploiting a notion of *progress* exhibited by many systems. This notion of progress makes it possible to store only a (small) subset of all the reachable states at any given time during the state space exploration. To apply the sweep-line method, a *progress measure* must be provided for the model as formalised below, where S denotes the set of all states (markings), $\rightarrow^*$ the reachability relation on the markings of the CPN model, and $\mathcal{R}(M_0)$ denotes the states reachable from the initial marking M_0.

Definition 12. *A **progress measure** is a tuple $\mathcal{P} = (O, \sqsubseteq, \psi)$ such that O is a set of **progress values**, $\sqsubseteq$ is a total order on O, and $\psi : S \rightarrow O$ is a **progress mapping**. $\mathcal{P}$ is **monotonic** if $\forall s, s' \in \mathcal{R}(M_0) : s \rightarrow^* s' \Rightarrow \psi(s) \sqsubseteq \psi(s')$. Otherwise, P is **non-monotonic**.*

The subsets of states that need to be stored at the same time while exploring the state space are determined via a *progress value* assigned to each state, and the method explores the states in a least-progress-first order. The sweep-line method explores states with a given progress value before progressing to the states with a higher progress value. When the method proceeds to consider states with a higher progress value, all the states with a lower progress values can be discarded from memory. If it should turn out during the exploration that the system regresses (a non-monotonic progress measure), then the method will mark states at the end of such *regress edges* as *persistent* (i. e., stores them permanently in memory) in order to ensure termination of the exploration. In the presence of regression, the sweep-line method may visit the same state multiple times (for details, see [10]).

The structure of PA-CPNs and services testers can be exploited in different ways for defining progress measures. The control flow in the service modules is one source of progress as there is a natural progression from the entry point of the service towards the exit point. The life-cycle of a principal is another potential source of progress as there will often be an overall intended order in which the services are to be invoked, and this will be reflected in the life-cycle variables of the principal. Finally, the service testers are also a source of progress as they will inherently progress from the start towards the end of the test.

The progress measure for a CPN can be defined by a *progress expression*, which has places of the CPN in it as variables. The progress value of a concrete marking is then defined by evaluating the progress expression where each place takes the value of that place in that concrete marking. We will show how to define such progress expressions for a PA-CPN with service testers. First, we show how to define progress expressions for service testers and service modules based on the block tree of their underlying control flow nets. We then show how to augment a progress expression for a service level module to take into account also the $\langle\langle\texttt{driver}\rangle\rangle$ places, and finally we show how to combine the progress expressions of the individual modules to obtain a progress expression for the complete PA-CPN model with the service testers.

The basic idea is that evaluating a progress expression in a given state (marking) will result in a progress value quantifying how far the model has progressed in the given state. For the example service tester in Fig. 7, the progress expression can be defined as a place-wise sequence of expressions reflecting that the token initially on d0 moves towards place d3 as the execution of the test progresses. This can be captured by the progress expression below, where $\text{Driver}_{\text{BT}}$ denotes a block tree of the underlying control flow net of the module Driver:

$$PME(\text{Driver}_{\text{BT}}) = (|\text{d3}|, |\text{d2}|, |\text{d1}|, |\text{d0}|) \tag{1}$$

Evaluating this expression (i.e., replacing each place with its multi-set of tokens) in a state s with a token on d1 results in the progress value $(0, 0, 1, 0)$ while evaluating the expression in a state s' with a token on d2 results in the progress value $(0, 1, 0, 0)$. Two such progress values (sequences) can be compared via lexicographic ordering, meaning that the position of the elements represents their significance. In this case, s' is larger than s reflecting that s' represents a state in which the driver has progressed further than in s.

Consider now the Send service module in Fig. 3 and the underlying control flow net (highlighted with thick lines). Here, we may consider a state in which there is a token on place next to be a state in which the module has progressed further than in a state in which there is a token in place startSending – even if the service module may later regress by putting a token back on place startSending to send the next message. In this case, the progress expression becomes:

$$PME_{\mathsf{la}}(\mathsf{Send_{BT}}) = (|\mathsf{next}|, |\mathsf{startSending}|) \tag{2}$$

We can eliminate regression when going back to the start of a loop by viewing the loop-block as one unit and only record if the service level module is executing somewhere inside the loop. In this case, the progress expression becomes:

$$PME_{\mathsf{lu}}(\mathsf{Send_{BT}}) = (|\mathsf{next}| + |\mathsf{startSending}|) \tag{3}$$

The difference between Eqs. 2 and 3 lies in how loops are handled. The expression in Eq. 2 is *loop-aware* (la) as it takes the loop structure into account by treating each place within the loop as a separate element in the sequence. In contrast, Eq. 3 is *loop-unaware* (lu) as it does not explicitly record on which place the token is present - only that a token is somewhere in the loop.

We generalise the above idea by inductively defining progress measure expressions on the block tree of the underlying control flow net of service tester and service level modules. We use $a \cdot b = (a_1, \ldots, a_n, b_1, \ldots, b_m)$ to denote the concatenation of two sequences $a = (a_1, \ldots, a_n)$ and $b = (b_1, \ldots, b_m)$. Basically, we can define a progress expression for each block based on the progress expressions of its sub-blocks. The non-trivial part of this definition is that the entry and exit places can be shared among different blocks, since this is where blocks are glued together; each place should be accounted for in the progress expression exactly once and at the right position in order to avoid unnecessary regression. In the following definition, we take care of an entry or exit place in the progress expression only when it is not safe in a block; if it is safe, it is accounted for outside the block. When chaining blocks to a sequence, however, some entry and exit places might not be accounted for at all: if the exit place of some block and the entry place of the subsequent block would be a safe exit in the first and a safe entry in the subsequent block, this place would not occur in the progress measure at all; so we need to insert such places between the progress measures of such blocks. To this end, we define the following expressions: For a block B_i with exit place x and a block B_{i+1} with entry place x, we define $S(B_i, B_{i+1}) = (|x|)$ if x is a safe exit place of B_i and a safe entry place of B_{i+1}; otherwise we define $S(B_i, B_{i+1}) = ()$ (the empty sequence). Likewise for a block B with entry place x we define $S_s(B) = (|x|)$ if x is a safe entry place of B, and $S_s(B) = ()$ otherwise; and for a block B with exit place x we define $S_e(B) = (|x|)$ if x is a safe exit place of B, and $S_s(B) = ()$ otherwise. This allows us to define the progress measure expressions for blocks and service level modules as follows.

Definition 13. *Let B be a block tree for the underlying control flow net of a module CPN. The loop-aware $PME_{la}(B)$ and loop-unaware $PME_{lu}(B)$ **progress measure expressions** are defined inductively over the block tree B by:*

Case B:atomic *For an atomic block B, $PME_{la}(B) = PME_{lu}(B) = ()$.*

Case B:sequence *Let* $B_1, B_2 \ldots B_n$ *be the subblocks of B and* $\mathsf{lx} \in \{\mathsf{la}, \mathsf{lu}\}$, *then:* $PME_{\mathsf{lx}}(B) = PME_{\mathsf{lx}}(B_n) \cdot S(B_{n-1}, B_n) \cdot PME_{\mathsf{lx}}(B_{n-1}) \ldots PME_{\mathsf{lx}}(B_2) \cdot S(B_1, B_2) \cdot PME_{\mathsf{lx}}(B_1)$

Case B:choice *Let* $B_1, B_2 \ldots B_n$ *be the subblocks of B and* $\mathsf{lx} \in \{\mathsf{la}, \mathsf{lu}\}$, *then:* $PME_{\mathsf{lx}}(B) = PME_{\mathsf{lx}}(B_1) \cdot PME_{\mathsf{lx}}(B_2) \cdots PME_{\mathsf{lx}}(B_n)$

Case B:loop *Let* B_1 *and* B_2 *be the sub-blocks of a loop block B with entry place s and exit place e and places* $P = \{p_1, \ldots, p_m\}$

$$PME_{\mathsf{la}}(B) = (|e|) \cdot PME_{\mathsf{la}}(B_1) \cdot (|s|) \tag{4}$$

$$PME_{\mathsf{lu}}(B) = (|p_1| + |p_2| + \ldots + |p_m|) \tag{5}$$

Let CPN_{SLM} *be a service level module with block tree B and with the unique input driver place ds and the unique output driver place de. The progress measure expression for* CPN_{SLM} *is defined as:*

$$PME_{\mathsf{lx}}(CPN_{SLM}) = (|de|) \cdot S_e(B) \cdot PME_{\mathsf{lx}}(B) \cdot S_s(B) \cdot (|ds|) \tag{6}$$

Note that for the service level modules we also take the ⟨⟨driver⟩⟩ places connected to the ⟨⟨service⟩⟩ and the ⟨⟨return⟩⟩ transition into account. For the service level module in Fig. 3 this results in the following progress expression:

$$PME_{\mathsf{la}}(Send) = (|\mathsf{endSend}|, |\mathsf{next}|, |\mathsf{startSending}|, |\mathsf{message}|) \tag{7}$$

$$PME_{\mathsf{lu}}(Send) = (|\mathsf{endSend}|, |\mathsf{next}| + |\mathsf{startSending}|, |\mathsf{message}|) \tag{8}$$

The place endSend is at the beginning of the progress expression since most progress has been made when the execution of the service has terminated in comparison to a state in which the service is to be started.

A progress expression for the complete PA-CPN model can be obtained by concatenating the progress expressions for the service tester and the service level modules. The exact order of the progress expressions for the modules in the concatenation is arbitrary, but the progress expressions for the service testers come first since they drive the execution and make the most significant progress.

If the service testers do not contain any loop constructs and when using loop-unaware progress expressions for all service modules, the combined progress expression obtained in the above way is monotonic. When the service testers have loops or when using loop-aware progress expressions, however, the combined progress expression for the complete system might not be monotonic.

Experimental Results. Table 1 shows experimental results on the protocol example for different configurations (number of transmitted messages) and channel characteristics (lossy/non-lossy) with the loop-aware and the loop-unaware progress measures. We consider exploration of the complete state space since the sweep-line method in the worst-case explores all states in order to check a property. The loop-unaware progress measure is monotonic which means that the number of explored states (in this case) equals the number of reachable states of the respective example (for completeness, it is listed in the second column).

Table 1. Verification using loop-aware and loop-unaware progress measure

Config	loop-unaware PM					loop-aware PM			
	Reachable	Explored	Peak	Ratio	Time	Explored	Peak	Ratio	Time
1:noloss	156	156	77	49.3	<1 s	165	63	40.3	<1 s
1:lossy	186	186	99	53.2	<1 s	196	78	41.9	<1 s
3:noloss	2,222	2,222	2,014	90.6	<1 s	2,790	1,582	71.2	<1 s
3:lossy	2,928	2,928	2,700	92.2	<1 s	4,037	2,187	75.7	<1 s
7:noloss	117,584	117,584	115,373	98.1	216 s	143,531	86,636	73.6	32 s
7:lossy	160,620	160,620	158,888	98.1	532 s	263,608	124,661	77.6	80 s

The loop-aware progress measure is not monotonic and hence some states might be visited (explored) multiple times. Therefore, the number of explored states is higher than the reachable states of the respective example. The ratio columns give the ratio in percent between the peak number of states stored (with the respective progress measure) and the number of reachable states. It can be seen that the runtime as well the peak memory use are better when using the loop-aware progress measure. The loop-aware measure provides better performance since the send service has a loop as the top-level control flow construct and, in this case, the peak memory use is reduced to between 40 and 77 %.

8   Related Work

PetriCode and PA-CPNs have been designed and developed with four main requirements on the code generation in mind: *platform independence*, *code integration*, *readability*, and *scalability*. PetriCode was evaluated against these requirements in [7,8]. A fifth requirement was *verifiability*, which means that the model used for code generation can be used also for verifying the correctness of the protocol itself, which was demonstrated in [7,11] and in this paper. We do not discuss the requirements on PetriCode in detail here, but use them to guide the comparison of our approach to related work.

Even though CPNs have been primarily used for modelling and verifying protocols, there exist approaches supporting code generation from CPNs – and more generally from high-level Petri Nets (HLPNs). Kaim et al. [12] discuss general aspects of generating code from low-level and high-level Petri nets with the purpose of executing the code outside the simulation environment where it was created. Kaim et al. discuss both centralised and parallel approaches to interpretation of models. A main aspect of the parallel approach is a structural analysis of the model in order to identify subnets that can be mapped to processes. In the PetriCode approach, the structural pragmatics provided by the modeller and the structural restrictions of PA-CPNs provide similar information. In contrast to PetriCode, Kaim et al. do not consider code integration and readability of the generated code.

The approach of Philippi [13] is a hybrid of a simulation-based and a structural analysis approach to code generation for HLPNs. The motivation for the hybrid approach is to produce more readable code than a pure simulation approach would because fewer checks are needed in the code. Philippi targets the Java platform only and is therefore not platform independent in its basic form. The generated code can be integrated into third party code in that the API of the generated code is defined by UML class diagrams. Philippi does not discuss the scaling to large applications. Lassen et al. [14] aim to generate readable code by creating code with constructs that are similar to what human programmers would have created. Since the approach of Lassen is based on Java annotations, the approach is tailored to the Java programming language and does not provide a generic infrastructure that supports code generation for different platforms.

Reinke [15] studies, in the context of the functional programming language Haskell, how to use language embedding for mapping constructs from HLPNs into Haskell code. The focus of Reinke is on generating code for a HLPN simulator and is not aimed at providing a general mechanism for generating readable code and on integrating the code into a larger application. Kummer et al. [16] are concerned with the execution of reference nets in the context of the Renew tool, which is based on the Java platform. Reference nets as supported by Renew are known to be verifiable [17], but the approach is specifically tailored to the Java platform. The work does not focus on integration at the code level but rely on service-oriented means for integrating the code into larger applications [18].

Mortensen [19] explores a simulation-based approach extracting the generated simulation code from CPN Tools. As such, the work of Mortensen is aimed at making a Standard ML implementation of the modelled system and not on conducting verification of the models or to target multiple platforms. Furthermore, being a simulation-based approach, the goal from the outset is not to generate code that is intended for humans to read. The use of a simulation-based approach also means that there is a considerable performance overhead due to enabling checks in the code. The approach of Kristensen et al. [20] is similar to the approach in [19]. PP-CPNs are used in [21] for code generation targeting the Erlang language but the approach is not designed to address readability of the generated code. Furthermore, the approach is tailored to the Erlang platform and is not easily adapted to other platforms even though PP-CPNs and the intermediary representation of control flow graphs are independent of the target language. Jørgensen et al. [22] propose an approach for generating BPEL code. The approach is targeted at BPEL and does not support multiple platforms or address verifyability, code integration, readability and scalability.

9 Conclusions and Future Work

PA-CPNs are at the core of the PetriCode approach, which has been discussed and evaluated in earlier work [3–8,11]. This paper completes the development of the PetriCode approach by providing a formal definition of PA-CPNs and hence establishing the formal foundation of our approach. By carefully restricting the class of CPNs and adding annotations, we have shown that it is possible to generate the code for the software and to verify the protocol based on the same model. PA-CPNs have been designed specifically for the domain of protocol software. The structure of PA-CPNs could probably be adjusted to other domains than protocol software: these domains might need a slightly different structure and possibly a different or not fixed number of levels of modules and some additional pragmatics. But, before defining such a more general class of annotated CPNs, we would need to have a look at more examples from other domains.

PetriCode aims at generating code from verified models, where verification is done by standard techniques for CPNs. PetriCode did not aim at developing new verification techniques itself. In future work, it might be interesting to look at results on workflow nets and controllability or operability [23, 24] for protocols. In this paper, we demonstrated, however, that the same model can be used for code generation and verification; and, we have shown that the structure of PA-CPNs can be exploited to improve the performance of existing verification techniques by automatically computing a progress measure for the sweep-line state space exploration method.

Note that the PetriCode code generator itself is not verified yet. Techniques such as the one presented by Blech et al. [25] could be explored for verifying the code generators for the different target languages of PetriCode. But due to the template-based approach and the platform independence of PetriCode, this would be an ambitious project in its own right. Another option to guaranteeing the correctness of the generated code would be, not to verify the code generator itself, but to apply model-based testing [26]: we could use the service testers not only for the verification of the protocol system; we could use them also for generating code for these tests (if the testers do not access the LCV places of the services). The generated tests could then be run with the generated protocol software and the results compared to the outcome in the model. In this way, it would be guaranteed that the result of these tests are the same in the model and the generated code.

References

1. Jensen, K., Kristensen, L.: Coloured Petri Nets - Modelling and Validation of Concurrent Systems. Springer, Heidelberg (2009)
2. Billington, J., Gallasch, G.E., Han, B.: A Coloured Petri Net approach to protocol verification. In: Desel, J., Reisig, W., Rozenberg, G. (eds.) Lectures on Concurrency and Petri Nets. LNCS, vol. 3098, pp. 210–290. Springer, Heidelberg (2004)
3. Kristensen, L.M., Simonsen, K.I.F.: Applications of Coloured Petri Nets for functional validation of protocol designs. In: Jensen, K., van der Aalst, W.M.P., Balbo, G., Koutny, M., Wolf, K. (eds.) Transactions on Petri Nets and Other Models of Concurrency VII. LNCS, vol. 7480, pp. 56–115. Springer, Heidelberg (2013)
4. Simonsen, K.I.F., Kristensen, L.M., Kindler, E.: Generating protocol software from CPN models annotated with pragmatics. In: Iyoda, J., de Moura, L. (eds.) SBMF 2013. LNCS, vol. 8195, pp. 227–242. Springer, Heidelberg (2013)

5. Simonsen, K.I.F.: PetriCode: a tool for template-based code generation from CPN models. In: Counsell, S., Núñez, M. (eds.) SEFM 2013. LNCS, vol. 8368, pp. 151–163. Springer, Heidelberg (2014)
6. Simonsen, K.: Code generation from pragmatics annotated Coloured Petri Nets. Ph.D. thesis. Technical University of Denmark (2014)
7. Simonsen, K.I.F., Kristensen, L.M.: Implementing the websocket protocol based on formal modelling and automated code generation. In: Magoutis, K., Pietzuch, P. (eds.) DAIS 2014. LNCS, vol. 8460, pp. 104–118. Springer, Heidelberg (2014)
8. Simonsen, K.: An evaluation of automated code generation with the PetriCode approach. In: Proceedings of PNSE 2014, vol. 1160. CEUR Workshop Proceedings, pp. 295–312. CEUR-WS.org (2014)
9. Simonsen, K., Kristensen, L., Kindler, E.: Pragmatics annotated Coloured Petri Nets for protocol software generation and verification. In: Proceedings of PNSE 2015, vol. 1372. CEUR Workshop Proceedings, pp. 79–98 (2015)
10. Jensen, K., Kristensen, L., Mailund, T.: The sweep-line state space exploration method. Theor. Comput. Sci. **429**, 169–179 (2012)
11. Simonsen, K.I.F., Kristensen, L.M.: Towards a CPN-based modelling approach for reconciling verification and implementation of protocol models. In: Machado, R.J., Maciel, R.S.P., Rubin, J., Botterweck, G. (eds.) MOMPES 2012. LNCS, vol. 7706, pp. 106–125. Springer, Heidelberg (2013)
12. Kaim, W.E., Kordon, F.: Code generation. In: Girault, C., Valk, R. (eds.) Petri Nets for System Engineering, pp. 433–470. Springer, Heidelberg (2003)
13. Philippi, S.: Automatic code generation from high-level Petri-Nets for model driven systems engineering. J. Syst. Softw. **79**(10), 1444–1455 (2006)
14. Lassen, K.B., Tjell, S.: Translating colored control flow nets into readable Java via annotated Java workflow nets. In: Proceedings of 8th CPN Workshop, pp. 127–146 (2007)
15. Reinke, C.: Haskell-coloured Petri Nets. In: Koopman, P., Clack, C. (eds.) International Workshop on Implementation of Functional Languages. LNCS, vol. 1868, pp. 165–180. Springer, Heidelberg (1999)
16. Kummer, O., Wienberg, F., Duvigneau, M., Schumacher, J., Köhler, M., Moldt, D., Rölke, H., Valk, R.: An extensible editor and simulation engine for Petri Nets: RENEW. In: Cortadella, J., Reisig, W. (eds.) ICATPN 2004. LNCS, vol. 3099, pp. 484–493. Springer, Heidelberg (2004)
17. Mascheroni, M., Wagner, T., Wüstenberg, L.: Verifying reference nets by means of hypernets: a plugin for renew. In: Proceedings of PNSE 2010. Berichte des Fachbereichs Informatik. Universität Hamburg, pp. 39–54 (2010)
18. Betz, T., et al.: Integrating web services in Petri Net-Based agent applications. In: Proceedings of PNSE 2013, vol. 989. CEUR Workshop Proceedings, pp. 97–116 (2013)
19. Mortensen, K.H.: Automatic code generation method based on Coloured Petri Net models applied on an access control system. In: Nielsen, M., Simpson, D. (eds.) ICATPN 2000. LNCS, vol. 1825, pp. 367–386. Springer, Heidelberg (2000)
20. Kristensen, L.M., Mechlenborg, P., Zhang, L., Mitchell, B., Gallasch, G.E.: Model-based development of a course of action scheduling tool. Int. J. Softw. Tools Technol. Transf. **10**, 5–14 (2008)
21. Kristensen, L.M., Westergaard, M.: Automatic structure-based code generation from Coloured Petri Nets: a proof of concept. In: Kowalewski, S., Roveri, M. (eds.) FMICS 2010. LNCS, vol. 6371, pp. 215–230. Springer, Heidelberg (2010)

22. van der Aalst, W.M.P., Jørgensen, J.B., Lassen, K.B.: Let's go all the way: from requirements via Colored Workflow Nets to a BPEL implementation of a new bank system. In: Meersman, R., Tari, Z. (eds.) OTM 2005. LNCS, vol. 3760, pp. 22–39. Springer, Heidelberg (2005)

23. Schmidt, K.: Controllability of open workflow nets. In: Enterprise Modelling and Information Systems Architectures, Proceedings of the Workshop in Klagenfurt, 24–25 October 2005, pp. 236–249 (2005)

24. Massuthe, P., et al.: Can i find a partner? undecidability of partner existence for open nets. Inf. Process. Lett. **108**(6), 374–378 (2008)

25. Blech, J., Glesner, S., Leitner, J.: Formal verification of Java code generation from UML models. In: Fujaba Days 2005, pp. 49–56 (2005)

26. Utting, M., Pretschner, A., Legeard, B.: A taxonomy of model-based testing approaches. Softw. Test. Verification Reliab. **22**(5), 297–312 (2012)

A Petri Net-Based Approach to Model and Analyze the Management of Cloud Applications

Antonio Brogi[1], Andrea Canciani[1], Jacopo Soldani[1(✉)], and PengWei Wang[2]

[1] Department of Computer Science, University of Pisa, Pisa, Italy
soldani@di.unipi.it
[2] School of Computer Science and Technology,
Donghua University, Shanghai, China

Abstract. How to flexibly manage complex applications over heterogeneous clouds is one of the emerging problems in the cloud era. The OASIS Topology and Orchestration Specification for Cloud Applications (TOSCA) aims at solving this problem by providing a language to describe and manage complex cloud applications in a portable, vendor-agnostic way. TOSCA permits to define an application as an orchestration of nodes, whose types can specify states, requirements, capabilities and management operations — but not how they interact each another. In this paper we first propose how to extend TOSCA to specify the behaviour of management operations and their relations with states, requirements, and capabilities. We then illustrate how such behaviour can be naturally modelled, in a compositional way, by means of open Petri nets. The proposed modelling permits to automate different analyses, such as determining whether a deployment plan is valid, which are its effects, or which plans allow to reach certain system configurations.

1 Introduction

Available cloud technologies permit to run on-demand distributed software systems at a fraction of the cost which was necessary just a few years ago. On the other hand, how to flexibly deploy and manage such applications over heterogeneous clouds is one of the emerging problems in the cloud era.

In this perspective, OASIS recently released the *Topology and Orchestration Specification for Cloud Applications* (TOSCA [24,25]), a standard to support the automation of the deployment and management of complex cloud-based applications. TOSCA provides a modelling language to specify, in a portable and vendor-agnostic way, a cloud application and its deployment and management. An application can be specified in TOSCA by instantiating component types, by connecting a component's requirements to the capabilities of other components,

This work is an extended version of [8]. It has been partly supported by the EU-FP7-ICT-610531 project SeaClouds.

© Springer-Verlag Berlin Heidelberg 2016
M. Koutny et al. (Eds.): ToPNoC XI, LNCS 9930, pp. 28–48, 2016.
DOI: 10.1007/978-3-662-53401-4_2

and by orchestrating components' operations into plans defining the deployment and management of the whole application.

Unfortunately, the current specification of TOSCA [24] does not permit to describe the behaviour of the management operations of an application. Namely, it is not possible to describe the order in which the management operations of a component must be invoked, nor how those operations depend on the requirements and affect the capabilities of that component. As a consequence, the verification of whether a plan to deploy an application is valid must be performed manually, with a time-consuming and error-prone process.

In this paper, we first propose a way to extend TOSCA to specify the behaviour of management operations and their relations with states, requirements, and capabilities. We define how to specify the management protocol of a TOSCA component by means of finite state machines whose states and transitions are associated with conditions on (some of) the component's requirements and capabilities. Intuitively speaking, those conditions define the consistency of component's states and constrain the executability of component's operations to the satisfaction of requirements.

We then illustrate how the management protocols of TOSCA components can be naturally modelled, in a compositional way, by means of open Petri nets [2,18]. This allows us to obtain the management protocol of an arbitrarily complex cloud application by combining the management protocols of its components. The proposed modelling permits to automate different analyses, such as determining whether a deployment plan is valid, which are its effects, or which plans allow to reach certain system configurations.

The rest of the paper is organized as follows. Section 2 introduces the needed background (TOSCA and open Petri nets), while Sect. 3 illustrates a scenario motivating the need for an explicit, machine-readable representation of management protocols. Section 4 describes how TOSCA can be extended to specify the behaviour of management operations, how such behaviour can be naturally and compositionally modelled by means of open Petri nets, and how the proposed modelling permits to automate different types of analysis. Related work is discussed in Sect. 5, while some concluding remarks are drawn in Sect. 6.

2   Background

2.1   TOSCA

TOSCA [24] is an emerging standard whose main goals are to enable (i) the specification of portable cloud applications and (ii) the automation of their deployment and management. In this perspective, TOSCA provides an XML-based modelling language which allows to specify the structure of a cloud application as a typed topology graph, and deployment/management tasks as plans. More precisely, each cloud application is represented as a `ServiceTemplate` (Fig. 1), which consists of a `TopologyTemplate` and (optionally) of management `Plans`.

The `TopologyTemplate` is a typed directed graph that describes the topological structure of the composite cloud application. Its nodes (`NodeTemplate`s)

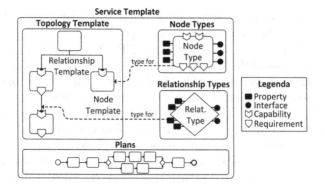

Fig. 1. TOSCA `ServiceTemplate`.

model the application components, while its edges (`RelationshipTemplates`) model the relations between those application components. `NodeTemplates` and `RelationshipTemplates` are typed by means of `NodeTypes` and `RelationshipTypes`, respectively. A `NodeType` defines (i) the observable properties of an application component C, (ii) the possible states of its instances, (iii) the requirements needed by C, (iv) the capabilities offered by C to satisfy other components' requirements, and (v) the management operations of C. `RelationshipTypes` describe the properties of relationships occurring among components.

On the other hand, `Plans` enable the description of application deployment and/or management aspects. Each `Plan` is a workflow that orchestrates the operations offered by the application components (i.e., `NodeTemplates`) to address (part of) the management of the whole cloud application[1].

2.2 (Open) Petri Nets

Before providing a formal definition of open Petri nets (Definition 2), we recall the definition of Petri nets just to introduce the employed notation. We instead omit to recall other very basic notions about Petri nets (e.g., marking of a net, firing of transitions, etc.) as they are well-know and easy to find in literature [23].

Definition 1. *A* Petri net *is a tuple* $\mathcal{P} = \langle P, T, \bullet\cdot, \cdot\bullet, M_0 \rangle$ *where* P *is a set of places,* T *is a set of transitions (with* $P \cap T = \varnothing$*),* $\bullet\cdot, \cdot\bullet : T \to 2^P$ *are functions assigning to each transition its input and output places, and* $M_0 : P \to \mathbb{N}$ *is the initial marking of* $\mathcal{P}$*.*

According to [2], an open Petri net is an ordinary Petri net with a distinguished set of (open) places that are intended to represent the interface of the net towards the external environment, meaning that the environment can put or remove tokens from those places. In this paper, we will employ a subset of open

---

[1] A more detailed and self-contained introduction to TOSCA can be found in [10].

Petri nets, where transitions consume at most one token from each place, and where the environment can both add/remove tokens to/from all open places.

Definition 2. *An* open Petri net *is a pair* $\mathcal{Z} = \langle \mathcal{P}, I \rangle$, *where* $\mathcal{P} = \langle P, T, \bullet\cdot, \cdot\bullet, M_0 \rangle$ *is an ordinary Petri net, and* $I \subseteq P$ *is the set of* open *places. The places in* $P \backslash I$ *will be referred to as* internal *places.*

3   Motivating Scenario

Consider a developer who wants to deploy and manage the web services *Send-SMS* and *Forex* on a TOSCA-compliant cloud platform. She first describes her services in TOSCA, and then selects the third-party components (i.e. `NodeTypes`) needed to run them. For instance, she indicates that her services will run on a *Tomcat* server installed on an *Ubuntu* operating system, which in turn runs on an *AmazonEC2* virtual machine. Figure 2 illustrates the resulting `TopologyTemplate`, according to the Winery graphical notation [19]. For the sake of simplicity, and without loss of generality, in the following we focus only on the lifecycle interface [10] of each `NodeType` instantiated in the topology (i.e., the interface containing the operations to install, configure, start, stop, and uninstall a component).

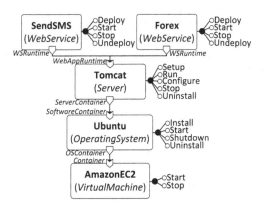

Fig. 2. Motivating scenario.

Suppose that the developer wants to describe the automation of the deployment of the *SendSMS* and *Forex* services by writing a TOSCA `Plan`. Since TOSCA does not include any representation of the management protocols of (third-party) `NodeTypes`, developers may produce invalid `Plans`. For instance, while Fig. 3 illustrates three seemingly valid `Plans`, only the third is a valid plan. The other `Plans` cannot be considered valid since (a) *Tomcat*'s `Configure` operation cannot be executed before *Tomcat* is running, and (b) *Tomcat* cannot be installed when the *Ubuntu* operating system is not running.

While the validity of `Plans` can be manually verified, this is a time-consuming and error-prone process. In order to enable the automated verification of the

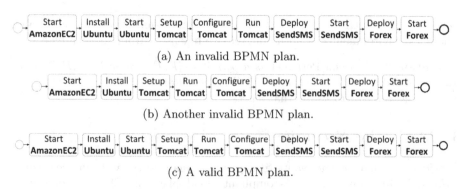

(a) An invalid BPMN plan.

(b) Another invalid BPMN plan.

(c) A valid BPMN plan.

Fig. 3. Deployment Plans.

validity of Plans, TOSCA should be extended so as to permit specifying the behaviour of and the relations among NodeTypes' management operations.

4 Modelling Management Protocols

While a TOSCA NodeType can be described by means of its states, requirements, capabilities, and management operations, there is currently no way to specify how management operations affect states, how operations or states depend on requirements, or which capabilities are concretely provided in a certain state.

The objective of the next section is precisely to propose a way to extend TOSCA to specify the behavior of management operations and their relations with states, requirements, and capabilities.

4.1 Management Protocols in TOSCA

Let N be a TOSCA NodeType, and let us denote its states, requirements, capabilities, and management operations with S_N, R_N, C_N, and O_N, respectively.

We want to permit describing whether and how the management operations of N depend on other operations of the same node as well as on operations of the other nodes providing the capabilities that satisfy the requirements of N.

– The first type of dependencies can be easily described by specifying the relationship between states and management operations of N. More precisely, the order with which the operations of N can be executed can be described by means of a transition relation τ, that specifies whether an operation o can be executed in a state s, and which state is reached by executing o in s.
– The second type of dependencies can be described by associating transitions and states with (possibly empty) sets of requirements to indicate that the corresponding capabilities are assumed to be provided. More precisely, the requirements associated with a transition t specify which are the capabilities that must be offered by other nodes to allow the execution of t. The

requirements associated with a state of a `NodeType` N specify which are the capabilities that must (continue to) be offered by other nodes in order for N to (continue to) work properly.

To complete the description, each state s of a `NodeType` N also specifies the capabilities provided by N in s.

Definition 3. *Let* $N = \langle S_N, R_N, C_N, O_N, \mathcal{M}_N \rangle$ *be a* `NodeType`, *where* $S_N, R_N, C_N,$ *and* O_N *are the sets of its states, requirements, capabilities, and management operations.* $\mathcal{M}_N = \langle \overline{s}, \rho, \gamma, \tau \rangle$ *is the* management protocol *of* N, *where*

- $\overline{s} \in S_N$ *is the initial state,*
- ρ *is a function indicating, for each state* $s \in S_N$, *which conditions on require-ments must hold (i.e.,* $\rho(s) \subseteq R_N$, *with* $\rho(\overline{s}) = \varnothing)^2$,
- γ *is a function indicating which capabilities of* N *are concretely offered in a state* $s \in S_N$ *(i.e.,* $\gamma(s) \subseteq C_N$, *with* $\gamma(\overline{s}) = \varnothing$*), and*
- $\tau \subseteq S_N \times 2^{R_N} \times O_N \times S_N$ *is a set of quadruples modelling the transition relation (i.e.,* $\langle s, H, o, s' \rangle \in \tau$ *means that in state* s, *and if condition* H *holds,* o *is executable and leads to state* s'*).*

Syntactically, to describe $\mathcal{M}_N$ we slightly extend the syntax[3] for describing a TOSCA `NodeType`. Namely, we enrich the description of an instance state by introducing the nested elements `ReliesOn` and `Offers`. `ReliesOn` defines ρ (of Definition 3) by enabling the association between states and assumed require-ments, while `Offers` defines γ by indicating the capabilities offered in a state. Furthermore, we introduce the element `ManagementProtocol`, which allows to specify the `InitialState` $\overline{s}$ of the protocol, as well as the `Transitions` defining the transition relation τ.

The management protocols of the `NodeTypes` in the motivating sce-nario of Sect. 3 are shown in Fig. 4, where $\mathcal{M}_{WS}$ is the management pro-tocol for `WebServices`, $\mathcal{M}_S$ for `Server`, $\mathcal{M}_{OS}$ for `OperatingSystem`, and $\mathcal{M}_{VM}$ for `VirtualMachine`. Consider for instance the management proto-col $\mathcal{M}_S$ of `NodeType` `Server` defining the *Tomcat* server. Its states S_N are `Unavailable` (initial state), `Stopped`, and `Working`, the only requirement in R_N is `ServerContainer`, the only capability in C_N is `WebAppRuntime`, and its man-agement operations are `Setup`, `Uninstall`, `Run`, `Stop`, and `Configure`. States `Unavailable` and `Stopped` are not associated with any requirement or capa-bility. State `Working` instead specifies that the capability corresponding to the `ServerContainer` requirement must be provided (by some other node) in order for `Server` to (continue to) work properly. State `Working` also specifies that `Server` provides the `WebAppRuntime` capability when in such state. Finally, all transitions (but those involving operations `Stop` and `Configure`) constrain their firability by requiring the capability that satisfies `ServerContainer` to be offered (by some other node).

---

[2] Without loss of generality, we assume that the initial state of a management protocol has no requirements and does not provide any capability.

[3] A more detailed syntax for extended `NodeTypes` can be found in [7].

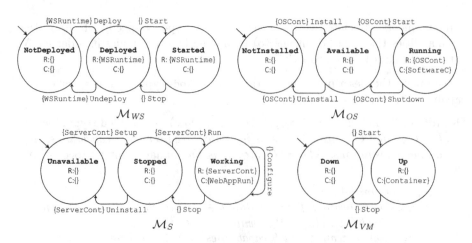

Fig. 4. Management protocols of the NodeTypes in our motivating scenario.

Note that Definition 3 permits to define operations that have non-deterministic effects when applied in a state (e.g., a state can have two outgoing transitions corresponding to the same operation and leading to different states). This form of non-determinism is not acceptable in the management of a TOSCA application [10]. We will thus focus on *deterministic* management protocols, i.e. protocols ensuring deterministic effects when performing an operation in a state.

Definition 4. *Let* $N = \langle S_N, R_N, C_N, O_N, \mathcal{M}_N \rangle$ *be a* NodeType. *The management protocol* $\mathcal{M}_N = \langle \overline{s}, \rho, \gamma, \tau \rangle$ *is* deterministic *if and only if*

$$\forall \langle s_1, H_1, o_1, s_1' \rangle, \langle s_2, H_2, o_2, s_2' \rangle \in T: s_1 = s_2 \land o_1 = o_2 \Rightarrow s_1' = s_2'$$

4.2 Encoding Management Protocols in Petri Nets

A (deterministic) management protocol $\mathcal{M}_N$ of a NodeType N can be easily encoded by an open Petri net. Each state of $\mathcal{M}_N$ is mapped into an internal place of the Petri net, and each capability and requirement of N is mapped into an open place of the same net. Furthermore, each transition $\langle s, H, o, s' \rangle$ of $\mathcal{M}_N$ is mapped into a Petri net transition t with the following inputs and outputs:

(i) The input places of t are the places denoting s, the requirements that are needed but not already available in s (i.e., $(\rho(s') \cup H) - \rho(s)$), and the capabilities that are provided in s but not in s' (i.e., $\gamma(s) - \gamma(s')$).

(ii) The output places of t are the places denoting s', the requirements that were needed but are no more assumed to hold in s' (i.e., $(\rho(s) \cup H) - \rho(s')$), and the capabilities that are provided in s' but not in s (i.e., $\gamma(s') - \gamma(s)$).

The initial marking of the obtained net prescribes that the only place initially containing a token is that corresponding to the initial state $\overline{s}$ of $\mathcal{M}_N$.

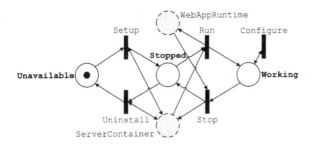

Fig. 5. Example of Petri net translation.

Definition 5. *Let* $N = \langle S_N, R_N, C_N, O_N, \mathcal{M}_N \rangle$ *be a* NodeType, *with* $\mathcal{M}_N = \langle \overline{s}, \rho, \gamma, \tau \rangle$. *The management protocol* $\mathcal{M}_N$ *is encoded into an open Petri net* $\mathcal{Z}_N = \langle \mathcal{P}_N, I_N \rangle$, *with* $\mathcal{P}_N = \langle P_N, T_N, \bullet\cdot, \cdot\bullet, M_0 \rangle$ *and* $I_N \subseteq P_N$, *as follows.*

- $P_N = S_N \cup R_N \cup C_N$, *i.e. the set* P_N *of places contains a separate place for each state in* S_N, *for each requirement in* R_N, *and for each capability in* C_N.
- $I_N = R_N \cup C_N$, *i.e. the set* $I_N \subset P_N$ *of open places contains the places denoting the requirements in* R_N *and the capabilities in* C_N.
- $T_N = \tau$ *(i.e., the set* T_N *contains a net transition* t *for each transition* $\langle s, H, o, s' \rangle \in \tau$*), and* $\forall t = \langle s, H, o, s' \rangle \in T_N$
  (i) $\bullet t = \{s\} \cup ((\rho(s') \cup H) - \rho(s)) \cup (\gamma(s) - \gamma(s'))$, *i.e. the set* $\bullet t$ *of input places contains the place* s, *the places denoting the requirements in* $(\rho(s') \cup H) - \rho(s)$, *and those denoting the capabilities in* $\gamma(s) - \gamma(s')$.
  (ii) $t\bullet = \{s'\} \cup ((\rho(s) \cup H) - \rho(s')) \cup (\gamma(s') - \gamma(s))$, *i.e. the set* $t\bullet$ *of output places contains the place* s', *the places denoting the requirements in* $(\rho(s) \cup H) - \rho(s')$, *and those denoting the capabilities in* $\gamma(s') - \gamma(s)$.
- *The initial marking* M_0 *of* $\mathcal{Z}_N$ *is defined as follows:*

$$\forall p \in P_N . M_0(p) = \begin{cases} 1 & \text{if } p \text{ denotes } \overline{s} \\ 0 & \text{otherwise} \end{cases}$$

The above definition ensures that the Petri net encoding of a management protocol satisfies the following properties:

- There is a one-to-one correspondence between the marking of the internal places of the Petri net and the states of a management protocol. Namely, there is exactly one token in the internal place denoting the current state, and no tokens in the other internal places.
- Each operation can be performed if and only if all the necessary requirements are available in the source state, and no capability required by any connected component is disabled in the target state.

Consider for instance the management protocol $\mathcal{M}_S$ (Fig. 4), whose corresponding Petri net is shown in Fig. 5. Each state in $\mathcal{M}_S$ is translated into an internal place (represented as a circle), while the `ServerContainer` requirement and the `WebAppRuntime` capability are translated into open places (represented as dashed circles). Additionally, protocol transitions are translated into net transitions. For example, the transition ⟨`Stopped`,{`ServerContainer`}, `Run`, `Working`⟩ is translated into a Petri net transition, whose inputs places are `Stopped` and `ServerContainer`, and whose outputs places are `Working` and `WebAppRuntime`.

4.3 Modelling the Management of a `ServiceTemplate`

We now show how the Petri net modelling the management protocol of a TOSCA `TopologyTemplate` (specifying a whole cloud-based application) can be obtained, in a compositional way, from the Petri nets modelling the management protocols of the `NodeTypes` in such `TopologyTemplate`.

We first need to model (by open Petri nets working as a *capability controllers*) the `Relationship-Templates` that define in a `TopologyTemplate` the association between the requirements of a `NodeTypes` and the capabilities of other `NodeTypes`. To do that, we first define an utility *binding* function that returns the set of requirements with which a capability is associated.

Definition 6. *Let S be a* `ServiceTemplate`, *and let c be a capability offered by a* `NodeType` *in S. We define $b(c, S) = \{r_1, \ldots, r_n\}$, where $r_1, \ldots, r_n$ are the requirements connected to c in S by means of* `RelationshipTemplates`.

We now exploit function b to define *capability controllers*. On the one hand, the controller must ensure that once a capability c is available, the nodes exposing the connected requirements $r_1, \ldots, r_n$ are able to simultaneously exploit it. This is obtained by adding a transition $c_\uparrow$ able to propagate the token from place c to places $r_1, \ldots, r_n$ (i.e., the input place of $c_\uparrow$ is c, and its output places are $r_1, \ldots, r_n$). On the other hand, the controller has also to ensure that the capability is not removed while at least another node is actively assuming its availability (with a condition on a connected requirement). Thus, we introduce a transition $c_\downarrow$ whose input places are $r_1, \ldots, r_n$ and whose output place is c.

Definition 7. *Let S be a* `ServiceTemplate`, *and let c be a capability offered by a* `NodeType` *instantiated in S. Let $r_1, \ldots, r_n$ be the requirements exposed by the nodes in S such that $b(c, S) = \{r_1, \ldots, r_n\}$. The controller of c is an open Petri net $\mathcal{Z}_c = \langle \mathcal{P}_c, I_c \rangle$, with $\mathcal{P}_c = \langle P_c, T_c, \bullet \cdot, \cdot \bullet, M_0 \rangle$, defined as follows.*

- *The set P_c of places contains a separate place for the capability c and for each requirement $r_1, \ldots, r_n$. It also contains a place r_c that witnesses the availability of the capability c.*
- *The set I_c coincides with P_c.*
- *The set T_c contains only two Petri net transitions $c_\uparrow$ and $c_\downarrow$.*
  - *The input and output places of $c_\uparrow$ are the place c, and the places $r_1, \ldots, r_n$ and r_c, respectively (i.e., $\bullet c_\uparrow = \{c\}$ and $c_\uparrow \bullet = \{r_1, \ldots, r_n\} \cup \{r_c\}$).*
  - *The input and output places of $c_\downarrow$ are the places $r_1, \ldots, r_n$ and r_c, and the place c, respectively (i.e., $\bullet c_\uparrow = \{r_1, \ldots, r_n\} \cup \{r_c\}$ and $c_\uparrow \bullet = \{c\}$).*
- *The initial marking M_0 of $\mathcal{Z}_c$ is $\forall p \in P_c . M_0(p) = 0$.*

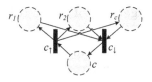

Fig. 6. Example of *capability controller.*

An example of controller (for a capability c connected to two requirements r_1 and r_2) is illustrated in Fig. 6.

We can now compose the nets modelling the management protocols of the NodeTypes instantiated in a ServiceTemplate's topology by interconnecting them with the above introduced controllers. The composition is quite simple: We just collapse the open places corresponding to the same requirements/capabilities.

Definition 8. *Let S be a* ServiceTemplate. *We encode S with an open Petri net $\mathcal{Z}_S = \langle \mathcal{P}_S, I_S \rangle$, where $\mathcal{P}_S = \langle P_S, T_S, \bullet\cdot, \cdot\bullet, M_0 \rangle$, as follows.*

- *For each node N in the topology of S, we encode its management protocol with an open Petri net $\mathcal{Z}_N$ obtained as shown in Definition 5.*
- *For each capability c exposed by a NodeTemplate in S, we create an open Petri net $\mathcal{Z}_c$ (acting as its controller) as shown in Definition 7.*
- *We then compose the above mentioned nets by taking their disjoint union and merging the places denoting the same requirement r or capability c.*
- *The initial marking M_0 is the union of the markings of the collapsed nets.*

For example, Fig. 7 shows the net obtained for the motivating scenario in Sect. 3. For the sake of readability, in the figure we omit, for each capability c, the place r_c of its controller.

A very convenient property of the obtained encoding is that it is *safe* (i.e., the number of tokens in each place does not exceed one, for any marking M that is reachable from the initial marking M_0 [23]). To prove it, we need to further characterize the Petri net encoding we provided through Definitions 5, 7 and 8.

Property 1. Let S be a ServiceTemplate, and let $\mathcal{Z}_S$ be its Petri net encoding.

$$\mathcal{Z}_S \text{ is safe.}$$

Proof. The property follows from the properties (i), (ii), and (iii) shown in Lemma 1 (see Appendix). More precisely, (i) proves that the internal places denoting node states can contain at most one token, (ii) proves that each open place denoting a capability c (as well as the corresponding place r_c) can contain at most one token, and (iii) proves that each open place denoting a requirement can contain at most one token. Therefore, all places in $\mathcal{Z}_S$ can contain at most one token (in any reachable marking), thus making the whole net safe [23]. □

4.4   Analyzing the Management of a `ServiceTemplate`

The Petri net encoding of the management of a `ServiceTemplate` S permits us defining what is a *valid plan* according to such management. Essentially, thanks to the encoding of capability controllers and to the way we compose these controllers with management protocol encodings, the obtained net ensures that no requirement can be assumed to hold if the corresponding capability is not provided, and that no capability can be removed if at least one of the corresponding requirements is assumed to hold. This permits to consider a plan valid if and only if it corresponds to a firing sequence in the net encoding of S.

Definition 9. *Let S be a `ServiceTemplate` and let $\mathcal{Z}_S = \langle \mathcal{P}_S, I_S \rangle$, with $\mathcal{P}_S = \langle P_S, T_S, \bullet\cdot, \cdot\bullet, M_0 \rangle$, be the Petri net encoding of S. A sequence $o_1 o_2 ... o_m$ of management operations is a* valid sequential plan *for S if and only if there is a firing sequence $t_1 t_2 \ldots t_n$ (with $t_i \in T_S$) from the initial marking M_0 such that*

$$o_1 \cdot o_2 \cdot \ldots \cdot o_m = \lambda(t_1) \cdot \lambda(t_2) \cdot \ldots \cdot \lambda(t_n),$$

where $\cdot$ indicates the concatenation operator[4] *and:*

$$\lambda(t) = \begin{cases} \epsilon & \text{if } t \text{ denotes a } c_\uparrow \text{ or } c_\downarrow \text{ transition} \\ o & \text{if } t \text{ denotes a management protocol transition } \langle s, H, o, s' \rangle \end{cases}$$

It is easy to see now that plan (c) of Fig. 3 is valid since, for instance,

> *AmazonEC2*:**Start Container**↑ *Ubuntu*:**Install** *Ubuntu*:**Start SoftwareContainer**↑ *Tomcat*:**Setup** *Tomcat*:**Run** *Tomcat*:**Configure WebAppRuntime**↑ *SendSMS*:**Deploy** *SendSMS*:**Start** *Forex*:**Deploy** *Forex*:**Start**

is a corresponding firing sequence for the Petri net in Fig. 7. Conversely, plans (a) and (b) in Fig. 3 are not valid as there are no corresponding firing sequences. Intuitively speaking, (a) is not valid since after firing, for instance,

> *AmazonEC2*:**Start Container**↑ *Ubuntu*:**Install** *Ubuntu*:**Start SoftwareContainer**↑ *Tomcat*:**Setup**

transition *Tomcat*:**Configure** cannot be fired. It indeed requires a token in the **Working** place, but that place is empty and it is not possible to add tokens to it without firing *Tomcat*:**Run**. On the other hand, (b) is not valid since after firing

> *AmazonEC2*:**Start Container**↑ *Ubuntu*:**Install**

transition *Tomcat*:**Setup** cannot fire. It requires a token in the place denoting the **ServerContainer** requirement, but that place is empty and it is not possible to add tokens to it without firing **SoftwareContainer**↑, which in turn cannot fire as it misses a token in the place denoting the *Ubuntu*'s **SoftwareContainer** capability (and no token can be added to such place without firing *Ubuntu*:**Start**).

We can easily extend the definition of validity from sequential plans to generic workflow **Plans**, by constraining all their sequential traces to be valid.

---

[4] The empty string ϵ is the neutral element of $\cdot$, hence controllers' net transitions are ignored (as $\lambda(t) = \epsilon$ when t denotes a $c_\uparrow$ or $c_\downarrow$ transition).

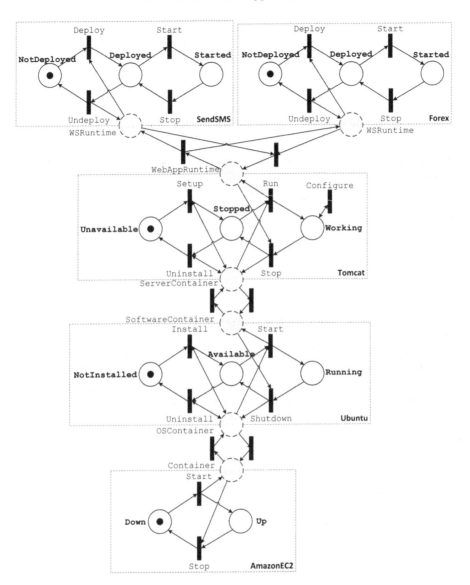

Fig. 7. Petri net encoding for the motivating scenario in Sect. 3.

Definition 10. *Let S be a* ServiceTemplate, *and let $\mathcal{Z}_S$ be its Petri net encoding. A workflow* Plan P *is valid for S if and only if all its sequential traces are valid sequential plans for S (see Definition 9).*

However, the above Definition 10 does not ensure that all traces end up in the same setting of the ServiceTemplate. Two different traces can reach two different markings with a different token assignment for the internal places. This would mean that, by differently inter-leaving the activities in a workflow `Plan`, the nodes in a `ServiceTemplate` can end up in different states (thus potentially activating different capabilities and assuming different requirements). This is not acceptable in the management of a TOSCA application, as we would expect a `Plan` to have deterministic effects (independently of the inter-leaving of the activities that compose such `Plan`). We thus define the notion of *deterministic* `Plans`, after introducing that of internally equivalent markings.

Definition 11. *Let* $\mathcal{Z} = \langle \mathcal{P}, I \rangle$, *with* $\mathcal{P} = \langle P, T, \bullet\cdot, \cdot\bullet, M_0 \rangle$, *be an open Petri net. Two markings* $M_1, M_2 : P \to \mathbb{N}$ *are internally equivalent* $(M_1 \equiv_M M_2)$ *if and only if*

$$\forall p \in P \backslash I. M_1(p) = M_2(p)$$

Definition 12. *Let* S *be a* `ServiceTemplate`, *and let* $\mathcal{Z}_S = \langle \mathcal{P}_S, I_S \rangle$, *with* $\mathcal{P}_S = \langle P_S, T_S, \bullet\cdot, \cdot\bullet, M_0 \rangle$, *be the Petri net encoding of* S. *Let also* P *be a valid workflow* `Plan` *for* S. P *is also* deterministic *if and only if for each pair* M_1, M_2 *of markings reached by executing two finite, complete[5] sequential traces of* P

$$M_1 \equiv_M M_2.$$

The effects of a plan on the states of the components of a TOSCA `ServiceTemplate`, as well as on the requirements that are satisfied and the capabilities that are available, can then be directly determined from the marking that is reached performing the corresponding firing sequence. We thus first characterize the states, requirements, and capabilities that are active in a marking (Definition 13), and we then employ such characterization to list the effects of a deterministic `Plan` (Remark 1).

Definition 13. *Let* S *be a* `ServiceTemplate`, *and let* $\mathcal{Z}_S = \langle \mathcal{P}_S, I_S \rangle$, *with* $\mathcal{P}_S = \langle P_S, T_S, \bullet\cdot, \cdot\bullet, M_0 \rangle$, *be the Petri net encoding of* S. *Let also* $N_i = \langle S_{N_i}, R_{N_i}, C_{N_i}, O_{N_i}, \mathcal{M}_{N_i} \rangle$, *with* $\mathcal{M}_{N_i} = \langle \bar{s}, \rho, \gamma, \tau \rangle$, *be a node in* S. *Finally, let* M *be a marking.*

– *The* active states *in* M *are*

$$A_S^M = \{ s \mid s \in P_S \setminus I_S \wedge M(s) = 1 \}.$$

– *The* assumed requirements *in* M *are*

$$A_R^M = \{ r \mid M(r) = 0 \wedge r \in b(c, S) \wedge M(r_c) = 1 \}.$$

– *The* offered capabilities *in* M *are*

$$A_C^M = \{ c \mid M(c) = 1 \vee M(r_c) = 1 \}.$$

Remark 1. Let S be a `ServiceTemplate` and let $\mathcal{Z}_S$ be its Petri net encoding. Let also P be a deterministic `Plan`, and let M_0 and M be the initial marking and a marking equivalent to the markings reached by performing the (complete) sequential traces of P in M_0.

---

[5] A sequential trace for a `Plan` P is *complete* if and only if its first and last operation correspond to an initial and to a final activity of P.

- The requirements that are assumed after P are A_R^M (where the newly assumed ones are $A_R^M \backslash A_R^{M_0}$), while those that are no more assumed are $A_R^{M_0} \backslash A_R^M$.
- The capabilities that are offered after P are A_C^M (where the newly added ones are $A_C^M \backslash A_C^{M_0}$), while those that are no more offered are $A_C^{M_0} \backslash A_C^M$.

Please note that it is possible to consider as initial marking any other (reachable) marking so as to analyze maintenance plans (starting from non-initial states) besides deployment plans. Obviously, the very same properties and techniques also apply in this case.

Additionally, various classical notions in the Petri net context assume a specific meaning in the context of TOSCA applications. For example the problem of finding whether there is a plan which achieves a specific goal (e.g., bringing some components of an application to specific states or making some capabilities available) can be reduced in a straightforward way to the coverability problem [23] on the associated Petri net. To show it, we first define the notion of *goal*, that is a marking putting exactly one token in the places denoting the states and capabilities that have to be active.

Definition 14. Let S be a `ServiceTemplate`, and let $N_i = \langle S_{N_i}, R_{N_i}, C_{N_i}, O_{N_i}, M_{N_i} \rangle$, with $M_{N_i} = \langle \bar{s}, \rho, \gamma, \tau \rangle$, be a node in S. A goal for planning in $\mathcal{Z}_S$ is a pair $G = \langle S_G, C_G \rangle$ such that

(a) $S_G \subseteq \bigcup_i S_{N_i}$ is the set of states to be reached, and
(b) $C_G \subseteq \bigcup_i C_{N_i}$ is the set of capabilities to be offered.

A valid sequential plan P for S reaches the goal $G = \langle S_G, C_G \rangle$ if and only if

(a) $\forall s \in S_G . s \in S_{N_i} \Rightarrow s$ is the current state of N_i, and
(b) $\forall c \in C_G . c \in C_{N_i} \wedge s$ is the current state of $N_i \Rightarrow c \in \gamma(s)$.

Theorem 1. Let S be a `ServiceTemplate`, and let $\mathcal{Z}_S$ be the Petri net encoding of S. Finding a valid sequential plan for S that reaches a goal G corresponds to solving a coverability problem in $\mathcal{Z}_S$.

Proof. Let $G = \langle S_G, C_G \rangle$. We can easily build a marking $M_G : P_S \to \{0, 1\}$ as follows:

$$\forall p \in P_S . M_G(p) = \begin{cases} 1 & \text{if } p \in S_G \\ 1 & \text{if } p = r_c \wedge c \in C_G \\ 0 & \text{otherwise} \end{cases}$$

From the above, it follows that finding a sequential plan that reaches the goal G corresponds to solving the coverability problem for the marking M_G. □

Theorem 2. Let S be a `ServiceTemplate`, and let G be a goal. Finding a valid sequential plan for S that reaches G can be solved with polynomial space.

Proof. The proof follows from the facts that the Petri net encoding $\mathcal{Z}_S$ of S is safe, that finding a sequential plan in $\mathcal{Z}_S$ that reaches G corresponds to solving a coverability problem, and that coverability in safe Petri nets is PSPACE-complete [12]. □

Another classical notion in the Petri net context that assumes a specific meaning is that of *reversibility* [23]: The Petri net encoding of a `ServiceTemplate` S is *reversible* if and only if it is always possible to softly reset the application, i.e. if whatever (valid) sequence of operations we perform, we can always get back to the initial state of S by performing another (valid) sequence of operations. This is a very convenient property, because it guarantees that it is always possible to generate a sequential plan for any reachable goal from any application state.

Definition 15. *Let S be a `ServiceTemplate`, and let $\bar{s}_S$ be its initial configuration (i.e., the configuration in which all the management protocols of its nodes are in their initial state). We say that S is* softly resettable *if and only if for each valid sequential plan for S*

$$o_1 o_2 ... o_m$$

there exists a continuation

$$o_{m+1} o_{m+2} ... o_{m+n}$$

such that

$$o_1 o_2 ... o_m o_{m+1} o_{m+2} ... o_{m+n}$$

is a valid sequential plan for S such that the firing of $o_1 o_2 ... o_m o_{m+1} o_{m+2} ... o_{m+n}$ from $\bar{s}_S$ leads to $\bar{s}_S$.

Theorem 3. *Let S be a `ServiceTemplate`, and let $\mathcal{Z}_S$ be the Petri net encoding of S.*

$$S \text{ is softly resettable} \Leftrightarrow \mathcal{Z}_S \text{ is reversible.}$$

Proof. By Definition 15, S is softly resettable if and only if the following condition holds: (C) For each valid sequence $o_1 o_2 ... o_n$, we can always determine a longer valid sequence $o_1 o_2 ... o_m o_{m+1} ... o_{m+n}$ such that by firing it in the initial configuration $\bar{s}_S$ we end up in the same configuration $\bar{s}_S$.

Notice that $\bar{s}_S$ corresponds to the initial marking of the Petri net encoding $\mathcal{Z}_S$, and that a valid sequence of operations corresponds to a firing sequence in $\mathcal{Z}_S$. Thus, condition C corresponds to saying that whatever firing sequence we can perform in the initial marking, we can always find a longer firing sequence that (starts and) ends up in the initial marking. This in turn corresponds to saying that $\mathcal{Z}_S$ is reversible (since whatever marking we can reach with a sequence of firings, we can always come back to the initial marking).   □

5   Related Work

Automating application management is a well-known problem in computer science. With the advent of cloud computing, it has become even more prominent because of the complexity of both applications and platforms [11]. This is witnessed by the proliferation of so-called *configuration management systems*, like Chef (https://www.chef.io/chef/) or Puppet (https://puppetlabs.com/). These systems provide a domain-specific language to model the desired configuration for a machine and employ a client-server model in which a server holds the model and the client ensures this configuration is met. However, the lack of a machine readable representation of management protocols of application components inhibits the possibility of automating verification on components' configurations and dependencies.

A large body of research has been devoted to model interacting systems by means of finite state machines, Petri nets, and other formal models (e.g., [5,16]). Our approach to protocol specification and analysis brings some similarities for instance with [3,14,22,26], that employ high-level Petri nets for protocol specification, and exploit notions like firability, reachability, and coverability, to analyse such protocols. For instance, [3] employs "numeric" Petri nets to model and analyse communication protocols. Such nets generalize tokens into tuples of variables to model fields in protocol messages, introduce net data variables to store "global values", and associate conditions and operations with transitions to permit checking and editing net variables. As the problem we address is simpler, we do not need a complex system like [3] since we just need to synchronize the management of connected components, by allowing each component to determine whether a needed capability is actually offered. Similar considerations apply to [14,22,26].

A detailed comparison with other existing approaches is beyond the scope of this paper[6]. We focus next on the subset of approaches more closely related to ours, tailored to model the behaviour of cloud application management.

A first attempt to master the complexity of the cloud is given by the Aeolus component model [15]. The Aeolus model is specifically designed to describe several characteristics of cloud application components (e.g., dependencies, non-functional requirements, etc.), as well as the fact that component interfaces might vary depending on the internal component state. However, the model only allows to specify what is offered and required in a state. Our approach instead allows developers to clearly separate the requirements ensuring the consistency of a state from those constraining the applicability of a management operation. This allows developers to easily express transitions where requirements are affecting only the applicability of an operation and not the consistency of a state (e.g., the transition ⟨Unavailable, {ServerContainer}, Setup, Stopped⟩ of the management protocol $\mathcal{M}_S$ in Fig. 4). Such a kind of transitions cannot be easily modelled in Aelous. Furthermore, Aelous and other emerging solutions like Juju (https://jujucharms.com/) and Engage [17], differ from our approach since they are geared towards the deployment of cloud applications, thus not including also their maintenance. Additionally, Aelous, Juju, and Engage are currently not integrated with any cloud interoperability standard, thus limiting their applicability to only some supported cloud platforms. Our approach, instead, intends to model the entire lifecycle of a cloud application component, and achieves cloud interoperability by relying on the TOSCA standard [24].

---

[6] A more detailed discussion on existing approaches exploiting Petri nets for protocol engineering can be found in [13].

To this end, TOSCA offers a rich type system permitting to match, adapt and reuse existing solutions [10]. Since our proposal extends this type system, it can also be exploited to refine existing reuse techniques, like [9,27]. Currently, these techniques are matchmaking and adapting (fragments of) existing `ServiceTemplates` to implement a desired `NodeType` by checking whether the features of the latter are all offered by the former. To overcome syntactic differences, ontologies may be employed to check whether two different names are denoting the same concept. However, these techniques are behaviour-unaware: There is no way to determine whether the behaviour of the identified (fragment of) `ServiceTemplate` is coherent with that of the desired `Node-Type`. Since our approach permits describing the behaviour of management operations, it can be exploited to extend the aforementioned techniques to become behaviour-aware.

It is also worth highlighting that we could directly compose the finite state machines specifying management protocols, and model valid plans as the language accepted by the composite finite state machine [6]. However, the size of the latter grows exponentially with the number of application components. This results in a high computational complexity, even if we exploit composition-oriented automata (e.g., *interface automata* [1]). On the other hand, with open Petri nets [2,18], we have a very simple composition approach, and the exponential growth only affects the amount of reachable markings (instead of the size of the net). A simpler composition approach is even more convenient since cloud applications can change over time. For instance, to add another web service to our motivating scenario, our approach just requires to add the open Petri net encoding its management protocol, and to connect the open places denoting its requirement with the corresponding $c_\uparrow$ and $c_\downarrow$ transitions. On the other hand, with an automata based approach, the composition would be much harder, as it requires to compute the Cartesian product of the automatons' states.

6 Conclusions

In this paper we have proposed an extension of TOSCA that permits to specify the behaviour of management operations of cloud-based applications, and their relations with states, requirements, and capabilities. We have then shown how the management protocols of TOSCA components can be naturally modelled, in a compositional way, by means of open Petri nets, and that such modelling permits to automate different analyses, such as determining whether a plan is valid, which are its effects, or which plans allow to reach certain system configurations.

Please note that, while some of those Petri-net analyses have an exponential time complexity in the worst case, they still constitute a significant improvement with respect to the state of the art, where the validity of deployment plans can be verified only manually, after delving through the documentation of application components. Please also note that our approach builds on top of, but is not limited to, TOSCA. It can be easily adapted to other stateful behaviour models of systems that describe states, requirements, capabilities, and operations.

We see different possible extensions of our work. We are currently working on a prototype implementation of our approach, which includes a graphical user interface to support the definition of valid TOSCA specifications that include management protocols. The graphical user interface will compile the management protocols of a TOSCA application into a PNML file [4], hence enabling to plug-in different PNML processing environments (e.g., LoLa, ProM, or WoPeD, just to mention some) to implement the analyses described in Sect. 4.4. Another interesting direction for future work is to investigate the applicability of more sophisticated fault diagnosis analyses (like [20,21]) to identify the reasons why a plan may not be valid (besides just showing the points in which a plan may get stuck, as we currently do). Finally, we want to extend the matchmaking and adaptation techniques we previously proposed [9,27] by including the behaviour information coming from management protocols.

Appendix

The objective of this appendix is to provide the properties of the Petri net encoding of a `ServiceTemplate` (see Definition 8) that are needed to prove its safeness (see Proposition 1). First, since each node N_i in a `ServiceTemplate` S can be in a unique state, exactly one of the internal places denoting its states contains one token, while the others contain no token. This holds at any given time, and thus in any marking that can be reached from the initial marking of the Petri net encoding of $\mathcal{Z}_S$. In short, (i) each internal place of the net encoding a `ServiceTemplate` contains at most one token. The same holds also for the open places modeling (ii) capabilities and (iii) requirements.

Lemma 1. *Let S be a `ServiceTemplate` and let $\mathcal{Z}_S = \langle \mathcal{P}_S, I_S \rangle$, with $\mathcal{P}_S = \langle P_S, T_S, \bullet\cdot, \cdot\bullet, M_0 \rangle$, be the Petri net encoding of S. Let also M be a marking reachable from the initial marking M_0 of $\mathcal{Z}_S$. For each node $N_i = \langle S_{N_i}, R_{N_i}, C_{N_i}, O_{N_i}, \mathcal{M}_{N_i} \rangle$ (with $\mathcal{M}_{N_i} = \langle \overline{s}, \rho, \gamma, \tau \rangle$) in S, the following properties hold:*

(i) $\exists s' \in S_{N_i}.M(s') = 1 \ \wedge \ \forall s \in S_{N_i}.s \neq s' \Rightarrow M(s) = 0$ *or, equivalently:*

$$\Sigma_{s \in S_{N_i}} M(s) = 1$$

(ii) *Let s be the current state of a node N_i (i.e. $s \in S_{N_i} \wedge M(s) = 1$). For any capability $c \in C_{N_i}$, the number of tokens in the open places r_c and c is:*

$$c \notin \gamma(s) \Leftrightarrow M(c) + M(r_c) = 0$$
$$c \in \gamma(s) \Leftrightarrow M(c) + M(r_c) = 1$$

(iii) *Let s be the current state of a node N_i (i.e. $s \in S_{N_i} \wedge M(s) = 1$). For any requirement $r \in R_{N_i}$ bound to a capability c (i.e., $r \in b(c, S)$), the number of tokens in the open places r and r_c is:*

$$r \notin \rho(s) \Leftrightarrow (M(r) = M(r_c) = 0) \vee (M(r) = M(r_c) = 1)$$
$$r \in \rho(s) \Leftrightarrow M(r) = 0 \wedge M(r_c) = 1$$

Proof. The proofs for (i), (ii), and (iii) are listed below.

(i) For each node N_i, the places denoting its states are internal to $\mathcal{Z}_S$. Hence, their input and output transitions are not changed by the merge process, which in turn means that only the net transitions (encoding the protocol transitions) of the same node N_i can add/remove tokens to/from them.

By construction, the above mentioned transitions always input exactly one token from an internal place and output exactly one token to an internal place (potentially the same). This guarantees that the total number of tokens in the internal places of a single node cannot change:

$$\Sigma_{s \in S_{N_i}} M(s) = \Sigma_{s \in S_{N_i}} M'(s),$$

where M' is a marking reached by firing a transition in M.

The above, along with the fact that the initial marking M_0 of $\mathcal{Z}_S$ includes a token only in the places denoting the initial states of the nodes in S (i.e., for each node N_i, $\Sigma_{s \in S_{N_i}} M_0(s) = 1$), implies that any sequence of firings starting from the initial marking will preserve exactly one token in the internal places denoting the states of each node.

(ii) First, we show that the property holds in the initial marking M_0 of $\mathcal{Z}_S$. According to the definition of management protocols (Definition 3), $\gamma(\overline{s}) = \varnothing$, which means that (in order for the property to hold) the initial marking M_0 of the open places must be empty (i.e., for each capability c, $M(c) + M(r_c) = 0$). This follows from the construction of $\mathcal{Z}_S$ (Definition 8), thus the property holds for M_0.

Since the property holds for the initial marking, we can prove that it holds for every reachable marking, by showing that no transition can invalidate the property. We will thus consider it as invariant.

Consider the capability c of a node N_i. The places mentioned in the property (i.e., c and r_c) are connected to the $c_\uparrow$ and $c_\downarrow$ transitions, and to the transitions of N_i that input/output a token to/from c. These are the only transitions that might affect the invariant, since the transitions connected to the requirements managed by the controller of c cannot change the marking of c nor that of r_c.

The $c_\uparrow$ and $c_\downarrow$ transitions cannot affect the invariant, since they do not change the total number of tokens in c and r_c. This is because, whenever $c_\uparrow$ fires, it removes one token from c, but it also adds one token to r_c (and to all of the other r_i places). Symmetrically, whenever $c_\downarrow$ fires, it removes one token from r_c (and from each of the other r_i places), but it also adds one token to c.

Thus, the only transitions that might invalidate the invariant are the transitions of the node N_i that input/output one token to/from c. Since all these transitions move a token from a state s to a state s', they can be classified as follows:

(a) c is either provided in both s and s' or in neither of them (i.e., $c \in \gamma(s) \cap \gamma(s') \vee c \notin \gamma(s) \cup \gamma(s')$);

(b) c is provided in s', but it is not provided in s (i.e., $c \in \gamma(s') - \gamma(s)$);

(c) c is provided in s, but it is not provided in s' (i.e., $c \in \gamma(s) - \gamma(s')$).

Each of these cases is consistent with the property that we want to prove.

(a) In the first case, transitions do not affect c at all, as (by construction) they are not even connected to c. They thus preserve the sum $M(c) + M(r_c)$, as well as the truth value of $c \in \gamma(\cdot)$.

(b) In the second case, transitions lead to a state s' such that $c \in \gamma(s')$, but they also add a token to c. If the invariant held before the transition (i.e., $M(c) + M(r_c) = 0$ with $M(s) = 1 \wedge c \notin \gamma(s)$), it also holds after the transition, because the sum becomes $M(c) + M(r_c) = 1$ with $M(s') = 1 \wedge c \in \gamma(s)$.

(c) The third case is precisely the opposite of the second one, since transitions lead to a state s' such that $c \notin \gamma(s')$ and they remove a token from c. If the invariant held before the transition (i.e., $M(c) + M(r_c) = 1$ with $M(s) = 1 \wedge c \in \gamma(s)$), then it also holds after the transition. The sum indeed becomes $M(c) + M(r_c) = 1$ with $M(s') = 1 \wedge c \notin \gamma(s)$.

In conclusion, since the invariant holds for M_0 and none of the transitions can invalidate it, by induction (over the length of a firing sequence) it holds for any reachable marking.

(iii) The proof of the property follows the same line as the one for (ii). Namely, the property can be proved to hold for any reachable marking by induction over the length of a firing sequence, by showing that it holds for the initial marking M_0, and that none of the transitions can invalidate such property.

□

References

1. de Alfaro, L., Henzinger, T.A.: Interface automata. In: Proceedings of ESEC/FSE-9, pp. 109–120. ACM (2001)

2. Baldan, P., Corradini, A., Ehrig, H., Heckel, R.: Compositional semantics for open Petri nets based on deterministic processes. Math. Struct. Comput. Sci. **15**(01), 1–35 (2005)

3. Billington, J., Wheeler, G.R., Wilbur-Ham, M.C.: PROTEAN: a high-level petri net tool for the specification and verification of communication protocols. IEEE Trans. Softw. Eng. **14**(3), 301–316 (1988)

4. Billington, J., et al.: The petri net markup language: concepts, technology, and tools. In: van der Aalst, W.M.P., Best, E. (eds.) ICATPN 2003. LNCS, vol. 2679, pp. 483–505. Springer, Heidelberg (2003)

5. Bochmann, G.V., Sunshine, C.A.: A survey of formal methods. In: Green Jr., P.E. (ed.) Computer Network Architectures and Protocols. Applications of Communications Theory, pp. 561–578. Springer, Heidelberg (1982)

6. Brogi, A., Canciani, A., Soldani, J.: Modelling and analysing cloud application management. In: Dustdar, S., Leymann, F., Villari, M. (eds.) ESOCC 2015. LNCS, vol. 9306, pp. 19–33. Springer, Heidelberg (2015). http://dx.doi.org/10.1007/978-3-319-24072-5_2

7. Brogi, A., Canciani, A., Soldani, J.: Modelling the behaviour of management operations in TOSCA. Technical report, University of Pisa, July 2015

8. Brogi, A., Canciani, A., Soldani, J., Wang, P.: Modelling the behaviour of management operations in cloud-based applications. In: Moldt, D. (ed.) Proceedings of the International Workshop on Petri Nets and Software Engineering (PNSE 2015), CEUR Workshop Proceedings, vol. 1372, pp. 191–205. CEUR-WS.org (2015)

9. Brogi, A., Soldani, J.: Finding available services in TOSCA-compliant clouds. Science of Computer Programming 115–116, 177–198, Special Section on Foundations of Coordination Languages and Software (FOCLASA 2012), Special Section on Foundations of Coordination Languages and Software (FOCLASA 2013) (2016)

10. Brogi, A., Soldani, J., Wang, P.W.: TOSCA in a nutshell: promises and perspectives. In: Villari, M., Zimmermann, W., Lau, K.-K. (eds.) ESOCC 2014. LNCS, vol. 8745, pp. 171–186. Springer, Heidelberg (2014)

11. Buyya, R., Yeo, C.S., Venugopal, S., Broberg, J., Brandic, I.: Cloud computing and emerging IT platforms: vision, hype, and reality for delivering computing as the 5th utility. Future Gener. Comput. Syst. 25(6), 599–616 (2009)

12. Cheng, A., Esparza, J., Palsberg, J.: Complexity results for 1-safe nets. In: Shyamasundar, R.K. (ed.) FSTTCS 1993. LNCS, vol. 761, pp. 326–337. Springer, Heidelberg (1993)

13. Cheung, T.Y.: Petri nets for protocol engineering. Comput. Commun. 19(14), 1250–1257 (1996)

14. Courtiat, J.P., Ayache, J.M., Algayres, B.: Petri nets are good for protocols. SIGCOMM Comput. Commun. Rev. 14(2), 66–74 (1984)

15. Cosmo, R., Mauro, J., Zacchiroli, S., Zavattaro, G.: Aeolus: a component model for the cloud. Inf. Comput. 239, 100–121 (2014)

16. Diaz, M.: Modeling and analysis of communication and cooperation protocols using Petri net based models. Comput. Netw. 6(6), 419–441 (1982)

17. Fischer, J., Majumdar, R., Esmaeilsabzali, S.: Engage: a deployment management system. In: Proceedings of PLDI 2012, pp. 263–274. ACM (2012)

18. Kindler, E.: A compositional partial order semantics for Petri net components. In: Azéma, P., Balbo, G. (eds.) ICATPN 1997. LNCS, vol. 1248, pp. 235–252. Springer, Heidelberg (1997)

19. Kopp, O., Binz, T., Breitenbücher, U., Leymann, F.: Winery - modeling tool for TOSCA-based cloud applications. In: Basu, S., Pautasso, C., Zhang, L., Fu, X. (eds.) ICSOC 2013. LNCS, vol. 8274, pp. 700–704. Springer, Heidelberg (2013)

20. Lohmann, N.: Why does my service have no partners? In: Bruni, R., Wolf, K. (eds.) WS-FM 2008. LNCS, vol. 5387, pp. 191–206. Springer, Heidelberg (2009)

21. Lohmann, N., Fahland, D.: Where did i go wrong? In: Sadiq, S., Soffer, P., Völzer, H. (eds.) BPM 2014. LNCS, vol. 8659, pp. 283–300. Springer, Heidelberg (2014)

22. Morgan, E.T., Razouk, R.R.: Interactive state-space analysis of concurrent systems. IEEE Trans. Software Eng. 10, 1080–1091 (1987)

23. Murata, T.: Petri nets: properties, analysis and applications. Proc. IEEE 77(4), 541–580 (1989)

24. OASIS: Topology and Orchestration Specification for Cloud Applications (2013). http://docs.oasis-open.org/tosca/TOSCA/v1.0/TOSCA-v1.0.pdf

25. OASIS: TOSCA Simple Profile in YAML (2014). http://docs.oasis-open.org/tosca/TOSCA-Simple-Profile-YAML/v1.0/TOSCA-Simple-Profile-YAML-v1.0.pdf

26. Paule, C., Eckert, H.: The NEt Simulation SYstem NESSY: Summary and Example. Ges. fur Mathematik u, Datenverarbeitung (1985)

27. Soldani, J., Binz, T., Breitenbcher, U., Leymann, F., Brogi, A.: ToscaMart: a method for adapting and reusing cloud applications. J. Syst. Softw. 113, 395–406 (2016)

Non-interference Notions Based on Reveals and Excludes Relations for Petri Nets

Luca Bernardinello$^{(\boxtimes)}$, Görkem Kılınç, and Lucia Pomello

Dipartimento di informatica, sistemistica e comunicazione,
Università degli Studi di Milano-Bicocca,
Viale Sarca 336, U14, Milano, Italy
luca.bernardinello@unimib.it

Abstract. We introduce two families of relations on the transitions of a Petri net. The first one is an adaptation of the "reveals" relation previously defined on occurrence nets for fault diagnosis applications. Here, this relation is considered for modeling positive information flow, which arises when the occurrence of a transition gives the information that another transition already occurred or will occur. The second one, called "excludes", is presented for modeling negative information flow, which arises when the occurrence of a transition gives information on the non-occurrence of another transition, in the past or in the future. We consider the notion of non-interference proposed in the literature for formalizing security in distributed systems. On the basis of reveals and excludes relations we propose a collection of new notions of non-interference for ordinary Petri nets and compare them with notions already proposed in the literature.

Keywords: Information flow · Non-interference · Reveals · Excludes · Petri nets · Unfolding

1 Introduction

Information flow is the transfer of a piece of information from an entity to another in a system. It can occur, for example, among variables of a program or among components of a distributed system. Information flow can be used to rule the behavior of a system, to guarantee the correct synchronization of tasks, to implement a communication protocol, and so on. However, information flow can be undesirable when it unintentionally leaks a piece of information to some unauthorized entities.

In this paper, we distinguish two kinds of information flow in Petri nets. The first one arises when the occurrence of a transition gives the information that another transition has already occurred or will inevitably occur in the future. We call this *positive information flow*. The second one is based on deducing information about non-occurrence of a transition. More specifically, this kind of information flow arises when the occurrence of a transition means that another

© Springer-Verlag Berlin Heidelberg 2016
M. Koutny et al. (Eds.): ToPNoC XI, LNCS 9930, pp. 49–70, 2016.
DOI: 10.1007/978-3-662-53401-4_3

transition did not occur or cannot occur in the future. We call this *negative information flow*.

We introduce two families of relations on the transitions of Petri nets which model the two kinds of information flow that are mentioned above. The *reveals* relation, with its variants, models positive information flow. The reveals relation was originally defined on the events of an occurrence net for the aim of fault diagnosis in [17]. In this paper, we redefine it on the transitions of a Petri net. Informally, a transition reveals another transition if its occurrence implies that the other one has already occurred or will occur inevitably in the future. We also present two parametric variants. The first one, called *extended-reveals*, is defined between sets of transitions. The second one is called *repeated reveals* and it considers the repeated occurrences of transitions. *Excludes* is a new relation which models negative information flow in Petri nets. Informally, two transitions exclude each other if they never appear together in the same run. We also distinguish *future/past excludes* with respect to the future and past occurrences of transitions.

In the literature there are several formal notions concerning information flow such as non-deducibility [26], opacity [7,8,20], anonymity [25] and *non-interference*. Here, we apply the newly introduced relations to study formal notions of unwanted information flow, based on non-interference notion within the theory of Petri nets, and compare our approach with existing approaches.

Non-interference was first defined for deterministic programs [15]. Later, several adaptations were proposed for more abstract settings, like transition systems, usually related to observational semantics [12,13,21,23,24].

Broadly speaking, these approaches assume that the actions performed in a system belong to two types, conventionally called *high* (hidden) and *low* (observable). A system is then said to be free from interference if a user, which knows the structure of the system, by interacting only via low actions, cannot deduce information about which high actions have been performed. This approach was formalized in terms of 1-safe Petri nets in [9], relying on known observational equivalences, including bisimulation.

In [22] a special kind of non-interference, called *intransitive non-interference*, is introduced in which there are not only two kinds of actions but also an intermediate kind called *downgrading*. The idea of having downgrading actions is that whenever one of such actions occurs it declassifies the high actions executed before it. Intransitive non-interference has been formalized in elementary net systems in [16] and studied in [5,6] on Place/Transition nets.

Similarly to Busi and Gorrieri [9], in this paper we analyze systems that can perform high and low level actions without considering downgrading actions. We rely on a progress assumption which was ignored in non-interference notions in the literature.

We propose a collection of new non-interference notions for ordinary Petri nets among which a system analyzer or designer can choose with respect to security needs. The new non-interference notions deal with positive information flow as well as negative information flow, regarding both past and future occurrences and are based on unfoldings and on reveals and excludes relations which are formally defined in Sect. 3.

The first non-interference notion we introduce is called *Reveals based Non-Interference (RNI)* and states that a net is secure if no low transition reveals any high transition (Sect. 4.1). We also propose more restrictive notions called *k-Extended-Reveals based Non-Interference (k-ERNI)* and *n-Repeated-Reveals based Non-Interference (n-ReRNI)*; these are based on observation of multiple occurrences of low transitions (Sects. 4.2 and 4.3). In Sect. 4.4, *Improved-Positive/Negative Non-Interference (I-PNNI)* is introduced on the basis of both reveals and future/past-excludes relations between low and high transitions, capturing both positive and negative information flow. The new notions are discussed and compared with each other while they are introduced. In Sect. 5, we compare, on the basis of examples, the new introduced notions with the ones already introduced in the literature and mentioned at the beginning of Sect. 4. Finally, Sect. 6 concludes the paper and discusses some possible developments.

2   Basic Definitions

Let $R \subseteq I \times I$ be a binary relation, the transitive closure of R is denoted by R^+; the reflexive and transitive closure of R is denoted by R^*.

A *net* is a triple $N = (B, E, F)$, where B and E are disjoint sets, and $F \subseteq (B \times E) \cup (E \times B)$ is called the *flow relation*. The pre-set of an element $x \in B \cup E$ is the set $^\bullet x = \{y \in B \cup E : (y, x) \in F\}$. The post-set of x is the set $x^\bullet = \{y \in B \cup E : (x, y) \in F\}$.

An (ordinary) Petri net $N = (P, T, F, m_0)$ is defined by a net (P, T, F), and an initial marking $m_0 : P \to \mathbb{N}$. The elements of P are called *places*, the elements of T are called *transitions*. A net is finite if the sets of places and of transitions are finite.

A *marking* is a map $m : P \to \mathbb{N}$. A marking m is safe if $m(p) \in \{0, 1\}$ for all $p \in P$. Markings represent global states of a net.

A transition t is *enabled* at a marking m, denoted $m[t\rangle$, if, for each $p \in {}^\bullet t$, $m(p) > 0$. Let t be enabled at m; then, t can fire in m producing the new marking m', denoted $m[t\rangle m'$ and defined as follows:

$$m'(p) = \begin{cases} m(p) - 1 & \text{for all } p \in {}^\bullet t \setminus t^\bullet \\ m(p) + 1 & \text{for all } p \in t^\bullet \setminus {}^\bullet t \\ m(p) & \text{in all other cases} \end{cases}$$

A marking q is *reachable* from a marking m if there exist transitions $t_1 \ldots t_{k+1}$ and intermediate markings $m_1 \ldots m_k$ such that: $m[t_1\rangle m_1[t_2\rangle m_2 \ldots m_k[t_{k+1}\rangle q$. The set of markings reachable from m will be denoted by $[m\rangle$. If all the markings in $[m_0\rangle$ are safe, then $N = (P, T, F, m_0)$ is said to be *1-safe* (or, shortly, safe). N is called *1-live* iff $\forall t \in T$ $\exists m \in [m_0\rangle$ such that $m[t\rangle$. Let $t_1, t_2 \in T$ and $m \in [m_0\rangle$, t_1 is *in conflict with* t_2 at m if they are both enabled at m and the firing of one of them disables the other one.

In the rest of the paper, we will consider systems modeled by 1-live Petri nets, in which the underlying nets are finite and all transitions have non-empty presets, i.e., all have input places.

Let $N = (B, E, F)$ be a net, and $x, y \in B \cup E$. If there exist $e_1, e_2 \in E$, such that $e_1 \neq e_2$, $e_1 F^* x$, $e_2 F^* y$, and there is $b \in {}^\bullet e_1 \cap {}^\bullet e_2$, then we write $x \# y$.

A net $N = (B, E, F)$, possibly infinite, is an *occurrence net* if the following restrictions hold:

1. $\forall x \in B \cup E : \neg(x F^+ x)$
2. $\forall x \in B \cup E : \neg(x \# x)$
3. $\forall e \in E : \{x \in B \cup E \mid x F^* e\}$ is finite
4. $\forall b \in B : |{}^\bullet b| \leq 1$

The set of minimal elements of an occurrence net N with respect to F^* will be denoted by $\circ N$. The elements of B are called *conditions* and the elements of E are called *events*. If $x \# y$ in an occurrence net, then we say that x and y are in *conflict*. Let $e \in E$ be an event in an occurrence net; then the *past* of e is the set of events preceding e in the partial order given by F^*: $\uparrow e = \{t \in E \mid t F^* e\}$. An occurrence net represents the alternative histories of a process; therefore its underlying graph is acyclic, and paths branching from a condition, corresponding to a choice between alternative behaviors, never converge. A *run* of an occurrence net $N = (B, E, F)$ is a set R of events which is closed with respect to the past, and free of conflicts: (1) for each $e \in R$, $\uparrow e \subseteq R$; (2) for each $e_1, e_2 \in R$, $\neg(e_1 \# e_2)$. A run is maximal if it is maximal with respect to set inclusion.

Let $N_i = (P_i, T_i, F_i)$ be a net for $i = 1, 2$. A map $\pi : P_1 \cup T_1 \to P_2 \cup T_2$ is a *morphism* from N_1 to N_2 if:

1. $\pi(P_1) \subseteq P_2$; $\pi(T_1) \subseteq T_2$
2. $\forall t \in T_1$ the restriction of π to ${}^\bullet t$ is a bijection from ${}^\bullet t$ to ${}^\bullet \pi(t)$
3. $\forall t \in T_1$ the restriction of π to $t^\bullet$ is a bijection from $t^\bullet$ to $\pi(t)^\bullet$

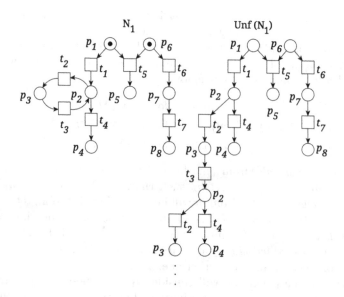

Fig. 1. A Petri net and its unfolding

A *branching process* of a Petri net $N = (P, T, F, m_0)$ is a pair (O, π), where $O = (B, E, G)$ is an occurrence net, and π is a morphism from O to N such that:

1. $\forall p \in P \ m_0(p) = |\pi^{-1}(p) \cap {}^\circ O|$
2. $\forall x, y \in E$, if ${}^\bullet x = {}^\bullet y$ and $\pi(x) = \pi(y)$, then $x = y$

A branching process $\Pi_1 = (O_1, \pi_1)$ is a prefix of $\Pi_2 = (O_2, \pi_2)$ if there is an injective morphism f from O_1 to O_2 which is a bijection when restricted to ${}^\circ O_1$, and such that $\pi_1 = \pi_2 f$.

Any finite Petri net N has a unique branching process which is maximal with respect to the prefix relation. This maximal process, called the *unfolding* of N, will be denoted by $\mathrm{Unf}(N) = ((B, E, F), \lambda)$, where λ is the morphism from (B, E, F) to N [11]. In Fig. 1, a Petri net with its infinite unfolding is illustrated.

The set of events of an unfolding $\mathrm{Unf}(N) = ((B, E, F), \lambda)$ corresponding to a specific transition t of a given Petri net $N = (P, T, F, m_0)$ will be denoted $E_t = \{e \in E : \lambda(e) = t\}$.

The following definitions concern the *reveals* relations, originally introduced for occurrence nets in [17] and applied to diagnostics problems. These notions have been further studied in [1,2].

Definition 1 [17]. *Let $O = (B, E, F)$ be an occurrence net, $\Omega \subseteq 2^E$ be the set of its maximal runs, and e_1, e_2 be two of its events. Event e_1 reveals e_2, denoted $e_1 \triangleright e_2$, iff $\forall \sigma \in \Omega, e_1 \in \sigma \implies e_2 \in \sigma$.*

Definition 2 [1]. *Let $O = (B, E, F)$ be an occurrence net, $\Omega \subseteq 2^E$ be the set of its maximal runs, and A, B two sets of events. A extended-reveals B, $A \twoheadrightarrow B$, iff $\forall w \in \Omega, A \subseteq w \implies B \cap w \neq \emptyset$.*

The reveals relation can be expressed as extended-reveals relation between singletons: $a \triangleright b$ can be written as $\{a\} \twoheadrightarrow \{b\}$.

Example 1. In the occurrence net given in Fig. 2, $e_2 \triangleright e_4$ and $e_4 \triangleright e_2$. $e_6 \triangleright e_4$ but $e_4 \not\triangleright e_6$ since after e_4, e_7 can occur instead of e_6.

In the same occurrence net, the occurrence of e_1 does not necessarily mean that e_5 will occur, however e_1 together with e_2 extended-reveals e_5, denoted $\{e_1, e_2\} \twoheadrightarrow \{e_5\}$. The occurrence of e_4 reveals neither e_6 nor e_7. However, it reveals that either e_6 or e_7 will occur, denoted $\{e_4\} \twoheadrightarrow \{e_6, e_7\}$.

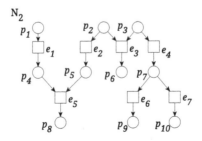

Fig. 2. An occurrence net.

3 Reveals and Excludes Relations on Petri Nets

In this section, we first introduce a *reveals* and an *extended-reveals* relation on the set of transitions of a Petri net, relying on the corresponding relations on occurrence nets as recalled in Sect. 2. We then define a parametric relation, called *repeated-reveals*, again on the set of transitions of a Petri net. Reveals, extended-reveals and repeated-reveals will be used here to model positive information flow.

We then define a relation between transitions, called *excludes*, which will be used to model negative information flow.

We will assume progress in the behavior of nets, which means that a constantly enabled transition occurs if it is not disabled by another transition. In other words, we consider only maximal runs in the unfolding.

In the rest of this section, $N = (P, T, F, m_0)$ will denote a 1-live Petri net, $\text{Unf}(N) = ((B, E, F), \lambda)$ its unfolding and Ω the set of all its maximal runs.

Definition 3. *Let* $t_1, t_2 \in T$ *be two transitions. Then* t_1 *reveals* t_2, *denoted* $t_1 \triangleright_{tr} t_2$, *iff* $\forall \omega \in \Omega \ \ E_{t_1} \cap \omega \neq \emptyset \implies E_{t_2} \cap \omega \neq \emptyset$.

We say transition t_1 reveals transition t_2 if each maximal run which contains an occurrence of t_1 also contains at least one occurrence of t_2. This means that for each observation of t_1, t_2 has been already observed or will be observed.

The reveals relation on transitions is *reflexive* and *transitive*.

Example 2. In the net N_1, in Fig. 1, t_3 reveals both t_2 and t_1. In order to fire t_3 we must first fire t_1 and t_2. In fact, in the unfolding, $\text{Unf}(N_1)$, given in Fig. 1, for each occurrence of t_3 there is at least one occurrence of t_2 and similarly, for each occurrence of t_3 there is at least one occurrence of t_1. However, t_1 does not reveal t_2 or t_3, since there is a run in which t_1 occurs and neither t_2 nor t_3 occurs.

Transition t_1 also reveals transition t_6 because when t_1 fires, t_5 cannot fire anymore and, since the net progresses, t_6 must eventually fire. Since we do not assume strong fairness, $t_1 \not\triangleright_{tr} t_4$, after the occurrence of t_1, t_2 and t_3 can loop forever. Reveals relation is not only about past occurrences. Observing t_1 does not tell us when t_6 fires. It might have fired already or it will fire in the future. $t_1 \triangleright_{tr} t_6$ tells us that when t_1 occurs, an occurrence of t_6 is inevitable.

When one transition alone does not give much information about the behavior of the net, a set of transitions together could do. Extended-reveals deals with this.

Definition 4. *Let* $W, Z \subseteq T$. *Then* W *extended-reveals* Z, *denoted* $W \twoheadrightarrow_{tr} Z$, *iff* $\forall \omega \in \Omega$

$$\bigwedge_{t \in W} (\omega \cap E_t \neq \emptyset) \implies \bigvee_{t \in Z} (\omega \cap E_t \neq \emptyset)$$

A set of transitions W extended-reveals another set of transitions Z, if each maximal run, which contains at least an occurrence of each transition in W, also contains at least an occurrence of a transition in Z.

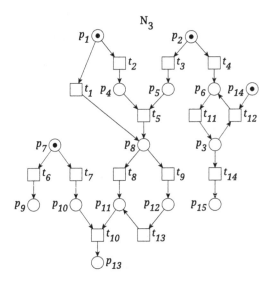

Fig. 3. Examples of extended reveals

The reveals relation on transitions, $t_1 \rhd_{tr} t_2$, corresponds to the extended-reveals relation between singletons, $\{t_1\} \twoheadrightarrow_{tr} \{t_2\}$.

Example 3. In the net shown in Fig. 3, t_2 alone does not reveal t_5, whereas t_2 and t_3 together tell us that t_5 will fire, denoted as $\{t_2, t_3\} \twoheadrightarrow_{tr} \{t_5\}$. In the same net, the occurrence of t_5 tells us that either t_8 or t_9 will fire, denoted as $\{t_5\} \twoheadrightarrow_{tr} \{t_8, t_9\}$. Similarly, $\{t_7, t_8\} \twoheadrightarrow_{tr} \{t_{10}\}$, i.e., there is no maximal run which includes occurrences of t_7, t_8 and not t_{10}.

Proposition 1. *Let* $t_1, t_2 \in T$. $t_1 \rhd_{tr} t_2 \iff \forall e_1 \in E_{t_1} : \{e_1\} \twoheadrightarrow E_{t_2}$.

Proof. Suppose first that $\forall e_1 \in E_{t_1} : \{e_1\} \twoheadrightarrow E_{t_2}$. By using Definition 2 (extended-reveals between events), we rewrite $\forall e_1 \in E_{t_1} : \{e_1\} \twoheadrightarrow E_{t_2}$ into

$$\forall e_1 \in E_{t_1}, \forall \omega \in \Omega : \{e_1\} \subseteq \omega \implies E_{t_2} \cap \omega \neq \emptyset.$$

By moving the universal quantifier $\forall \omega \in \Omega$ to the beginning of the statement. $\forall e_1 \in E_{t_1} : \{e_1\} \subseteq \omega \implies E_{t_1} \cap \omega \neq \emptyset$, we get

$$\forall \omega \in \Omega : E_{t_1} \cap \omega \neq \emptyset \implies E_{t_2} \cap \omega \neq \emptyset.$$

With this, we have achieved the definition of $t_1 \rhd_{tr} t_2$.

Suppose now that $t_1 \rhd_{tr} t_2$. From Definition 3, we can rewrite $t_1 \rhd_{tr} t_2$ as

$$\forall \omega \in \Omega : E_{t_1} \cap \omega \neq \emptyset \implies E_{t_2} \cap \omega \neq \emptyset.$$

The above statement can be rewritten equivalently as:

$$\forall \omega \in \Omega, \forall e_1 \in E_{t_1} : \{e_1\} \cap \omega \neq \emptyset \implies \exists e_2 \in E_{t_2} : \{e_2\} \cap \omega \neq \emptyset.$$

This means that each occurrence of t_1 appears together with at least one occurrence of t_2 in the same maximal run. So the statement becomes:

$$\forall \omega \in \Omega, \forall e_1 \in E_{t_1} : \ \{e_1\} \cap \omega \neq \emptyset \implies E_{t_2} \cap \omega \neq \emptyset.$$

Note that for each $e_1 \in E_{t_1}$ it is possible to have different occurrences of t_2 for different runs. This is in accordance with the definition of extended-reveals between events. Consequently we can write: $\forall e_1 \in E_{t_1} : \ \{e_1\} \rightarrowtail E_{t_2}$. □

Repeated occurrences of the same transition can give more information about the behavior of a net than only one occurrence.

Definition 5. *Let R be the set of all runs of N, $t_1, t_2 \in T$ be two transitions, and n be a positive integer. Let $R_{t_i}^n = \{\omega \in R : \ |\omega \cap E_{t_i}| = n\}$ and $\Omega_{t_i}^n$ denote the set of maximal runs in $R_{t_i}^n$ with respect to set inclusion (i.e., $\Omega_{t_i}^n \subseteq R_{t_i}^n$ such that if $u, v \in \Omega_{t_i}^n \wedge u \subseteq v$ then $u = v$).*

If $\Omega_{t_1}^n \neq \emptyset$ then t_1 n − repeated reveals t_2, denoted $t_1 \vartriangleright_{tr}^n t_2$, iff $\forall \omega \in \Omega_{t_1}^n \ E_{t_2} \cap \omega \neq \emptyset$.

If $\Omega_{t_1}^n = \emptyset$ then $t_1 \vartriangleright_{tr}^n t_2$ is not defined.

Notation. $t_1 \ntriangleright_{tr}^n t_2$ will denote that there is at least one run in $\Omega_{t_1}^n$ such that t_1 appears n times and t_2 does not appear. $\neg(t_1 \vartriangleright_{tr}^n t_2)$ will denote that either $t_1 \vartriangleright_{tr}^n t_2$ is not defined, or $t_1 \ntriangleright_{tr}^n t_2$.

Example 4. Let us consider N_3 in Fig. 3. Transition t_{11} does not reveal t_{12}; however if two occurrences of t_{11} are observed, then t_{12} must have occurred, therefore t_{11} 2-Repeated reveals t_{12}, denoted $t_{11} \vartriangleright_{tr}^2 t_{12}$, whereas $t_{11} \ntriangleright_{tr}^1 t_{12}$ since after the first occurrence of t_{11}, t_{14} can fire instead of t_{12}.

Since t_{11} can fire at most twice, neither $t_{11} \vartriangleright_{tr}^3 t_{12}$ nor $t_{11} \ntriangleright_{tr}^3 t_{12}$ is defined; therefore $\neg(t_{11} \vartriangleright_{tr}^3 t_{12})$.

Proposition 2. *Let R be the set of all runs of N and $t_1, t_2 \in T$.*

$$t_1 \vartriangleright_{tr}^1 t_2 \implies t_1 \vartriangleright_{tr} t_2.$$

Proof. Let $R_{t_1}^1 = \{\omega \in R : \ |\omega \cap E_{t_1}| = 1\}$ and $\Omega_{t_1}^1$ be the set of maximal runs in $R_{t_1}^1$. If $t_1 \vartriangleright_{tr}^1 t_2$, then $\Omega_{t_1}^1 \neq \emptyset$ and $\forall \omega \in \Omega_{t_1}^1 \ \omega \cap E_{t_2} \neq \emptyset$. Let σ be an arbitrary maximal run of $\mathrm{Unf}(N)$. Suppose that $\sigma \cap E_{t_1} \neq \emptyset$ then we can always take a run $\omega \in \Omega_{t_1}^1$ such that $\omega \subseteq \sigma$. Then we know that σ contains at least one occurrence of t_2 and so $t_1 \vartriangleright_{tr} t_2$. □

The implication of the previous proposition does not hold in the other direction. In fact, consider the net in Fig. 4, $t_1 \vartriangleright_{tr} t_2$, $t_1 \vartriangleright_{tr} t_3$, $t_1 \ntriangleright_{tr}^1 t_2$ and $t_1 \ntriangleright_{tr}^1 t_3$. The main difference is that we consider only maximal runs for reveals relation. For this net there is only one maximal run which contains t_1 (twice), t_2 and t_3. However, there is a run in $\Omega_{t_1}^1$ in which t_1 appears and t_2 does not appear, as well as a run in which t_1 appears and t_3 does not appear. All runs in $\Omega_{t_1}^2$, i.e., including t_1 twice, contain both t_2 and t_3, i.e., $t_1 \vartriangleright_{tr}^2 t_2$ and $t_1 \vartriangleright_{tr}^2 t_3$.

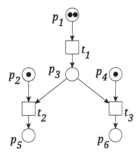

Fig. 4. Examples of reveals on transitions

Proposition 3. *Let $t_1, t_2 \in T$. If $t_1 \rhd_{tr}^n t_2$ and $\Omega_{t_1}^{n+1} \neq \emptyset$ then $t_1 \rhd_{tr}^{n+1} t_2$.*

Proof. Let R be the set of all runs of N, $R_{t_1}^n = \{\omega \in R : |\omega \cap E_{t_1}| = n\}$ and $\Omega_{t_1}^n$ be the set of maximal runs in $R_{t_1}^n$. If $t_1 \rhd_{tr}^n t_2$, then $\Omega_{t_1}^n \neq \emptyset$ and $\forall \omega \in \Omega_{t_1}^n \ \omega \cap E_{t_2} \neq \emptyset$. Let $\sigma \in \Omega_{t_1}^{n+1}$, we can always choose a run $\omega \in \Omega_{t_1}^n$ such that $\omega \subseteq \sigma$. Then we know that $\sigma \cap E_{t_2} \neq \emptyset$, so $t_1 \rhd_{tr}^{n+1} t_2$.   □

The next relation we introduce is called *excludes* and it models what we call negative information flow. Two transitions exclude each other if they never occur in the same run. This means that the occurrence of one implies non-occurrence of the other one.

Definition 6. *Let $t_1, t_2 \in T$. t_1 excludes t_2, denoted $t_1 \ \underline{ex} \ t_2$, iff $\forall \omega \in \Omega$ $E_{t_1} \cap \omega \neq \emptyset \implies E_{t_2} \cap \omega = \emptyset$.*

By definition, excludes is a symmetric relation. Moreover, it does not coincide with conflict relation. Transitions which are in conflict at a reachable marking can still appear in the same maximal run, so they may not exclude each other.

Example 5. Transitions t_2 and t_4 of N_1 in Fig. 1 are in conflict whereas $\neg(t_2 \ \underline{ex} \ t_4)$. In the unfolding in the same figure, it is possible to see a maximal run including occurrences of both.

$t_5 \ \underline{ex} \ t_4$ although they are not in conflict.
$t_7 \ \underline{ex} \ t_5$, $t_5 \ \underline{ex} \ t_1$ but $\neg(t_7 \ \underline{ex} \ t_1)$, indeed the relation is not transitive.

Excludes relation is not the opposite of reveals. Clearly, if $t_1 \ \underline{ex} \ t_2$ then $t_1 \not\rhd_{tr} t_2$, but the implication does not hold in the other direction. For example, in N_1 of Fig. 1, $t_1 \not\rhd_{tr} t_2$ and $\neg(t_1 \ \underline{ex} \ t_2)$. However, there is an interesting relation between excludes and extended-reveals relations.

Proposition 4. *Let $t_1, t_2 \in T$. $t_1 \ \underline{ex} \ t_2 \iff \{t_1, t_2\} \rhd_{tr} \emptyset$.*

Proof. Suppose $\{t_1, t_2\} \rhd_{tr} \emptyset$. By Definition 4, we have $\forall \omega \in \Omega : (\omega \cap E_{t_1} \neq \emptyset \wedge \omega \cap E_{t_2} \neq \emptyset) \implies \omega \cap \emptyset \neq \emptyset$. Since the consequent is false, we have $\forall \omega \in \Omega : \omega \cap E_{t_1} = \emptyset \vee \omega \cap E_{t_2} = \emptyset$ which is equivalent to $t_1 \ \underline{ex} \ t_2$.   □

Existence of excludes relation between two transitions tells that they can never appear in the same maximal run together. This refers to all past and future occurrences of the two transitions. However, we are not only interested in two transitions excluding each other in general, but also in cases in which the occurrence of a transition guarantees that another transition will never appear in the future, although it might have occurred in the past, or that it might occur in the future but did not occur in the past. We then define *future-excludes* and *past-excludes*. The former focuses on the future occurrences while the latter focuses on the past occurrences.

Definition 7. *Let $e \in E$, $\downarrow e = \{e' \in E : e < e'\}$. Let $t_1, t_2 \in T$; t_1 future-excludes t_2, denoted $t_1 \; \underline{ex}_f \; t_2$, iff $\forall e \in E_{t_1}, \forall e' \in E_{t_2} : \downarrow e \cap E_{t_2} = \emptyset \wedge \neg(e \; \mathbf{co} \; e')$, i.e., t_2 never occurs after t_1 or concurrently with t_1.*

Example 6. In Fig. 5, $t_2 \; \underline{ex}_f \; t_3$ since occurrence of t_2 disables t_3 forever, however after occurrence of t_3, t_2 can still fire in the future, therefore $\neg(t_3 \; \underline{ex}_f \; t_2)$. Similarly, in this net, $t_2 \; \underline{ex}_f \; t_1$. It is easy to see that t_1 can occur many times until t_2 occurs, and after the occurrence of t_2, it can never occur again.

Note that, unlike excludes, future-excludes is not symmetric.

Definition 8. *Let $e \in E$, $\uparrow e = \{e' \in E : e' < e\}$. Let $t_1, t_2 \in T$; t_1 past-excludes t_2, denoted $t_1 \; \underline{ex}_p \; t_2$, iff $\forall e \in E_{t_1}, \forall e' \in E_{t_2} : \uparrow e \cap E_{t_2} = \emptyset \wedge \neg(e \; \mathbf{co} \; e')$, i.e., t_2 never occurs before t_1 or concurrently with t_1.*

Example 7. In Fig. 5, $t_3 \; \underline{ex}_p \; t_2$ since an occurrence of t_3 means that t_2 did not fire in the past (after t_2, t_3 can never fire again). However $\neg(t_2 \; \underline{ex}_p \; t_3)$. Similarly, in this net, $t_1 \; \underline{ex}_p \; t_2$. It is easy to see that t_1 and t_3 can occur many times before t_2 occurs, so $\neg(t_2 \; \underline{ex}_p \; t_1)$; however after the occurrence of t_2, they can never occur again, thus t_2 cannot appear in the past of t_1 or t_3.

Proposition 5. *Let $t_1, t_2 \in T$. $t_1 \; \underline{ex}_f \; t_2 \Longleftrightarrow t_2 \; \underline{ex}_p \; t_1$.*

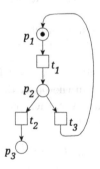

Fig. 5. Examples of excludes

Proof. We first prove that $t_1 \underline{ex}_f t_2 \implies t_2 \underline{ex}_p t_1$ by contradiction. Assume $t_1 \underline{ex}_f t_2$ and $\neg(t_2 \underline{ex}_p t_1)$. So, $\forall e_1 \in E_{t_1} : \downarrow e_1 \cap E_{t_2} = \emptyset$ and $\forall e_1 \in E_{t_1}, \forall e_2 \in E_{t_2} : \neg(e_1 \text{ co } e_2)$. Since $t_1 \underline{ex}_f t_2$ implies that $\neg(e_1 \text{ co } e_2)$ for all occurrences of t_1 and t_2, the unsatisfied requirement for $t_2 \underline{ex}_p t_1$ is that there exists $e_2 \in E_{t_2}$ such that $\uparrow e_2 \cap E_{t_1} \neq \emptyset$. This means that: $\exists e_1' \in E_{t_1}, \exists e_2' \in E_{t_2} : e_1' < e_2'$, i.e., there is an occurrence of t_1 in the past of an occurrence of t_2, which is in contradiction with: $\forall e_1 \in E_{t_1} : \downarrow e_1 \cap E_{t_2} = \emptyset$, which means that t_2 cannot occur after t_1. Hence $t_1 \underline{ex}_f t_2 \implies t_2 \underline{ex}_p t_1$.

In the other direction, assume that $t_2 \underline{ex}_p t_1$ and $\neg(t_1 \underline{ex}_f t_2)$. So, $\forall e_2 \in E_{t_2} : \uparrow e_2 \cap E_{t_1} = \emptyset$ and $\forall e_2 \in E_{t_2}, \forall e_1 \in E_{t_1} : \neg(e_2 \text{ co } e_1)$. Since $t_2 \underline{ex}_p t_1$ implies that $\neg(e_2 \text{ co } e_1)$ for all occurrences of t_1 and t_2, the unsatisfied requirement for $t_1 \underline{ex}_f t_2$ is that there exists $e_1 \in E_{t_1}$ such that $\downarrow e_1 \cap E_{t_2} \neq \emptyset$. This means that:

$$\exists e_1' \in E_{t_1}, \exists e_2' \in E_{t_2} : e_1' < e_2',$$

i.e., there is an occurrence of t_1 in the past of an occurrence of t_2, which is in contradiction with:

$$\forall e_2 \in E_{t_2} : \uparrow e_2 \cap E_{t_1} = \emptyset,$$

which means that t_1 cannot occur before t_2. Hence $t_2 \underline{ex}_p t_1 \implies t_1 \underline{ex}_f t_2$. $\square$

Proposition 6. *Let* $t_1, t_2 \in T$. $t_1 \underline{ex} t_2 \iff (t_1 \underline{ex}_f t_2 \wedge t_1 \underline{ex}_p t_2)$.

Proof. By Definition 6, $t_1 \underline{ex} t_2$ means

$$\forall \omega \in \Omega : E_{t_1} \cap \omega \neq \emptyset \implies E_{t_2} \cap \omega = \emptyset.$$

This means that t_1 can never be in the same run with t_2. So,

$$\forall e_1 \in E_{t_1}, \forall e_2 \in E_{t_2} : \neg(e_1 \text{ co } e_2) \wedge \neg(e_1 < e_2) \wedge \neg(e_2 < e_1).$$

By using Proposition 5, we can rewrite the above statement as: $t_2 \underline{ex}_p t_1 \wedge t_1 \underline{ex}_p t_2$ or, equivalently, $t_1 \underline{ex}_f t_1 \wedge t_2 \underline{ex}_f t_1$. Both formulas mean that t_1 and t_2 cannot occur concurrently or one after the other. So the statements $t_1 \underline{ex} t_2$ and $(t_1 \underline{ex}_f t_2 \wedge t_1 \underline{ex}_p t_2)$ are equivalent. $\square$

4 Non-interference with Petri Nets

In dealing with non-interference, one usually starts by classifying actions into *high* and *low*, and assumes that an "ordinary" user, who knows the structure of the system, can observe only the latter.

We will distinguish two kinds of information flow: *positive* and *negative*. As discussed in Sect. 1, the former arises when the occurrence of a high level transition can be deduced from the low level behavior of the system, whereas a negative information flow is concerned with the non-occurrence of a high transition.

Several non-interference notions have been proposed for Petri nets. The less restrictive notion, introduced in [12,13], and also studied on 1-safe Petri nets in [9], is *Strong Nondeterministic Non-Interference (SNNI)*, a trace-based property (trace as sequence of event occurrences), that intuitively says that a system is secure if produces the same sequences of low transitions even when high transitions are prevented from occurring. More restrictive notions are based on bisimulation [9,12,13].

Place Based Non-Interference (PBNI), introduced in [9], and other variants of it [10], are based on the absence of some kinds of specific places in the net, called causal and conflict places. A causal place is a place such that a low transition consumes from it a token produced by a high transition. A conflict place is a place such that at least one low transition and one high transition consume a token from it. A net is considered to be *PBNI* secure in the absence of such places. *PBNI* is one of the strongest among the known non-interference notions for Petri nets.

In [9] the authors provide a survey and a comparison of non-interference notions for 1-safe Petri nets. In the next section we will compare SNNI and PBNI with the alternatives introduced in this paper.

Non-interference has been studied also in unbounded P/T nets [6] both for systems with only high and low transitions and for systems with downgrading transitions.

All these notions seem to aim mainly at deducing past occurrences of high transitions: for example they all consider system N_6 in Fig. 7 secure, whereas, assuming progress, after the occurrence of l, a low user can deduce that h is inevitable.

The notions we propose not only capture information flow about past occurrences of high transitions, but also about inevitable or impossible future occurrences of them. The mere ability to deduce that some high transition has occurred is not always a security threat, provided the low user cannot know which one occurred.

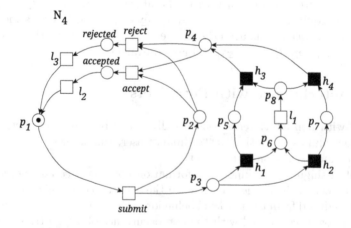

Fig. 6. A net modeling paper submission and evaluation.

Let us illustrate this issue by an example. The net in Fig. 6 represents a system in which a user can repeatedly submit a paper to a committee, each time receiving a judgment (accept or reject). From now on, the black squares represent high transitions. The review process can follow either of two paths, and we do not want the user to know which one was chosen. When the user receives an answer, he knows that some high transition occurred, but he cannot infer which one.

For this reason, the new notions we are going to introduce in the following will consider such a system secure, whereas it is not secure with respect to *SNNI*, and the other above recalled notions.

In the sequel, $N = (P, T, F, m_0)$ will denote a 1-live Petri net such that $T = H \cup L$, $H \cap L = \emptyset$, $L, H \neq \emptyset$, where H is the set of high transitions and L is the set of low transitions. $\mathrm{Unf}(N) = ((B, E, F), \lambda)$ will denote the unfolding of N. R will denote the set of all runs of N whereas Ω the set of all maximal runs. For all $t \in T$, $E_t = \{e \in E : \lambda(e) = t\}$.

4.1   Non-interference Based on Reveals

Reveals-based Non-Interference requires that no low transition reveals any high transition.

Definition 9. *N is secure with respect to* Reveals-based Non-Interference (RNI) *iff* $\forall l \in L, \forall h \in H : l \not\rhd_{tr} h$.

Example 8. N_4 in Fig. 6 is *RNI* secure. N_5 and N_6 in Fig. 7 are not since in both nets a low transition reveals a high transition: $l \rhd_{tr} h$. An observer who knows the net can deduce that h has already fired in N_5 by observing l. For N_6, again by observing l, he can deduce that h will fire inevitably. N_7 in Fig. 7 is also not secure because the observation of l_1 tells that h has already fired or will fire inevitably, since l_2 cannot fire anymore.

RNI does not capture negative information flow. N_8 in Fig. 7 is secure with respect to *RNI* since it cannot capture the negative information flow between h

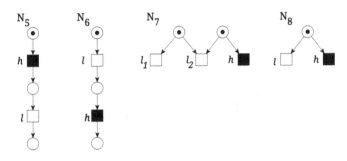

Fig. 7. Reveals based Non Interference (RNI)

and l, i.e., an observer can deduce that h has not fired and will not fire in the future by observing the occurrence of l. In Sect. 4.4, we will introduce a notion which deals with this kind of information flow.

4.2   Non-interference Based on Extended-Reveals

As explained in Sect. 3, a transition may not tell much about the behavior of the net, whereas a set of transitions together can give some more information. Extended-reveals deals with this relation. We propose to use this relation in order to define a new non-interference notion in which the occurrences of a set of low transitions together give information about some high transitions.

Definition 10. *Let k be a positive integer such that $1 \leq k \leq |L|$. N is secure with respect to k-Extended-Reveals based Non-Interference (k-ERNI) iff $\forall h \in H$, $\forall A \subseteq L$ such that $|A| \leq k \wedge \exists \omega \in \Omega : A \subseteq \lambda(\omega)$, it holds $A \not\rightarrow_{tr} \{h\}$.*
N is ERNI secure if it satisfies the above condition for $k = |L|$.

Intuitively, we say that a net is *k-ERNI* secure, if an attacker is not able to deduce information about the hidden part of the net by observing occurrences of k low transitions. If a net is *k-ERNI* secure then it is secure with respect to all *n-ERNI* where $1 \leq n \leq k$.

Example 9. N_9 in Fig. 8 is not secure with respect to *2-ERNI*. When l_2 and l_3 occur, an observer can deduce that h will occur, i.e., $\{l_2, l_3\} \rightarrow_{tr} \{h\}$. In the net in Fig. 9, no low transition alone reveals a high transition as well as no pair of low transitions reveals a high transition. However, $\{l_2, l_4, l_6\} \rightarrow_{tr} \{h_1\}$, i.e., by observing that all these three transitions occurred, an observer can deduce that h_1 will inevitably occur. Thus, this net is *2-ERNI* secure whereas it is not *3-ERNI* secure.

Obviously, *1-ERNI* coincides with *RNI*, where no low transition alone reveals a high transition. Moreover, *k-ERNI* $\subseteq$ *RNI*, for $k \geq 1$. N_9 is *RNI* secure since none of the low transitions reveals a high transition alone.

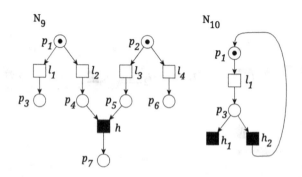

Fig. 8. Extended Reveals based Non Interference (ERNI)

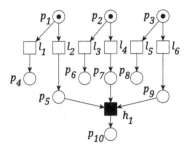

Fig. 9. ERNI and k-ERNI

4.3   Non-interference Based on Repeated-Reveals

Another case can be the one in which an attacker is not able to deduce information by observing low transitions and this is because only repeated occurrence
of a low transition gives information about the hidden part of the net. Thus, we
assume that the attacker can count the occurrences of low transitions and so he
can deduce information about the high transitions.

Definition 11. *Let $n > 0$. N is secure with respect to n-Repeated-Reveals based
Non-Interference (n-ReRNI) iff $\forall l \in L$, $\forall h \in H$, $\forall m \leq n$ such that $\Omega_l^m \neq \emptyset$:
$\neg(l \triangleright_{tr}^m h)$.*
    N is ReRNI iff it is n-ReRNI for all $n > 0$.

Proposition 7. $n - ReRNI \implies (n - 1)$-ReRNI

The proof follows from the definition.

*Example 10. N_{10} in Fig. 8 is not 2-ReRNI secure. Although the first occurrence
of l_1 does not reveal a high transition, by observing its second occurrence an
observer can deduce that h_2 occurred. However, the net is RNI secure as well
as ERNI secure. In the net in Fig. 10 $l_1 \triangleright_{tr}^3 h_2$ therefore the net is not 3-ReRNI
secure. If the transition h_3 was absent, then every maximal run would include at
least one occurrence of h_2 and then, even without observing l_1, the occurrence
of h_2 would be inevitable.*

The following proposition is directly derived from Proposition 2.

Proposition 8. *If a net is RNI secure then it is 1-ReRNI secure.*

However, the previous implication does not hold in the opposite direction. Consider the net in Fig. 4 and let t_1 be a low transition, t_2 and t_3 be high transitions.
This net is 1-ReRNI secure since the first occurrence of t_1 does not reveal information about t_2 and t_3, as discussed in Example 4. However the net is not RNI
secure since $t_1 \triangleright_{tr} t_2$ and $t_1 \triangleright_{tr} t_3$. Note that this net is not secure with respect
to 2-ReRNI since the second occurrence of t_1 reveals both t_2 and t_3, i.e. $t_1 \triangleright_{tr}^2 t_2$
and $t_1 \triangleright_{tr}^2 t_3$.

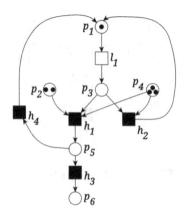

Fig. 10. Repeated Reveals based Non Interference (ReRNI)

In general, k-$ERNI$ and n-$ReRNI$ are not comparable since they are parametric notions which are based on observing different aspects: k-$ERNI$ considers occurrences of different low transitions together whereas n-$ReRNI$ considers multiple occurrences of the same low transition. Both k-$ERNI$ and n-$ReRNI$ catch positive information flow about the past or future occurrences of high transitions, whereas they allow negative information flow. In the following, we will introduce a notion considering both positive and negative information flow.

4.4 Improved-Positive/Negative Non-interference Based on Reveals and Excludes

Until now we have explored positive information flow on Petri nets. In order to catch negative information flow, related to non-occurrence of high transitions, we need to consider the excludes relation, as introduced in Definition 6. In [4], we have defined *Positive/Negative Non-interference (PNNI)*, on the basis of reveals and excludes relations, which catches both positive and negative information flow. Here, we propose a stronger version. The intuition is explained on the example below.

Example 11. Let us consider the net in Fig. 5. If $t_1, t_2 \in L$ and $t_3 \in H$, then the net is *PNNI* secure since none of the low transitions reveals or excludes t_3. In fact, a transition excludes another transition only if they can never occur together in the same run. In this example, both low transitions t_1 and t_2 can occur together with the high transition t_3. However, a transition might exclude another in the future (resp. past) and not in the past (resp. future).

In Fig. 5, t_3 can occur in the past of t_2 but not in its future. Consequently, an observer can deduce that t_3 will never occur in the future once t_2 occurs: $t_2 \underline{\mathrm{ex}}_f t_3$ whereas $\neg(t_2 \underline{\mathrm{ex}} t_3)$.

PNNI does not catch this kind of flow because "not excludes" does not mean "not excludes in the future and in the past". So we will require the negation of both $\underline{ex}_f$ and $\underline{ex}_p$ between high and low transitions instead of only $\underline{ex}$.

Definition 12. *N is secure with respect to* Improved-Positive/Negative Non-Interference (I-PNNI) *iff* $\forall l \in L, \forall h \in H : l \not\rightarrow_{tr} h \wedge \neg(l \; \underline{ex}_f \; h) \wedge \neg(l \; \underline{ex}_p \; h)$.

Example 12. Let us consider the net in Fig. 5 and let $t_1, t_2 \in L$ and $t_3 \in H$. Then the net is not secure with respect to *I-PNNI* because $t_2 \; \underline{ex}_f \; t_3$, whereas it is *PNNI* secure.

Obviously *I-PNNI* is stronger than *RNI*.

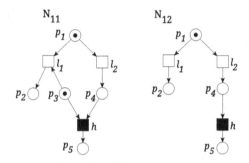

Fig. 11. Improved Positive/Negative Non Interference (I-PNNI)

Example 13. Both N_{11} and N_{12} in Fig. 11 are not *I-PNNI* secure since a low transition l_1 excludes a high transition h (both in the future and in the past). Thus, by observing an occurrence of l_1, one can deduce that h did not occur and will not occur. N_{13} in Fig. 12 is not secure with respect to *I-PNNI* because of negative information flow: l_2 excludes h_1, as well as h_2. An observer can deduce that none of the high transitions occurred and they will not occur in the future by observing l_2 or l_3. This net is *RNI*, *ERNI* and *ReRNI* secure.

In the same figure, N_{14} is *I-PNNI* secure. No low transition reveals a high transition, as well as no low transition excludes a high transition in the past or in the future. However, an observer can deduce that h_1 will inevitably occur by observing the occurrences of both l_2 and l_3, i.e., $\{l_2, l_3\} \rightarrow_{tr} \{h_1\}$. In other words, this net is not 2-*ERNI* while it is *RNI* and *ReRNI* secure.

Neither *I-PNNI* nor k-*ERNI* is stronger than the other for any k. The net N_{15} in Fig. 13 is both *ERNI* and *I-PNNI* secure, whereas N_{16} in Fig. 13 is not *I-PNNI* secure, however it is *ERNI* secure. N_{14} of Fig. 12 is *I-PNNI* secure, whereas it is not secure with respect to 2-*ERNI* as it is discussed in Example 13.

Similarly, neither *I-PNNI* nor n-*ReRNI* is stronger than the other one for any n. A net which is both *I-PNNI* and *ReRNI* secure is the one in Fig. 6. The net in Fig. 10 is not secure with respect to 3-*ReRNI* whereas it is *I-PNNI* secure. If we add to the net another low transition l_2 which consumes a token from p_5,

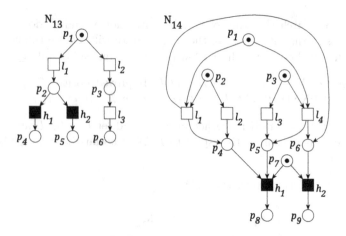

Fig. 12. A comparison among notions of non interference

the net becomes not secure with respect to *I-PNNI* as well as with respect to *RNI*, since l_2 reveals h_1. N_{13} in Fig. 12 is not *I-PNNI* secure whereas it is *ReRNI* secure.

5   Comparison of Non-interference Notions

We have introduced new notions of non-interference for Petri nets. These notions are based on the reveals and the excludes relations and on the progress assumption.

One major difference between these notions with the existing ones, recalled in Sect. 4, is that the new notions explicitly consider the information flow both about the past and the future occurrences of high transitions. For example, if a low user can tell that the occurrence of a high transition is inevitable in the future, such a system is considered to be not secure according to the notions we have here introduced, whereas it is considered secure by *SNNI* and *PBNI*.

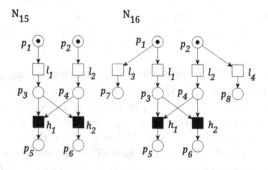

Fig. 13. A comparison among notions of non interference

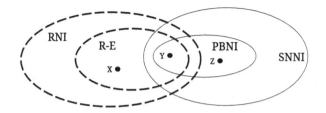

Fig. 14. Relations among notions of non interference

Similarly, for the negative information flow, we consider both past and future non-occurrences of high transitions.

Another important difference is shown by N_4 in Fig. 6. This net is not secure according to *SNNI* even if a low user cannot infer which high transitions actually occurred. On the other hand, it is secure with respect to all non-interference notions based on reveals and excludes, since these require the capability of differentiating among the high transitions. Figure 14 illustrates the relation between our notions and the other notions we have discussed so far. For the sake of simplicity, we only consider the weakest (*SNNI*) and the strongest (*PBNI*) notions from the ones recalled in Sect. 4 and compare them with the weakest of the new notions, i.e., *RNI*, and with the intersection set, denoted *R-E* in Fig. 14, of the new notions *RNI*, *k-ERNI*, *n-ReRNI*, *PNNI* and *I-PNNI*.

We will examine three examples to discuss the differences of these classes.

A net which is secure with respect to all notions based on reveals and excludes and which is not secure with respect to *SNNI* is denoted by X in Fig. 14 and it is the one in Fig. 6. We consider this net secure since an observer cannot differentiate among the high transitions even if he can know some high actions have been performed (or will be performed). However, this net is not secure with respect to *SNNI*.

The net denoted by Y in Fig. 14 is secure with respect to all non-interference notions based on reveals and excludes as well as with respect to *PBNI*. This net can be N_{15} in Fig. 13. This net is secure since no low transition reveals a high transition (alone or together with another transition) as well as no low transition excludes a high transition. Thus there is neither positive nor negative information flow. It is also secure with respect to *PBNI* due to the fact that there is no active causal or active conflict place.

Two nets which are secure with respect to *PBNI* but not secure with respect to any of the non-interference notions based on reveals and excludes, denoted by Z in Fig. 14, are for example N_6 in Fig. 7 and N_{12} in Fig. 11.

6   Conclusion

In this paper, we have introduced two new relations with their variants and applied them into the formal notion of non-interference in Petri nets. The first one is an adaptation to Petri nets of the *reveals* relation, previously defined on occurrence nets and applied in fault diagnosis. In particular, we have introduced a class of parametrized reveals relations for modeling positive information flow in Petri nets. The second relation is called *excludes* and it has been introduced here with the aim of modeling negative information flow.

On the basis of the new relations, we have proposed a collection of new notions of non-interference for Petri nets, and compared them with notions already proposed in the literature. In this approach, the transitions of a system net are partitioned into two disjoint sets: the low and the high transitions. A system net is considered *secure*, or *free from interference*, if, from the observation of the occurrence of a low transition, or a set of low transitions, it is not possible to infer information on the occurrence of a high transition. Our new non-interference notions rely on net unfolding and on reveals and excludes.

The notion of *RNI* states that a net is secure if no low transition reveals any high transition. We have shown that this notion captures some situations which were not captured by the existing notions. We also propose more restrictive notions: k-*ERNI* based on observing occurrences of multiple low transitions and n-*ReRNI* based on the ability of the low user to count the occurrences of a low transition.

By adding the *excludes* relation to the picture, we allow one to infer negative information, namely the fact that a high transition has not occurred and will not occur. This is the basis of *I-PNNI*. The paper includes a comparison between the notions introduced here and those found in the literature on the subject.

The notions proposed in this paper, and further variants of them, should now be tested on more realistic cases. Our aim is to build a collection of different non-interference properties, so that a system designer, or a system analyzer, can choose those more appropriate to a specific case. A generalization could be a non-interference notion based on a parametric reveals relation between multisets of transitions.

We are currently exploring algorithms to check non-interference. In particular, we consider using finite prefixes of net unfoldings, similarly to [3]. In [19], a method based on finite prefixes of net unfoldings has been proposed by adapting the diagnosis algorithm introduced in [18] to the problem of checking reveals and excludes relations. We are also interested in further investigating the excludes relation and the possibility to apply it in different contexts.

Acknowledgements. This work was partially supported by MIUR and by MIUR - PRIN 2010/2011 grant 'Automi e Linguaggi Formali: Aspetti Matematici e Applicativi', code H41J12000190001.

References

1. Balaguer, S., Chatain, T., Haar, S.: Building tight occurrence nets from reveals relations. In: Caillaud, B., Carmona, J., Hiraishi, K. (eds.) 11th International Conference on Application of Concurrency to System Design, ACSD 2011, Newcastle Upon Tyne, UK, pp. 44–53. IEEE, 20–24 June 2011. http://doi.ieeecomputersociety.org/10.1109/ACSD.2011.16

2. Balaguer, S., Chatain, T., Haar, S.: Building occurrence nets from reveals relations. Fundam. Inform. **123**(3), 245–272 (2013). http://dx.doi.org/10.3233/FI-2013-809

3. Baldan, P., Carraro, A.: Non-interference by unfolding. In: Ciardo, G., Kindler, E. (eds.) PETRI NETS 2014. LNCS, vol. 8489, pp. 190–209. Springer, Heidelberg (2014)

4. Bernardinello, L., Kılınç, G., Pomello, L.: Non-interference notions based on reveals and excludes relations for Petri nets. In: Proceedings of the International Workshop on Petri Nets and Software Engineering (PNSE 2015), Brussels, Belgium, pp. 59–78, 22–23 June 2015

5. Best, E., Darondeau, P.: Deciding selective declassification of Petri nets. In: Degano, P., Guttman, J.D. (eds.) Principles of Security and Trust. LNCS, vol. 7215, pp. 290–308. Springer, Heidelberg (2012)

6. Best, E., Darondeau, P., Gorrieri, R.: On the decidability of non interference over unbounded Petri nets. In: Chatzikokolakis, K., Cortier, V. (eds.) Proceedings 8th International Workshop on Security Issues in Concurrency, SecCo 2010, Paris, France, vol. 51, pp. 16–33. EPTCS, 30 August 2010. http://dx.doi.org/10.4204/EPTCS.51.2

7. Bryans, J., Koutny, M., Mazaré, L., Ryan, P.Y.A.: Opacity generalised to transition systems. Int. J. Inf. Sec. **7**(6), 421–435 (2008). http://dx.doi.org/10.1007/s10207-008-0058-x

8. Bryans, J., Koutny, M., Ryan, P.Y.A.: Modelling opacity using Petri nets. Electr. Notes Theor. Comput. Sci. **121**, 101–115 (2005). http://dx.doi.org/10.1016/j.entcs.2004.10.010

9. Busi, N., Gorrieri, R.: A survey on non-interference with Petri nets. In: Desel, J., Reisig, W., Rozenberg, G. (eds.) Lectures on Concurrency and Petri Nets. LNCS, vol. 3098, pp. 328–344. Springer, Heidelberg (2004)

10. Busi, N., Gorrieri, R.: Positive non-interference in elementary and trace nets. In: Cortadella, J., Reisig, W. (eds.) ICATPN 2004. LNCS, vol. 3099, pp. 1–16. Springer, Heidelberg (2004)

11. Engelfriet, J.: Branching processes of Petri nets. Acta Inf. **28**(6), 575–591 (1991). http://dx.doi.org/10.1007/BF01463946

12. Focardi, R., Gorrieri, R.: A classification of security properties for process algebras. J. Comput. Secur. **3**(1), 5–34 (1995)

13. Focardi, R., Gorrieri, R.: Classification of security properties (Part I: information flow). In: FOSAD [14], pp. 331–396

14. Focardi, R., Gorrieri, R. (eds.): FOSAD 2000. LNCS, vol. 2171, pp. 331–396. Springer, Heidelberg (2001)

15. Goguen, J.A., Meseguer, J.: Security policies and security models. In: IEEE Symposium on Security and Privacy, pp. 11–20 (1982)

16. Gorrieri, R., Vernali, M.: On intransitive non-interference in some models of concurrency. In: Aldini, A., Gorrieri, R. (eds.) FOSAD 2011. LNCS, vol. 6858, pp. 125–151. Springer, Heidelberg (2011)

17. Haar, S.: Unfold and cover: qualitative diagnosability for Petri nets. In: Proceedings of 46th IEEE Conference on Decision and Control (2007)

18. Haar, S., Rodríguez, C., Schwoon, S.: Reveal your faults: it's only fair! In: Carmona, J., Lazarescu, M.T., Pietkiewicz-Koutny, M. (eds.) 13th International Conference on Application of Concurrency to System Design, ACSD 2013, Barcelona, Spain, pp. 120–129. IEEE, 8–10 July 2013. http://dx.doi.org/10.1109/ACSD.2013.15

19. Kılınç, G.: Formal notions of non-interference and liveness for distributed systems. Ph.D. thesis, Universitdegli Studi di Milano-Bicocca (2015)

20. Mazaré, L.: Using unification for opacity properties. In: Proceedings of WITS, pp. 165–176 (2004)
21. Roscoe, A.W.: CSP and determinism in security modelling. In: IEEE Symposium on Security and Privacy, pp. 114–127. IEEE Computer Society (1995)
22. Rushby, J.: Noninterference, transitivity, and channel-control security policies. Technical report. http://www.csl.sri.com/papers/csl-92-2/
23. Ryan, P.Y.A.: Mathematical models of computer security. In: Focardi, R., Gorrieri, R. (eds.) [14], pp. 1–62
24. Ryan, P.Y.A., Schneider, S.A.: Process algebra and non-interference. In: CSFW, pp. 214–227. IEEE Computer Society (1999)
25. Schneider, S., Sidiropoulous, A.: CSP and anonymity. In: Martella, G., Kurth, H., Montolivo, E., Bertino, E. (eds.) ESORICS 1996. LNCS, vol. 1146, pp. 198–218. Springer, Heidelberg (1996)
26. Sutherland, D.: A model of information. In: Proceedings of National Computer Security Conference, pp. 175–183 (1986)

Validating DCCP Simultaneous Feature Negotiation Procedure

Somsak Vanit-Anunchai[✉]

School of Telecommunication Engineering, Institute of Engineering,
Suranaree University of Technology, Nakhon Ratchasima 30000, Thailand
somsav@sut.ac.th

Abstract. This paper investigates the feature negotiation procedure of the Datagram Congestion Control Protocol (DCCP) in RFC 4340 using Coloured Petri Nets (CPNs). After obtaining a formal executable CPN model of DCCP feature negotiation, we analyse it using state spaces. The experimental result reveals that simultaneous negotiation may be incorrect and broken on even a lossless FIFO channel. In the undesired terminal states, the confirmed feature values of the client and the server do not match. To fix this problem we suggest two solutions. Firstly, sending a Change option when an endpoint changes its preference. Secondly, an endpoint in STABLE does not discard non-reordered Confirm options. We have applied our suggested changes to the constructed CPN models. The formal verification of the revised models shows that the undesired terminal states have been eliminated.

Keywords: Datagram Congestion Control Protocol · Feature negotiation · Coloured Petri Nets · State space analysis

1 Introduction

In 2006, the Internet Engineering Task Force (IETF) published a set of standards for the Datagram Congestion Control Protocol (DCCP) [15] comprising RFC 4336 [7]; RFC 4340 [16]; RFC 4341 [8] and RFC 4342 [10]. RFC 4336 discusses problems and disadvantages of existing transport protocols and the motivation for designing a new transport protocol for unreliable datagrams. RFC 4340 specifies reliable connection management procedures; reliable negotiation of options; acknowledgement and optional mechanisms used by the congestion control mechanisms. RFC 4340 also provides the extension for modular congestion control, called *Congestion Control Identification* (CCID) but the congestion control mechanisms themselves are specified in other RFCs. Currently there are three published standards, RFC 4341, CCID2: TCP-like congestion control [8], RFC 4342, CCID3: TCP-Friendly Rate Control [10] and CCID4: RFC 5622 TCP-Friendly Rate Control for Small Packets [9].

This work is supported by Research Grant no. TRG5380023 from the Thai Network Information Center Foundation and the Thailand Research Fund.

M. Koutny et al. (Eds.): ToPNoC XI, LNCS 9930, pp. 71–91, 2016.
DOI: 10.1007/978-3-662-53401-4_4

Unlike TCP, DCCP does not impose flow control on the data transfer. But state information such as the sequence number sent and received is still used in order to trace packet loss which is crucial for congestion control. From the sequence number variables, a sequence number validity window is set up [16] to protect against attacks. Thus *connection management procedures* specified in RFC 4340 are used to set up and clear the state information. Apart from the reliable connection management, both sides must choose congestion control mechanisms and agree upon the same CCID. This requires a reliable negotiation procedure called *Feature Negotiation* which is also specified in RFC4340. If both sides are not aware of reaching an agreement with different CCIDs, the situation will be very harmful[1] and currently there is no recovery mechanisms. Hence it is vital to verify that the DCCP feature negotiation procedure works correctly. In this paper we use Coloured Petri Nets (CPNs) [13,14] to formally model and analyse DCCP feature negotiation procedures.

Formal methods [1] are techniques based on mathematically defined syntax and semantics for the specification, development and verification of software and hardware systems. They remove ambiguities and are indispensable for checking correctness of high-integrity systems. Coloured Petri Net (CPN) [13,14] is a formal method which is widely used [2,3,6,18] to model and analyse concurrent and complex systems. An important advantage of CPNs is its graphical notation with abstract data types providing a high level of expressive modelling power. CPNs and their analysis techniques have been used to verify many industrial scale protocols such as the Wireless Application Protocol (WAP) [11], TCP [12], DCCP [22] and SCTP [24]. The application of CPNs and related techniques for validation of the protocol design were illustrated in [17]. In addition to focusing on the four projects: the DYMO routing protocol, Generic Access Network (GAN) Architecture, Routing Interoperability protocol (RIP) and Edge Router Discovery Protocol (ERDP), they reviewed various work related to validation of the protocol design.

DCCP connection management operating over reordering channels with no loss was studied in [22] using Coloured Petri Nets. Later, the work [22] was extended by including DCCP simultaneous open procedure (RFC 5596) and Network Address Translators (NAT) in [23]. However, regarding DCCP feature negotiation procedure, there are very few articles [20,21] investigating it. The background information on feature negotiation was summarized and the algorithms for processing the feature negotiation options were illustrated in [20]. Interaction between the DCCP feature negotiation and the protocol procedures was discussed in [21]. As far as we are aware of, DCCP feature negotiation has not been formally modelled and analysed before.

The contribution of this paper is threefold. First, as far as we are aware of this paper presents the first formal executable model of DCCP feature negotiation. Second, the formal analysis helps us identify an error in the specification.

---

[1] It is difficult to justify the consequence when the CCIDs of both side do not match because it depends on the applications. However, we envisage that the receiver could submit garbage to the application while no one realizes the problem.

Third, conducting the state space analysis provides us insight as to the causes the error. We suggest two solutions to fix the error. After incorporating the suggested changes, our analysis shows the absence of undesired terminal states.

This paper is organised as follows. Section 2 provides an overview of the protocol and packet format. Section 3 briefly describes the DCCP feature negotiation procedure. The description of the CPN model of DCCP feature negotiation is described in Sect. 4, which starts with modelling assumptions and specification interpretation. Section 5 discusses analysis result and insight. Section 6 discusses the lessons learned and perspectives. Section 7 presents the conclusion of this paper and future work. We assume that the readers have knowledge of Coloured Petri Nets [13,14] and CPN Tools [5].

2   DCCP Overview

The Internet protocol architecture is organized into five layers known as the TCP/IP reference model. While TCP is a transport protocol that provides the reliable delivery of a byte stream, DCCP is a transport protocol for the timely but unreliable delivery of datagrams. DCCP can be viewed as an upgraded version of UDP equipped with new facilities for connection management, acknowledgement, feature negotiation and congestion control.

DCCP exchange packets over the Internet Protocol between a client and a server. The protocol uses 11 packets to setup and release connections and

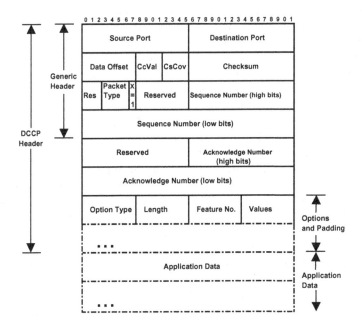

Fig. 1. DCCP packet format.

transfer data. RFC 4340 [16] defines a DCCP packet as a sequence of 32 bit words comprised of a DCCP Header and an Application Data area as shown in Fig. 1. The header comprises a generic header (applicable to all packets), followed by an acknowledgement number (if any) and then the options field. The length of the Option and Application Data fields can vary.

The DCCP header contains source and destination port numbers, and a checksum. A data offset indicates the length in 32-bit words from the beginning of the Header to the beginning of the Application data. CCVal is a value used by the congestion control mechanisms [10]. Checksum Coverage (CsCov) specifies the part of the packet being protected by the checksum. The Packet Type field specifies the type of the packet: Request, Response, Data, DataAck, Ack, CloseReq, Close, Reset, Sync, SyncAck and Listen. Request and Data packets do not include acknowledgement numbers. The sequence numbers of Data packets and the sequence numbers and acknowledgement numbers of Ack and DataAck packets can be reduced to 24-bit short sequence numbers when setting the Extend Sequence Number (X) field to 0.

The Options field contains state information or commands for applications to negotiate various features such as the Congestion Control Identifier (CCID) and the width of the Sequence Number validity window [16].

3   Feature Negotiation Procedure

DCCP allows both the client and the server to negotiate their parameters called *features* using the options field. The option field shown in Fig. 1 is a multiple of 32-bit words which may contain more than one option. Because each option consists of a multiple of 8 bits, the field may need to be padded to the word boundary. The first byte is an option type. The second byte is the length in bytes of each option including the option type field, the length and data of the option. The data part comprises a feature number and feature values. The feature negotiation can happen any time but is typically done during connection establishment. Each entity can initiate the negotiation of two kinds of feature numbers: *local features* (L)-the initiator's features and *remote features* (R)-the other side's features. Four particular options are dedicated to feature negotiations; Change L, Confirm L, Change R and Confirm R. The option types have values of 32, 33, 34 and 35, respectively. The format of Confirm or Change Options including a feature number and feature values are shown in Fig. 2(a). Figure 2(b) shows the six 8-bit values representing a Change L option when negotiating CCID. The meaning of each 8-bit value is shown in Fig. 2(c).

The feature number identifies the feature. For instance, 1 refers to CCID and 2 means short sequence numbers are allowed. The complete list of features is given in [16]. To reach agreement on a feature value, a reconciliation rule known to both sides is required. Currently, RFC 4340 defines two reconciliation rules: server priority and non-negotiable. Figure 3 shows a typical message sequence chart of each rule.

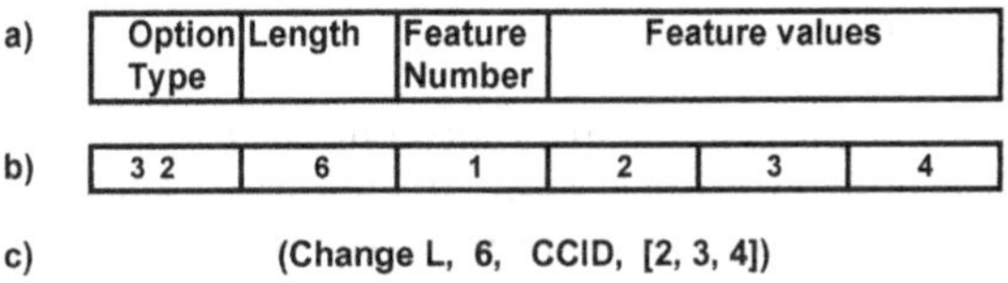

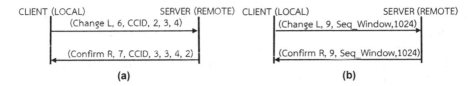

Fig. 2. Option format in DCCP header and an example of a Change L option.

CLIENT (LOCAL)   SERVER (REMOTE)   CLIENT (LOCAL)   SERVER (REMOTE)
            (Change L, 6, CCID, 2, 3, 4)   (Change L, 9, Seq_Window,1024)

            (Confirm R, 7, CCID, 3, 3, 4, 2)   (Confirm R, 9, Seq_Window,1024)
                      (a)   (b)

Fig. 3. Examples of the feature negotiation: (a) the server priority (b) the non-negotiable.

The server priority rule: This rule is applied when the feature value is a fixed-length byte string. During negotiation, DCCP entity keeps an ordered preference list of the feature values. The initiator sends a Change option containing its preference list. The receiver responds with the Confirm option containing an agreed value followed by its preference list. Thus the agreed value will appear twice in the Confirm option. The agreed value is defined as the first element in the server's list that matches any element in the client's list. If there is no match, the agreed value remains the existing feature value.

For example, the client sends *32,6,1,2,3,4* corresponding to Change L(32), length(6), CCID(1), the client's preference list(2,3,4). This means the client proposes to change its CCID and the preferred CCIDs are CCID#2, CCID#3 and CCID#4 respectively. The server responds *35,7,1,3,3,4,2* corresponding to Confirm R(35), length(7), CCID (1), agreed value (3) and the server's preference list (3,4,2). According to the client's and server's preference lists in this example, the client must use CCID#3.

Non-negotiable rule: The Change and Confirm options under this rule contain only one feature value which is a byte string. After receiving the Change L from the feature local, the feature remote must accept the valid value and reply with Confirm R containing this value. If the received feature value is invalid, the feature remote must send an empty Confirm R. This non-negotiable rule must not be used with Change R and Confirm L options.

For example the client sends *32,9,3,0,0,0,0,4,0* corresponding to Change L(32), length(9), Sequence number window (3), value of window size(1024). The server replies with *35,9,3,0,0,0,0,4,0*.

3.1   Finite State Machines

The feature negotiation procedures are represented by state diagrams. Figure 4 shows the state diagram for *feature local*. It comprises three states: STABLE; CHANGING; and UNSTABLE. The entity in the STABLE state always knows its feature value and expects the other to agree on the same value. When the local receives Change R, it calculates a new agreed value and replies Confirm L. On the other hand the Confirm R received will be discarded.

After the entity in STABLE sends the first Change L command, it enters the CHANGING state and goes back to the STABLE state upon receiving a Confirm R or a empty Confirm R. If the local in CHANGING does not get a reply from the other side, it keeps retransmitting the Change L option.

When the preference list is changed by its user while the entity is in the CHANGING state, it enters the UNSTABLE state. Here it ignores the on-going negotiation but starts a new negotiation by sending a Change command with the new preference list before going back to the CHANGING state.

The state diagram for *feature remote* can be obtained by interchanging *L*s and *R*s in Fig. 4. Thus each entity consists of three state machines working together: connection management, feature local and feature remote. It is possible that one side initiates Change L while the other side initiates Change R of the same feature. According to Fig. 4 when the local in CHANGING receives Change R, it computes a new agreed value and replies with a Confirm L. This situation is called *simultaneous negotiation*. The specification also allows the preferences to be changed any time.

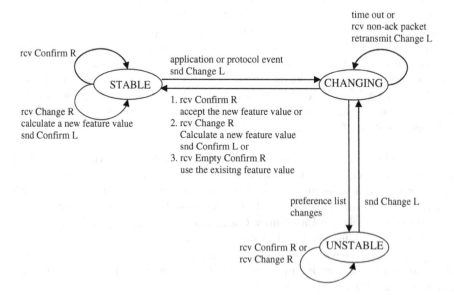

Fig. 4. DCCP feature negotiation state diagram - redrawn from [16].

3.2   Important Rules of Feature Negotiation

Although the feature negotiation procedures explained in the previous section sound simple, the real situation may be very complex when packets are reordered and lost. Moreover, the negotiation for the same feature can be simultaneously initiated by both sides and the preference lists can be changed any time. To cope with this, the RFC specifies some rules intended to provide reliable signalling so that both sides reach agreement on the feature value.

Non-reordered Change and Confirm Options. The RFC specifies that any Change and Confirm options in packets that do not arrive in strictly increasing order must be ignored. According to the related pseudo-code and algorithms, the strictly increasing order rule is only enforced for packets that contain the Change and Confirm options. An ordered packet with the Change and/or Confirm options may have a sequence number less than GSR if the later packets do not contain any Change or Confirm options.

In order to check the order of arrival, the RFC specifies another two variables: Feature Greatest Sequence Number Received (FGSR) and Feature Greatest Sequence Number Sent (FGSS). If the received packet's sequence number is less than or equal to FGSR, Change or Confirm options received must be ignored. If the acknowledgement number is less than FGSS or the packet contains no acknowledgement, the Confirm option received must be ignored.

Because DCCP-Data with short sequence numbers is vulnerable to attack, any option attached to DCCP-Data that might cause the connection to be reset shall be ignored. Thus both Change and Confirm options received in DCCP-Data must be ignored in all circumstances. FGSR is updated when the entity receives a valid packet containing non-reordered Change or Confirm options. FGSS is updated when the entity sends a Change Option during a transition from STABLE or UNSTABLE to CHANGING.

Retransmission. Change options must be retransmitted when the sender does not receive a non-reordered Confirm option within a specific period. The Confirm option must be generated only when a non-reordered Change option is received. Retransmission of options may be achieved by either generating a new packet (DCCP-Ack or DCCP-Sync) or by including the appropriate option field in a packet that is about to be transmitted. Retransmission continues until a non-reordered Confirm option is received or the connection is closed.

4   CPN Model of DCCP Feature Negotiation (DCCP-FN)

4.1   Modelling Assumptions and Specification Interpretation

We make the following assumptions regarding DCCP feature negotiation when creating our model.

1. We assume the medium to be First-in First-out (FIFO) channels with no loss. There are three reasons supporting this assumption. Firstly, RFC 4340 requires that the reordered Change and Confirm Options are ignored. This requirement is fulfilled by the two checking algorithms specified in RFC4340. It implies that actually DCCP feature negotiation protocol operates over FIFO channels. Secondly, the assumption of FIFO channel makes the model simpler. We can abstract away irrelevant details such as sequence number, acknowledgement number, state variables FGSS and FGSR. Thirdly, reordering and/or lossy channels can mask out inherent errors such as unspecified receptions which could appear when protocol operates over FIFO channels with no loss. Thus, protocol validation shall be started from operating over the FIFO channels with no loss; FIFO channels with loss; reordering channels with no loss; and reordering channels with loss, respectively. Our current analysis considers only FIFO channels with no loss.

2. According to [21], RFC 4340 separated the feature negotiation and protocol state machines as independent but they are not actually separate from each other. We agree with [21] that they are not independent but this paper models and analyses only the state machines of the feature negotiation. Without loss of generality, instead of modelling three FSMs (connection management, feature local and feature remote) at each side, only one FSM (Fig. 4) (either the feature local's or the feature remote's FSM) is required. In particular we assign the feature local's FSM to the client and the feature remote's FSM to the server. This assumption makes the CPN model readable and easy to understand.

3. A DCCP packet is modelled by an option type and a list of feature values (preference list). Other fields such as packet type and sequence-acknowledgement numbers are omitted because they do not affect the operation of the feature negotiation.

4. RFC4340 allows many options to be sent in one packet and many features to be negotiated at the same time. Following an incremental approach [3], as a first step we consider the negotiation of *Congestion Control Identification* (CCID) that uses the server-priority reconciliation rule because the ability to negotiate the suitable congestion control mechanism is the main objective of DCCP.

5. Our model does not include the mandatory options, invalid options and unknown feature numbers.

6. RFC 4340 specifies that the preference list can be changed any time. It is unclear what should happen if the preference list is changed while the endpoint is in STABLE. However according to [20], the endpoint can remain in STABLE if it changes the preference list without changing the preferred value. Thus we assume that the endpoint remains in STABLE after it changes the preference list. However we investigate the scenario when the endpoint changes the preference list without changing the preferred value.

4.2   Model Structure

Our model structure is inspired by [22,26] which model and analyse DCCP connection management. However, the feature negotiation procedure was not included in [22,26]. Our DCCP feature negotiation model comprises three hierarchical levels as shown in Fig. 5(a). The first level page is Main_FN. This page is linked to the second level pages named FN_Local and FN_Remote. The third level has six pages. Each one is named by a DCCP feature negotiation state. Figure 6 shows declarations which define the data associated with the model. The CPN diagram in the first level page, Fig. 5(b), comprises two substitution transitions (represented by double-line rectangles), four places (represented by ellipses) and arcs connecting places and transitions. The substitution transition on the left models the client (Local) and the one on the right models the server (Remote). Both communicate via two places named Remote2Local and Local2Remote in the middle of Fig. 5(b). Each place models a unidirectional and First-in First-out channel typed by List_Option_Field. List_Option_Field is a list of product sets named Option_Field defined in Fig. 6. Option_Field comprises Option_Type and Preference_List sets also defined in Fig. 6. Through these places, tokens (which are values taken from the type of the place) are transferred between Local and Remote.

Places FN_State_Local and FN_State_Remote, typed by FN_CB, model the states of the feature negotiation procedure. The FN_CB is defined as a product comprising colour sets FN_State, Confirmed_Value and Preference_List.

The substitution transitions Local and Remote in Fig. 5(b) are linked to the second level pages named FN_Local in Fig. 7 and FN_Remote in Fig. 11. Each of the second level CPN pages comprises three substitution transitions, named by

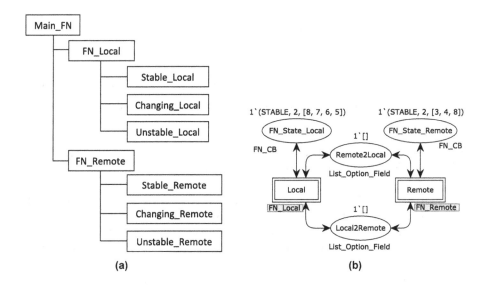

Fig. 5. (a) The DCCP-FN hierarchy page (b)The Main_FN overview page.

```
 1: (* Feature Negotiations *)
 2: colset E = with e;
 3: colset CCID = int with 2..255;
 4: colset Confirmed_Value = CCID;
 5: colset Preference_List = list CCID;
 6: colset Option_Type = with ChangeL | ConfirmL
 7:                            | ChangeR | ConfirmR;
 8: colset Option_Field = product Option_Type
 9:                            * Preference_List;
10: colset List_Option_Field = list Option_Field;
11: colset FN_State = with STABLE | CHANGING | UNSTABLE;
12: colset FN_CB = product FN_State * Confirmed_Value
13:                            * Preference_List;
```

Fig. 6. Declarations for the CPN model.

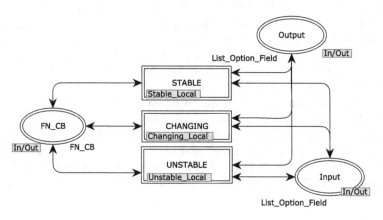

Fig. 7. The FN_Local page.

the feature negotiation states and linked to the CPN pages in the third level. Each CPN page of the third level corresponds to states in FSMs (Fig. 4). We can directly map each state transition in Fig. 4 onto each transition on the third level CPN page.

Stable_Local Page. Figure 8 captures the behaviour when Local is in the STABLE state. Transition ApplicationEvent models when the protocol receives a command to start the negotiation. It sends a ChangeL option and enters the CHANGING state. When receiving a ChanngeR option, transition Rcv_ChangeR computes the new confirmed feature value. Local sends a ConfirmL option containing this new confirmed value and remains in STABLE. Note that the preference list in the received ChangeR has a higher priority than the one kept in the client's state. Transition Rcv_ConfirmR discards any received ConfirmR option. The last transition PreferenceChanges replaces a new preference list in the client's state and Local remains in the STABLE state.

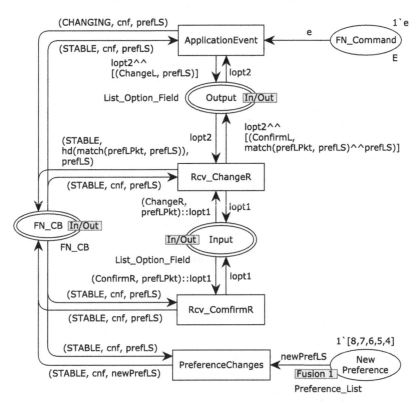

Fig. 8. The Stable_Local page.

Changing_Local Page. The transitions of the CHANGING state in FSMs (Fig. 4) are mapped to the transitions in Fig. 9. Transition `PreferenceChanges` puts a new preference list into the client's state and `Local` enters the UNSTABLE state. Transition `Retransmission` keeps retransmitting the ChangeL option. Because the retransmission is not used in this paper, `MaxRetransLocal` is set to 0. After receiving a ChangeR option, transition `Rcv_ChangeR` computes the new confirmed feature value, returns a ConfirmL option containing the new confirmed value and changes `Local`'s state to STABLE. The preference list in the received ChangeR has a higher priority than the one kept in the client's state. When receiving the ConfirmR option that does not contain any confirmed feature value, transition `Rcv_EmptyConfirmR` keeps the existing confirmed value in the client's state and enters the STABLE state. After receiving a ConfirmR option, transition `Rcv_ConfirmR` not only changes `Local`'s state to STABLE but also checks if the received confirmed feature value is correct. If it is incorrect, the `Local` uses the default feature value. If the new value is correct, the `Local` replaces the new value into its state variables.

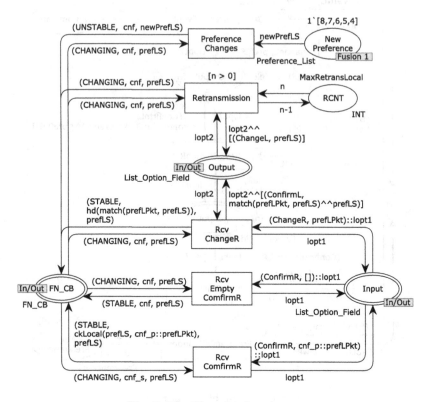

Fig. 9. The Changing_Local page.

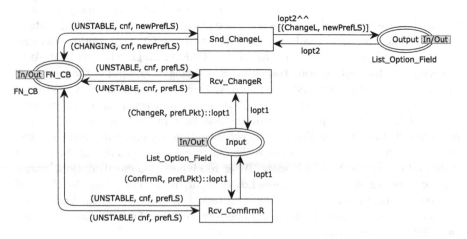

Fig. 10. The Unstable_Local page.

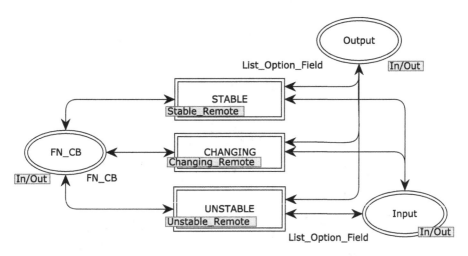

Fig. 11. The FN_Remote page.

Unstable_Local Page. The transitions of the UNSTABLE state in FSMs (Fig. 4) are mapped to the transitions in Fig. 10. Transition Snd_ChangeL sends the ChangeL option containing the new preference list and changes Local's state to CHANGING. When receiving any ChangeR option, transition Rcv_ChangeR keeps ignoring it. Similarly, if any ConfirmR option is received, transition Rcv_Co-nfirmR discards it.

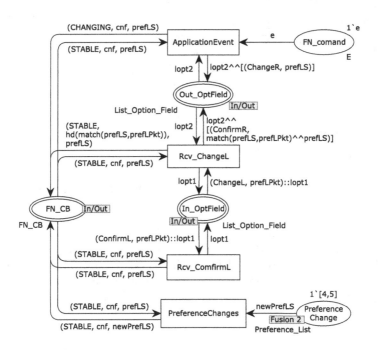

Fig. 12. The Stable_Remote page.

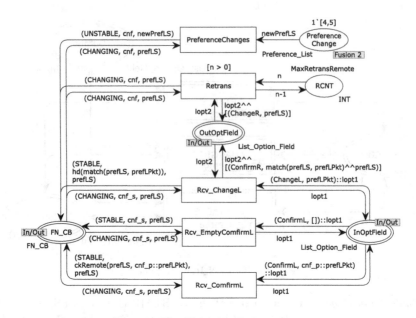

Fig. 13. The Changing_Remote page.

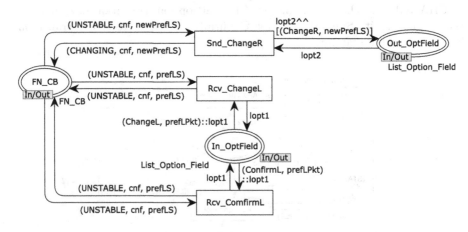

Fig. 14. The Unstable_Remote page.

Figures 12, 13 and 14 are the third level CPN pages representing the behaviour of Remote in the STABLE, CHANGING and UNSTABLE states, respectively. It behaves similar to Local but with two differences. First, "L"s (Local) interchanges with "R"s (Remote). Second, the preference list in Remote has a higher priority than the one in the received option because we assign Remote's FSM to the server.

5 Analysis of DCCP-FN CPN Model

5.1 Initial Configurations

Our DCCP feature negotiation model is analysed using CPN Tools [5,14] version 4.0 on an Intel i5-4300U 1.90 GHZ with 4 GB RAM. To analyse a particular scenario, the CPN model needs to be initialised by distributing initial tokens to the places FN_State_Local and FN_State_Remote in Fig. 5(b); the places FN_Command and NewPreference in Stable_Local (Fig. 8) as well as the places FN_Command and NewPreference in Stable_Remote (Fig. 12). The channel places Remote2Local and Local2Remote initially contain an empty list. The presence of an e-token in the place FN_Command allows the entity to start the feature negotiation procedure. The analysis in this paper assumes no retransmission.

With reference to assumption 4 in Sect. 4.1, we choose to model and analyse the negotiation of the feature CCID. This feature uses the reconciliation rule based on server priority. The default feature value is 2 which represents TCP-like congestion control. Although currently the standard specifies only CCID2 (RFC4341), CCID3 (RFC4342) and CCID4 (RFC5622), we make up CCID numbers in each preference list for the purpose of validating the feature negotiation procedure. Table 1 shows the preference lists we used in our experiments before and after the preference has been changed. The resolved values before and after the preference changed under the server-priority reconciliation rule are also shown in Table 1. According to [20] the endpoint can remain in the STABLE state if it changes the preference list without changing the preferred value. Therefore at the client (Local) we keep the old preference list but add the new feature value (4) at the end of the list.

Table 1. An agreed feature value before and after preference lists have been changed.

			Client (Local)	
			before	after
			[8, 7, 6, 5]	[8, 7, 6, 5, 4]
Server (Remote)	before	[3,4,8]	8	4
	after	[4, 5]	5	4

5.2 Analysis Result

Table 2 shows the initial configurations and analysis results of twelve possible scenarios. The scenarios (cases) are classified according to which sides are allowed to initiate the negotiation and which sides change their preference lists. Our CPN model allows simultaneous negotiation and both sides can change their preference lists in Case 12. The total number of states, arcs in each case are shown in the sixth and seventh columns. Columns 8, 9 and 10 show the terminal markings of

Table 2. Initial configurations of twelve possible scenarios and analysis result.

| | Initial markings | | | | | | Terminal markings | | |
| | FN_Command | | Change of preference list | | Nodes | Arcs | Type I | Type II | Type III |
Case (1)	Local (2)	Remote (3)	Local (4)	Remote (5)	(6)	(7)	(8)	(9)	(10)
1	1'e	empty	disable	disable	4	3	1	0	0
2	empty	1'e	disable	disable	4	3	1	0	0
3	1'e	1'e	disable	disable	20	26	1	0	0
4	1'e	empty	enable	disable	19	22	2	1	0
5	empty	1'e	enable	disable	10	11	2	0	0
6	1'e	1'e	enable	disable	106	169	2	1	0
7	1'e	empty	disable	enable	10	11	2	0	0
8	empty	1'e	disable	enable	19	22	2	1	0
9	1'e	1'e	disable	enable	106	169	2	1	0
10	1'e	empty	enable	enable	50	77	3	1	0
11	empty	1'e	enable	enable	52	78	3	2	0
12	1'e	1'e	enable	enable	553	1,043	3	3	1

each scenario. All terminal markings have both sides in STABLE and no packets left in the channels and hence there is no unspecified reception. The terminal markings are classified into 3 types. Type-I is the desired terminal state, where both client and server reach the same feature value. Type-II is the undesired terminal state, where both sides reach different feature values but an endpoint knows that the agreed value is wrong. Type-III is also the undesired terminal state, where both sides reach different feature values and both endpoints do not know that their feature values do not match.

5.3   Discussion

Figure 15 shows a scenario leading to a Type-II terminal state in which after sending the first Change L Option, the client changes its preference list and sends the second Change L in the UNSTABLE state. When receiving the Confirm R of the first Change L in the CHANGING state, the client enters the STABLE state and then ignores the Confirm R of the second Change L. The agreed feature value in the first Confirm R is outdated and different from the feature value in the server. However when comparing the preference list in the first Confirm R option with the preference list in the client's state information, the client is able to know that the agreed value is wrong. Obviously in this case the client should resend the Change option or reset the connection.

Figure 16 illustrates a scenario leading to an undesired Type-III terminal state. This is the center of our attention in this paper. This scenario can happen when both sides initiate the negotiation simultaneously and both sides change their preference list (Case 12). We notice that all Confirm options in Fig. 16 are discarded. It becomes one way communication with no acknowledgement. Figure 16 can be viewed as three attempts of negotiation. Two attempts are simultaneously initiated from both sides. This can happen during DCCP simultaneous open procedure. Preference list changed in the CHANGING state causes

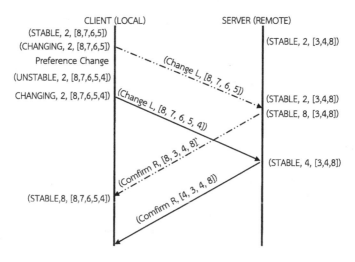

Fig. 15. A scenario leading to an undesired terminal marking Type-II.

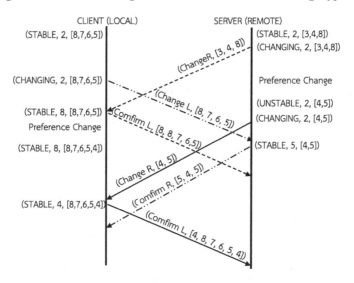

Fig. 16. A scenario leading to an undesired terminal marking Type-III.

the third attempt of negotiation. All three calls do not receive any reply. The root of the problem is that the new preference list from the other side cannot pass through. In our opinion the main objective of the DCCP feature negotiation protocol is to exchange the preference lists. After the preference list of the other side is known, the agreed feature value can be correctly computed. Because both entities in Fig. 16 are not aware that their agreed feature values are different, Type-III terminal state is worse than Type-II.

Table 3. Analysis results of the revised CPN models (solution A and B).

	Solution A					Solution B				
			Terminal markings					Terminal markings		
Case	nodes	arcs	Type I	Type II	Type III	nodes	arcs	Type I	Type II	Type III
(1)	(2)	(3)	(4)	(5)	(6)	(7)	(8)	(9)	(10)	(11)
1	10	11	2	0	0	4	3	1	0	0
2	10	11	2	0	0	4	3	1	0	0
3	131	218	4	0	0	20	26	1	0	0
4	83	124	2	2	0	18	22	2	0	0
5	131	218	4	0	0	10	11	2	0	0
6	1,170	2,255	4	4	0	106	170	2	1	0
7	131	218	4	0	0	10	11	2	0	0
8	83	124	2	2	0	18	22	2	0	0
9	1,170	2,255	4	4	0	106	170	2	1	0
10	1,170	2,255	4	4	0	48	76	3	0	0
11	1,032	2,047	4	0	0	49	77	3	0	0
12	9,539	2,117	4	4	0	553	1,046	4	4	0

We suggest two solutions to fix this problem. Solution A is when the preference list is changed (either major or minor change), the endpoint shall send a Change option to inform the other side. If the preference list is changed in the STABLE state, the endpoint shall send a Change option and enter the CHANGING state. Solution B is that the endpoint does not discard non-reordered Confirm options in the STABLE state. Table 3 shows the analysis results of the revised CPN models that incorporate solutions A and B. According to Table 3, both solutions can rectify the problem of the Type-III terminal state (Column 6 and 11) but the Type-II terminal states (Column 5 and 10) persist. Although Solution B seems to alleviate the problem of the Type-II terminal states, we prefer Solution A. Solution B requires changing the endpoint's behaviour in the STABLE state which is the essence of the protocol. We still do not know its side effect[2] when the protocol operates in a different environment such as working together with connection management procedures and operating over reordering and/or lossy channels. On the other hand, Solution A involves only re-initiate the negotiation in which case there should be no side effect.

6   Lessons Learned and Perspectives

We created the first version (unpublished) of the feature negotiation CPN model similar to the one presented in this paper. The CPN model and analysis result

---

[2] The solution that fixes errors in an environment may cause other errors in a different environment.

were limited because the protocol simply operated on the FIFO lossless channel and did not include the algorithm for checking the non-reordered options specified in RFC4340. Because we found that the feature negotiation and connection management state machines were not independent, the CPN model of DCCP connection management [25] was extended to include the feature negotiation procedure. We also combined FIFO/Reordering/Lossy channels into a single model [4] so that we were able to select the channel type and conduct the analysis without switching to different models.

To combine the feature negotiation with DCCP connection management, we considered two modelling approaches. First, to avoid the state explosion we maintained the existing transitions of DCCP connection management but modified the arc inscriptions. The feature negotiation state machines and related algorithms were modelled using ML functions embedded in the arc inscriptions. Second, we added new transitions to represent the feature negotiation state machines. The option fields were extracted and transferred between the connection management and the feature negotiation procedures via two buffer places. Because the second approach induced a huge number of states, we chose the first approach to keep the state space analyzable. The sweep-line analysis [19] revealed not only the errors we discussed in this paper but also an error caused by the interaction between connection management and feature negotiation.

Although we were able to analyse the CPN model using the sweep-line, the first approach had an important drawback. The model was too complex and too difficult to understand. Despite of the model complexity, we could determine whether the errors are genuine or not by tracing and investigating the counter examples. We divided the errors into two groups. The first group contains the errors caused by the protocols themselves. These errors appear even when the protocol operates over an ideal (FIFO without loss) channel. The second group has the errors caused by the imperfection (reordering, lossy, duplicated packets) of the channel. We argue that the error of the first group is more severe than those of the second group. When we revised the CPN model of the feature negotiation without connection management, a similar error that we discovered using the sweep-line analysis persisted. In our view, the simplified FIFO model has the advantages of readability and less modelling mistakes. Nevertheless, the simple model and simple analysis technique can reveal the error.

7   Conclusion and Future Work

This paper presented a Coloured Petri Net model and analysis of DCCP feature negotiation procedure operating over FIFO with no loss channels. The analysis result show that the protocol could fail in an undesired state (Type-III) where the feature values of both sides do not match and both sides are not aware of the mismatch. Usually when the protocol operates over reordering and/or lossy channels, it is possible that the protocol fails due to the channel imperfection. However if the protocol operates over the ideal channels (FIFO with no loss), the error indicates the flaw in the protocol itself. We proposed and validated two solutions that can rectify the problem.

The terminal state (Type-III) occurs when both sides change their preference lists during the simultaneous feature negotiation. Although the odds of this scenario is low, given the large number of potential connections in the Internet, we consider that this defect could be a serious threat.

This paper presented the abstract model with a lot of assumptions. In the future we would like to present the refined models which relax some of these assumptions. In particular we are interested to continue analysing the combined model which includes both connection management and feature negotiation procedures operating over reordering and lossy channels.

Acknowledgements. This work is supported by Research Grant no. TRG5380023 from the Thai Network Information Center Foundation and the Thailand Research Fund. The author is thankful to anonymous reviewers. Their constructive feedback has helped the author improve the quality of this paper.

References

1. Babich, F., Deotto, L.: Formal methods for the specification, analysis of communication protocols. IEEE Commun. Surv. **4**(1), 2–20 (2002). Third Quarter
2. Billington, J., Diaz, M., Rozenberg, G. (eds.): Application of Petri Nets to Communication Networks. LNCS, vol. 1605. Springer, Heidelberg (1999)
3. Billington, J., Gallasch, G.E., Han, B.: A Coloured Petri Net approach to protocol verification. In: Desel, J., Reisig, W., Rozenberg, G. (eds.) Lectures on Concurrency and Petri Nets. LNCS, vol. 3098, pp. 210–290. Springer, Heidelberg (2004)
4. Billington, J., Vanit-Anunchai, S., Gallasch, G.E.: Parameterised Coloured Petri Net channel models. Trans. Petri Nets Other Models Concurrency **3**, 71–97 (2009)
5. CPN Tools home page. http://cpntools.org
6. Figueiredo, J.C.A., Kristensen, L.M.: Using Coloured Petri Nets to investigate behavioural and performance issues of TCP protocols. In: Second Workshop and Tutorial on Practical Use of Coloured Petri Nets and Design/CPN, DAIMI PB-541, pp. 21–40. Department of Computer Science, University of Aarhus, 11–15 October 1999
7. Floyd, S., Handley, M., Kohler, E.: Problem statement for the Datagram Congestion Control Protocol (DCCP), RFC 4336, March 2006. http://www.rfc-editor.org/rfc/rfc4336.txt
8. Floyd, S., Kohler, E., Profile for Datagram Congestion Control Protocol (DCCP) congestion control ID 2: TCP-like congestion control, RFC 4341, March 2006. http://www.rfc-editor.org/rfc/rfc4341.txt
9. Floyd, S., Kohler, E.: Profile for Datagram Congestion Control Protocol (DCCP) congestion control ID 4: TCP-Friendly Rate Control for Small Packets (TFRC-SP), RFC 5622, August 2009. http://www.rfc-editor.org/rfc/rfc5622.txt
10. Floyd, S., Kohler, E., Padhye, J., Profile for Datagram Congestion Control Protocol (DCCP) congestion control ID 3: TCP-Friendly Rate Control (TFRC), RFC 4342, March 2006. http://www.rfc-editor.org/rfc/rfc4342.txt
11. Gordon, S.: Verification of the WAP transaction layer using Coloured Petri Nets. Ph.D. thesis, Institute for Telecommunications Research and Computer Systems Engineering Centre, School of Electrical and Information Engineering, University of South Australia, Adelaide, Australia, November 2001

12. Han, B.: Formal specification of the TCP service and verification of TCP connection management. Ph.D. thesis, Computer Systems Engineering Centre, School of Electrical and Information Engineering, University of South Australia, Adelaide, Australia, December 2004
13. Jensen, K., Kristensen, L.M.: Colored Petri Nets: a graphical language for formal modeling and validation of concurrent systems. Commun. ACM **58**(6), 61–70 (2015)
14. Jensen, K., Kristensen, L.M.: Coloured Petri Nets: Modelling and Validation of Concurrent Systems. Springer, Heidelberg (2009)
15. Kohler, E., Handley, M., Floyd, S.: Designing DCCP: congestion control without reliability. In: Proceedings of the 2006 ACM Conference on Applications, Technologies, Architectures, and Protocols for Computer Communications (SIGCOMM 2006), pp. 27–38, Pisa, Italy, 11–15 September 2006
16. Kohler, E., Handley, M., Floyd, S.: Datagram Congestion Control Protocol, RFC 4340, March 2006. http://www.rfc-editor.org/rfc/rfc4340.txt
17. Kristensen, L.M., Inge, K., Simonsen, F.: Applications of Coloured Petri Nets for functional validation of protocol designs. Trans. Petri Nets Other Models Concurrency **7**, 56–115 (2013)
18. Kristensen, L.M., Jørgensen, J.B., Jensen, K.: Application of Coloured Petri Nets in system development. In: Desel, J., Reisig, W., Rozenberg, G. (eds.) Lectures on Concurrency and Petri Nets. LNCS, vol. 3098, pp. 626–685. Springer, Heidelberg (2004)
19. Kristensen, L.M., Mailund, T.: A generalised sweep-line method for safety properties. In: Eriksson, L.-H., Lindsay, P.A. (eds.) FME 2002. LNCS, vol. 2391, pp. 549–567. Springer, Heidelberg (2002)
20. University of Aberdeen, Electronics Research Group, School of Engineering: Background on Feature Negotiation. http://www.erg.abdn.ac.uk/users/gerrit/dccp/notes/feature_negotiation/background.html
21. University of Aberdeen, Electronics Research Group, School of Engineering: Why feature negotiation and protocol state machine are not independent. http://www.erg.abdn.ac.uk/users/gerrit/dccp/notes/feature_negotiation/dependencies.html
22. Vanit-Anunchai, S.: An investigation of the datagram congestion control protocol's connection management and synchronisation procedures. Ph.D. thesis, Computer Systems Engineering Centre, School of Electrical and Information Engineering, University of South Australia, Adelaide, Australia, November 2007
23. Vanit-Anunchai, S.: Analysis of two-layer protocols: DCCP simultaneous-open and hole punching procedures. In: Choppy, C., Sun, J. (eds.) 1st French Singaporean Workshop on Formal Methods and Applications (FSFMA 2013). OpenAccess Series in Informatics (OASIcs), vol. 31, pp. 3–17. Schloss Dagstuhl-Leibniz-Zentrum fuer Informatik, Dagstuhl, Germany (2013)
24. Vanit-Anunchai, S.: Validating SCTP simultaneous open procedure. In: Arbab, F., Sirjani, M. (eds.) FSEN 2013. LNCS, vol. 8161, pp. 233–249. Springer, Heidelberg (2013)
25. Vanit-Anunchai, S., Billington, J., Gallasch, G.E.: Analysis of the datagram congestion control protocol's connection management procedures using the sweep-line method. Int. J. Softw. Tools Technol. Transfer **10**(1), 29–56 (2008). http://dx.doi.org/10.1007/s10009-007-0050-1
26. Vanit-Anunchai, S., Billington, J., Kongprakaiwoot, T.: Discovering chatter and incompleteness in the datagram congestion control protocol. In: Wang, F. (ed.) FORTE 2005. LNCS, vol. 3731, pp. 143–158. Springer, Heidelberg (2005)

Integrating Petri Net Semantics in a Model-Driven Approach: The Renew Meta-Modeling and Transformation Framework

David Mosteller[✉], Lawrence Cabac[✉], and Michael Haustermann[✉]

Faculty of Mathematics, Informatics and Natural Sciences,
Department of Informatics, University of Hamburg, Hamburg, Germany
{mosteller,cabac,haustermann}@informatik.uni-hamburg.de

Abstract. This paper presents an approach to the development of modeling languages and automated generation of specific modeling tools based on meta-models. Modeling is one of the main tasks in engineering. Graphical modeling helps the engineer not only to understand the system but also to communicate with engineers and with other stakeholders that participate in the development (or analytic) process.

In order to be able to provide adequately adapted modeling techniques for a given domain, it is useful to support the development of techniques that are designed for their special purpose, i.e. domain-specific modeling languages (DSML). For this purpose meta-modeling comes in handy. Meta-models provide a clear abstract syntax and model-driven design approaches allow for rapid prototyping of modeling languages. However, the transformation and also the original (source model) as well as the transformed (target) model often do not provide a clear semantics.

We present an approach to model-driven development that is based on Petri nets: high- and low-level Petri nets in various formalisms can be used as target models. The presented approach uses ontology-based meta-models, code and graphical templates, as well as custom and predefined transformation engines. The RMT framework provides the generation of modeling tools and the transformation into executable and/or analyzable models based on the defined Petri net semantics.

Keywords: RENEW · Petri nets · Model-Driven development · Meta-modeling

1 Introduction

Meta-modeling enables us to build models in a more abstract way than we are used to today. For many purposes we prefer languages that solve a specific modeling quest. While there are several well-established modeling techniques with a clear semantics, the purpose of the incorporated languages is more or less fixed. In UML annotations can, in combination with profiles, enhance the expressiveness. However, it is difficult to build lean languages that cover exactly those

© Springer-Verlag Berlin Heidelberg 2016
M. Koutny et al. (Eds.): ToPNoC XI, LNCS 9930, pp. 92–113, 2016.
DOI: 10.1007/978-3-662-53401-4_5

domain aspects that are required in a certain context. In addition, normally no tool exists that directly supports those languages with specific language constructs. To make a language easy to use, one usually needs direct tool support. The development of tools for building graphical models was a challenge some years ago. Nowadays it is relatively easy within environments such as Eclipse and its meta-modeling plugins[1]. Even extensions that allow a simulation of models built with those languages are available. However, these execution environments are usually relatively restricted and do not scale. This is due to the fact that the execution engine has to be built separately.

The development of a DSML and a corresponding modeling tool includes a whole range of tasks. In this contribution we will address: (1) providing the possibility to define an abstract syntax to allow users to build a special purpose language, (2) providing a graphical environment to allow users to build special language constructs for their specific language concepts (based on textual and graphical representations), (3) providing a tool set that allows practitioners to build models based on the previously defined languages and (4) providing a simulation environment (more specifically an environment based on the reference net formalism [15]) that allows users to execute and simulate their models. The presented approach to developing modeling languages and tools (RMT approach) is extensively applied within our approach to developing agent-oriented software based on Petri nets (P*AOSE approach, [3,18,22]), in which the mutual interplay of modeling languages is omnipresent. It is, however, equally applicable to other domains.

The P*AOSE approach is an agile model-based approach for the development of multi-agent systems. Various aspects of the system are modeled using multiple modeling techniques, which in turn are transformed into Petri net models. The resulting agent-oriented application is composed of these Petri net models, which are executed using our agent framework MULAN/CAPA [8,24] running on the RENEW simulator [5,16]. The approach to software development requires specialized techniques and transformations to allow adequate modeling of the different aspects of agent-oriented software. This requirement is addressed with the RMT approach.

We provide a prototype, which offers the possibility to develop modeling languages and to generate corresponding modeling tools. The RENEW Meta-Modeling Framework (RMT framework)[2] was applied in several settings. The RMT framework constitutes a further development step of the model-driven approach, which has already been envisioned and partly applied during the development of the Agent Role Modeler (ARM, [6]). The ARM tool, which was developed without appropriate meta-modeling tool support, provides the modeling facility for agent organizations and knowledge bases.

In contrast to other approaches we concentrate on the definition of the semantics of the models by providing a mapping to Petri net models; i.e. we provide

---

[1] Eclipse Modeling Framework, EMF, https://www.eclipse.org/modeling/emf/.

[2] RMT: RENEW Meta-Modeling and Transformation Framework, tools and examples: http://www.paose.net/wiki/Metamodeling.

a transformational Petri net semantics for the specialized modeling techniques (DSML). While the semantics of models are provided by the transformation to Petri nets, the syntax is inspired by the agent-oriented approach. The abstract syntax is defined by the agent ontologies that are applied here as meta-models. The Semantic Language (SL, [10]) defines the meta-language for all meta-models that are applied: the abstract syntax, the concrete syntax and the tool configurations as well as style-sheets.

The remainder of this paper is structured as follows: Sect. 2 briefly introduces the P*AOSE approach (PETRI NET-BASED, AGENT- AND ORGANIZATION-ORIENTED SOFTWARE ENGINEERING). The conceptual background, which comprises the model-driven tool development, encompassing meta-modeling, graphical modeling, transformations and semantical issues, is discussed with respect to the requirements and specification of our solution in Sect. 3. The example presented in Sect. 4 demonstrates the approach and the applications of Petri nets as well as the application of other techniques during DSML development. Section 5 elaborates on the wider context of model-driven development and the approach of providing transformational semantics for modeling languages with Petri nets. In Sect. 6 we will summarize our results and give an outlook on our further research directions opened by these results.

2 Petri Net-Based, Agent- and Organization-oriented Software Engineering

The P*AOSE [3] is a conceptual approach to the development of Petri net-based multi-agent applications (MAA). It combines concepts from agent-orientation and organizational modeling with well-grounded techniques from Petri net theory. The P*AOSE provides a system decomposition based on agents and interactions. Beyond the fundamental properties commonly associated with object-oriented systems, such as states and encapsulation, agents feature additional capabilities, such as adaptivity and also intelligence to a certain extent. They interact with their environment only through message communication and capture knowledge about their environments using ontologies, which is shared among the agents throughout conversations.

The technical framework of the P*AOSE – the MULAN framework [24] – is implemented with Java Reference nets, which is a Petri net formalism that features Java inscriptions, net instantiation as well as synchronous channels. The main objective of the framework is to provide a means of designing multi-agent systems focusing on distributed and concurrent execution using the Reference net formalism as a graphical programming language. Execution is provided by RENEW's simulation environment. Concurrency is an intrinsic feature of the Petri net processes implemented in Reference nets, while bidirectional exchange of information is provided by synchronous channels. Cross platform communication is enabled by the MULAN/CAPA framework [8].

Beyond Java Reference nets the P*AOSE provides specific models to capture different facets of a MAS in development. It offers various modeling techniques to model all dimensions of the application (compare with [4]). For the system overview we provide the Coarse Design Diagram (CDD), for the agent interactions we use Agent Interaction Protocol Diagrams (AIP, a variant of Sequence Diagrams). The agent roles are defined using Agent Role Models (ARM), which also include an application setup. Ontologies are modeled through Concept Diagrams (CD, simplified Class Diagrams). All diagrams are supported by modeling tools that are accompanied by generators, which transform the declarative models into application (source code) artifacts. The Coarse Design Diagrams are used to generate complete folder structures of plugins that are compilation-ready. These folders provide - among configuration files and build scripts - also the skeletons for the ARMs, AIPs and CDs. Refined Agent Role Models are transformed into the initial Agents' knowledge bases, which are used to instantiate agents – implemented as high-level Petri nets. Agent Interaction Diagrams are used to generate the agent protocols as Petri net skeletons. The Concept Diagrams are also used to generate Java classes (and other languages such as JavaScript), which are used for a convenient implementation of the agent communication.

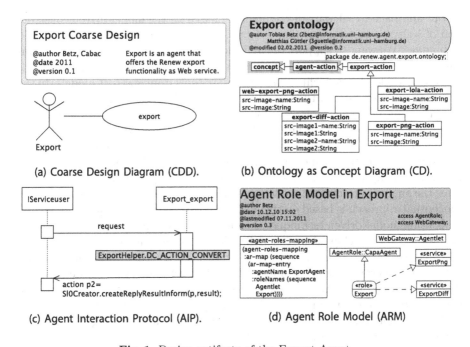

Fig. 1. Design artifacts of the Export Agent.

Figure 1 shows all four models for the Export Agent application. This example is a rather minimalist one. It contains only one agent and one interaction. The agent offers the export services as agent services and in conjunction with the WebGateway [1] also as Web services. The ontology only consists in the four agent-actions that trigger different services. The Agent Role Model actually shows that only two services[3] are offered as agent services (*ExportPng* and *ExportDiff*). This model also contains the specification of the *ExportAgent*, which consists of two roles: the *Agentlet* role and *Export* role.

All presented models are supported by modeling tools – implemented as RENEW plugins – that are accompanied by generators (or transformers) of source code artifacts. All tools have been developed as individual tools with individual approaches and each technique can be regarded as domain-specific modeling language. In this context the RMT framework provides a systematic and model-based approach to the engineering of modeling languages and thus simplifies the development of DSML. Some of the modeling techniques already use means that are available in the RMT framework. For instance, the Coarse Design Diagram uses graphical components for the concrete syntax and the Agent Role Model already applies the meta-model based approach for the definition of the abstract syntax.

3   Conceptual Approach

As our approach to software development is based on the model-driven construction of software systems our aim is to provide a tool chain using model-driven techniques. We want to support the agile development of graphical modeling languages. Therefore, we rely on the concepts of software language engineering [14] and apply model-driven techniques to generate tools from abstract models. In the following we elaborate on the techniques required to realize a framework based on generating modeling tools. RENEW provides the basis for our meta-modeling framework. It serves as a graphical framework for the flexible construction of graphical models and at the same time provides the execution and simulation environment of Petri net models, which serve as target languages that provide the transformational semantics for the designed languages. This approach facilitates the analysis of Petri net models and the validation of model properties. Our conceptual approach is based on the idea of bootstrapping the required modeling tools using model-driven techniques. Following the concepts of software language engineering the development of modeling languages encompasses three aspects: *abstract syntax, concrete syntax* and *semantics*. Translating these concepts into the area of generative tool development leads to a set of descriptions defining the different aspects of software languages [20]: structure, constraints, representation and behavior. The structure (abstract syntax) and the representation (concrete syntax) of modeling languages will be addressed in the following section. The behavior (semantics) is covered in Sect. 3.2.

3.1   Meta-modeling and Tool Generation

In this section we elaborate on the first part of the DSML development process. First we need to define the syntax of the new language (or technique). The

---

[3] Note that the diagram elements are partly collapsed, i.e. the role and the services.

abstract syntax of a language is specified by a meta-model, which defines the structure of the language. Our tool set, which is based on RENEW, supports the modeling of the abstract syntax directly through the technique of Concept Diagrams (cf. [3, Chap. 12]). Concept Diagrams are simplified Class Diagrams, which are usually used to design type hierarchies or agent ontologies (in the context of P*AOSE). In the context of this work the type hierarchies of Concept Diagrams are utilized to model the meta-models of the designed DSML, i.e. the abstract syntax.

Additionally, in order to define the representation of the elements we also need to define the concrete syntax. The concrete syntax, i.e. the representation of the syntactic elements, is defined through a mapping from the syntactic element to its graphical representation (representational mapping). The representational mapping includes concrete graphical or textual syntax as well as serialization representations. Typically, if the language should not be restricted to graphical standard figures, the layout, concrete form, etc. has to be defined in a way that is close to the implementation language. However, we also provide the possibility that the syntactic elements may be defined directly within the RENEW environment using the graphical user interface. Each provided artifact that specifies the graphical representation is stored as a template drawing and the representational mapping refers not to an implementation but to a template (graphical component). Alternatively, some standard elements are provided. These can be configured in terms of style sheets to define the representation for the language constructs.

In addition to the abstract and the concrete syntax, we need to configure the user interface of the modeling tool that provides the modeling facility. In the RENEW environment the modeling tool is integrated as a plugin. The configuration is done by defining another mapping for task bar tool buttons and their design together with some general information about the modeling tool, such as the file extension or the ordering of tool buttons in the task bar.

The RENEW plugins that provide the modeling facility for the style sheets and the tool configurations are themselves meta-model based. They have been generated – in a bootstrapping fashion – using the RMT approach.

Figure 2 shows the defining artifacts of a modeling language's syntax at the top. These artifacts are expressed within the scope of the meta-meta-model – the RMT meta-model – and can thus be used to generate a domain-specific modeling tool, which then provides the possibility to design a model, using the technique; e.g. a (domain-specific) modeling language.

A modeler may use the generated tool to model, store and retrieve graphical models (diagrams) in the syntax of the newly developed modeling language[4]. For operational or analytic models, however, it is not enough to be able to provide graphical descriptions of the models. In these cases we need to define a clear semantics. Following the idea of the model-driven architecture (MDA) the semantic interpretation of a source model can be defined through a transformation into

---

[4] In the following we will address these models as *domain models* or *source models*.

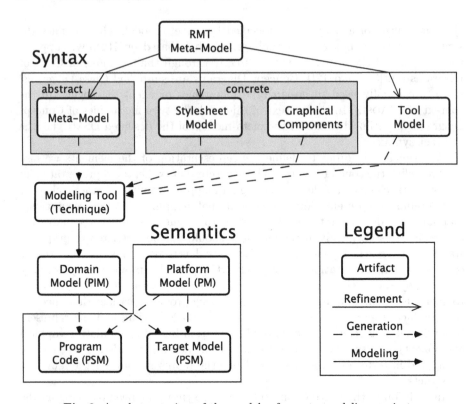

Fig. 2. An abstract view of the models of a meta-modeling project.

specific target models using a generator as shown in the lowermost part of Fig. 2, which refers to the schematic view of Petrasch et al. [23, p. 107].

We elaborate on this in the following section. But before we present the approach to the definition of the semantics, we stress the flexibility of the given approach, up to this point. The meta-modeling approach in itself offers a high degree of flexibility. By changing (augmenting, modifying or restricting) the meta-model we are able to quickly produce variations of modeling techniques, which may subsequently be compared with each other (cf. Sect. 4.2). Additionally, we are able to change the representation of the modeling language by either changing the representational mapping or by editing the graphical components. Especially the latter can be done by someone without profound knowledge of the development details, who can thus create his own representation.

3.2 Transforming Source Models to Target Models

The semantics of a modeling language is defined – as semantic mapping, cf. [11] – either through formalization, through an operationalization or through the transformation into other models that already have a formal or an operational semantics. As we use the RENEW environment as a basis for our approach, we transform given source models to Petri net models, i.e. our *target languages* are Petri net formalisms. Nevertheless, the RMT approach is not restricted to behavioral modeling languages. By choosing the proper target languages, modeling structural properties can be performed by applying the same approach. The focus here, however, lies on the specification of the behavioral properties of modeling languages. RENEW has the ability to simulate Java Reference nets [15], which combine the modeling power of Petri nets with concepts from the object-oriented programming language Java, such as states, encapsulation etc. We present an example of generated Java Reference net code in Sect. 4.2.

In Figs. 2 and 3 we can identify the domain specific model (source model), which is transformed into a target model (Platform Specific Model, PSM) within the application domain layer (M1). The RENEW environment together with its provided Petri net formalisms serves as Platform Model (PM, compare with Fig. 2). In the context of model-driven development, the source model is often described as Platform Independent Model (PIM).

The transformation process is depicted in Fig. 3 as a schematic Petri net. Transitions represent actions provided by either the RMT tool set (generation, transformation, execution or analysis) or by the source model developer (modeling). Reserve arcs in presets of transitions indicate that artifacts are not being

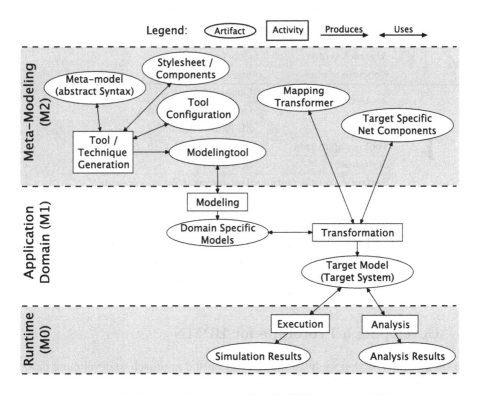

Fig. 3. Artifacts and process within the RMT usage workflow.

consumed by the actions. Artifacts that are necessary for the development of the modeling language are provided by the language developer using the RMT framework. These artifacts comprise the syntax meta-models, the transformer and the semantic elements provided as net components [3, Chap. 5]. Net components are Petri net snippets that are used as patterns to be mapped by a generator and combined to constitute the target models. In this sense the model transformation process can be characterized as a pattern-oriented transformation following the categorization of Petrasch et al. [23, p. 132].

Besides supporting the agile development of graphical languages, the RMT approach also provides a high level of flexibility regarding the semantic transformation. The semantic targets for the syntactic elements are defined as net components, which can be easily modified or exchanged. We are even able to provide several target mapping sets of net components, which can be expressed using distinct formalisms. Thus, we are able to transform one source model into multiple forms of target models. For instance, a transformation of a workflow description into a PT net model is desirable for analytic examination, while a transformation into a colored Petri net can be included for simulation/execution within a real world application.

Table 1. Applied techniques in the RMT framework.

Objective	Technique/Artifact
Abstract syntax	Concept diagram
Concrete syntax	Standard figure[a]
	Custom figure
	Component/Template
	SL figure (default)
Tool configuration	SL model
Stylesheet	SL model
Semantic transformation	Transformer/Net components

[a] Standard figures may be customized through style sheets.

Table 1 summarizes the techniques applied (or artifacts used) for each objective. There are four possible ways to define the elements of the concrete syntax. With the exception of the Custom Figure and the Transformer all objectives are satisfied through model-based means.

4   Developing a Prototype for BPMN

In the previous section we introduced a conceptual approach to developing modeling languages. We now show the concept in practice and demonstrate the concrete models, which are utilized in the development process. We have chosen to present as an example, the well-known modeling technique BPMN (Business Process Model and Notation, [21]), in order to demonstrate the approach.

In Sect. 4.1 we develop a (rather simple) modeling language that implements a subset of BPMN. We show how model transformations can be used to generate Petri net models, which provide formal semantics to the abstract BPMN models. The generated Petri net models can be referred to for analyzing a BPMN process.

In a subsequent step a more specific modeling language is developed in Sect. 4.2. This second language – the BPMN$_{AIP}$ formalism – enriches concepts from BPMN with domain-specific elements from the context of P*AOSE (see Sect. 2). The intention is to demonstrate the flexibility of the RMT approach and the appropriateness for agile, rapid and prototypical model-driven language development.

4.1   BPMN

We start with a simple subset of BPMN. Since BPMN has been described extensively in the context of modeling, meta-modeling and also in the context of Petri nets, we do not need to go into detail about the underlying semantics. A mapping of syntactic elements of BPMN to PT net components has been proposed by Dijkman et al. [7]. Using these Petri net mappings, we can focus on the aspects of agile language development instead. We concluded in Sect. 3.1 that a modeling language is based on the specifications of abstract and concrete (graphical) syntax.

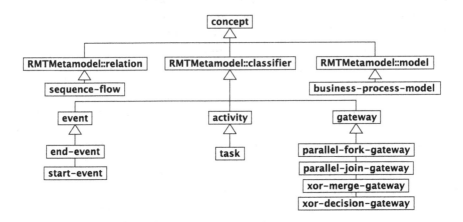

Fig. 4. A meta-model for a subset of BPMN language constructs.

Figure 4 shows a meta-model for the chosen fragment of BPMN. All concepts defined in this meta-model are instances of three basic concepts from the RMT meta-model: *model, classifier, relation*. In Fig. 4 it is also shown that the three basic concepts are themselves instances of the single core concept (*concept*). The developed BPMN language defines a model type, the *business-process-model*.

Events, *activities* and two different *gateways*, one for parallel processing and one with exclusive alternatives are also defined. The concepts can be connected through the *sequence-flow* relation. These concepts alone define the abstract syntax of the simplified BPMN formalism.

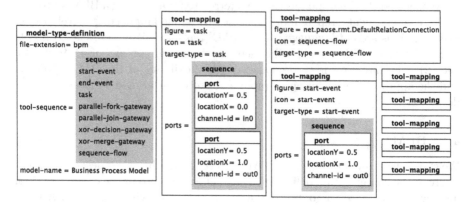

Fig. 5. The tool configuration model for the BPMN modeling tool (with partly collapsed tool mappings).

In order to complete the modeling language and generate the respective supporting modeling tool, the RMT approach requires additional information. One part is the visual representation of graphical constructs. These are developed using the built-in graphical constructs of the RENEW drawing framework. Each graphical figure is stored in a separate drawing file (template) and can be used as syntactic element for modeling later on. Other information required is a specification of properties for the modeling tool. An example of a tool configuration as SL Model is shown in Fig. 5. This model contains basic properties such as a model name and a file extension as well as a set of tool mappings. The latter define mappings from concepts of the meta-model (*target-type*) to graphical constructs (net components). Connectors of the constructs are specified as *ports*, relative to their position. All elements of the tool configuration are expressed in Semantic Language (SL), which can be compared to Yaml or JSON Tool configurations are defined using the SLEditor plugin for RENEW, which provides a UML-like representation as well as editing support for the modeler.

Figure 6 shows the graphical components representing the syntactic elements of the BPMN language alongside with the RENEW UI, which presents the loaded palette for the BPMN drawing tools. The graphical components are defined in separate template drawings. The templates define the concrete syntax for the BPMN technique. This concludes the specifications for the modeling language and enables us to generate the plugin for the modeling tool. During the generation process the RMT generator (automatically) prepares the images that are used for the tool buttons on the basis of the graphical templates. The icon

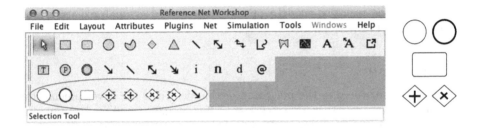

Fig. 6. The RENEW UI with the tool palette providing BPMN elements.

images of parallel and alternative gateways were slightly modified as shown in the encircled part of Fig. 6 to better distinguish the complementary constructs of split and join figures.

Using the generated BPMN plugin we are now able to model with this new technique using the RENEW editor. Figure 7 shows a ticket workflow described in BPMN. The process reflects the lifecycle of support tickets in a conventional issue tracking system. Issues are created and at some point assigned to the holder of a certain role. They can be either rejected or accepted, in which case the corresponding task will be carried out by the assignee. Later on, the task may be discontinued (*unassigned*) or completed (*finish*).

With the mapping of Dijkman et al. [7] for the transformation to Petri nets we are able to transform the given workflow to a PT net model. The generated Petri net is displayed in Fig. 8. It constitutes the transformational semantics of the BPMN process in the context of the RENEW simulation environment. In

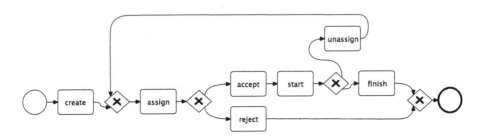

Fig. 7. The lifecycle of tickets in a issue tracking system, modeled as BPMN.

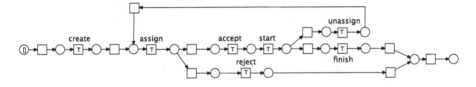

Fig. 8. The target model of the lifecycle of tickets as PT net.

consequence, the resulting model can now be executed or analyzed using, for instance, the RENEW simulator.

4.2   BPMN$_{AIP}$

The example presented in the preceding section describes the development of a modeling language together with a corresponding modeling tool (as RENEW plugin) following the RMT approach. Based on meta-models, the approach provides a high level of flexibility in all stages of the development of modeling languages. This enables language developers to rapidly prototype specific languages, evaluate them and adapt them according to their needs. To further illustrate this flexibility, we now present a domain-specific variation of BPMN, called BPMN$_{AIP}$, which is used within the P*AOSE approach.

We use BPMN$_{AIP}$ to model agent interaction protocols. In contrast to Agent Interaction Protocol Diagrams (a variation of Sequence Diagrams [3, Chap. 13]), the BPMN$_{AIP}$ formalism allows shifting the focus to the internal agent processes. The presented agent-specific extensions have been proposed by Haustermann [12] in order to augment a subset of BPMN for the use within the P*AOSE approach. With the RMT approach it is possible to refine the BPMN language in an agile process and develop a corresponding modeling language (BPMN$_{AIP}$), which satisfies the demands of a given domain-specific context.

BPMN$_{AIP}$ extends the BPMN subset in the previous section by incoming (drawn as white envelopes) and outgoing (black envelopes) message events and special tasks for agent-specific operations. The *dc-exchange-task* represents the synchronous or asynchronous call of an internal service. The *kb-access-task* serves for accessing the agent's internal knowledge base. To use these constructs in the modeling tool, they have to be added to the meta-model. Figure 9 shows the extensions of the meta-model in Fig. 4[5]. With these extensions the modeling tool can already be used with the added constructs. The generated modeling tool uses a standard representation and standard task bar tool buttons to allow the running of early tests if the developer provides none. In order to define a customized concrete syntax, analogous to the previous example, a representation template drawn with the RENEW tool, a button icon generated from the template image and a tool mapping entry in the tool configuration as shown in Fig. 5 are sufficient.

In addition to the agent-specific constructs, BPMN$_{AIP}$ also has a domain-specific semantics. The semantics is based on the MULAN/CAPA agent framework that is applied in the P*AOSE approach, which uses Petri nets to implement agents and the agents' behavior. Therefore, the semantic net components for the target models are tailored to fit within the framework used.

In order to obtain another semantics it is possible to provide a different set of net components. The RMT framework is able to handle multiple transformation engines and multiple sets of net components. For the BPMN$_{AIP}$ formalism a variation of the MULAN net components by Cabac are used [3, Chap. 5]. Table 2

---

[5] Elements already defined in the BPNM meta-model are depicted in gray.

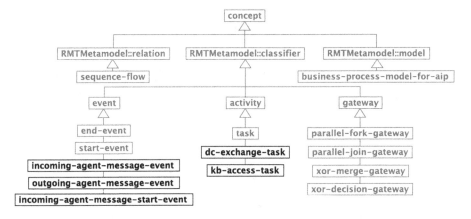

Fig. 9. BPMN$_{AIP}$ extensions to the BPMN meta-model (cf. Fig. 4).

visualizes the mapping from BPMN$_{AIP}$ elements to Petri net components. Basically, the mapping is very similar to the one proposed by Dijkman [7] although the target model's underlying formalism is the Java Reference net formalism. Additionally, some well-established agent-related elements have been added.

Figure 10 shows an adaptation of the ticket service example using BPMN$_{AIP}$. The Ticket Agent provides the management of the ticket status. It can delegate tasks to other agents (see Fig. 10a). In this example the task of exporting some drawing to an image is assigned to an Export Agent (as described by Cabac et al. [1]), which is informed about the assignment by a message. This message results in an instantiation of the process depicted in Fig. 10b. The Export Agent checks its knowledge base if it can export the drawing and delegates the task to

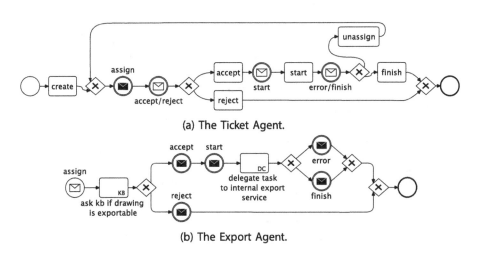

Fig. 10. The ticket workflow.

Table 2. Semantic mapping for BPMN$_{AIP}$ elements

an internal service if possible. The Ticket Agent changes the status of the ticket according to the messages it receives as a response from the Export Agent.

Using the described semantics, the two agent processes in Fig. 10 are transformed by the RMT-based BPMN$_{AIP}$ modeling tool into the Petri nets shown in Fig. 11. These nets are protocol net skeletons, which have to be completed with additional implementation details in order to be runnable with the framework used. The figure illustrates the structure of the generated nets. The nets have been beautified and inscriptions have been enlarged for improved readability.

5 Related Work

The proper design of a modeling language presents many challenges. Harel and Rumpe [11] are concerned about the common misunderstandings that are widespread among the users and developers of modern modeling languages, such as UML. The authors point out that there is often no clear distinction between syntax and semantics while this distinction is crucial to obtain a rigid definition of a language's semantics. The authors express that "... a language consists of a syntactic notation (syntax), which is a possibly infinite set of legal elements, together with the meaning of those elements, which is expressed by relating the syntax to a semantic domain" [11, p. 65]. We agree on the need for a clear distinction between syntactic and semantic domain. The RMT approach emphasizes the explication of each domain by covering abstract syntax, concrete syntax and semantic mappings, each in separate models (cf. Sect. 3). Our description of the semantic domain profits from the expressive power of Petri nets, which provides the formal specification and the operational behavior of the models. Harel and Rumpe advise against mistaking behavior for semantics. "The semantic domain is not to be taken lightly: It specifies the very concepts that exist in the universe of discourse. As such, it serves as an abstraction of reality, capturing the decisions about the kinds of things the language should express" [11, p. 67]. They see no principal difference between textual and graphical modeling languages but the latter require more effort to obtaining a rigid definition. They see little hope for developing formal semantics that cover the full UML standard in its whole complexity. With the RMT framework we take a different approach. We focus on the prototypical development of specific modeling languages, which can be experimentally investigated and refined, yet, in each stage provide a rigid specification. We rely on the expressiveness and the formal semantics of various Petri net formalisms. This enables us to study the semantics of existing modeling languages and those that are yet to be developed (i.e. DSML). Alongside a rigid and clear definition of the semantics of a modeling language, we aim for an agile, incremental approach.

In this publication we motivate the rapid and prototypical development of domain-specific modeling languages. There are a number of related publications on prototyping domain-specific languages (DSL), each focusing on different aspects or application domains. Blunk et al. [2] see the best gain for prototyping DSL as an extension of a general purpose programming language.

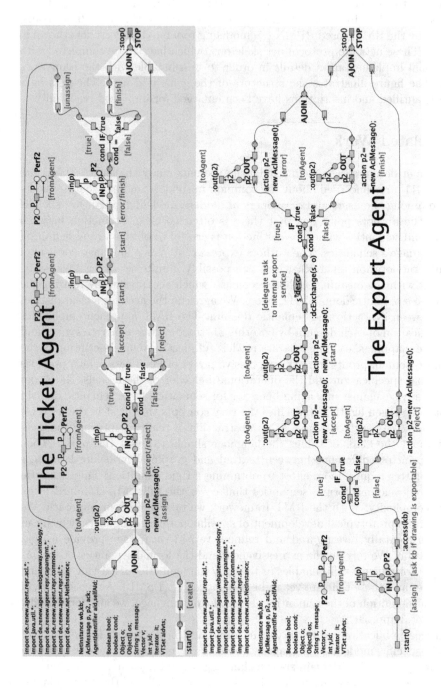

Fig. 11. Generated protocol net skeletons.

Sadilek et al. [26] stress the increasing demand for supporting agile approaches to the development of DSML. They "argue that for prototyping a DSML on the platform independent level, its semantics should not only be described in a transformational but also in an operational fashion" [26, p. 63]. However, they use the Query View Transformation (QVT) language to implement operational semantics of Petri nets rather than exploiting their operational semantics to formalize the semantics of a second modeling language, as done here. Rouvoy et al. [25] specialize on the domain of architecture description languages (ADLs) and develop a modular framework for prototyping ADLs based on the Scala language. The method presented here emphasizes the high degree of automation through generative methods, the automated generation of modeling tools and also the automated transformation of abstract models to Petri nets.

Nytun et al. [20] provide a categorization of different approaches to automated tool generation in the context of meta-modeling and DSML. The authors examine various meta-modeling approaches according to the four categories: structure, constraints, representation and behavior. With the RMT approach we cover most of these aspects by utilizing concept diagrams, representational mappings and Petri net-based target models. At the current time we do not provide any means to define constraints, but we plan to introduce constraints in the future.

Fill and Karagiannis examine the conceptualization of modeling methods using as an example the ADOxx platform [9]. ADOxx is an enterprise level meta-modeling platform. Their analysis focuses especially on four aspects of modeling languages regarding their conceptualization: visualization, transformation, simulation and querying. Concerning visualization the authors distinguish approaches that make no implications on the representation of constructed modeling languages from other approaches that provide pre-defined representations. For the RMT approach there are - besides using the default SL Figures or customized implementations - two ways of assigning representations to a modeling language, either by using the graphical drawing capabilities of RENEW or by the application of style sheets to standard constructs. Following Fill and Karagiannis transformation refers to import and export formats, e.g. XML. "The transformation of model contents to specific data formats is often needed to exchange models between different tools, feed the information contained in models to other systems, or create reports about model contents via document formats." [9, p. 14]. In the context of P*AOSE various types of target models are applied (cf. Sect. 2). The main focus in our approach is on providing Petri net transformations that enable the simulation of models within RENEW. Concerning serialization, the RMT approach features SL import and export[6]. The term simulation in the context of ADOxx is extended to algorithms for the purpose of model evaluation (e.g. path analysis), while in the context of the RMT framework an interactive simulation is supported directly within the RENEW environment. Additionally, plugins can be used to perform analysis of the transformed target models.

---

[6] A plugin to support the exchange of models through XMI serializations is currently in development.

Through the definition of customized analyzers, queries on models could be performed but, currently, we do not focus on this aspect in the development of the RMT framework.

With the claim of addressing general problems of defining DSML semantics, our goal is to develop a Petri net-based framework by combining techniques of meta-modeling with Petri nets engineering. With the Event Coordination Notation (ECNO), Kindler [13] takes a model-driven approach that uses Petri net models to implement local components behavior. The collaboration of components is defined in abstract coordination diagrams. The implementation is based on the wide-spread Eclipse Modeling Framework (EMF). In combination with the EMF, the graphical modeling framework (GMF) can be used to automatically generate specific modeling tools from meta-models. The idea of generating domain-specific tools from models was adopted for this work, but we try to take a minimalist approach instead of overcharging the tool with features, thus increasing complexity. The intrinsic complexity is a point of criticism concerning meta-modeling frameworks [25, p. 14].

Dijkman et al. [7] show a mapping of BPMN constructs to Petri nets and elaborate on the semantics of such transformations. On the basis of that work a tool exists for converting BPMN models to PNML and a tool for converting BPMN to YAWL. With the flexible tool presented in this work the languages can be quickly adopted and the concerns about problems in evaluating BPMN models using Petri net semantics can be empirically investigated. Lohmann et al. [17] provide a basis for analyzing different business process modeling languages with respect to their realizability using Petri net semantics for BPEL, BPMN, EPC, YAWL. This can be a good starting point for further research using our approach. The RMT framework has been applied by Möllers [19] for the development of a modeling tool for the design and execution of Deployment Diagrams. Möllers has also implemented and applied an XMI (XML Metadata Interchange) exchange format for Deployment Diagrams.

6   Conclusion

In this contribution we present the RMT approach, which enables us to develop modeling languages and modeling tools by applying concepts of model-driven development. The key aspects of this approach are the use of meta-models for automatic tool generation and transformation of models by exploiting the formal semantics of Petri nets. In the context of P*AOSE the transformation of abstract models to Petri net implementation artifacts is applied in order to develop multi-agent applications (cf. Sect. 2). Based on our continuously developed graphical modeling tool and Petri net simulation environment RENEW [5,16] we provide the technical realization of the RMT approach. The RMT framework provides the means to describe modeling languages building on the concepts of software language engineering (cf. Sect. 3). The abstract syntax, concrete syntax and tool configurations are provided as model-based specifications of the desired modeling languages and tool behavior. The semantics is defined as transformation-based operational semantics using Petri net formalisms as target models. With this environment we are able to provide the representation directly within our graphical framework, leading to appropriate language constructs, which can be designed for special purposes that fit the needs and expectations of its users. With the RMT approach the users are able to develop and adapt their own languages/modeling techniques, define constructs based on graphical representations and finally generate modeling tools, which empower them to draw models in domain-specific languages.

Depending on the chosen and intended formalism, we could even go one step further. We are able to simulate the transformed models directly, if an operational semantics exists that can be mapped to the formalisms we already have implemented within the RENEW context. For experimental environments where users want to define a special purpose language that suits exactly their current needs, we can provide a powerful tool set.

While the prototypical development of languages is already quite fast, we now have to address the question of sustainable meta-modeling-based tools. We have already successfully applied the RMT framework several times within our P*AOSE approach. In this context we expect that further new modeling languages can be developed in a prototyping approach. In the future we wish to provide the means to support hierarchical modeling within the RMT framework. With the Nets-within-Nets paradigm [27] the concepts to support hierarchical target models already exist. Since the whole P*AOSE approach is Petri net-based, the direct support by simulation of target models within RENEW is implicitly given. The prototyping approach of languages empowers us to evaluate several languages in order to improve specific frameworks that are already at hand.

Acknowledgment. We thank Dr. Daniel Moldt and the TGI group of the Department of Informatics, University of Hamburg for their support, constructive criticism and fruitful discussions.

References

1. Betz, T., Cabac, L., Duvigneau, M., Wagner, T., Wester-Ebbinghaus, M.: Software engineering with Petri nets: a Web service and agent perspective. In: Haddad, S., Yakovlev, A. (eds.) ToPNoC IX. LNCS, vol. 8910, pp. 41–61. Springer, Heidelberg (2014). http://dx.doi.org/10.1007/978-3-662-45730-6_3
2. Blunk, A., Fischer, J.: Prototyping domain specific languages as extensions of a general purpose language. In: Haugen, Ø., Reed, R., Gotzhein, R. (eds.) SAM 2012. LNCS, vol. 7744, pp. 72–87. Springer, Heidelberg (2013). http://dx.doi.org/10.1007/978-3-642-36757-1_5
3. Cabac, L.: Modeling Petri Net-Based Multi-Agent Applications, Agent Technology - Theory and Applications, vol. 5. Logos Verlag, Berlin (2010). http://www.sub.uni-hamburg.de/opus/volltexte/2010/4666/
4. Cabac, L., Dörges, T., Duvigneau, M., Moldt, D., Reese, C., Wester-Ebbinghaus, M.: Agent models for concurrent software systems. In: Bergmann, R., Lindemann, G., Kirn, S., Pěchouček, M. (eds.) MATES 2008. LNCS (LNAI), vol. 5244, pp. 37–48. Springer, Heidelberg (2008). http://dx.doi.org/10.1007/978-3-540-87805-6_5

5. Cabac, L., Haustermann, M., Mosteller, D.: Renew 2.5 – towards a comprehensible integrated development environment for Petri net-based applications. In: Kordon, F., Moldt, D. (eds.) PETRI NETS 2016. LNCS, vol. 9698, pp. 101–112. Springer, Heidelberg (2016). doi:10.1007/978-3-319-39086-4_7

6. Cabac, L., Mosteller, D., Wester-Ebbinghaus, M.: Modeling organizational structures and agent knowledge for Mulan applications. In: Haddad, S., Yakovlev, A. (eds.) ToPNoC IX. LNCS, vol. 8910, pp. 62–82. Springer, Heidelberg (2014). http://dx.doi.org/10.1007/978-3-662-45730-6_4

7. Dijkman, R.M., Dumas, M., Ouyang, C.: Semantics and analysis of business process models in BPMN. Inf. Softw. Technol. 50(12), 1281–1294 (2008). doi:10.1016/j.infsof.2008.02.006

8. Duvigneau, M., Moldt, D., Rölke, H.: Concurrent architecture for a multi-agent platform. In: Giunchiglia, F., Odell, J.J., Weiss, G. (eds.) AOSE 2002. LNCS, vol. 2585, pp. 59–72. Springer, Heidelberg (2003). http://dx.doi.org/10.1007/3-540-36540-0_5

9. Fill, H.G., Karagiannis, D.: On the conceptualisation of modelling methods using the ADOxx meta modelling platform. Enterp. Model. Inf. Syst. Architect. 8(1), 4–25 (2013). https://www.emisa-journal.org/emisa/article/view/99

10. FIPA, Foundation for Intelligent Physical Agents: FIPA SL Content Language Specification, December 2002. http://fipa.org/specs/fipa00008/

11. Harel, D., Rumpe, B.: Meaningful modeling: what's the semantics of "semantics"? IEEE Comput. 37(10), 64–72 (2004). http://dx.doi.org/10.1109/MC.2004.172

12. Haustermann, M.: BPMN-Modelle für petrinetzbasierte agentenorientierte Softwaresysteme auf Basis von Mulan/Capa. Master thesis. University of Hamburg, Department of Informatics, Vogt-Kölln Str. 30, D-22527 Hamburg, September 2014

13. Kindler, E.: Coordinating interactions: the event coordination notation. Technical report 05, DTU Compute - Department of Applied Mathematics and Computer Science, Technical University of Denmark, May 2014. http://orbit.dtu.dk/en/publications/p(714667a1-4786-4b68-969e-c011187a6ab8).html

14. Kleppe, A.: Software Language Engineering: Creating Domain-Specific Languages Using Metamodels. Pearson Education, Boston (2008)

15. Kummer, O.: Referenznetze. Logos Verlag, Berlin (2002). http://www.logos-verlag.de/cgi-bin/engbuchmid?isbn=0035&lng=deu&id=

16. Kummer, O., Wienberg, F., Duvigneau, M., Cabac, L., Haustermann, M., Mosteller, D.: Renew - the Reference Net Workshop, June 2016. http://www.renew.de/. release 2.5

17. Lohmann, N., Verbeek, E., Dijkman, R.: Petri net transformations for business processes – a survey. In: Jensen, K., van der Aalst, W.M.P. (eds.) Transactions on Petri Nets and Other Models of Concurrency II. LNCS, vol. 5460, pp. 46–63. Springer, Heidelberg (2009). http://dx.doi.org/10.1007/978-3-642-00899-3_3

18. Moldt, D.: Petrinetze als Denkzeug. In: Farwer, B., Moldt, D. (eds.) Object Petri Nets, Processes, and Object Calculi. pp. 51–70. No. FBI-HH-B-265/05 in Report of the Department of Informatics, University of Hamburg, Department of Computer Science, Vogt-Kölln Str. 30, D-22527 Hamburg, August 2005

19. Möllers, K.S.M.: Entwicklung eines P*AOSE-Werkzeugs zur Dynamisierung von Verteilungsdiagrammen. Bachelor thesis, University of Hamburg, Department of Informatics, Vogt-Kölln Str. 30, D-22527 Hamburg (2014)

20. Nytun, J.P., Prinz, A., Tveit, M.S.: Automatic generation of modelling tools. In: Rensink, A., Warmer, J. (eds.) ECMDA-FA 2006. LNCS, vol. 4066, pp. 268–283. Springer, Heidelberg (2006). http://dx.doi.org/10.1007/11787044_21

21. OMG, Object Management Group: Business Process Model and Notation (BPMN) - Version 2.0.2, December 2013. http://www.omg.org/spec/BPMN/2.0.2
22. PAOSE-Website: Organization-oriented Software Engineering. University of Hamburg, Department of Informatics, Theoretical Foundations Group, June 2016. http://www.paose.net
23. Petrasch, R., Meimberg, O.: Model Driven Architecture: eine praxisorientierte Einführung in die MDA. dpunkt-Verlag, Heidelberg (2006)
24. Rölke, H.: Modellierung von Agenten und Multiagentensystemen - Grundlagen und Anwendungen, Agent Technology - Theory and Applications, vol. 2. Logos Verlag, Berlin (2004). http://logos-verlag.de/cgi-bin/engbuchmid?isbn=0768&lng=eng&id=
25. Rouvoy, R., Merle, P.: Rapid prototyping of domain-specific architecture languages. In: Larsson, M., Medvidovic, N. (eds.) International ACM SIGSOFT Symposium on Component-Based Software Engineering (CBSE 2012), Bertinoro, Italie, pp. 13–22. ACM, June 2012. http://dx.doi.org/10.1145/2304736.2304741
26. Sadilek, D.A., Wachsmuth, G.: Prototyping visual interpreters and debuggers for domain-specific modelling languages. In: Schieferdecker, I., Hartman, A. (eds.) ECMDA-FA 2008. LNCS, vol. 5095, pp. 63–78. Springer, Heidelberg (2008). http://dx.doi.org/10.1007/978-3-540-69100-6_5
27. Valk, R.: Object Petri Nets. In: Desel, J., Reisig, W., Rozenberg, G. (eds.) Lectures on Concurrency and Petri Nets. LNCS, vol. 3098, pp. 819–848. Springer, Heidelberg (2004). http://dx.doi.org/10.1007/978-3-540-27755-2_23

Mining Conditional Partial Order Graphs
from Event Logs

Andrey Mokhov[1(✉)], Josep Carmona[2], and Jonathan Beaumont[1]

[1] Newcastle University, Newcastle, UK
{andrey.mokhov,j.r.beaumont}@ncl.ac.uk
[2] Universitat Politècnica de Catalunya, Barcelona, Spain
jcarmona@cs.upc.edu

Abstract. Process mining techniques rely on *event logs*: the extraction of a process model (*discovery*) takes an event log as the input, the adequacy of a process model (*conformance*) is checked against an event log, and the *enhancement* of a process model is performed by using available data in the log. Several notations and formalisms for event log representation have been proposed in the recent years to enable efficient algorithms for the aforementioned process mining problems. In this paper we show how *Conditional Partial Order Graphs* (CPOGs), a recently introduced formalism for compact representation of families of partial orders, can be used in the process mining field, in particular for addressing the problem of compact and easy-to-comprehend representation of event logs with data. We present algorithms for extracting both the control flow as well as the relevant data parameters from a given event log and show how CPOGs can be used for efficient and effective visualisation of the obtained results. We demonstrate that the resulting representation can be used to reveal the hidden interplay between the control and data flows of a process, thereby opening way for new process mining techniques capable of exploiting this interplay. Finally, we present open-source software support and discuss current limitations of the proposed approach.

1 Introduction

Event logs are ubiquitous sources of process information that enabled the rise of the *process mining* field, which stands at the interface between formal methods, concurrency theory, machine learning, and data visualisation [1]. A *process* is a central notion in process mining and in computing science in general, and the ability to automatically discover and analyse evidence-based process models is of utmost importance for many government and business organisations. Furthermore, this ability is gradually becoming a necessity as the digital revolution marches forward and traditional process analysis techniques based on the explicit construction of precise process models are no longer adequate for continuously evolving large-scale real-life processes, because our understanding of them is often incomplete and/or inconsistent.

© Springer-Verlag Berlin Heidelberg 2016
M. Koutny et al. (Eds.): ToPNoC XI, LNCS 9930, pp. 114–136, 2016.
DOI: 10.1007/978-3-662-53401-4_6

At present, the process mining field is mainly focused on three research directions: (i) the *discovery* of a process model, typically, a Petri Net or a BPMN (Business Process Model and Notation); (ii) the *conformance* analysis of a process model with respect to a given event log; and (iii) the *enhancement* of a process model using additional information (i.e., *data*) contained in an event log. The bulk of research in these directions has been dedicated to the design of the algorithmic foundation and associated software tools with many notable successes, such as, e.g. the PROM framework [2].

However, a more basic problem of *event log representation and visualisation* received little attention to date, despite the fact that effective visualisation is essential for achieving a good understanding of the information contained in an event log. Indeed, even basic *dotted charts* prove very useful for describing many aspects of event logs even though they are just simple views of event log traces plotted over time [3].

In this paper we discuss the application of *Conditional Partial Order Graphs* (CPOGs) for event log representation and visualisation. The CPOG model has been introduced in [4] as a compact graph-based formalism for complex concurrent systems, whose behaviour could be thought of as a collection of multiple partial order scenarios (see a formal definition in Sect. 4). The key idea behind our approach is to convert a given event log into a collection of partial orders, which can then be compactly described and visualised as a CPOG, as explained in the motivating example in Sect. 2. CPOGs are less expressive than Petri Nets and have important limitations, such as the inability to represent cyclic behaviour, but they are well-suited for representing inherently acyclic event logs.

We see CPOGs not as the end product of process mining, but as a convenient intermediate representation of event logs that provides much better clarity of visualisation as well as better compactness, which is important for the efficiency of algorithms further in the process mining pipeline. Furthermore, CPOGs can be manipulated using algorithmically efficient operations such as *overlay* (combining several event logs into one), *projection* (extracting a subset of interesting traces from an event log), *equivalence checking* (verifying if two event logs describe the same behaviour) and others, as formalised in [5].

The contributions of this paper[1] are:

- We propose two methods for mining compact CPOG representations from event logs, see Sect. 5. The methods are based on the previous research in CPOG synthesis [4], and on a novel concurrency oracle introduced in Sect. 5.2.
- We propose techniques for extracting data parameters from the information typically contained in event labels of a log and for using these parameters for annotating derived CPOG models, thereby providing a direct link between the control and data aspects of a system under observation, see Sect. 6.
- We present an opensource implementation of the CPOG mining methods as a WORKCRAFT plugin [7] and as a command line tool PGMINER [8], see Sect. 7.

---

[1] This paper is an extended version of [6].

– We evaluate our implementation on several event logs known to the process
  mining community, see Sect. 7.3. The experimental results show that the current implementation is capable of handling large real-life logs in reasonable
  time and highlight the areas where future research work is needed. We review
  and discuss related work in Sect. 8.

2   Motivating Example

We start by illustrating the reasons that motivate us to study the application
of CPOGs in process mining, namely: (i) the ability of CPOGs to compactly
represent complex event logs and clearly illustrate their high-level properties,
and (ii) the possibility of capturing event log meta data as part of a CPOG
representation, thereby taking advantage of the meta data for the purpose of
explaining the process under observation.

Consider an event log $L = \{abcd, cdab, badc, dcba\}$. One can notice that the
order between events a and b always coincides with the order between events
c and d. This is an important piece of information about the process, which
however may not be immediately obvious when looking at the log in the text
form. To visualise the log one may attempt to use existing process mining techniques and discover a graphical representation for the log, for example in the
form of a Petri Net or a BPMN. However, an exact Petri Net representation of
event log L is cumbersome and difficult to understand. Furthermore, existing
Petri Net based process mining techniques perform very poorly on this log. To
compare the models discovered from this log by several popular process mining
methods, we will describe the discovered behaviour by regular expressions, where
operators $\|$ and $\cup$ denote interleaving and union, respectively.

The α-algorithm [9] applied to L produces a Petri Net accepting the behaviour $a \cup b \cup c \cup d$, which clearly cannot reproduce any of the traces in L.
Methods aimed at deriving block-structured process models [10,11] produce
a connected Petri Net that with the help of *silent* transitions reproduces the
behaviour $a \| b \| c \| d$, which is a very imprecise model accepting all possible
interleavings of the four events. The region-based techniques [12] discover the
same behaviour as the block-structured miners, but the derived models are not
connected. One can use classical synthesis techniques to exclude wrong continu-
ations (such as $acbd$, $acdb$, etc.), from the resulting Petri Net [13], however, this
process is hard to automate and still leads to inadequately complex models.

CPOGs, however, can represent L exactly and in a very compact form, as
shown in Fig. 1(a). Informally, a CPOG is an overlay of several partial orders
that can be extracted from it by assigning values to variables that appear in the
conditions of the CPOG vertices and arcs. For example, the upper-left graph
shown in Fig. 1(b) (assignment $x = 1$, $y = 1$) corresponds to the partial order
containing the causalities $a \prec b$, $a \prec d$, $b \prec c$, $c \prec d$. One can easily verify that
the model is precise by trying all possible assignments of variables x and y and
checking that they generate the traces $\{abcd, cdab, badc, dcba\}$ as desired, and
nothing else. See Fig. 1(b) for the corresponding illustration. The compactness

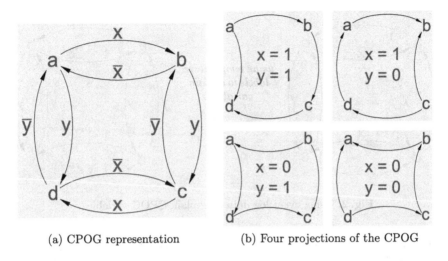

(a) CPOG representation   (b) Four projections of the CPOG

Fig. 1. Exact CPOG representation of log $L = \{abcd, cdab, badc, dcba\}$

of the CPOG representation is due to the fact that several event orderings are overlayed on top of each other taking advantage of the similarities between them. See Sects. 4 and 5 for a formal introduction to CPOGs and synthesis algorithms that can be used for mining CPOGs from event logs.

It is worth mentioning that CPOGs allow us to recognise *second-order relations* between events. These are relations that are not relating events themselves, but are relating relations between events: indeed, the CPOG in Fig. 1(a) clearly shows that the relation between a and b is equal to the relation between c and d, and the same holds for pairs (a, d) and (b, c). In principle, one can go even further and consider third-order relations and so forth. The practical use of such a relation hierarchy is that it may help to extract an event hierarchy from event logs, thereby simplifying the resulting representation even further.

One may be unsatisfied by the CPOG representation in Fig. 1(a) due to the use of 'artificial' variables x and y. Where do these variables come from and what exactly do they correspond to in the process? We found out that additional data which is often present in event logs can be used to answer such questions. In fact, as we will show in Sect. 6, it may be possible to use easy-to-understand predicates constructed from the data instead of 'opaque' Boolean variables.

For example, consider the same event log L but augmented with temperature data attached to the traces:

- $abcd, t = 25°$
- $cdab, t = 30°$
- $badc, t = 22°$
- $dcba, t = 23°$

With this information at hand we can now explain what variable x means. In other words, we can open the previously opaque variable x by expressing it as a predicate on temperature t: $x = t \geq 25°$

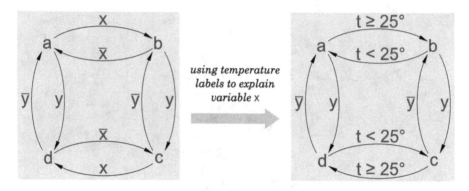

Fig. 2. Using event log data to explain CPOG variables

One can subsequently drop x completely from the CPOG by using conditions $t \geq 25°$ and $t < 25°$ in place of x and $\overline{x}$, respectively, as shown in Fig. 2.

In summary, we believe that CPOGs bring unique event log visualisation capabilities to the process mining field. One can use CPOGs as an intermediate representation of event logs, which can be exact as well as more comprehensible both for humans and for software tools further in the process mining pipeline.

3   Event Logs

In this section we introduce the notion of an *event log*, which is central for this paper and for the process mining field. We also discuss important quality metrics that are typically used to compare methods for event log based process mining.

Table 1 shows a simple event log, which contains not only event information but also *data* in the form of *event attributes*. The underlying traces of the log are $\{abcd, cdab, badc, dcba\}$, just as in the previous section, and they correspond to 'case IDs' 1, 2, 3 and 4, respectively. We assume that the set of attributes is fixed and the function *attr* maps pairs of events and attribute names to the corresponding values. For each *event e* the log contains the case ID $case(e)$, the activity name $act(e)$, and a set of attributes, e.g. $attr(e, timestamp)$. As an example, $case(e_7) = 2$, $act(e_7) = a$, $attr(e_7, timestamp) = $ "10-04-2015 10:28pm", and $attr(e_7, cost) = 19$ in Table 1. Given a set of events E, an *event log* is a multiset of *traces* E^* of events, where events are identified by the activities act.

Process mining techniques use *event logs* containing footprints of real process executions for discovering, analysing and extending formal process models, which reveal real processes in a system [1]. The process mining field has risen around a decade ago, and since then it has evolved in several directions, with process discovery being perhaps the most difficult challenge, as demonstrated by a large number of existing techniques. Discovered process models are typically ranked across the following quality metrics, some of which are mutually exclusive:

– *fitness:* the ability of the model to reproduce the traces in the event log (in other words, not too many traces are lost);

Table 1. An example event log

Event	Case ID	Activity	Timestamp	Temperature	Cost	Risk
1	1	a	10-04-2015 9:08am	25.0	17	Low
2	2	c	10-04-2015 10:03am	28.7	29	Low
3	2	d	10-04-2015 11:32am	29.8	16	Medium
4	1	b	10-04-2015 2:01pm	25.5	15	Low
5	1	c	10-04-2015 7:06pm	25.7	14	Low
6	1	d	10-04-2015 9:08pm	25.3	17	Medium
7	2	a	10-04-2015 10:28pm	30.0	19	Low
8	2	b	10-04-2015 10:40pm	29.5	22	Low
9	3	b	11-04-2015 9:08am	22.5	31	High
10	4	d	11-04-2015 10:03am	22.0	33	High
11	4	c	11-04-2015 11:32am	23.2	35	High
12	3	a	11-04-2015 2:01pm	23.5	40	Medium
13	3	d	11-04-2015 7:06pm	28.8	43	High
14	3	c	11-04-2015 9:08pm	22.9	45	Medium
15	4	b	11-04-2015 10:28pm	23.0	50	High
16	4	a	11-04-2015 10:40pm	23.1	35	Medium

- *precision* of the representation of the event log by the model (the opposite of fitness, i.e. not too many new traces are introduced);
- *generalisation:* the ability of the model to generalise the behaviour covered by the event log;
- *simplicity:* the *Occam's Razor* principle that advocates for simpler models.

We present new methods for CPOG mining from event logs and analyse their performance. A qualitative study with respect to the above metrics is beyond the scope of this paper and is left for future research.

4   Conditional Partial Order Graphs

Conditional Partial Order Graphs (CPOGs) were introduced for the compact specification of concurrent systems comprised from multiple behavioural scenarios [4]. CPOGs are particularly effective when scenarios of the system share common patterns, which can be exploited for the automated derivation of a compact combined representation of the system's behaviour. CPOGs have been used for the design of asynchronous circuits [14] and processor microcontrollers [15]. In this paper we demonstrate how CPOGs can be employed in process mining.

4.1   Basic Definitions

A CPOG is a directed graph (V, E), whose *vertices* V and *arcs* $E \subseteq V \times V$ are labelled with Boolean functions, or *conditions*, $\phi : V \cup E \to (\{0,1\}^X \to \{0,1\})$, where $\{0,1\}^X \to \{0,1\}$ is a Boolean function on a set of Boolean *variables* X.

Figure 3 (the top left box) shows an example of a CPOG H containing 4 vertices $V = \{a, b, c, d\}$, 6 arcs and 2 variables $X = \{x, y\}$. Vertex d is labelled with condition $x + y$ (i.e. 'x OR y'), arcs (b, c) and (c, b) are labelled with conditions x and y, respectively. All other vertices and arcs have trivial conditions 1 (trivial conditions are not shown for clarity); we call such vertices and arcs *unconditional*.

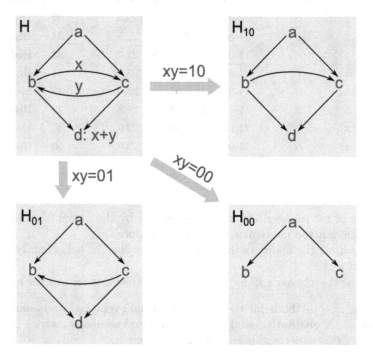

Fig. 3. A CPOG and the associated family of graphs

There are $2^{|X|}$ possible assignments of variables X, called *codes*. Each code induces a subgraph of the CPOG, whereby all the vertices and arcs, whose conditions evaluate to 0 are removed. For example, by assigning $x = y = 0$ one obtains graph H_{00} shown in the bottom right box in Fig. 3; vertex d and arcs (b, c) and (c, b) have been removed from the graph, because their conditions are equal to 0 when $x = y = 0$. Different codes can produce different graphs, therefore a CPOG with $|X|$ variables can potentially specify a *family* of $2^{|X|}$ graphs. Figure 3 shows two other members of the family specified by CPOG H: H_{01} and H_{10}, corresponding to codes 01 and 10, respectively, which differ only in the direction of the arc between vertices b and c. Codes will be denoted in a bold font, e.g. $\mathbf{x} = 01$, to distinguish them from vertices and variables.

It is often useful to focus only on a subset $C \subseteq \{0,1\}^X$ of codes, which are meaningful in some sense. For example, code 11 applied to CPOG H in Fig. 3 produces a graph with a loop between vertices b and c, which is undesirable if arcs are interpreted as causality. A Boolean *restriction function* $\rho : \{0,1\}^X \rightarrow \{0,1\}$ can be used to compactly specify the set $C = \{\mathbf{x} \mid \rho(\mathbf{x}) = 1\}$ and its complement $DC = \{\mathbf{x} \mid \rho(\mathbf{x}) = 0\}$, which are often referred to as the *care* and *don't care* sets [16]. By setting $\rho = \overline{xy}$ one can disallow the code $\mathbf{x} = 11$ as $\rho(11) = 0$, thereby restricting the family of graphs specified by CPOG H to three members only, which are all shown in Fig. 3.

The *size* $|H|$ of a CPOG $H = (V, E, X, \phi, \rho)$ is defined as:

$$|H| = |V| + |E| + |X| + \left| \bigcup_{z \in V \cup E} \phi(z) \cup \rho \right|,$$

where $|\{f_1, f_2, \ldots, f_n\}|$ stands for the size of the smallest circuit [17] that computes all Boolean functions in the set $\{f_1, f_2, \ldots, f_n\}$.

4.2   Families of Partial Orders

A CPOG $H = (V, E, X, \phi, \rho)$ is *well-formed* if every allowed code $\mathbf{x}$ produces an acyclic graph $H_{\mathbf{x}}$. By computing the transitive closure $H_{\mathbf{x}}^*$ one can obtain a *strict partial order*, an irreflexive and transitive relation on the set of *events* corresponding to vertices of $H_{\mathbf{x}}$.

We can therefore interpret a well-formed CPOG as a specification of a family of partial orders. We use the term *family* instead of the more general term *set* to emphasise the fact that partial orders are *encoded*, that is each partial order $H_{\mathbf{x}}^*$ is paired with the corresponding code $\mathbf{x}$. For example, the CPOG shown in Fig. 3 specifies the family comprising the partial order H_{00}^*, where event a precedes concurrent events b and c, and two total orders H_{01}^* and H_{10}^* corresponding to sequences $acbd$ and $abcd$, respectively.

The *language* $\mathcal{L}(H)$ *of a CPOG* H is the set of all possible linearisations of partial orders contained in it. For example, the language of the CPOG shown in Fig. 3 is $\mathcal{L}(H) = \{abc, acb, abcd, acbd\}$. One of the limitations of the CPOG model is that it can only describe finite languages. However, this limitation is irrelevant for the purposes of this paper since event logs are always finite.

It has been demonstrated in [18] that CPOGs are a very efficient model for representing families of partial orders. In particular, they can be exponentially more compact than *Labelled Event Structures* [19] and *Petri Net unfoldings* [20]. Furthermore, for some applications CPOGs provide more comprehensible models than other widely used formalisms, such as *Finite State Machines* and *Petri Nets*, as has been shown in [4,5]. This motivated the authors to investigate the applicability of CPOGs to process mining.

4.3   Synthesis

In the previous sections we have demonstrated how one can extract partial orders from a given CPOG. However, the opposite problem is more interesting: *derive the smallest CPOG description for a given a set of partial orders.* This problem is called *CPOG synthesis* and it is an essential step in the proposed CPOG-based approach to process mining.

A number of CPOG synthesis methods have been proposed to date. The simplest method is based on graph colouring [4] and produces CPOGs with all conditions having at most one literal. Having at most one literal per condition is a serious limitation for many applications, but we found that the method works well for process mining. A more sophisticated approach, which produces CPOGs with more complex conditions has been proposed in [21], however, it has poor scalability and cannot be applied to large process mining instances. The most scalable approach to date, as confirmed by the experiments in Sect. 7.3, has been developed in [22] and is based on simulated annealing. All encoding methods are supported by open-source modelling framework WORKCRAFT [7], which we used in our experiments. In general, the CPOG synthesis problem is still in active research phase and new approximate methods are currently being developed. A promising direction for overcoming this challenge is based on reducing the CPOG synthesis problem to the problem of Finite State Machine synthesis [23].

5   From Event Logs to CPOGs

When visualising behaviour of an event log, it is difficult to identify a single technique that performs well for any given log due to the *representational bias* exhibited by existing process discovery algorithms. For example, if the event log describes a simple workflow behaviour, then the α-algorithm [9] is usually the best choice. However, if non-local dependencies are present in the behaviour, the α-algorithm will not be able to find them, and then other approaches, e.g. based on the theory of regions [12,24,25], may deliver best results. The latter techniques in turn are not robust when dealing with *noisy event logs*, for which other approaches may be more suitable [26,27]. There are many event logs for which none of the existing process discovery techniques seem to provide a satisfactory result according to the quality metrics presented in Sect. 3; for instance, see our simple motivating example in Sect. 2.

In this section we describe two approaches for translating a given event log L into a compact CPOG representation H. The first approach, which we call the *exact CPOG mining*, treats each trace as a totally ordered sequence of events and produces a CPOG H such that $L = \mathcal{L}(H)$. This approach does not introduce any new behaviours, hence the discovered models are *precise*.

The second approach attempts to exploit the concurrency between the events in order to discover *simpler* and *more general* models, hence we call it the *concurrency-aware CPOG mining*. This approach may in fact introduce new behaviours, which could be interpreted as new possible interleavings of the traces contained in the given event log L, hence producing a CPOG H that overapproximates the log, i.e. $L \subseteq \mathcal{L}(H)$. Both approaches satisfy the *fitness* criteria, that is, the discovered models cover all traces of the event log.

5.1 Exact CPOG Mining

The *exact CPOG mining* problem is stated as follows: given an event log L, derive a CPOG H such that $L = \mathcal{L}(H)$. This can be trivially reduced to the CPOG synthesis problem. Indeed, each trace $t = e_1 e_2 \cdots e_m$ can be considered a total order of events $e_1 \prec e_2 \prec \cdots \prec e_m$. Therefore, a log $L = \{t_1, t_2, \cdots, t_n\}$ can be considered a set of n total orders and its CPOG representation can be readily obtained via CPOG synthesis. The solution always exists, but it is usually not unique. If uniqueness is desirable one can fix the assignment of codes to traces, in which case the result of synthesis can be presented in the *canonical form* [5].

For example, given event log $L = \{abcd, cdab, badc, dcba\}$ described in Sect. 2, the exact mining approach produces the CPOG shown in Fig. 1. As has already been discussed in Sect. 2, the resulting CPOG is very compact and provides a more comprehensible representation of the event log compared to conventional models used in process mining, such as Petri Nets or BPMNs.

When a given event log contains concurrency, the exact CPOG mining approach may lead to suboptimal results. For example, consider a simple event log $L = \{abcd, acbd\}$. If we directly synthesise a CPOG by treating each trace of this log as a total order, we will obtain the CPOG H shown in Fig. 4 (left). Although $L = \mathcal{L}(H)$ as desired, the CPOG uses a redundant variable x to distinguish between the two total orders even though they are just two possible linearisations of the same partial order, where $a \prec b$, $a \prec c$, $b \prec d$, and $c \prec d$. It is desirable to recognise and extract the concurrency between events b and c, and use the information for simplifying the derived CPOG, as shown in Fig. 4 (right). Note that the simplified CPOG H' still preserves the language equality: $L = \mathcal{L}(H')$.

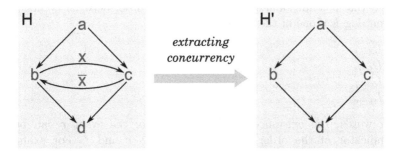

Fig. 4. CPOG mining from event log $L = \{abcd, acbd\}$

Since exact CPOG mining is a special case of the general CPOG synthesis problem (all given partial orders are in fact total orders), it is reasonable to expect that more efficient methods exist. The authors are unaware of such methods at present, but believe that this may be an interesting topic for research.

5.2   Concurrency-Aware CPOG Mining

This section presents an algorithm for extracting concurrency from a given event log and using this information for simplifying the result of the CPOG mining. Classic process mining techniques based on Petri Nets generally rely on the α-algorithm for concurrency extraction [1]. We introduce a new concurrency extraction algorithm, which differs from the classic α-algorithm in two aspects. On the one hand, it is more conservative when declaring two given events concurrent, which may lead to the discovery of more precise process models. On the other hand, it considers not only adjacent events in a trace as candidates for the concurrency relation but all event pairs, and therefore can find concurrent events even when the distance between them in traces is always greater than one, as we demonstrate below by an example. This method works particularly well in combination with CPOGs due to their compactness, however, we believe that it can also be useful in combination with other formalisms.

First, let us introduce convenient operations for extracting subsets of traces from a given event log L. Given an event e, the subset of L's traces containing e will be denoted as L_e, while the subset of L's traces not containing e will be denoted as $L_{\bar{e}}$. Clearly, $L_e \cup L_{\bar{e}} = L$. Similarly, given events e and f, the subset of L's traces containing both of them with e occurring before f will be denoted as $L_{e \to f}$. Note that $L_e \cap L_f = L_{e \to f} \cup L_{f \to e}$, i.e. if two events appear in a trace, they must be ordered one way or another. For instance, if $L = \{abcd, acbd, abce\}$ then $L_e = \{abce\}$, $L_{\bar{a}} = \emptyset$, $L_{a \to b} = L$, and $L_{a \to d} = \{abcd, acbd\}$. An event e is *conditional* if $L_e \neq \emptyset$ and $L_e \neq L$, otherwise it is *unconditional*. A conditional event will necessarily have a non-trivial condition (neither 0 nor 1) in the mined CPOG. Similarly, a pair of events e and f is *conditionally ordered* if $L_{e \to f} \neq \emptyset$ and $L_{e \to f} \neq L_e \cap L_f$. Otherwise, e and f are *unconditionally ordered*.

We say that a conditional event r *indicates* the order between events e and f in an event log L if one of the following holds:

- $L_r \subseteq L_{e \to f}$
- $L_r \subseteq L_{f \to e}$
- $L_{\bar{r}} \subseteq L_{e \to f}$
- $L_{\bar{r}} \subseteq L_{f \to e}$

In other words, the existence or non-existence of the event r can be used as an indicator of the order between the events e and f. For example, if $L = \{abcd, acbd, abce\}$, then e indicates the order between b and c. Indeed, whenever we observe event e in a trace we can be sure that b occurs before c in that trace: $L_e \subseteq L_{b \to c}$. This notion leads to a simple concurrency oracle.

Definition 1 (Concurrency oracle). *Two events e and f are concurrent if they are conditionally ordered and no event r indicates their order.*

Intuitively, the order between two truly concurrent events should not be indicated by anything, i.e. it should have no side effects. Indeed, if one of the orderings is in any sense special and there is an indicator of this, then the events are not really concurrent, or at least they are *not always concurrent*. CPOGs are capable of expressing such *conditional concurrency* in a compact form. The *indicates relation* has been inspired by and is similar to the *reveals relation* from [28].

The above concurrency oracle is built on the simplest possible indicator – a single event whose occurrence happens to distinguish the order between two other events. We found this oracle to be very useful and efficient in practice, but it may be too weak in certain cases, in particular, similarly to the α-algorithm it declares all events concurrent in the motivation example from Sect. 2, resulting in a very imprecise process model $a \parallel b \parallel c \parallel d$. Fortunately, we can strengthen the oracle by using second-order relations between events as indicators.

We say that a pair of events (r, s) *indicates* the order between events e and f in an event log L if one of the following holds:

- $L_{r \to s} \subseteq L_{e \to f}$
- $L_{r \to s} \subseteq L_{f \to e}$

In other words, the order between the events r and s can be used as an indicator of the order between the events e and f. For example, if $L = \{abcd, cdab, badc, dcba\}$, then the order between events a and b indicates the order between events c and d (and vice versa). Indeed, whenever a occurs before b in a trace, we know that c occurs before d: $L_{a \to b} = L_{c \to d}$. We can use such second-order indicates relation for defining a more conservative concurrency oracle.

Definition 2 (Rank-2 concurrency oracle). *Two conditionally ordered events e and f are concurrent if (i) no event r indicates their order, and (ii) no pair of events (r, s) indicates their order.*

One can consider more sophisticated combinations of events and the order between them in the definition of the concurrency oracle, hence leading to a *hierarhcy of rank-N oracles*. Indeed, the order can be indicated by a triple $\{r, s, t\}$ of events, or a combination of an event r and an ordering $s \to t$, etc. A detailed investigation of the hierarchy of concurrency oracles is beyond the scope of this paper, but we believe that the hierarchy may be useful for choosing the right precision of the obtained models during process discovery.

The following example, suggested by an anonymous reviewer, highlights the difference between the proposed concurrency oracles and the α-algorithm.

Consider event log $L = \{xay_1y_2y_3bz, xby_1y_2y_3az, xy_1y_2y_3abz, xy_1y_2y_3baz\}$. The α-algorithm does not declare events a and y_2 concurrent, because they never appear adjacent in a trace (i.e. they are not in the so-called *directly-follows* relation). The proposed simple oracle however does declare them concurrent; in fact the whole chain $y_1 \prec y_2 \prec y_3$ is declared concurrent to both a and b, hence compressing the event log into one partial order $x \prec (a \parallel b \parallel y_1 \prec y_2 \prec y_3) \prec z$. The rank-2 oracle is very conservative in this example and does not declare any events concurrent; indeed, the ordering $a \to y_1$ is very rare (it appears only in the first trace) and can therefore be used as an indicator of $a \to b$, etc. The sensitivity of rank-N oracles to such rare combinations may be a disadvantage in some cases. To deal with this problem one can set a threshold for discarding rare indicators, a common approach when dealing with noisy event logs.

We are now ready to describe the algorithm for concurrency-aware CPOG mining. The algorithm takes an event log L as input and produces a CPOG H such that $L \subseteq \mathcal{L}(H)$.

1. Extract the concurrency: find all conditionally ordered pairs of events e and f, such that the order between them is not indicated by any events or pairs of events (when using the rank-2 oracle). Call the resulting set of concurrent pairs of events C.
2. Convert each trace $t \in L$ into a partial order p by relaxing the corresponding total order according to the set C. Call the resulting set of partial orders P.
3. Perform the exact CPOG synthesis on the obtained set of partial orders P to produce the resulting CPOG H.

Note that the resulting CPOG H indeed satisfies the condition $L \subseteq \mathcal{L}(H)$, since we can only add new linearisations into H in step (2) of the algorithm, when we relax a total order corresponding to a particular trace by discarding some of the order relations.

Let us now apply the algorithm to the previous examples. Given log $L = \{abcd, cdab, badc, dcba\}$ from Sect. 2, the algorithm does not find any concurrent pairs, because the order between each pair of events is indicated by the order between the complementary pair of events (e.g. $L_{a \to b} = L_{c \to d}$). Hence, $C = \emptyset$ and the result of the algorithm coincides with the exact CPOG mining, as shown in Sect. 2. Given log $L = \{abcd, acbd\}$ from Sect. 5.1, the algorithm finds one pair of concurrent events, namely (b, c), which results in collapsing of both traces of L into the same partial order with trivial CPOG representation shown in Fig. 4 (right).

6   From Control Flow to Data

As demonstrated in the previous section, one can derive a compact CPOG representation from a given event log using CPOG mining techniques. The obtained representations however rely on opaque Boolean variables, which make the result difficult to comprehend. For example, Fig. 1(a) provides no intuition on how a particular variable assignment can be interpreted with respect to the process under observation. The goal of this section is to present a method for the automated extraction of useful data labels from a given event log (in particular from available event attributes) and using these labels for constructing 'transparent' and easy-to-comprehend predicates, which can substitute the opaque Boolean variables. This is similar to the application of conventional machine learning techniques for learning 'decision points' in process models or in general for the automated enhancement of a given model by leveraging the available data present in the event log [1].

More formally, given an event log L and the corresponding CPOG H our goal is to explain how a particular condition f can be interpreted using data available in L. Note that f can be as simple as just a single literal $x \in X$ (e.g. the arc $a \to b$ in Fig. 1(a)), in which case our goal is to explain a particular Boolean variable; however, the technique introduced in this section is applicable to any Boolean function of the CPOG variables $f : \{0, 1\}^X \to \{0, 1\}$, in particular, one can use the technique for explaining what the restriction function ρ corresponds to in the process, effectively discovering the process *invariants*. We achieve the goal by constructing an appropriate instance of the *classification problem* [29].

Let $n = |E|$ be the number of different events in L, and k be the number of different event attributes available in L. Remember that attributes of an event e can be accessed via function $attr(e)$, see Sect. 3. Hence, every event e in the log defines a *feature vector* $\hat{e}$ of dimension k where the value at i-th position corresponds to the value of the i-th attribute[2] of e. For instance, the feature vector $\hat{e}_1$ corresponding to the event e_1 in Table 1 is ("10-04-2015 9:08am", 25.0, 17, Low). Some features may need to be abstracted before applying the technique described below to produce better results, e.g. timestamps may be mapped to five discrete classes: *morning, noon, afternoon, evening* and *night*.

Table 2. Binary classification problem for function f and event log L.

Feature vectors	Class
$\{\hat{e} \mid e \in \sigma \land \sigma \in L_f\}$	True
$\{\hat{e} \mid e \in \sigma \land \sigma \in L_{\bar{f}}\}$	False

The key observation for the proposed method is that all traces in the log L can be split into two disjoint sets, or *classes*, with respect to the given function f: (i) set L_f, containing the traces where f evaluates to 1, and (ii) set $L_{\bar{f}}$ containing the traces where f evaluates to 0. This immediately leads to an instance of the *binary classification problem* on n feature vectors, as illustrated in Table 2. In other words, every event belonging to a trace where the function f evaluates to 1 is considered to belong to the class we learn, that is, the class labelled as True in Table 2 (the remaining events do not belong to this class). Several methods can be applied to solve this problem, including *decision trees* [30], *support vector machines* [31], and others. In this work we focus on decision trees as they provide a convenient way to extract predicates defined on event attributes, which can be directly used for substituting opaque CPOG conditions. The method is best explained by way of an example.

Consider the event log in Table 1, which contains a few data attributes for each event. The traces underlying the log are $\{abcd, cdab, badc, dcba\}$. Figure 1(a) shows the corresponding CPOG produced by the CPOG mining techniques presented in the previous section. Let us try to find an interpretation of the variable

---

[2] We assume a total order on the set of event attributes.

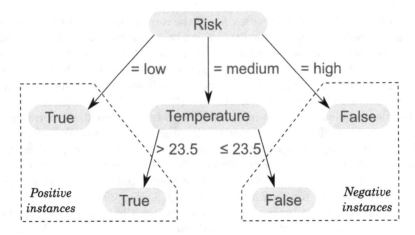

Fig. 5. Decision tree built for function $f = x$ in the CPOG of Fig. 1(a).

x by applying the above procedure with $f = x$. The set L_f equals to $L_{a \rightarrow b}$, i.e. it contains traces 1 and 2, wherein event a occurs before event b and therefore $f = 1$. Therefore, feature vectors $\hat{e}_1 - \hat{e}_8$ provide the positive instances of the class to learn (the first eight events of the log belong to traces 1 and 2), while feature vectors $\hat{e}_9 - \hat{e}_{16}$ provide the negative ones. The decision tree shown in Fig. 5 is a possible classifier for this function, which has been derived automatically using machine learning software WEKA [32]. By combining the paths in the tree that lead to positively classified instances, one can derive the following predicate for f: $risk = low \lor (risk = medium \land temperature > 23.5)$. This predicate can be used to substitute the opaque variable x in the mined CPOG.

One can use the same procedure for deriving the explanation for all variables and/or conditions in a CPOG, thereby providing a much more comprehensible representation for the event log. Note that for complementary functions, taking the negation of the classification description will suffice, e.g. $\bar{x}$ in Fig. 1(a) can be substituted with predicate $risk \neq low \land (risk \neq medium \lor temperature \leq 23.5)$. Alternatively, one can derive the predicate for a complementary function by combining paths leading to the negative instances; for example, for $f = \bar{x}$ the resulting predicate is $risk = high \lor (risk = medium \land temperature \leq 23.5)$.

The learned classifier can be tested for evaluating the quality of representation of the learned concept. If the quality is unacceptable then the corresponding condition may be left unexplained in the CPOG. Therefore in general the data extraction procedure may lead to partial results when the process contains concepts which are 'difficult to learn'. For example, in the discussed case study the condition $f = y$ could not be classified exactly.

A coarse-grain alternative to the technique discussed in this section is to focus on *case attributes* instead of event attributes. Case attributes are attributes associated with a case (i.e., a trace) as a whole instead to individual events [1].

Furthermore, the two approaches can be combined with the aim of improving the quality of obtained classifiers.

7   Tool Support and Experiments

The techniques presented in this paper have been implemented as a plugin for the WORKCRAFT framework [7,33], which is a collection of opensource tools for design, verification and analysis of concurrent systems. In this section we will describe our backend tools, frontend capabilities, and will analyse the performance of the current implementation on a set of realistic process mining benchmarks.

7.1   Backend Tools

We rely on three backend tools: PGMINER [8], SCENCO [34] and WEKA [35].

PGMINER is a contribution of this paper, developed specifically for the efficient concurrency-aware mining of CPOGs from event logs as described in Sect. 5.2. It can handle event logs with multiple occurrences of an event in a trace, by splitting such traces into scenarios that are free from event repetitions, which is essential for our current implementation (this is further discussed in Sect. 7.2). An important feature of the tool is that the results are represented in an algebraic form using the algebra of Parameterised Graphs introduced in [5] (hence the name, PGMINER). This avoids the quadratic explosion of the representation due to transitive arcs appearing after the concurrency extraction step. PGMINER has been implemented as a process mining library written in Haskell [36] and can be run as a standalone command line tool or via the WORKCRAFT frontend.

SCENCO is a collection of CPOG synthesis algorithms that have been developed in a series of publications and integrated in WORKCRAFT: graph colouring based single literal synthesis [4], SAT-based synthesis [21], and heuristic synthesis [22]. We use SCENCO for encoding collections of partial orders produced by PGMINER. As discussed in Sect. 7.3, CPOG synthesis is the main bottleneck of the current process mining implementation. Our future work will be dedicated to the development of a custom CPOG synthesis algorithm specialised for collections of partial orders obtained from process logs after concurrency extraction.

WEKA is a collection of opensource machine learning and data mining algorithms. In the current workflow WEKA is used for extracting meaningful conditions from event log data, as discussed in Sect. 6. Our future work includes integration of WEKA into WORKCRAFT for better interoperability with other methods.

7.2   Details of Current Implementation

WORKCRAFT [7,33] is a collection of software tools united by a common modelling infrastructure and a graphical user interface. WORKCRAFT suppors several interpreted graph models: Petri Nets, Finite State Machines, digital circuits, dataflow structures, xMAS communication networks, and CPOGs, the latter being particularly important for this work. It provides a unified frontend for visual editing and simulation of interpreted graph models, as well as facilities for processing these models by established model-checking and synthesis tools.

WORKCRAFT features a plugin for CPOGs, providing an interface which allows a user to create and edit CPOGs by using a graphical editor, or by describing graphs algebraically using the algebra of parameterised graphs [5]. It is possible to convert between the graphical and algebraic representations automatically.

The authors developed a *process mining plugin* for WORKCRAFT that provides the functionality for importing event logs, manipulating them in the graphical editor, performing concurrency extraction using PGMINER, and synthesising compact CPOG models using SCENCO.

An event log can be imported either directly, in which case each trace is treated as a total order of events, or indirectly via PGMINER, in which case the log undergoes the concurrency extraction procedure leading to a more compact representation and allowing for handling bigger event logs. The current implementation treats multiple occurrences of the same event as different events, e.g., trace (a, b, a, b, c, b, c) is interpreted as $(a_1, b_1, a_2, b_2, c_1, b_3, c_2)$. This can have a negative impact on the concurrency extraction procedure; to avoid this PGMINER provides a method for splitting traces into scenarios which are free from repeated events. For the example at hand this leads to splitting the trace into three sub-traces (a, b), (a, b, c), and (b, c), i.e. whenever a current sub-trace cannot be extended without repeating an event, a new sub-trace is started.

A collection of partial orders can be synthesised into a compact CPOG model using the SCENCO plugin. Our experiments have shown that only heuristic CPOG synthesis [22] can cope with event logs of realistic sizes. Other, more sophisticated encoding methods are not scalable enough. Once a CPOG representation of an event log is obtained, the user can analyse it visually and investigate the meaning of encoding variables using the CPOG projection functionality provided in WORKCRAFT or by performing data mining in WEKA.

7.3   Experiments

Table 3 summarises the experimental results. All benchmark logs come from the process mining community: artificial logs derived from the simulation of a process model (Caise2014, BigLog1, Log1, Log2), a real-life log containing the jobs sent to a copy machine (DigitalCopier), a software log (softwarelog), and real-life logs in different other contexts [37] (documentflow, incidenttelco, purchasetopay, svn_log, telecom). Some of the logs are challenging even for prominent process mining software, and they were therefore chosen as a realistic challenge for testing the capabilities of the developed tools. Note that the '# events' column reports the number of different events after cyclic traces are split by PGMINER.

As can be seen from the table, there are normally a lot more traces than partial orders, thanks to the successful concurrency extraction by PGMINER.

Table 3. Summary of experimental results

Benchmark	Log parameters				Tool runtime				CPOG size		
	File size	# traces	# events	# partial orders	Direct import	Indirect import	Concurrency extraction	CPOG encoding	# arcs	# vars	# gates
BigLog1-100	21Kb	100	22	16	<1 sec	<1 sec	<1 sec	1 sec	33	5	103
BigLog1-500	102Kb	500	22	27	3 sec	<1 sec	<1 sec	1 sec	37	5	174
BigLog1-1000	204Kb	1000	22	26	6 sec	<1 sec	<1 sec	2 sec	37	5	149
Caise2014	25Kb	100	40	401	2 sec	88 sec	1 sec	-	-	-	-
softwarelog	4Kb	5	210	167	<1 sec	1 sec	<1 sec	19 sec	464	8	1751
DigitalCopier-300	70Kb	300	33	15	9 sec	<1 sec	<1 sec	2 sec	37	4	56
DigitalCopier	173Kb	750	33	9	35 sec	<1 sec	<1 sec	1 sec	45	4	78
DigitalCopierMod	116Kb	1000	15	6	4 sec	<1 sec	<1 sec	1 sec	18	3	1
documentflow	208Kb	12391	70	651	2 min	11 sec	1 sec	-	-	-	-
incidenttelco-100	17Kb	100	20	25	<1 sec	<1 sec	<1 sec	4 sec	61	5	225
incidenttelco	161Kb	956	22	77	8 sec	1 sec	<1 sec	8 sec	97	7	641
Log1-filtered	3.6Mb	5000	47	402	-	3 min	13 sec	-	-	-	-
Log2	2Mb	10000	22	32	8.25 min	1 sec	1 sec	1 sec	38	5	194
purchasetopay	232Kb	10487	21	20	3.7 min	1 sec	<1 sec	1 sec	34	5	140
svn_log	24Kb	765	13	92	3 sec	1 sec	<1 sec	2 sec	69	7	581
telecom	15Kb	1000	38	122	2 sec	1 sec	<1 sec	4 sec	194	7	937

However, two cases, namely Caise2014 and softwarelog, are exceptions: they contain traces with particularly many event repetitions which leads to a significant increase of the logs due to the log splitting heuristic described in Sect. 7.2.

The experiments show that PGMINER, when used as a standalone command line tool, is very scalable and can efficiently handle most logs (see column 'Concurrency extraction'). Indeed, most execution times are below or around 1 s, and only Log1-filtered (a 3.6 Mb log) takes 13 s to be processed.

WORKCRAFT is less scalable, as one would expect from a feature-rich graphical editor. Direct import of some logs takes minutes and Log1-filtered cannot be directly imported at all. Indirect import of logs, which is performed by invoking PGMINER first, is more scalable: all logs can be imported this way with most execution times being around 1 s.

CPOG synthesis is the bottleneck of the presented process mining approach. It is a hard computational problem and even heuristic solutions do not currently scale well; in particular, cases with more than 200 partial orders could not be handled. Note that synthesised CPOGs are typically sparse; the number of vertices $|V|$ coincides with the number of events in a log, and as can be seen from the table, the number of arcs $|E|$ in resulting CPOGs is often close to $|V|$. The sparseness of synthesised CPOGs should be exploited by future synthesis tools.

Figure 6 shows an example of a mined model for the DigitalCopierMod log, which is a modified version of DigitalCopier: a new event *BackupImage* was added to demonstrate concurrency extraction, while multiple occurrences of other events were eliminated. The CPOG model was produced by WORKCRAFT from a log containing 1000 traces in under 1 s; note that we manually improved the layout and added colours to enhance the readability. The bottom subfigure shows a projection obtained by setting $x = 0$ and $y = 1$. One can easily compute CPOG projections with WORKCRAFT when exploring CPOG process models.

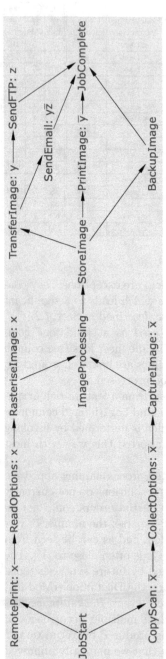

(a) Process model. Note the restriction function $\rho = z \Rightarrow y$, i.e. setting $y = 0$ and $z = 1$ is forbidden.

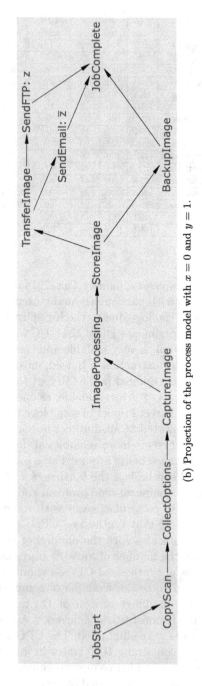

(b) Projection of the process model with $x = 0$ and $y = 1$.

Fig. 6. Visualisation example: CPOG models of the DigitalCopierMod log.

8   Related Work and Discussion

Process mining is a vibrant research field and there are a few relevant research works that are worth discussing and comparing with the proposed CPOG-based representation of event logs. [38] is very close to our work in spirit: it convincingly advocates for using event structures as a unified representation of process models and event logs. As has been recently shown in [18], CPOGs can be exponentially more compact than event structures, therefore we believe that the approach presented in [38] can benefit from the extra compactness provided by CPOGs.

The authors of [39] introduce *trace alignment*, a technique for aligning traces of an event log thereby producing a better visual representation. It uses a matrix representation where rows correspond to traces and columns correspond to positions within each trace. Trace alignment is a powerful visualisation technique that aims to maximise the consensus of the event positions across different traces. In contrast to CPOGs, trace alignment does not compress the information encountered in the traces, nor does it provide a bridge between the control flow and data as proposed in this paper. Furthermore, the trace alignment matrix is a final process mining representation, whilst CPOGs are intended as an intermediate representation and can be used to algebraically operate on event logs.

Another relevant research direction [40,41] relies on the notion of partially-ordered event data and introduces techniques for conformance checking of this type of event representations. In particular, [40] presents the notion of partially-ordered trace (*p-trace*). As in the case of CPOGs, a p-trace allows for explicit concurrency between events of the same trace. P-traces can be computed by careful inspection of the event timestamps. The techniques to extract p-traces are extended in [41] in order to deal with data. However, the use of data attributes is narrower compared to the approach presented in this paper: data attributes are split into read/write accesses to data values, and simple rules to extract concurrency and dependency are introduced to take into account the role of a data access within a trace. We believe that the techniques for relating control flow and data presented in this paper may be applied in the scope of [40,41].

As discussed in the previous section, several challenges need to be faced before the presented techniques can be adopted in industrial process mining solutions, e.g. the complexity of CPOG synthesis algorithms, the fine-tuning of parameters of the data mining techniques, and some others. Due to the inability of CPOGs to directly represent cyclic behavior, we currently only focus on using CPOGs for visualisation and as an intermediate representation of event logs, which can be further transformed into an appropriate process mining formalism, such as Petri Nets or BPMNs. Although some syntactic transformations already exist to transform CPOGs into contextual Petri Nets [33], we believe that finding new methods for discovery of process mining models from CPOGs is an interesting direction for future research.

Another future research direction is to consider CPOGs as compact algebraic objects that can be used to efficiently manipulate and compare event logs [5]. Since a CPOG corresponding to an event log can be exponentially smaller, this may help to alleviate the memory requirements bottleneck for current process mining tools that store 'unpacked' event logs in memory.

Event logs are not the only suitable input for the techniques presented in this paper: we see an interesting link with the work on *discovery of frequent episodes*, e.g. as reported recently in [42]. *Episodes* are partially ordered collections of events (not activities), and as such they can also be represented by CPOGs. This may help to compress the information provided by frequent episodes, especially if one takes into account the fact that current algorithms may extract a large number of episodes, which then need to be visualised for human understanding.

9   Conclusions

This paper describes the first steps towards the use of CPOGs in the field of process mining. In particular, the paper presented the automatic derivation of the control flow part of the CPOG representation from a given event log, and then the incorporation of meta data contained in the log as conditions of the CPOG vertices and arcs. We have implemented most of the reported techniques and some preliminary experiments have been carried out.

The future work includes addressing the challenges described in the previous section, as well as an evaluation of how derived CPOGs can be useful in practice for understanding event data.

Acknowledgments. The authors would like to thank Alessandro de Gennaro and Danil Sokolov for their help with the integration of the developed process mining tools into WORKCRAFT. Many organisations supported this research work: Andrey Mokhov was supported by Royal Society Research Grant 'Computation Alive' and EPSRC project UNCOVER (EP/K001698/1); Josep Carmona was partially supported by funds from the Spanish Ministry for Economy and Competitiveness (MINECO) and the European Union (FEDER funds) under grant COMMAS (ref. TIN2013-46181-C2-1-R); Jonathan Beaumont is currently a PhD student sponsored by a scholarship from the School of Electrical and Electronic Engineering, Newcastle University, UK.

References

1. van der Aalst, W.: Process Mining: Discovery, Conformance and Enhancement of Business Processes. Springer, Heidelberg (2011)
2. The PROM framework homepage (2010). http://www.promtools.org/
3. Song, M., van der Aalst, W.M.P.: Supporting process mining by showing events at a glance. In: Proceedings of Annual Workshop on Information Technologies and Systems (WITS), pp. 139–145 (2007)
4. Mokhov, A.: Conditional partial order graphs. Ph.D. thesis, Newcastle University (2009)
5. Mokhov, A., Khomenko, V.: Algebra of parameterised graphs. ACM Trans. Embed. Comput. Syst. (TECS) **13**(4s), 143 (2014)
6. Mokhov, A., Carmona, J.: Event log visualisation with conditional partial order graphs: from control flow to data. In: Proceedings of the International Workshop on Algorithms and Theories for the Analysis of Event Data, ATAED, Brussels, Belgium, 22–23 June, pp. 16–30 (2015)

7. The WORKCRAFT framework homepage (2009). http://www.workcraft.org

8. The PGMINER tool repository (2015). https://github.com/tuura/process-mining

9. van der Aalst, W.M.P., Weijters, T., Maruster, L.: Workflow mining: discovering process models from event logs. IEEE TKDE **16**(9), 1128–1142 (2004)

10. Buijs, J.C.A.M., van Dongen, B.F., van der Aalst, W.M.P.: A genetic algorithm for discovering process trees. In: Proceedings of the IEEE Congress on Evolutionary Computation, CEC, Brisbane, Australia, 10–15 June, pp. 1–8 (2012)

11. Leemans, S.J.J., Fahland, D., van der Aalst, W.M.P.: Discovering block-structured process models from event logs - a constructive approach. In: Colom, J.-M., Desel, J. (eds.) PETRI NETS 2013. LNCS, vol. 7927, pp. 311–329. Springer, Heidelberg (2013)

12. Carmona, J., Cortadella, J., Kishinevsky, M.: New region-based algorithms for deriving bounded Petri nets. IEEE Trans. Comput. **59**(3), 371–384 (2010)

13. Bergenthum, R., Desel, J., Lorenz, R., Mauser, S.: Synthesis of Petri nets from finite partial languages. Fundam. Inf. **88**(4), 437–468 (2008)

14. Mokhov, A., Sokolov, D., Yakovlev, A.: Adapting asynchronous circuits to operating conditions by logic parametrisation. In: IEEE International Symposium on Asynchronous Circuits and Systems (ASYNC), pp. 17–24. IEEE (2012)

15. Mokhov, A., Rykunov, M., Sokolov, D., Yakovlev, A.: Design of processors with reconfigurable microarchitecture. J. Low Power Electron. Appl. **4**(1), 26–43 (2014)

16. de Micheli, G.: Synthesis and Optimization of Digital Circuits. McGraw-Hill Higher Education, New York (1994)

17. Wegener, I.: The complexity of Boolean functions. Johann Wolfgang Goethe-Universitat (1987)

18. Ponce-de-León, H., Mokhov, A.: Building bridges between sets of partial orders. In: Dediu, A.-H., Formenti, E., Martín-Vide, C., Truthe, B. (eds.) LATA 2015. LNCS, vol. 8977, pp. 145–160. Springer, Heidelberg (2015)

19. Nielsen, M., Plotkin, G., Winskel, G.: Petri nets, event structures and domains, part I. Theor. Comput. Sci. **13**, 85–108 (1981)

20. McMillan, K.: Using unfoldings to avoid the state explosion problem in the verification of asynchronous circuits. In: Proceedings of Computer Aided Verification Conference (CAV), vol. 663, p. 164 (1992)

21. Mokhov, A., Alekseyev, A., Yakovlev, A.: Encoding of processor instruction sets with explicit concurrency control. IET Comput. Digital Tech. **5**(6), 427–439 (2011)

22. de Gennaro, A., Stankaitis, P., Mokhov, A.: A heuristic algorithm for deriving compact models of processor instruction sets. In: International Conference on Application of Concurrency to System Design (ACSD) (2015)

23. Villa, T., Kam, T., Brayton, R.K., Sangiovanni-Vincentelli, A.L.: Synthesis of Finite State Machines: Logic Optimization. Springer, New York (2012)

24. Solé, M., Carmona, J.: Light region-based techniques for process discovery. Fundam. Inf. **113**(3–4), 343–376 (2011)

25. van der Werf, J.M.E.M., van Dongen, B.F., Hurkens, C.A.J., Serebrenik, A.: Process discovery using integer linear programming. In: ATPN, pp. 368–387 (2008)

26. Günther, C.W., van der Aalst, W.M.P.: Fuzzy mining – adaptive process simplification based on multi-perspective metrics. In: Alonso, G., Dadam, P., Rosemann, M. (eds.) BPM 2007. LNCS, vol. 4714, pp. 328–343. Springer, Heidelberg (2007)

27. Weijters, A.J.M.M., van der Aalst, W.M.P., Alves de Medeiros, A.K.: Process mining with the heuristics miner-algorithm. Technical Report WP 166, BETA Working Paper Series, Eindhoven University of Technology (2006)

28. Haar, S., Kern, C., Schwoon, S.: Computing the reveals relation in occurrence nets. Theor. Comput. Sci. **493**, 66–79 (2013)
29. Mitchell, T.M.: Machine Learning. McGraw Hill Series in Computer Science. McGraw-Hill, New York (1997)
30. Quinlan, J.R.: Induction of decision trees. Mach. Learn. **1**(1), 81–106 (1986)
31. Cortes, C., Vapnik, V.: Support-vector networks. Mach. Learn. **20**(3), 273–297 (1995)
32. Hall, M., Frank, E., Holmes, G., Pfahringer, B., Reutemann, P., Witten, I.H.: The WEKA data mining software: an update. ACM SIGKDD Explor. Newsl. **11**(1), 10–18 (2009)
33. Poliakov, I., Sokolov, D., Mokhov, A.: Workcraft: a static data flow structure editing, visualisation and analysis tool. In: Kleijn, J., Yakovlev, A. (eds.) ICATPN 2007. LNCS, vol. 4546, pp. 505–514. Springer, Heidelberg (2007)
34. The SCENCO tool website (2015). http://www.workcraft.org/scenco
35. The WEKA tool website (2015). http://www.cs.waikato.ac.nz/ml/weka
36. Marlow, S., et al.: Haskell 2010 language report (2010). http://www.haskell.org/
37. ActiTraC: Active Trace Clustering (2014). http://www.processmining.be/actitrac/
38. Dumas, M., García-Bañuelos, L.: Process mining reloaded: event structures as a unified representation of process models and event logs. In: Devillers, R., Valmari, A. (eds.) PETRI NETS 2015. LNCS, vol. 9115, pp. 33–48. Springer, Heidelberg (2015)
39. Jagadeesh Chandra Bose, R.P., van der Aalst, W.M.P.: Process diagnostics using trace alignment: opportunities, issues, and challenges. Inf. Syst. **37**(2), 117–141 (2012)
40. Lu, X., Fahland, D., van der Aalst, W.M.P.: Conformance checking based on partially ordered event data. In: Fournier, F., Mendling, J. (eds.) BPM 2014 Workshops. LNBIP, vol. 202, pp. 75–88. Springer, Heidelberg (2015)
41. Lu, X., Mans, R., Fahland, D., van der Aalst, W.M.P.: Conformance checking in healthcare based on partially ordered event data. In: Proceedings of the IEEE Emerging Technology and Factory Automation, ETFA, Barcelona, Spain, 16–19 September, pp. 1–8 (2014)
42. Leemans, M., van der Aalst, W.M.P.: Discovery of frequent episodes in event logs. In: Ceravolo, P., Russo, B., Accorsi, R. (eds.) SIMPDA 2014. LNBIP, vol. 237, pp. 1–31. Springer, Heidelberg (2014)

Conditions for Petri Net Solvable Binary Words

Kamila Barylska[2], Eike Best[1]([✉]), Evgeny Erofeev[1], Łukasz Mikulski[2],
and Marcin Piątkowski[2]

[1] Parallel Systems, Department of Computing Science,
Carl von Ossietzky Universität, 26111 Oldenburg, Germany
{eike.best,evgeny.erofeev}@informatik.uni-oldenburg.de
[2] Faculty of Mathematics and Computer Science,
Nicolaus Copernicus University, 87-100 Toruń, Poland
{kamila.barylska,lukasz.mikulski,marcin.piatkowski}@mat.umk.pl

Abstract. A word is called Petri net solvable if it is isomorphic to the reachability graph of an unlabelled Petri net. In this paper, the class of finite, two-letter, Petri net solvable, words is studied. Two conjectures providing different characterisations of this class of words are motivated and proposed. One conjecture characterises the class in terms of pattern-matching, the other in terms of letter-counting. Several results are described which amount to a partial proof of these conjectures.

Keywords: Binary words · Labelled transition systems · Petri nets · Synthesis

1 Introduction

The relationship between a Petri net and its reachability graph can be viewed from a system analysis or from a system synthesis viewpoint. In system analysis, a system could, for instance, be modelled by a marked Petri net whose (unique) reachability graph serves to facilitate its behavioural analysis [14]. We may get various kinds of interesting structural results for special classes of Petri nets. For example, if the given system is described by a marked graph, then its reachability graph enjoys a long list of useful properties (see, e.g., [7]). In system synthesis, a behavioural specification is typically given, and a system implementing it is sought. For example, one may try to find a Petri net whose reachability graph is isomorphic to a given labelled transition system [1]. We may get structural results of a different nature in this case. For example, [4] describes a structural characterisation of the class of marked graph reachability graphs in terms of a carefully chosen list of graph-theoretical properties.

In this paper, we investigate labelled transition systems which are finite and acyclic. The ultimate aim is to characterise, graph-theoretically, exactly which

K. Barylska, Ł. Mikulski and M. Piątkowski—Supported by the Polish Nat. Sci. Center (grant no. 2013/09/D/ST6/03928).
E. Best and E. Erofeev—Supported by DFG CAVER, ARS, and http://www. uni-oldenburg.de/en/scare/.

M. Koutny et al. (Eds.): ToPNoC XI, LNCS 9930, pp. 137–159, 2016.
DOI: 10.1007/978-3-662-53401-4_7

ones of them are synthesisable into an unlabelled place/transition Petri net
[11]. To our knowledge, such a characterisation is difficult and has not yet been
achieved in general. We begin to study the problem by restricting attention to a
limited special case: non-branching, linearly ordered, transition systems having
at most two edge labels. That is, we study the class of binary words, and our
aim is to characterise the Petri net synthesisable ones amongst them.

Region theory [1] provides an indirect characterisation of this class by means
of an algorithm based on solving systems of linear inequations and synthesising
a Petri net if possible. In this paper, we describe two alternative, more direct,
characterisations, and provide partial proofs in support of their validity. The
first condition characterises the class of Petri net synthesisable binary words
in terms of a pseudo-regular expression. The second condition characterises the
same class in terms of a letter-counting relationship. Both conditions seem to be
more efficient to check than by using the general synthesis algorithm.

In Sect. 2 we briefly recapitulate some basic definitions about labelled transition systems, Petri nets, and regions. Sections 3 and 4 describe our two conjectures and contain proofs that they are necessary for synthesisability. In Sect. 5, we
provide sufficiency proofs for special cases of these conjectures. Section 6 reduces
the problem to words of a special form, and Sect. 7 describes some pertinent
results about words of such forms. Section 8 concludes the paper.

2   Basic Concepts, and Region-Based Synthesis

2.1   Transition Systems, Words, and Petri Nets

A *finite labelled transition system* with initial state is a tuple $TS = (S, \rightarrow, T, s_0)$
with nodes S (a finite set of states), edge labels T (a finite set of letters), edges $\rightarrow$
$\subseteq (S \times T \times S)$, and an initial state $s_0 \in S$. A label t is enabled at $s \in S$, denoted by
$s[t\rangle$, if $\exists s' \in S \colon (s, t, s') \in \rightarrow$. A state s' is reachable from s through the execution
of $\sigma \in T^*$, denoted by $s[\sigma\rangle s'$, if there is a directed path from s to s' whose edges
are labelled consecutively by σ. The set of states reachable from s is denoted by
$[s\rangle$. A sequence $\sigma \in T^*$ is allowed, or firable, from a state s, denoted by $s[\sigma\rangle$,
if there is some state s' such that $s[\sigma\rangle s'$. For clarity, in case of long formulas
we write $|_r \alpha |_s \beta |_q$ instead of $r [\alpha\rangle s [\beta\rangle q$. Two labelled transition systems
$TS_1 = (S_1, \rightarrow_1, T, s_{01})$ and $TS_2 = (S_2, \rightarrow_2, T, s_{02})$ are isomorphic if there is a
bijection $\zeta \colon S_1 \rightarrow S_2$ with $\zeta(s_{01}) = s_{02}$ and $(s, t, s') \in \rightarrow_1 \Leftrightarrow (\zeta(s), t, \zeta(s')) \in \rightarrow_2$,
for all $s, s' \in S_1$.

A *word over* T is a sequence $w \in T^*$, and it is *binary* if $|T| = 2$. For a word w
and a letter t, $\#_t(w)$ denotes the number of times t occurs in w. A word $w' \in T^*$
is called a *subword* (or *factor*) of $w \in T^*$ if $\exists u_1, u_2 \in T^* \colon w = u_1 w' u_2$. A word
$w = t_1 t_2 \ldots t_n$ of length $n \in \mathbb{N}$ uniquely corresponds to a finite transition system
$TS(w) = (\{0, \ldots, n\}, \{(i-1, t_i, i) \mid 0 < i \leq n \wedge t_i \in T\}, T, 0)$.

An *initially marked Petri net* is denoted as $N = (P, T, F, M_0)$ where P is
a finite set of places, T is a finite set of transitions, F is the flow function
$F \colon ((P \times T) \cup (T \times P)) \rightarrow \mathbb{N}$ specifying the arc weights, and M_0 is the initial
marking (where a marking is a mapping $M \colon P \rightarrow \mathbb{N}$, indicating the number of

tokens in each place). A side-place is a place p with $p^{\bullet} \cap {}^{\bullet}p \neq \emptyset$, where $p^{\bullet} = \{t \in T \mid F(p,t)>0\}$ and ${}^{\bullet}p = \{t \in T \mid F(t,p)>0\}$. N is pure or side-place free if it has no side-places. A transition $t \in T$ is enabled at a marking M, denoted by $M[t\rangle$, if $\forall p \in P\colon M(p) \geq F(p,t)$. The firing of t leads from M to M', denoted by $M[t\rangle M'$, if $M[t\rangle$ and $M'(p) = M(p) - F(p,t) + F(t,p)$. This can be extended, as usual, to $M[\sigma\rangle M'$ for sequences $\sigma \in T^*$, and $[M\rangle$ denotes the set of markings reachable from M. The reachability graph $RG(N)$ of a bounded (such that the number of tokens in each place does not exceed a certain finite number) Petri net N is the labelled transition system with the set of vertices $[M_0\rangle$, initial state M_0, label set T, and set of edges $\{(M,t,M') \mid M, M' \in [M_0\rangle \wedge M[t\rangle M'\}$. If a labelled transition system TS is isomorphic to the reachability graph of a Petri net N, we say that N *PN-solves* (or simply *solves*) TS, and that TS is *synthesisable* to N. We say that N solves a word w if it solves $TS(w)$.

2.2 Basic Region Theory, and an Example

Let a finite labelled transition system $TS = (S, \rightarrow, T, s_0)$ be given. In order to synthesise – if possible – a Petri net with isomorphic reachability graph, T must, of course (since we do not consider any transition labels), be used directly as the set of transitions. For the places, $\frac{1}{2} \cdot (|S| \cdot (|S|-1))$ state separation problems and up to $|S| \cdot |T|$ event/state separation problems have to be solved, as follows:

- A *state separation problem* consists of a set of states $\{s, s'\}$ with $s \neq s'$, and for every such set, one needs a place that distinguishes them. Such problems are always solvable if $TS = TS(w)$ originates from a word w; for instance, we might simply introduce a counting place which has j tokens in state j.
- An *event/state separation problem* consists of a pair $(s,t) \in S \times T$ with $\neg(s[t\rangle)$. For every such problem, one needs a place p such that $M(p) < F(p,t)$ for the marking M corresponding to state s, where F refers to the arcs of the hoped-for net.

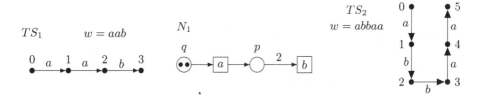

Fig. 1. TS_1 and TS_2 correspond to aab and $abbaa$, respectively. N_1 solves TS_1. No Petri net solution of TS_2 exists.

For example, in Fig. 1, TS_1 is PN-solvable, since the reachability graph of N_1 is isomorphic to TS_1. Note that N_1 has exactly two transitions a and b, which is true for any net solving a binary word over $\{a,b\}$. By contrast, TS_2 is not PN-solvable. The word *abbaa*, from which TS_2 is derived, is actually one of the two shortest non-solvable binary words (the other one being *baabb*, its dual under swapping a and b).

To see that *abbaa* is not PN-solvable, we may use the following argument. State $s = 2$ generates an event/state separation problem $\neg(s[a\rangle)$, for which we need a place q whose number of tokens in the marking corresponding to state 2 is less than necessary for transition a to be enabled. Such a place q has the general form shown in Fig. 2. We now show that such a place does not exist.

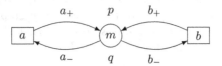

Fig. 2. A place with four arc weights a_-, a_+, b_-, b_+ and initial marking m. It is named p if used for preventing b and named q if used for preventing a.

In order to present this proof succinctly, it is useful to define the *effect* $\mathbb{E}(\tau)$ of a sequence $\tau \in T^*$ on place q. The effect of the empty sequence is $\mathbb{E}(\varepsilon) = 0$. The effect of a sequence $a\tau$ is defined as $\mathbb{E}(a\tau) = (a_+ - a_-) + \mathbb{E}(\tau)$, and similarly, $\mathbb{E}(b\tau) = (b_+ - b_-) + \mathbb{E}(\tau)$. For instance, $\mathbb{E}(abbaa) = 3 \cdot (a_+ - a_-) + 2 \cdot (b_+ - b_-)$. In general, $\mathbb{E}(\tau) = \#_a(\tau) \cdot \mathbb{E}(a) + \#_b(\tau) \cdot \mathbb{E}(b)$.

If q (as in Fig. 2) prevents a at the marking corresponding to state 2 in *abbaa* (cf. Fig. 1), then it must satisfy the following inequalities: $a_- \leq m$, since state 0 enables a; $a_- \leq m + \mathbb{E}(abba)$, since state 4 enables a; $m + \mathbb{E}(ab) < a_-$, since q prevents a at state 2. This set of inequalities cannot be solved in the natural numbers. Combine (0) and (2) to obtain $0 < -\mathbb{E}(ab)$; combine (4) and (2) to obtain $0 < \mathbb{E}(abba) - \mathbb{E}(ab) = \mathbb{E}(ab)$; contradiction.

2.3   Brief Estimation of the Complexity of the General Algorithm

In a word of length n, the equation system for a single event/state separation problem comprises $n + 1$ inequations, n for the states $0, \ldots, n - 1$, which guarantee that the corresponding transition is enabled, and one for the event/state separation itself. In binary words, we have $n + 2$ such problems, one for every state $0, \ldots, n - 1$ and two for the last state. A word w of length n is PN-solvable if and only if all $n + 2$ systems, each having $n + 1$ inequalities and five unknowns a_-, a_+, b_-, b_+, m, are solvable in $\mathbb{N}$.

Suppose that we solve this special case (with five unknowns) by Karmarkar's algorithm [10]. It seems that, solving $O(n)$ systems of inequalitites, we may roughly expect a running time of $O(n^3 \cdot L(n))$, i.e., cubic with a logarithmic factor $L(n) = \log(n) \cdot \log(\log(n))$.

For the remainder of the paper, we fix $T = \{a, b\}$.

3   A Pattern-Matching Condition

3.1   Minimal Unsolvable Words

If w is PN-solvable, then of all its subwords w' are. To see this, let the Petri net solving w be executed up to the state before w', take this as the new initial marking, and add a pre-place with $\#_a(w')$ tokens to a and a pre-place with $\#_b(w')$ tokens to b. Thus, the unsolvability of any proper subword of w entails the unsolvability of w. For this reason, the notion of a *minimal unsolvable word* is well-defined, namely, as an unsolvable word all of whose proper subwords are solvable. A complete list of minimal unsolvable words up to length 110 can be found, amongst some other lists, in [13]. Observe that in this list, every word starts and ends with the same letter. This is a consequence of (the contraposition of) the next proposition.

Proposition 1. SOLVABILITY OF aw AND wb IMPLIES SOLVABILITY OF awb
If both aw and wb are solvable, then awb is also solvable.

Proof: Assume that aw and wb are PN-solvable words over $\{a, b\}$. If $w = b^k$ (for $k \in \mathbb{N}$) then $awb = ab^{k+1}$ is obviously solvable, hence we assume that w contains at least one a. Let $N_1 = (P_1, \{a, b\}, F_1, M_{01})$ and $N_2 = (P_2, \{a, b\}, F_2, M_{02})$ be Petri nets such that N_1 solves aw and N_2 solves wb. We can assume that N_1 and N_2 are disjoint, except for their transitions a and b. Forming the union of N_1 and N_2 gives a net which is synchronised at a and b, and which allows all (and only) sequences allowed by both N_1 and N_2. We modify N_1 and N_2 before forming their union, as follows:

(i) In N_1, for each place p in $\bullet b \cap P_1$, add another $F_1(p, b)$ tokens; and if p in $\bullet a \cap P_1$, then add the quantity $F_1(p, b)$ both to $F_1(p, a)$ and to $F_1(a, p)$; otherwise, keep the arc weights unchanged. This allows an additional b in the end of the word awb. Since the last b in awb could have enabled a at the final state, we add a counting place q_a which is an input place for a with a unit arc weight and has $\#_a(aw)$ tokens on it initially. Thus, a remains disabled in awb exactly at states in which it was disabled before the modification and becomes permanently disabled after aw.

(ii) Modify N_2 by adding to each place q in $\bullet a \cap P_2$ another $F_2(q, a)$ tokens (this allows an additional a). Further, for each place p in $a^\bullet \cap P_2 \cap \bullet b$, add the quantity $F_2(a, p)$ both to $F_2(p, b)$ and to $F_2(b, p)$. The new arc weights lead to the same effect of b on p but prevent premature occurrences of b in the part wb (which could have been allowed by adding the tokens in front of b in the previous step). Moreover, if there is a place p in $\bullet a \cap \bullet b \cap P_2$, b could have been allowed at the very beginning of awb. To prevent this, add a new place p' to N_2, such that $F_2(a, p') = F_2(b, p') = F_2(p', b) = 1$ and $F_2(p', a) = M_0(p') = 0$. This place disables b at the beginning of awb and does not influence the behaviour of N_2 after the first a.

Define N as the union of the two nets thus modified, and see Fig. 3 for an example. (The added tokens are drawn as hollow circles.) In general, N solves

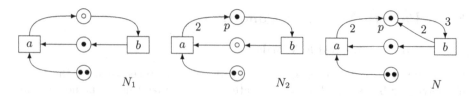

Fig. 3. N_1 (black tokens) solves $aw=abab$. N_2 (black tokens) solves $wb=babb$. N (redundant places omitted) solves $awb=ababb$. Arc weight change due to $p \in a^\bullet \cap P_2 \cap {}^\bullet b$.

awb in the following way: The initial a is allowed in N_1 by definition and in N_2 by the additional tokens. The subsequent w is allowed in both nets, and hence in their synchronisation. The final b is allowed in N_2 by definition and in N_1 by the additional tokens. No premature b is allowed by the arc weight increase, and no final additional a is allowed because N_1 does not allow it. All intermediate occurrences of a are regulated by the modification of N_1, and the same of b by the modification of N_2.   □

This proposition can be used for a remark on word reversal. If both aw, wb and their reversals are solvable, then both awb and its reversal are solvable. This follows directly from the previous proof. If one of the reversals of aw and wb is not solvable, however, then the reversal of awb is not necessarily solvable. Consider, for instance, $w = abba$, $aw = aabba$, $wb = abbab$, and $awb = aabbab$. Here, aw is solvable, but its reversal is $abbaa$, which is a subword of the reversal of awb.

3.2   A Pseudo-regular Expression for Unsolvable Words

Studying the list [13], it can first be observed that all words starting and ending with b are just mirror images of those starting and ending with a under swapping letters. More interestingly, all minimal unsolvable words starting and ending with the letter a happen to be of the following general form:

$$(a\,b\,\alpha)\, b^* \,(b\,a\,\alpha)^+ \,a\,, \quad \text{with } \alpha \in T^* \tag{1}$$

with a not being separated at the state between the b^* and the second bracket (and thus, before the first b in the second bracket, which exists because the bracket contains at least one instance of $ba\alpha$). For example, $abbaa$ satisfies (1) with $\alpha = \varepsilon$, the star $*$ being repeated zero times, and the plus $+$ being repeated once. Such words are generally PN-unsolvable:

Proposition 2. SUFFICIENT CONDITION FOR THE UNSOLVABILITY OF A WORD
If a word over $\{a, b\}$ has a subword of the form (1), then it is not PN-solvable.

Proof: Let s_0 be the state before the first a in (1), s the state before the first b in the second bracket, s' the state after this b, and r the state before the final a:

$$(|_{s_0} a\,b\,\alpha)\, b^* \,(|_s b\, |_{s'} a\,\alpha)^+ \,|_r a$$

For a word w having a subword of this form, we prove that such a subword cannot be solved (implying that w cannot be solved either). Because $ba\alpha$ occurs at least once in the second bracket, $s \neq r$, b is enabled at state s, and a is not enabled at s. Suppose that some place q as in Fig. 2 exists which separates a at s. Abbreviate $\mathbb{E}(ab\alpha)$ to E and $\mathbb{E}(b)$ to E_b. For q, we have the following inequalities:

$$
\begin{aligned}
(0)\quad & a_- \leq m \\
(s')\quad & a_- \leq m + E + k{\cdot}E_b + E_b & \text{for some fixed } k \geq 0 \\
(r)\quad & a_- \leq m + E + k{\cdot}E_b + \ell{\cdot}E & \text{for the same } k \text{ and some fixed } \ell > 0 \\
(s)\quad & 0 \leq -m - E - k{\cdot}E_b + a_- - 1 & \text{for the same } k
\end{aligned}
$$

(0) is true because s_0 enables a. (s') is true because s' enables a. (r) is true because r enables a; and $\ell > 0$ because of the $^+$. Finally, (s) is true because q disables a at state s. Adding $(s')+(s)$ gives $1 \leq E_b$. Adding $(0)+(s)$ gives $1 \leq -E - k{\cdot}E_b$, and using also $1 \leq E_b$ gives $1 \leq -E - k{\cdot}E_b \leq -E$. Adding $(r)+(s)$ gives $1 \leq \ell{\cdot}E$, contradicting $1 \leq -E$ because of $\ell > 0$. The system cannot be solved, and no place q separating a at s exists. □

3.3 Converses of Proposition 2, and Complexity Estimation

All words of the form (1) are unsolvable, but there exist unsolvable words which are not of this form. Nevertheless, it turns out that all *minimal* unsolvable words not only conform to (1), but are of an even simpler shape, as expressed in the following conjectures (and as will be elaborated in later parts of this paper; the facts from Sects. 5 and 6 are the justification of their partial correctness).

Conjecture 1. First converse of Proposition 2
Suppose a word over $\{a, b\}$ is non-PN-solvable and minimal with that property. Then it is (modulo swapping a and b) of the form given in (1). □

Basing on computer experiments partially supported by Proposition 5 (the fact on the existence of subwords aa and bb inside solvable words proven in Subsect. 6.2) we also feel that, without loss of generality, one can restrict (1) to α containing only letters b if the b^* part is not empty. More precisely:

Conjecture 1a. Strengthened converse of Proposition 2
Each minimal unsolvable word over $\{a, b\}$ conforms to one of the forms

$$
\left[\; ab \underbrace{b^j}_{\alpha} b^k ba \underbrace{b^j}_{\alpha} a \text{ with } j \geq 0, k \geq 1 \right] \quad \text{or} \quad \left[\; ab\alpha(ba\alpha)^\ell a \text{ with } \ell \geq 1 \right] \tag{2}
$$

(again, modulo swapping a and b). □

Using Conjecture 1, the problem of deciding the PN-solvability of a word v of length n can be reduced to a pattern-matching problem. Namely, we need to verify whether v contains a subword w of the form (1). Using an algorithm based on the Knuth-Morris-Pratt algorithm [8] (utilizing strict border arrays to search for the repetitions by processing all suffixes of v), this can be done in time $O(n^2 \log n)$. Using Conjecture 1a, subwords of the form $ab\alpha(ba\alpha)^\ell a$ with $\ell \geq 1$ can be recognised using the same technique (KMP-like algorithm). Let us notice that in this case the partial matched subword u_1 and the repeating subword $(u_2)^\ell$ are not separated by a block of the form b^k. Subwords of the form $abb^j b^k bab^j a$ ($j \geq 0, k \geq 1$) can be recognised in time $O(n)$ by counting distances between consecutive occurrences of a (at any moment we have to remember only the positions of two preceding occurrences of a). In contrast to the general case, using Conjecture 1a do not need any additional preprocessing or memory, and the solution takes time at most $O(n^2)$.

4   A Counting Condition

4.1   An Arithmetic Criterion for Unsolvable Words

Proposition 3. ANOTHER SUFFICIENT CONDITION FOR UNSOLVABILITY
Suppose $\alpha, \beta \in \{a, b\}^+$ and $w = \alpha\beta a$, where α starts with a, β starts with b, and

$$\#_a(\beta)\cdot\#_b(\alpha) \ \geq \ \#_a(\alpha)\cdot\#_b(\beta) \tag{3}$$

Then w is unsolvable.

Proof: Let s_0 be the state before α, s the state before β, and r the state before the final a:

$$w \ = \ |_{s_0} \alpha \,|_s \beta \,|_r a$$

If a place q separates a at s and has marking m at s_0, then for $E_\alpha = \mathbb{E}(\alpha) = \#_a(\alpha)\cdot E_a + \#_b(\alpha)\cdot E_b$ and $E_\beta = \mathbb{E}(\beta) = \#_a(\beta)\cdot E_a + \#_b(\beta)\cdot E_b$ we have:

$$
\begin{aligned}
&(0) \ a_- \leq m &&(\text{since } \alpha \text{ starts with } a)\\
&(r) \ a_- \leq m + E_\alpha + E_\beta &&(\text{since } r \text{ enables } a)\\
&(s) \ 0 \ \ \leq -m - E_\alpha + a_- - 1 &&(\text{since } \neg s[a))
\end{aligned}
$$

Adding (0)+(s) yields $1 \leq -E_\alpha$, hence (A): $-(\#_a(\alpha)E_a + \#_b(\alpha)E_b) \geq 1$.
Adding (r)+(s) yields $1 \leq E_\beta$, hence (B): $(\#_a(\beta)E_a + \#_b(\beta)E_b) \geq 1$.
Also, $E_b \geq 1$ because q prevents a at s, but a becomes enabled after one or more firings of b. Then,

$$
\begin{aligned}
-\#_a(\beta) \ &\geq \ \#_a(\beta)\#_a(\alpha)E_a + \#_a(\beta)\#_b(\alpha)E_b &&(\text{multiplying (A) by } \#_a(\beta))\\
&\geq \ \#_a(\beta)\#_a(\alpha)E_a + \#_a(\alpha)\#_b(\beta)E_b &&(\text{using (3) and } E_b \geq 1)\\
&\geq \ \#_a(\alpha) &&(\text{multiplying (B) by } \#_a(\alpha))
\end{aligned}
$$

However, $-\#_a(\beta) \geq \#_a(\alpha)$ implies $\#_a(\beta) = \#_a(\alpha) = 0$, and this is a contradiction since α contains at least one a. Thus, such a place q does not exist.   □

4.2 Converses of Proposition 3, and complexity estimation

Conjecture 2. FIRST CONVERSE OF PROPOSITION 3
If a word is of the form $w = \alpha\beta a$ where α starts with a and β starts with b, and if w is minimal non-PN-solvable, then inequation (3) holds. □

We also believe that for sufficiently long words that are of a special (as it turns out, interesting) shape, the $\geq$ in (3) can be strengthened to equality. More precisely,

Conjecture 2a. STRENGTHENED CONVERSE OF PROPOSITION 3
If $w = \alpha\beta a$ is of the form

$$w \;=\; \underbrace{ab^{x_1}a\ldots ab^{x_k-1}}_{\alpha} \mid_s \underbrace{ba\ldots ab^{x_n}}_{\beta}\, a \quad \text{with } n \geq 3 \text{ and } x_i \geq 1 \tag{4}$$

then a is not separable at state s iff $\#_a(\beta)\cdot\#_b(\alpha) = \#_a(\alpha)\cdot\#_b(\beta)$. □

The arithmetic criterion in Conjecture 2a tells us nothing about minimality. The word to be checked is assumed to start and end with the same letter. In a bad case, e.g., for $w = ab\ldots ab$, checking needs to be repeated two times. Each maximal subword, starting and ending with the same letter, can be divided into α and β at most in $n - 3$ different ways. For every such devision we need to go through the subword of length $n - 2$ once, in order to check the criterion. This amounts to time approximately $2(n-3)(n-2)$ and thus, time $O(n^2)$ in total. A solvability algorithm based on Conjecture 2 was recently (end of October 2015) implemented by Harro Wimmel and compared with the general synthesis APT algorithm [6,15]. It was briefly tested on 1024 words of length 1990. The special algorithm took about a minute to check solvability, while the general algorithm takes much longer (being general-purpose and actually constructing a solution if one exists). To our knowledge, testing only solvability with the general algorithm, without necessarily finding a solution, is only faster in the degree of the number of variables, which is constant for the separation problems.

A reasonable and possibly beneficial approach could be to use the algorithms described in Sects. 2.3, 3.3 and 4.2 in combination, depending on a particular task: The general algorithm yielding a Petri net solution if the given word is solvable; the pattern-matching algorithm checking minimal unsolvability (and possibly combinable with other efficient methods); and the counting algorithm checking solvability or unsolvability (but requiring, for minimality, several repetitions for subwords).

5 Special Cases of the Two Conjectures

In this section, we substantiate Conjectures 1 and 2 by providing partial proofs for the converses of Propositions 2 and 3. First, we prove the minimal unsolvability of words corresponding to the following two patterns, as special instances of (1):

$$ab b^x b^k bab^x a \quad \text{and} \quad ab b^x b(ab^x b)^d ab^x a \quad \text{with } x \geq 0, k \geq 1, d \geq 0 \tag{5}$$

The first pattern satisfies (1) with $\alpha = b^x$, the star * being repeated k times, and the plus $^+$ being repeated only once, while the second pattern satisfies (1) with $\alpha = b^x$, the star * being repeated zero times, and the plus $^+$ being repeated $d + 1$ times. Due to Proposition 2, all binary words of one of the forms in (5) are unsolvable. To prove that they are minimal with this property, we provide Petri nets (with initial markings) solving maximal proper prefixes and maximal proper suffixes of these words.

The Petri net N_1 on the left-hand side of Fig. 4, with appropriate values of parameters in the arc weights and initial marking, is a possible solution for a maximal prefix $abb^x b^k bab^x$ of the first form in (5). Place p_1 prevents b at the beginning, and p_2 restricts the total number of b's. Place q prevents a when it is necessary. This place has enough tokens on it for the initial a and for one more a after the block $bb^x b^k b$, and it does not enable a afterwards.

The maximal proper suffix $bb^x b^k bab^x a$ can be executed by the net N_2 on the right-hand side of Fig. 4. Initially only $x + k + 2$ firings of b are possible, which brings enough tokens on place q for a to occur. This first a adds x tokens on place p_1, which enables b again. The total number of b's is controlled by place p_2. When there is no tokens on p_2, a is enabled once more, and this last occurrence of a ends the execution of the suffix. Hence, words of the first form in (5) are minimally unsolvable.

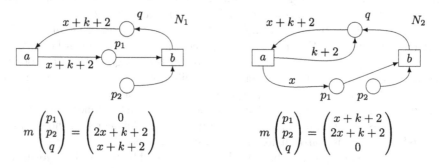

Fig. 4. N_1 solves the prefix $abb^x b^k bab^x$. N_2 solves the suffix $bb^x b^k bab^x a$.

The maximal proper prefix $abb^x b(ab^x b)^d ab^x$ of the second form in (5) can be solved by the net N_1 in Fig. 5. Place q in this net enables the initial a, and then disables it unless b has been fired $x + 2$ times. After the execution of block $bb^x b$ there are d tokens more than a needs to fire on place q. These surplus tokens allow a to be fired after each sequence $b^x b$, but not earlier. Place p_1 has initially 1 token on it, which is necessary for block $bb^x b$ after the first a, and this place has only $x + 1$ tokens after each next a, preventing b at states where a must occur. Places p_2 and p_3 prevent undesirable occurrences of b at the very beginning and at the very end of the prefix, respectively.

For the general form of suffix $bb^x b(ab^x b)^d ab^x a$ of the second form in (5), one can consider the Petri net N_2 on the right-hand side of Fig. 5 as a possible solution. Indeed, place q_1 prevents premature occurrences of a in the first block $bb^x b$, and enables a only after this and each next block $b^x b$. Doing so, it collects one additional token after each $b^x b$, which allows this place to enable the very last a after sequence b^x. The initial marking allows to execute the sequence $bb^x b$ in the beginning, and at most $x + 1$ b's in a row after that, thanks to place p_1. Place p_2 restricts the total number of b's allowing only block b^x at the end. Place q_2 serves for bounding the total number of occurrences of a, and it is necessary if $x = 0$ and $d = 0$. Thus we deduce that any word of the form $abb^x b(ab^x b)^d ab^x a$ with $x, d \geq 0$ is minimally unsolvable.

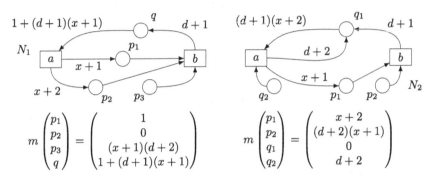

Fig. 5. N_1 solves the prefix $abb^x b(ab^x b)^d ab^x$. N_2 solves the suffix $bb^x b(ab^x b)^d ab^x a$.

Words of two forms in (5) correspond to two classes of minimally unsolvable words that were described in Conjecture 1a, the strengthened variant of Conjecture 1. Moreover, while the form $abb^x b(ab^x b)^d ab^x a$ is only a partial instance (for $\alpha = b^x$) of the more general form $ab\alpha(ba\alpha)^\ell a$ with $\ell \geq 1$ (see Conjecture 1a), pattern $abb^x b^k bab^x a$ coincides entirely with $abb^j b^{kb} a b^j a$, where $j \geq 0, k \geq 1$ (cf. (2)).

In support of Conjectures 2 and 2a, assume a minimally unsolvable word

$$w_1 = abb^x \mid_{s_1} b \ \ldots \ b^x \mid_{s_j} b \ \ldots \ b^x \mid_{s_{d+1}} bab^x a$$

of the second form in (5) to be given, with some fixed non-negative x and d. For any $1 \leq j \leq d + 1$ and state s_j, in $w_1 = \underbrace{ab \ldots b^x}_{\alpha} \mid_{s_j} \underbrace{b \ldots ab^x}_{\beta} a$ we have

$$\#_a(\beta) \cdot \#_b(\alpha) = (d+2-j) \cdot ((x+1) \cdot j) = j \cdot ((d+1-j) \cdot (x+1) + 1 + x) = \#_a(\alpha) \cdot \#_b(\beta)$$

By Proposition 3, a is not separated at such states s_j. On the other hand, expression (3) is fulfilled in w_1 as an equality, which corresponds to the strong variant of Conjecture 2.

The requirement $n \geq 3$ in (4) is important. In a minimally unsolvable word $w_2 = \underbrace{abb^x b^k}_{\alpha} \mid_r \underbrace{bab^x}_{\beta} a$ of the first form in (5), with $x \geq 0$ and $k \geq 1$, we have

$$\#_a(\beta) \cdot \#_b(\alpha) = 1 \cdot (x + k + 1) > 1 \cdot (x + 1) = \#_a(\alpha) \cdot \#_b(\beta)$$

According to Proposition 3, a is not separated at r, but (3) is satisfied as a strict inequality.

6   Limiting the Occurrence of Factors aa or bb

In this section, we show that the problem of characterising minimal unsolvable words w can be reduced to two cases, $w = b^{x_1}a \ldots ab^{x_n}$ or $w = ab^{x_1}a \ldots ab^{x_n}a$ (both with $x_1 \geq 1$). Observe that Conjecture 2a concerns the second case.

Since words in which a and b strictly alternate are easy to solve, it stands to reason to investigate the situations in which a letter occurs twice in a row. We show that in a minimal unsolvable word, the factors aa and bb are essentially limited to occur in some particular ways.

6.1   Factors aa or bb Starting an Unsolvable Word

If a word av is unsolvable and if av is minimal unsolvable, then, as a consequence of the next proposition, v definitely starts with a letter b. That is, no minimal unsolvable word can start with aa (nor with bb, for that matter).

Proposition 4. SOLVABLE WORDS STARTING WITH a CAN BE PREFIXED BY a *If a word av is PN-solvable then aav is, too.*

Proof: Let $N = (P, \{a, b\}, F, M_0)$ be a net solving av. We shall construct a net which solves aav. The idea is to obtain such a net by "unfiring" a once from the initial marking of N. Since this may lead to a non-semipositive marking which we would like to avoid, we will first normalise and modify the net N, obtaining another solution N' of av, and then construct a solution N'' for aav (cf. Fig. 6).

For normalisation, we assume that there are two places p_b and q_a; the first prevents b explicitly in the initial phase, and the second prevents a after the last occurrence of a. They are defined by $M_0(p_b) = 1$, $F(a, p_b) = 1$, $F(b, p_b) = \ell+1 = F(p_b, b)$, where ℓ is the number of a before the first b in av, and $M_0(q_a) = k$, $F(q_a, a) = 1$, where k is the number of a in av. (All other F values $= 0$.)

Let $NUF(a) = \{p \in a^\bullet \mid M_0(p) < F(a, p)\}$ be the set of places which do not allow the "unfiring" of a at M_0. Note that neither p_b nor q_a are in $NUF(a)$. Note also that for every $p \in NUF(a)$, $F(p, a) \leq M_0(p) < F(a, p)$ – the first because a is initially enabled, the second by $p \in NUF(a)$. That is, a has a positive effect on p. Without loss of generality, b has a negative effect on p (otherwise, thanks to the normalising place p_b, p could be deleted without changing the behaviour of N).

For every $p \in NUF(a)$ we add the quantity $F(a, p)$ uniformly to $M_0(p)$, to $F(p, b)$, and to $F(b, p)$, eventually obtaining $N' = (P', \{a, b\}, F', M_0')$, and we show that N' also solves av. First, both $M_0[a\rangle \wedge \neg M_0[b\rangle$ and $M_0'[a\rangle \wedge \neg M_0'[b\rangle$ (the former by definition, the latter by construction). For an inductive proof, suppose that $M_0[a\rangle M_1[\tau\rangle M$ and $M_0'[a\rangle M_1'[\tau\rangle M'$. We have $M[b\rangle$ iff $M'[b\rangle$ by construction. If $M[a\rangle$, then also $M'[a\rangle$, since $M \leq M'$. Next, suppose that $\neg M[a\rangle$; then there is some place q such that $M(q) < F(q, a)$. We show that, without loss of generality,

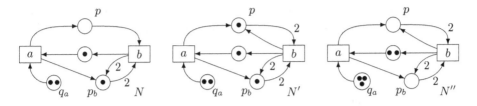

Fig. 6. N is normalised and solves $abab$. N' solves $abab$ as well. N'' solves $aabab$.

$q \notin NUF(a)$, so that q also disables a at M' in N'. If M disables a after the last a in av, we can take $q = q_a \notin NUF(a)$. If M disables a before its last occurrence in av, then q cannot be in $NUF(a)$, since b acts negatively on such places.

Now, we construct a net $N'' = (P', \{a, b\}, F', M_0'')$ from N' by defining $M_0''(p) = M_0'(p) - F'(a, p) + F'(p, a)$ for every place p. By construction, aav is a firing sequence of N''. Furthermore, M_0'' does not enable b because of p_b. □

6.2 Factors aa or bb Inside a Minimal Unsolvable Word

There can be factors aa or bb inside a minimal unsolvable word. However, the next proposition (together with the previous proposition) implies that we cannot have both – unless one of them is at the very end of the word, as in $abbaa$.

Proposition 5. NO aa AND bb INSIDE A MINIMAL UNSOLVABLE WORD
If a minimal non-PN-solvable word is of the form $u = a\alpha a$, then either α does not contain the factor aa or α does not contain the factor bb.

Proof: By contraposition. Assume that α contains a factor aa and a factor bb. Two cases are possible:

Case 1: There is a group of a's which goes after a group of b's. Let a^m and b^n be such groups, assume that a^m goes after b^n and that there are no groups of a or of b between them. Then u is of the following form

$$|_{s_0} \ \cdots \ |_q \ ab^n(ab)^k a^m \ |_r \ \cdots$$

where $n, m \geq 2$, $k \geq 0$. Recombine the letters in u to the following form:

$$|_{s_0} \ \cdots \ |_q \ (ab)b^{n-2}(ba)^{k+1} aa^{m-2} \ |_r \ \cdots$$

Since u ends with a, $(ab)b^{n-2}(ba)^{k+1}a$ is a proper subword of u. But it has the form $(abw)b^*(baw)^+a$, with $w = \varepsilon$, which implies its unsolvability by Proposition 2, contradicting the minimality of u.

Case 2: All groups of a precede all groups of b. In this case u is of the form

$$aa^{x_0}ba^{x_1}\ldots ba^{x_n}b^{y_0}ab^{y_1}ab^{y_2}\ldots ab^{y_m}a$$

where at least one of x_i and one of y_j is greater than 1. Consider $\ell = \max\{i \mid x_i > 1\}$. If $\ell = 0$, we get a contradiction to Proposition 4. Hence, $\ell > 0$. Let $t = \min\{j \mid y_j > 1\}$. Then u has the form

$$|_{s_0} a \ldots |_q ba^{x_\ell}(ba)^{n-\ell}(ba)^t b^{y_t} |_r \ldots a$$

Recombine the letters in u to the form

$$|_{s_0} a \ldots |_q (ba)a^{x_\ell-2}(ab)^{n-\ell+t+1}bb^{y_t-2} |_r \ldots a$$

Hence, u has a proper subword $(ba)a^{x_\ell-2}(ab)^{n-\ell+t+1}b$, which is of the form $(baw)a^*(abw)^+b$ with $w = \varepsilon$, implying its non-PN-solvability, due to Proposition 2 with inverted a and b. This again contradicts the minimality of u.   □

For these reasons, we are particularly interested in words of the following form:

$$\boxed{\text{either} \quad ab^{x_1}a \ldots ab^{x_n}a \quad \text{or} \quad b^{x_1}a \ldots ab^{x_n} \quad \text{where } x_i \geq 1 \text{ and } n > 1} \quad (6)$$

In the first form, there are no factors aa. If factors bb are excluded and the word starts and ends with an a, then we get words that are of the second form, except for swapping a and b.

7   Some Results About Words of the Form $b^{x_1}a \ldots ab^{x_n}$

Let $w = b^{x_1}a \ldots ab^{x_n}$ be a word with $n > 1$ and $x_i \geq 1$ for every $1 \leq i \leq n$, consisting of groups of letters b separated by single a's, and starting and ending with b. With a view to (6), it seems important to understand conditions

- for transforming solutions of w into solutions of aw,
- and for transforming solutions of w (or aw) into solutions of wa (or awa).

In the present section, we address the first of these tasks. The aim is to modify an existing solution of w to yield a solution of aw. Similar constructions in the previous sections were typically done by transforming the places of an existing Petri net into places of a new net. The proof technique employed in this section allows to create new regions from old ones by transforming a given solution involving quantities such as m, a_-, etc., into new quantities such as m', a'_-, etc. This is useful as there is not always a direct intuitive (pictorial) relationship between the new and the old places.

7.1   Side-Places in Words of the Form $b^{x_1}a \ldots ab^{x_n}$

If a word $w = b^{x_1}a \ldots ab^{x_n}$ can be solved, then side-places may be necessary to do it. For instance, $bbabbabababab$ cannot be solved side-place-freely. (More precisely: a side-place is needed in order to separate a at state 6.) However, we will show that in the worst case, only some side-places q around a, preventing a

at some state, are necessary. Also, such side-places are unnecessary if x_1 is small enough, in the sense that $x_1 \leq \min\{x_2, \ldots, x_{n-1}\}$. For example, $babbababab$ can be solved without any side-places. The "smallness" of x_1 is sufficient but not necessary. For instance, $bbabbabab$ has a side-place-free solution, even though $x_1 \not\leq \min\{x_2, \ldots, x_{n-1}\}$.

In the following, we assume w to be of the following form (7). The states s_i $(1 \leq i \leq n-1)$ denote the important states at which b has to be prevented, and the states r_k $(1 \leq k \leq n-1)$ denote the important states at which a has to be prevented. At or after the last group of b's, a can be prevented by a counting place, and at the final state, b can similarly be prevented by a counting place.

$$w = b^{x_1-1} \big|_{r_1} b \big|_{s_1} a\, b^{x_2-1} \big|_{r_2} b \big|_{s_2} a \,\cdots\, \big|_{s_{k-1}} a\, b^{x_k-1} \big|_{r_k} b \big|_{s_k} a \,\cdots\, \big|_{s_{n-1}} a\, b^{x_n} \quad (7)$$

Proposition 6. SIDE-PLACE-FREE SOLVABILITY WITH FEW INITIAL b'S
If $w = b^{x_1} ab^{x_2} a \ldots ab^{x_n}$ is solvable, then side-places are necessary, at worst, between a and q, where q is some place preventing a at one of the states r_k with $1 \leq k < n-1$. If $w = b^{x_1} ab^{x_2} a \ldots ab^{x_n}$ is solvable and $x_1 \leq \min\{x_2, \ldots, x_{n-1}\}$, then w is solvable side-place-freely.

Proof: The first claim follows from Lemmata 1 and 2 below. The second claim follows from Lemma 3. □

Lemma 1. SIDE-PLACE-FREENESS AROUND b
If $w = b^{x_1} a \ldots ab^{x_n}$ is solvable, then w is solvable without side-place around b.

Proof: We show that side-places around b are necessary neither for preventing any b (cf. **(A)** below), nor for preventing any a (cf. **(B)** below).

(A): Suppose some place p prevents b at some state s_k, for $1 \leq k \leq n-1$. (The only other state at which b must be prevented is state s_n, but that can clearly be done by a non-side-place, e.g. by an incoming place of transition b that has $\#_b(w) = \sum_{i=1}^{n} x_i$ tokens initially.) Note that $b_- > b_+$, because place p allows b to be enabled at the state preceding s_k but not at s_k. Similarly, $a_- < a_+$, because b is not enabled at state s_k but at the immediately following state, which is reached after firing a. From the form (7) of w, we have

$$
\begin{aligned}
b_+ &\leq m + x_1(b_+ - b_-) \\
b_+ &\leq m + (x_1 + x_2)(b_+ - b_-) + (a_+ - a_-) \\
&\cdots \\
b_+ &\leq m + (x_1 + \ldots + x_n)(b_+ - b_-) + (n-1)(a_+ - a_-) \\
0 &\leq -m - (x_1 + \ldots + x_k)(b_+ - b_-) - (k-1)(a_+ - a_-) + b_- - 1
\end{aligned}
\quad (8)
$$

The first n inequations assert the semipositivity of the marking of place p (more precisely, its boundedness from below by b_+, since p may be a side-place) at the n states $s_1, \ldots, s_n$. In our context, if these inequalities are fullfilled, then the marking is $\geq b_+$ at *all* states, as a consequence of $b_- \geq b_+$, $a_- \leq a_+$, and the special form of the word. The last inequality comes from $\neg(s_k[b\rangle)$.

We certainly have $0 \le b_+ < b_- \le m$, because of $b_- > b_+$ as noted above, and because b is initially enabled. If $b_+ = 0$, then p is not a side-place around b, and there is nothing more to prove (for p). If $b_+ \ge 1$, we consider the transformation

$$b'_+ = b_+ - 1 \text{ and } b'_- = b_- - 1 \text{ and } m' = m - 1$$

The relation $0 \le b'_+ < b'_- \le m'$ still holds for the new values. Also, all inequalities in (8) remain true for the new values: in the first n lines, 1 is subtracted on each side, and on the last line, the increase in $-m$ is offset by the decrease in b_-.

We have thus shown that subtracting one arc from b to p, one arc from p to b, and removing one initial token from p, leaves the region inequalities invariant. Thus, we get a solution preventing b with a 'smaller' side-place, and we can continue until eventually b_+ becomes zero. This finishes part **(A)** of the proof.

(B): A side-place around b might still be necessary to prevent a at some state. We show next that such side-places are also unnecessary. Suppose some place q as in Fig. 2 prevents a at state r_k, for $1 \le k \le n - 1$. Symmetrically to the previous case, we have $b_+ > b_-$. This is true because, while q does not have enough tokens to enable a at state r_k, it must have enough tokens to enable a at the directly following state (which we may continue to call s_k). But we also have (w.l.o.g.) $a_+ < a_-$. For $k \ge 2$, this follows from the fact that if the previous a (enabled at the state s_{k-1} just after r_{k-1}) acts positively on q, then q also has sufficiently many tokens to enable a at state r_k. For $k = 1$, it is possible to argue that $a_+ < a_-$ is valid without loss of generality. For suppose that q disables a only at r_1 and nowhere else. (This is no loss of generality because for the other states r_k, $k \ge 2$, copies of q can be used.) Then we may consider q' which is an exact copy of q, except that $a_+ = a_- - 1$ for q'. This place q' also disables a at state r_1 (because it has the same marking as q). Moreover, it does not disable a at any other state after r_1 because it always has $\ge a_- - 1$ tokens, and after the next b, $\ge a_-$ tokens, since $b_+ > b_-$.

Because of $b_+ > b_-$ and $a_+ < a_-$, place q also prevents a at all prior states in the same group of b's. Moreover, in the last (i.e. n'th) group of b's, a can easily be prevented side-place-freely. For place q with initial marking m, we have

$$
\begin{array}{rl}
a_+ & \le m + x_1(b_+ - b_-) + (a_+ - a_-) \\
a_+ & \le m + (x_1 + x_2)(b_+ - b_-) + 2(a_+ - a_-) \\
\cdots \\
a_+ & \le m + (x_1 + \ldots + x_{n-1})(b_+ - b_-) + (n - 1)(a_+ - a_-) \\
0 & \le -m - (x_1 + \ldots + x_k - 1)(b_+ - b_-) - (k - 1)(a_+ - a_-) + a_- - 1
\end{array}
\tag{9}
$$

The first $n - 1$ inequations assert the semipositivity of the marking of place q (more precisely, its boundedness from below by a_+, since q may be a side-place of a) at the $n - 1$ states just after the a's in (7). If they are fullfilled, then the marking is $\ge a_+$ at *all* states after the first a, as a consequence of $b_+ > b_-$ and the special form of the word. The last inequality asserts that place q prevents transition a at state r_k, hence effects the event/state separation of a at r_k.

If b_- is already zero, place q is not a side-place of b. Otherwise, we may perform the transformation

$$b'_+ = b_+ - 1 \text{ and } b'_- = b_- - 1 \text{ and } m' = m$$

because of $b_+ > b_-$ as noted above. The left-hand sides of the first $n-1$ inequalities in (9) do not decrease, and neither do the right-hand sides. The same is true for the last inequality. This finishes part **(B)** of the proof.   □

Lemma 2. SIDE-PLACE-FREENESS AROUND a, PREVENTING b
Suppose $w = b^{x_1}ab^{x_2}a\ldots ab^{x_n}$. If w is solvable by a net in which some place p separates b, then we may w.l.o.g. assume that p is not a side-place around a.

Proof: The equation system (8) is invariant under the transformation

$$a'_+ = a_+ - 1 \text{ and } a'_- = a_- - 1 \text{ and } m' = m$$

as neither left-hand sides nor right-hand sides change their values.   □

If some place q prevents transition a, then it may be a side-place between q and a. It may not always be possible to remove such a side-place. For instance, the word $w = bbabbababab$ is of the form (7), and any net solving it necessarily contains a side-place around transition a. The next lemma shows that the presence of a side-place around a may be due to there being "many" initial b's.

Lemma 3. SIDE-PLACE-FREENESS AROUND a, PREVENTING a
Suppose $w = b^{x_1}ab^{x_2}a\ldots ab^{x_n}$. If $x_1 \leq \min\{x_2,\ldots,x_{n-1}\}$ and if w is solvable by a net in which some place q prevents transition a at state r_k with $1 \leq k \leq n$, then we may w.l.o.g. assume that q is not a side-place around a.

Proof: For preventing a at state r_n, we only need a place with no input and a single output transition a (weight 1) which has $n-1$ tokens initially.
Suppose q prevents a at state r_k, with $1 \leq k \leq n-1$. From previous considerations, we know $a_+ \leq a_-$ and $b_+ > b_-$, and we may assume, from Lemma 1, that q is not a side-place around b, i.e., that $b_- = 0$. The initial marking m of q and the remaining arc weights a_+, a_-, b_+ satisfy the following system of inequations (which is the same as (9), except that it is simplified by $b_- = 0$):

$$
\begin{aligned}
a_+ &\leq m + x_1(b_+) + (a_+ - a_-) \\
a_+ &\leq m + (x_1 + x_2)(b_+) + 2(a_+ - a_-) \\
&\ldots \\
a_+ &\leq m + (x_1 + \ldots + x_{n-1})(b_+) + (n-1)(a_+ - a_-) \\
0 &\leq -m - (x_1 + \ldots + x_k - 1)(b_+) - (k-1)(a_+ - a_-) + a_- - 1
\end{aligned}
\tag{10}
$$

If $a_+ = 0$, then q is already of the required form. For $a_+ > 0$, we have two cases.

Case 1: $m > 0$ and $a_+ > 0$. Then consider the transformation

$$m' = m - 1 \text{ and } a'_+ = a_+ - 1 \text{ and } a'_- = a_- - 1$$

By $m > 0$ and $a_- \geq a_+ > 0$, we get new values $m', a'_+, a'_- \geq 0$. Moreover, (10) remains invariant under this transformation. So, q' serves the same purpose as q, and it has one incoming arc from a less than q. By repeating this procedure, we either get a place which serves the same purpose as q, or we hit Case 2.

Case 2: $m = 0$ and $a_+ > 0$. In this case, we consider the transformation

$$m' = m = 0 \text{ and } a'_+ = 0 \text{ and } a'_- = a_-$$

Such a transformation also guarantees $m', a'_+, a'_- \geq 0$. Also, the last line of (10) is clearly satisfied with these new values, since the value of its right-hand stays the same (for $k = 1$) or increases (for $k > 1$). To see that the first $n - 1$ lines of (10) are also true with the new values, and that we can, therefore, replace q by q', we may argue as follows. At any marking $\tilde{m}$ reached along the execution of w, we have the following:

$$\tilde{m}(q) \geq \tilde{m}(q') \geq 0 \tag{11}$$

These inequalities imply that the new place q' prevents a at r_k, whenever the old one, q, does, and that, moreover, no occurrences of a are excluded by the place q' where they should not be prohibited.

The first of the inequalities (11) holds because it holds initially (when $\tilde{m} = m$, then $\tilde{m}(q) = m = m' = \tilde{m}(q')$), and because the effect of a before the transformation is $(a_+ - a_-)$, and after the transformation, it is $(-a_-)$. In other words, a reduces the token count on q' more than it does so on q, while b has the same effect on q' as on q. To see the second inequality in (11), let $x = \min\{x_2, \ldots, x_{n-1}\}$. Then

$$a_- \leq x_1 \cdot b_+ \leq x \cdot b_+$$

The first inequality follows because $m = 0$ and q has enough tokens after the first x_1 occurrences of b in order to enable a. The second inequality follows from $x_1 \leq x$. But then, since a only removes a_- tokens from q' and the subsequent block of b's puts at least $x \cdot b_+$ tokens back on q', the marking on q' is always ≥ 0, up to and including the last block of b's. □

7.2 Solving Words aw from Words of the Form $w = b^{x_1} a \ldots ab^{x_n}$

Solving a word of the form $w = b^{x_1} a \ldots ab^{x_n}$ side-place-freely allows us to draw some conclusion about prepending a letter a to it. In fact, we have:

Proposition 7. SIDE-PLACE-FREE SOLVABILITY OF $b^{x_1} ab^{x_2} a \ldots ab^{x_n}$
$w = b^{x_1} ab^{x_2} a \ldots ab^{x_n}$ *is solvable side-place-freely iff* aw *is solvable.*

Proof: Lemmata 4 and 5 for ($\Rightarrow$), and Lemma 6 for ($\Leftarrow$). □

Lemma 4. PREVENTING a IN aw
Suppose $w = b^{x_1} ab^{x_2} a \ldots ab^{x_n}$ *is solvable side-place-freely. Then in* aw, *all occurrences of* a *can be separated side-place-freely.*

Proof: Because a can be prevented side-place-freely in w at any state r_k, the system (9) has a solution with $a_+ = 0$ and $b_- = 0$ for any fixed $1 \leq k \leq n - 1$. This refers to a pure input place q of a, which may or may not be an output place of b. In order to prevent a in aw side-place-freely, we need to consider the states r_k as before (but shifted to the right by one index position, still just before the last b of the k'th group of b's) and a correspondingly modified system as follows:

$$
\begin{array}{ll}
0 & \leq m' + (x_1 + \ldots + x_i) \cdot (b'_+) + (i + 1) \cdot (-a'_-) \quad \text{for all } 0 \leq i \leq n - 1 \\
0 & \leq -m' - (x_1 + \ldots + x_k - 1) \cdot (b'_+) - k \cdot (-a'_-) + a'_- - 1
\end{array}
\tag{12}
$$

where m', b'_+ and a'_- refer to a new pure place q' preventing a at state r_k in aw. The line with $i = 0$ was added because a must be enabled initially. Consider the transformation

$$m' = m + a_- \text{ and } b'_+ = b_+ \text{ and } a'_- = a_-$$

These values satisfy (12), provided m, b_+ and a_- (together with $a_+ = 0$ and $b_- = 0$) satisfy (9). The line with $i = 0$ follows from $m' = m + a_- \geq 0$. The other lines corresponding to $i \geq 1$ reduce to the corresponding lines in (9), since the additional $(-a_-)$ at the end of each line is offset by the additional $(+a_-)$ at the beginning of the line. The last line (which belongs to state r_k at which a is separated) corresponds to the last line of (9), because the decrease by a_- at the beginning of the line is offset by an increase by a_- in the term $k \cdot (-a'_-)$ (compared with $(k - 1) \cdot (-a_-)$ as in (9)). □

Note 1: In order to disable a at r_k, q could be replaced by a place q' obtained by duplicating q and changing the initial marking m to $m' = m + a_-$. Intuitively, this means that m' is computed from m by "unfiring" a once.

Note 2: Place q should not be removed as soon as q' is added, because q could also be preventing a at some other r_k. In that case, a new place q'' must be computed from q for this different value of k. We may forget about q only after all the relevant indices k have been processed.

Lemma 4 does not, by itself, imply that aw is solvable. We still need to consider the separations of b. Thus, consider an input place p of b in a side-place-free solution of w and suppose that p prevents b at state s_k. Suppose that we want to solve aw. If p is not also an output place of a, then it can simply be retained unchanged, and with the same marking, prevent b at corresponding states in aw and in w. However, if p is also an output place of a, "unfiring" a in the initial marking may lead to negative tokens on p. This is illustrated by the word $babbabb$ which has a side-place-free solution, as shown on the left-hand side of Fig. 7.

The places q_1, q_2 can be treated as in the above proof, that is, by changing their markings by "unfiring" a, yielding new places q'_1, q'_2 with marking $\{(q'_1, 3), (q'_2, 3)\}$. If we allowed negative markings, then a new place p' with initial marking $(p', -1)$ (and otherwise duplicating p) would do the job of solving $ababbabb$ (as in the middle of the figure). However, we shall need a more delicate argument in order to avoid negative markings.

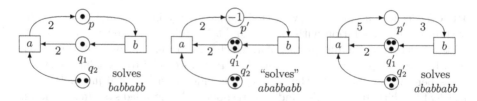

Fig. 7. Solving *babbabb* (l.h.s.), (almost) *ababbabb* (middle), and *ababbabb* (r.h.s.).

Let p' be a general new place which is supposed to prevent b at state s_k in aw. In order to check the general solvability of aw if w is side-place-freely solvable, we consider a general transformation

$$m' = m + \mu \ , \ b'_+ = b_+ + \beta_+ \ , \ b'_- = b_- + \beta_- \ , \ a'_+ = a_+ + \alpha_+ \ , \ a'_- = a_- + \alpha_-$$

where $\mu \geq -m$, $\beta_+ \geq -b_+$, $\beta_- \geq -b_-$, $\alpha_+ \geq -a_+$ and $\alpha_- \geq -a_-$, as well as a new inequation system:

$$\boxed{\begin{array}{ll} b'_+ & \leq \ m' + (x_1 + \ldots + x_i) \cdot (b'_+ - b'_-) + i \cdot (a'_+ - a'_-) \quad \text{for } 1 \leq i \leq n \\ 0 & \leq \ -m' - (x_1 + \ldots + x_k) \cdot (b'_+ - b'_-) - k \cdot (a'_+ - a'_-) + b'_- - 1 \end{array}}$$

This system has to be compared with a restricted form of (8) (setting $b_+ = a_- = 0$, since the solution of w is pure). Doing this by line-wise comparison, we get the following inequation system for the new value differences:

$$\boxed{\begin{array}{ll} \mu & \geq -m, \ \beta_+ \geq -b_+, \ \beta_- \geq -b_-, \ \alpha_+ \geq -a_+, \ \alpha_- \geq -a_- \\ \beta_+ & \leq \mu + (x_1 + \ldots + x_i) \cdot (\beta_+ - \beta_-) + i \cdot (\alpha_+ - \alpha_-) + a_+ \\ 0 & \leq -\mu - (x_1 + \ldots + x_k) \cdot (\beta_+ - \beta_-) - k \cdot (\alpha_+ - \alpha_-) - a_+ + \beta_- \end{array}} \quad (13)$$

The lines with i must be solved simultaneously for every $1 \leq i \leq n$ while the line with k must be solved individually for every $1 \leq k \leq n - 1$, in order to get a place preventing b at state s_k. This leads to the following lemma.

Lemma 5. SOLVING aw FROM w
Suppose $w = b^{x_1} a b^{x_2} a \ldots a b^{x_n}$ is solvable side-place-freely. Then aw is solvable.

Proof: Suppose that a pure place p with parameters b_- (arc into b), a_+ (arc from a) and m (initial marking) is given and suppose it separates b from s_k in w. This place solves (8) for that particular k. We distinguish two cases:

Case 1: $a_+ \leq m$. In this case, the place p can essentially be re-used for the same purpose in the solution (that we construct in this way) for aw, since (13) is solved by putting

$$\mu = -a_+ \ , \ \beta_+ = \beta_- = 0 \ , \ \alpha_+ = \alpha_- = 0$$

Hence, a place p' which differs from p only by its initial marking ($m' = m - a_+$ instead of m) separates b at s_k in aw.

Case 2: $a_+ > m$. In this case, (13) can be solved by

$$\mu = -m \ , \ \beta_+ = \beta_- = a_+ - m \ , \ \alpha_+ = \alpha_- = 0$$

That is, we may replace p by a place p' with zero initial marking and adding uniformly the value $a_+ - m$ to the incoming and outgoing arcs of b, creating a side-place around b.   □

For instance, in the solution of $babbabb$ shown on the left-hand side of Fig. 7, the place p from a to b satisfies $m=1$, $b_-=1$, $b_+=0$, $a_-=0$ and $a_+=2$. (13) is solved by $\mu = -1$, $\beta_- = 2$, $\beta_+ = 0$, $\alpha_- = 0$ and $\alpha_+ = 3$. Hence with $m'=m - 1$, $b'_-=b_- +2$, $b'_+=b_+$, $a'_-=a_-$ and $a'_+=a_+ +3$, the net shown on the right-hand side of Fig. 7 is a pure solution of $ababbabb$. (Place p' prevents b not only in states s_1 and s_2 but also in the initial state and in the final state.) There exist words such as $bbabbababab$, however, which can be solved but for which aw is not solvable. We have a converse of Lemma 5:

Lemma 6. Solving w side-place-freely from aw
    If $w=b^{x_1}ab^{x_2}a\ldots ab^{x_n}$ and aw can be solved, then w has a side-place-free solution.

Proof: Suppose that aw has a solution in which some place q', preventing a, is a side-place around a. Because q' prevents a, $a'_- > a'_+$ (unless it is the first a, but then we don't need q' in solving w). Because a is enabled initially, $m' \geq a'_-$. But then, the transformation $a''_- = a'_- - a'_+$, $a''_+ = 0$, $m'' = m' - a'_+$ yields another place q'' which is not a side-place around a but serves the same purpose as q'. The rest of the proof follows because the above transformations (removing side-places around b, or side-places around a which prevent b) do not introduce any new side-places around a.   □

8 Concluding Remarks

In this paper, the class of Petri net synthesisable binary words has been studied in depth. We have motivated, presented, and substantiated two conditions stating how such words could be characterised and how different algorithms could be devised for them. These algorithms can check solvability considerably more quickly than a general synthesis algorithm could. This has been confirmed both by the theoretical estimates contained in this paper and by experimental validation.

Several other facts are known about the class of two-letter PN-synthesisable words. It is easily seen that if a word is solvable side-place-freely, then so is the reverse word. Also, if a binary word is solvable, then it is solvable using places having exactly one outgoing transition. (This property is not shared by words with three or more letters, a counterexample being $abcbaa$.)

Moreover, PN-solvable words are balanced in the following sense. Referring to $w = b^{x_1}ab^{x_2}a \ldots ab^{x_n}$, call w balanced if there is some x such that $x_i \in \{x, x+1\}$ for all $2 \leq i \leq n - 1$. We can prove that if $w = b^{x_1}ab^{x_2}a \ldots ab^{x_n}$ is PN-solvable, then w is balanced, and moreover, $x_n \leq x + 1$. Presenting these, and other, properties of PN-solvability must however be left to future publications.

Once the conjectures are (hopefully) proved, it would be interesting to consider extensions and ramifications. For example, we know of no results characterising PN-solvable simple cycles, or PN-solvable acyclic labelled transition systems with few branching points, or with some other regular structure. The work described in [4] is an exception, a reason being that the cyclic structure of marked graph reachability graphs is particularly harmonious.

The present work could well be of interest in a wider context, as it might entail nontrivial necessary conditions for the solvability of an arbitrary labelled transition system. If the latter is solvable, then finding a PN-unsolvable structure in it may have a strong impact on its structure or shape. Also, words are persistent in the sense of [12] and tractable by the method described in [3]. However, they form (in some sense) a worst case and still lead to many region inequalities. It could therefore be interesting to check more closely whether the work described here can be of any benefit in enhancing the method described in [3].

Acknowledgments. We would like to thank Raymond Devillers, Thomas Hujsa, Uli Schlachter and Harro Wimmel for valuable comments. We also thank the anonymous reviewers for their remarks which allowed to improve the presentation of the paper.

Note added in proof. This paper extends [2] by Sect. 5 and a few other enhancements. At the time of revision (May 2016), the conjectures stated in Sects. 3.3 and 4.2 have been proved correct. These proofs are contained in [5,9].

References

1. Badouel, É., Darondeau, P.: Petri Net Synthesis, 339 p. Springer, Heidelberg (2015). ISBN 978-3-662-47966-7
2. Barylska, K., Best, E., Erofeev, E., Mikulski, Ł., Piątkowski, M.: On binary words being Petri net solvable. In: Carmona, J., Bergenthum, R., van der Aalst, W. (eds.) Proceedings of the ATAED 2015, pp. 1–15 (2015). http://ceur-ws.org/Vol-1371
3. Best, E., Devillers, R.: Synthesis of bounded choice-free Petri nets. In: Aceto, L., Frutos Escrig, D. (eds.) Proceedings of the 26th International Conference on Concurrency Theory (CONCUR 2015), LIPICS 2015 (2015). doi:10.4230/LIPIcs. CONCUR.2015.128, Schloss Dagstuhl - Leibniz-Zentrum für Informatik, Dagstuhl, 128–141
4. Best, E., Devillers, R.: Characterisation of the state spaces of marked graph Petri nets. In: Dediu, A.H., et al. (eds) Selected Extended Papers of LATA 2014, To appear in Information and Computation, 20 p. (2015)
5. Best, E., Erofeev, E., Schlachter, U., Wimmel, H.: Characterising Petri net solvable binary words. In: Kordon, F., Moldt, D. (eds.) PETRI NETS 2016. LNCS, vol. 9698, pp. 39–58. Springer, Heidelberg (2016). doi:10.1007/978-3-319-39086-4_4

6. Best, E., Schlachter, U.: Analysis of Petri nets and transition systems. In: Knight, S., Lanese, I., Lafuente, A.L., Vieira, H.T. (eds.) Proceedings of the 8th Interaction and Concurrency Experience, Electronic Proceedings in Theoretical Computer Science, vol. 189, pp. 53–67, June 2015. http://eptcs.web.cse.unsw.edu.au/paper.cgi?ICE2015.6

7. Commoner, F., Holt, A.W., Even, S., Pnueli, A.: Marked directed graphs. J. Comput. Syst. Sci. **5**(5), 511–523 (1971)

8. Cormen, T.H., Leiserson, C.E., Rivest, R.L., Stein, C.: Introduction to Algorithms, 3rd edn. The MIT Press, Cambridge (2009)

9. Erofeev, E., Barylska, K., Mikulski, L., Piątkowski, M.: Generating all minimal Petri net unsolvable binary words (2016). http://folco.mat.umk.pl/papers/generating-binary-muws.pdf

10. Karmarkar, N.: https://en.wikipedia.org/wiki/Karmarkar's_algorithm

11. Murata, T.: Petri Nets: properties, analysis and applications. Proc. IEEE **77**(4), 541–580 (1989)

12. Landweber, L.H., Robertson, E.L.: Properties of conflict-free and persistent Petri nets. JACM **25**(3), 352–364 (1978)

13. Piątkowski, M., et al.: http://folco.mat.umk.pl/unsolvable-words (2015)

14. Reisig, W.: Understanding Petri Nets: Modeling Techniques, Analysis Methods, Case Studies, 211 p. Springer, Hiedelberg (2013). ISBN 978-3-642-33278-4

15. Schlachter, U., et al.: https://github.com/CvO-Theory/apt (2013)

Self-tracking Reloaded: Applying Process Mining to Personalized Health Care from Labeled Sensor Data

Timo Sztyler[1]([⊠]), Josep Carmona[2], Johanna Völker[1],
and Heiner Stuckenschmidt[1]

[1] University of Mannheim, Mannheim, Germany
{timo,johanna,heiner}@informatik.uni-mannheim.de
[2] Universitat Politècnica de Catalunya, Barcelona, Spain
jcarmona@cs.upc.edu

Abstract. Currently, there is a trend to promote personalized health care in order to prevent diseases or to have a healthier life. Using current devices such as smart-phones and smart-watches, an individual can easily record detailed data from her daily life. Yet, this data has been mainly used for *self-tracking* in order to enable personalized health care. In this paper, we provide ideas on how process mining can be used as a fine-grained evolution of traditional self-tracking. We have applied the ideas of the paper on recorded data from a set of individuals, and present conclusions and challenges.

1 Introduction

Physical inactivity is a major risk factor for certain types of diseases. Indeed, physical activity does not only prevent or relieve diseases, but also improves public health and well being [6]. In this context, personalized health solutions and lifestyle monitoring can help to ensure that individuals are doing the right activity at the right time. However, the regular use of such methods is critical to achieve the desired result. Barriers for the adoption must be low, and using both software and devices should be as comfortable as possible.

Wearable devices such as smart-phones, smart-watches, and wristbands which do not affect people during their daily routine allow to setup a body sensor network. The provided sensor technology allows to monitor people all day long. In contrast, most of the available software requires substantial user input to specify, e.g., the current activity or even vital parameters like the heart rate or blood pressure.

The goal of our work is the development of an environment that monitors and analyzes the personal lifestyle of users and the provision of insightful visualizations. In this paper, we focus on deriving and analyzing personal process models through process mining [33] techniques as a central part of the system. The general goal will only be achievable if the recognition of a person's daily activities (such as different types of sports and desk work) can be automated.

M. Koutny et al. (Eds.): ToPNoC XI, LNCS 9930, pp. 160–180, 2016.
DOI: 10.1007/978-3-662-53401-4_8

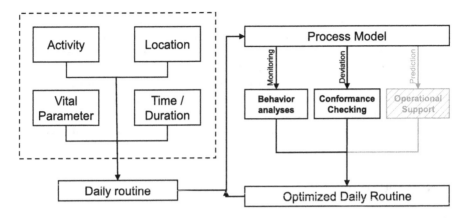

Fig. 1. Framework to optimize the daily routine and to achieve a healthier live. The framework illustrates the interaction of the individual and considered components of the activity recognition (left) and the process mining (right) domains. The latter comprises *Behavior Analyses*, *Conformance Checking* and *Operational Support*. In this paper, we focus on the first two aspects and consider *Operational Support* as future work.

In the following, we assume that this step is already addressed, i.e., with state of the art activity recognition techniques [18,31].

Figure 1 illustrates the main components of our framework in detail. The left part covers the activity recognition system that recognizes the performed physical activity based on data of on-body sensors. For that purpose, it collects context-related information, i.e., the current geographical location, local time, and vital parameter of the patient. Hence, this data represents a sequence of activities which can be considered as event log. The event log denotes the daily routine of an individual and can be transformed into a personal process model. Consequently, the process model enables to examine the daily routine regarding specific patterns, discrepancies, or to predict the next activity using common process mining techniques. This allows to reveal anomalous behavior and non-conformance regarding doctor's prescription. As a result, the daily routine can be optimized by recommendations and feedback or a caregiver can be informed. In this paper, we focus on the latter part of this problem: The mining of suitable process models from activity and location labels that have been extracted from an event log.

In the following, we consider different process formalisms when illustrating the techniques of this paper. The reason for this decision is twofold: On the one hand, we aim to present the process mining field in general terms. Thus, we want to use the best notation which is available to address our problem. On the other hand, the current situation of the process mining field enforces this decision, by not having a unified process notation that is superior in every dimension. For instance, it is well-known that *fuzzy models* are a good visualization aid. However, due to the lack of formal semantics, they cannot be used for the analysis of an underlying process, for which Petri nets are better suited.

The paper is structured as follows: In Sect. 2, the related work concerning health care, activity recognition, and process mining is summarized. Section 3 introduces background knowledge regarding process mining that is considered in the following sections. Section 4 describes the possibilities of discovering personal processes and extracting meaningful patterns and rules. Based on this, Sect. 5 outlines how to analyze and compare these processes to detect deviations and optimize the behavior of the related person. Section 6 describes the experiments of the introduced ideas concerning several different data sets. Finally, Sect. 7 covers the future work of this paper.

2   Related Work

In this paper, we aim to explore spatio-temporal data with process mining techniques to extract knowledge that facilitates personalized health care. Patients are often required to follow a well-defined exercise routine or have to be monitored as part of their treatment. Therefore, detecting wrong behavior or abnormal activities may help to prevent undesirable consequences [16,37]. Accurate information on people's behavior and their daily routine allows to support them [6].

The event log which results from common activity recognition techniques, describes the daily routine and can be transformed to a process model [35]. Research on Human Activity Recognition has shown that it is possible to determine common activities such as *preparing food* or *going to work* by relying on wearable and external sensors [18]. The wearable sensors are attached to the patient and are used to determine the physical activity by sensing the body movement [4]. In addition, external sensors are attached, e.g., to doors and items to recognize with which objects the patient interacts. Commonly, this is the case in a smart-home environment [30]. The result is a sequence of activities including the duration, location [22], and vital parameter [19].

We focus on wearable devices, i.e., smart-phones and smart-watches, because they provide variety of sensors and are carried all day long by many people [5]. Besides, the accelerometer which is very suitable enables continuous sensing over a complete day due to low power consumption.

Commonly, probabilistic approaches such as *Markov Logic Networks* or *Hidden Markov Models* are used to determine the performed activity or to predict an unobserved state, e.g., the next activity [17]. In this context, researchers also focus on pattern detection, i.e., analyzing a specific sequence of activities [17,27] to verify given references. In contrast, process mining enables to infer and extract routines that occur during the daily routine of a patient from a hidden structure. The techniques allow to perform a more analytical discussion regarding the performed healthcare process [23]. This means that the mentioned approaches do not exclude but can complement each other.

Several researchers of the processes mining area already addressed similar problems and developed techniques that are suitable for sequences of events and spatio-temporal data. For instance, Aztiria et al. showed that learning a habit is very similar to mine a process [3] and Agrawal et al. introduced algorithms that enable to mine sequential patterns that allow identifying common behavior [2,24]. However, these approaches focus only on the performed activities where we want also to consider the location and time of day. The combination of these dimensions may lead to valuable knowledge.

Concerning the dimensions, trajectory pattern mining enables to consider chronologically ordered geographical locations and the duration of movements between them. This facilitates to examine movement behavior but also the relation between time, location, and activity. Thus, the techniques discover highly frequented places as well as underlying patterns which might be related to other persons due to semantic relations [21]. However, current methods do not address rare cases and noise which is important concerning our scenario. So, behavior that occurs rarely may be a strong evidence for a specific diseases.

Considering the discrepancies between the daily routine of a patient and the desired behavior. Rozinat et al. [28] developed a fitness measure to expose the distinctions between a predefined model and the real behavior. Due to the limitations of this measure, Leoni et al. enhanced this approach by considering further dimensions. In detail, they describe costs and quantities for additional event data that allows to quantify conformance and analyze differences between model and reality [12].

However, a general problem is the handling of unstructured or flexible processes, as it is the case for the daily routine of an individual. In this context, Leotta identified that the human habits are flexible in their nature and addressed this problem by considering declarative models [20]. As a result, they developed a technique that enables to perform mining on declarative models of human habits. The work of this paper can be seen as an extension of Leotta's work where other formalisms like fuzzy maps are considered and the posterior analysis of the derived process is taken into account.

Finally, related to incorporating the modeling of context information like location in the process, Zhu et al. [39] presented a promising direction. In this work Petri nets are enriched with location constraints, and the semantic is extended to cope with this new dimension. For tool support, location-aware Petri nets are mapped to colored Petri nets so that the analysis can be done in CPN Tools [15]. Hence, it can be integrated with a Geographical Information System (GPS) at runtime. Unfortunately, so far there is no discovery technique for a location-aware Petri nets. A general framework to incorporate also other types of context in process models is presented by Serral et al. [29].

3   Preliminaries: Process Mining Techniques

In this section we provide the necessary background to understand the techniques which we consider in the following sections. We will focus on two main process mining disciplines: *process discovery* and *conformance checking*, which represent the core of process mining [33].

A log L is a finite set of traces over an alphabet A representing the footprints of the real process executions of a system S that is only (partially) visible through these runs. Process discovery techniques aim at extracting from a log L a process model M (e.g., a Petri net) with the goal to elicit the process underlying in S. By relating the behaviors of L, M and S, particular concepts can be defined [9]. A log is *incomplete* if $S\backslash L \neq \emptyset$. A model M *fits* log L if $L \subseteq B(M)$, where $B(M)$ denotes the behavior underlying M. A model is *precise* in describing a log L if $B(M)\backslash L$ is small. A model M represents a *generalization* of log L with respect to system S if some behavior in $S\backslash L$ exists in $B(M)$. Finally, a model M is *simple* when it has the minimal complexity in representing $B(M)$, i.e., the well-known *Occam's razor principle*.

Process discovery is challenging because the derived model has to be fitting, precise, general, and simple. Conformance checking techniques are meant to verify these criteria to assess the quality of a model in representing the information contained in a log. We focus on the *cost-based fitness analysis* [1] which allows to score deviations between log and model. An *optimal alignment* between a log trace and a model is a pair of traces denoting what is the best way for the log trace to be reproduced by the model. An alignment can be seen as a two-row matrix where the top row corresponds to "moves in the log" and the bottom row corresponds to "moves in the model". If a move in the model cannot be mimicked by a move in the log, or vice versa (denoted by the symbol $\gg$ in the corresponding matrix cell), then a fitness problem between the model and the log is revealed. In contrast, when log and model can execute the same activity, it denotes a fitting step. Considering an alignment, if only fitting steps appear then the trace can be reproduced by the model, otherwise a fitting problem is encountered. An example of alignment can be found below:

$$
\begin{array}{|c|c|c|c|c|}
\hline
a & \gg & b & d & e \\
\hline
a & c & b & \gg & e \\
\hline
\end{array}
$$

The first, third, and fifth column are fitting steps while the others denote fitting problems, also called *misalignments*. If unitary costs are assigned to misalignments, while fitting steps have cost zero, the previous example will have cost 2. In general, arbitrary costs can be assigned to the different types of misalignments. Considering the example, the misalignments $(\gg, c)$ and $(d, \gg)$ might have been the costs 1 and 2, respectively, whereas the rest of fitting steps have costs of zero. This will play a crucial role in the context of this paper. Techniques for computing alignments of imperative or declarative models with respect to logs exist in the literature [1,11].

4   The Discovery of Personal Processes

In this section we provide intuitive descriptions of what type of representations can be obtained through process discovery (Sect. 4.1) and how these representations can be enhanced to incorporate the information in the context of personal process behavior (Sect. 4.2).

4.1 Imperative and Declarative Representations of Personal Processes

Since a picture is worth a thousand words, the deployment of graphical representations of event data may lead to a precise awareness of the activities carried out by an individual. We believe that graphs are a strong visualization aid to understand aggregated behavior. Thus, we consider this direction as the first use case for understanding personal activity data. This deviates from the typical information that is provided by current tools for self-tracking individuals. In general, such tools focus only on showing numeric correlations between the tracked variables (e.g., eating vs. sport) or the evolution of single variables (weight over the week).

Interesting information a user can get periodically (every day or week) is the personal process model that describes the main activities and their dependencies. As introduced in a previous section, there exist two options for modeling process behavior: Imperative and declarative models.

Imperative process models tend to be well-suited for simple personal behavior, i.e., behavior that only denotes a reduced number of variants. This is especially true for elderly people where the number of performed activities is reduced and also the behavior is limited. However, even if the underlying process is less structured, this model still enables to discover frequent paths of activities. In this context, *fuzzy models* [14] or *heuristic nets* [36] may be good alternatives. Figure 2(a) illustrates an example of a fuzzy model showing the main behavior of a group of individuals during the working days. In this process model, nodes (representing the occurrence of activities) and arcs (denoting the activity ordering) are drawn in a way that frequent behavior is highlighted: the darker the background of a node (the thicker the arc), the more frequent was the related activity (arc) performed. Thus, it can be observed that particular patterns (subtraces) like MealPreparation → EatingDrinking → HouseWork → DeskWork are dominant in this model. In previous work, we have already used these models to infer interesting conclusions on the behavior of individuals, thus, the distinctions between working days and weekend behavior, across different type of users [32].

In contrast, declarative process models are adequate regarding flexible or unstructured behavior. Intuitively, declarative process models are denoted by a set of temporal constraints that relate pairs of activities [26]. Those constraints can be partitioned into existence, relation, negation, choice and branching templates, establishing the boundaries between observed and unobserved behavior. For the case of personal processes, declarative constraints seem to be very adequate representations, as it has been already acknowledged in recent work [20]. Figure 2(b) illustrates a declarative process model that results from the same log as Fig. 2(a). Considering both models, it is remarkable that the declarative model simplifies the information in a way which emphasizes meaningful rules. Thus, the declarative model covers three types of information. First, any pair of activities in the group {EatingDrinking, Movement, Transportation} is in choice relation, i.e., meaning that at least one of them should be present in any

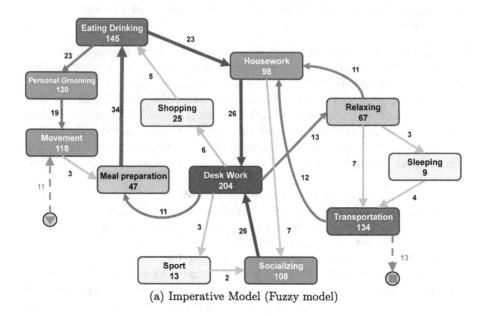

(a) Imperative Model (Fuzzy model)

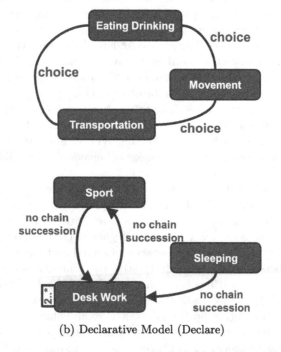

(b) Declarative Model (Declare)

Fig. 2. Main personal activities of a set of users during the week.

trace of the log. Second, the activity `DeskWork` has an existence constraint of 2 or more. Hence, in case of a workday this activity is repeated at least twice. Finally, the relation constraint *not chain succession* establishes nonexistence of immediate succession between activities, e.g., no trace exists where `DeskWork` directly follows `Sport`.

4.2   Model Enhancement Using Context-Related Information

The model of a personal process can also incorporate a geographical description of the process, i.e., the locations where the activities were performed, the frequency, and the relations between them. We focus on the chronological order and the relation between the location and the duration of the activity. Thus, it must be considered that the same activity can be performed in different locations and varying duration. This means that it is not possible to adjust easily the trajectory patterns [38]. Instead, it would be necessary to enhance the expressiveness of the trajectory patterns, so that it becomes possible to describe relations between the spatio-temporal data and activities. As a result, the enhanced models could help to optimize the daily routine concerning a healthier life by addressing, e.g., the type of movement between locations or providing beneficial locations for certain activities.

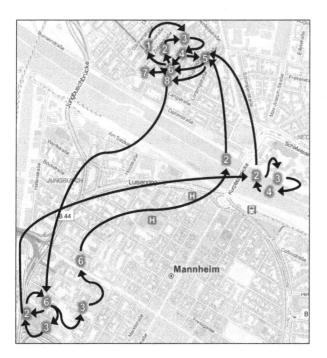

1) Shopping

2) Socializing

3) Meal Preparation

4) Eating/Drinking

5) Personal Grooming

6) Desk Work

7) Relaxing

8) Transportation

Fig. 3. Main personal activities for an individual including geographical position data: Numbers correspond to different activities, and arcs denote control-flow relations extracted from the activity data.

Algorithm 1. Personal activity-position map

Input: A_H : **location-enhanced event log**
$\qquad$ T_G : **maximum geographical distance for the same activity**
$\qquad$ T_F : **minimum number of elements in a cluster**
Output: a personal activity-position map

 1: $A_H \leftarrow \{\langle(act_{1,1}, lat_{1,1}, long_{1,1}, t_{1,1}), ..., (act_{1,n}, lat_{1,n}, long_{1,n}, t_{1,n})\rangle ...$
 2: $\qquad\qquad\qquad \langle(act_{m,1}, lat_{m,1}, long_{m,1}, t_{m,1}), ..., (act_{m,k}, lat_{m,k}, long_{m,k}, t_{m,k})\rangle\}$
$\qquad$ *{enhanced event log description as a set of enhanced traces}*
 3: $C \leftarrow [\,]$ *{empty list of clusters}*
 4: **for each** *trace* **in** A_H **do** *{initialize a cluster for each event in each trace}*
 5: $\quad$ **for each** $(act_i, lat_i, long_i, t_i)$ **in** *trace* **do**
 6: $\qquad$ $c_{new} \leftarrow$ newCluster$(a_i, lat_i, long_i)$
 7: $\qquad$ add c_{new} to C
 8: $\quad$ **end for**
 9: **end for**
10: $D \leftarrow (\,)$ *{geographical distance matrix of all clusters}*
11: **for each** $c_i, c_j \in C$: $(\forall x \in D : D(c_i, c_j) \leq x) \wedge D(c_i, c_j) < T_G$ **do** *{merge clusters that are close to each other and represent the same activity}*
12: $\quad$ $D(c_i, c_j) \leftarrow \infty$ *{forces to inspect each pair only once}*
13: $\quad$ **if** $label(c_i) = label(c_j)$ **then**
14: $\qquad$ $C \leftarrow C \setminus \{c_i, c_j\} \cup \{c_i \cup c_j\}$
15: $\qquad$ recompute *centroid* of the new cluster $\{c_i \cup c_j\}$
16: $\qquad$ $D \leftarrow$ update geographical distances matrix
17: $\quad$ **end if**
18: **end for**
19: **for each** $c_i \in C$ **do** *{remove clusters that cover an insufficient number of elements}*
20: $\quad$ **if** $|c_i| \leq T_F$ **then**
21: $\qquad$ $C \leftarrow C \setminus \{c_i\}$
22: $\quad$ **end if**
23: **end for**
24: $L \leftarrow ProjectAndRelabel(A_H, C)$ *{an event log is obtained from A_H with the activities from C}*
25: $(nodes, edges) \leftarrow FuzzyMap(L)$ *{a fuzzy miner is invoked on L}*

We combine the presented process model and a geographical map to arrange the performed activities with the related context information. As an example, we explain how to combine the imperative control-flow process models (see Fig. 2(a)) with the geographical position data to derive a *personal activity-position map*. This map illustrates geographically the control-flow with respect to the real geographical position of the activities. Compared with a trajectory-based graph, this map can be considered as a set of connected sub-graphs where each sub-graph represents the activities for a specific location.

$\qquad$ The computation of *personal activity-position maps* can be done by aligning the timing information (*start, end*) of an event with the corresponding time of the related geographical position. As a result, the locations that correspond to a specific activity can be extracted and analyzed. For instance, in Fig. 3, activity 2

Algorithm 2. ProjectAndRelabel Method

Input: A_H : **location-enhanced event log**
        C : **set of clusters**
Output: an event log
  1: $L \leftarrow \{\}$ {*empty event log*}
  2: **for each** *trace* **in** A_H **do** {*traverse the traces of the enhanced log*}
  3:    $\sigma \leftarrow$ empty trace
  4:    **for each** $(act_i, lat_i, long_i, t_i)$ **in** *trace* **do**
  5:      $c \leftarrow$ a cluster $x \in C$ originated from act_i and $(long_i, t_i) \in x$
  6:      **if** $|c| > 0$ **then**
  7:        $\sigma \leftarrow \sigma \cdot (label(c), t_i)$
  8:      **end if**
  9:    **end for**
 10:    **if** $\sigma \neq \epsilon$ **then**
 11:      $L \leftarrow L \cup \{\sigma\}$
 12:    **end if**
 13: **end for**
 14: **return** L

(Socializing) was performed in four different locations (nodes). Ideally, to have a simpler graph, the number of locations per activity should be small. Therefore, the locations for an activity can be computed by clustering a set of geographic coordinates and considering a fixed radius of k meters. The centroids as well as the frequency of the performed activities can be used to optimize the clusters. Finally, the nodes which correspond to activities in certain locations are displayed on top of a real map. Arcs from the control-flow are then routed from the corresponding locations in the map. Algorithm 1 describes this procedure in detail.

This algorithm needs as input the introduced enhanced event log A_H as well as the threshold values T_F and T_G. The thresholds specify the maximum geographical distance between the same activity for the same location (T_G), and the minimal cluster size that has to be considered (T_F). Then, the algorithm computes a set of clusters which contain events that share the same label and that are close enough in terms of their geographical position (lines 1–23). Subsequently, the *ProjectAndRelabel* method is applied (see Algorithm 2) where an event log is extracted. In general, this method simply traverses the traces in A_H, computing a normal trace (built of events with activity name and timestamp) that results from: (i) projecting only events that are covered by a cluster, and (ii) relabeling the events to guarantee that different clusters originated from the same activity will be represented by different activities in the derived event log. Then, in line 25 of Algorithm 1, a fuzzy miner is invoked, which returns the corresponding fuzzy model. Alternatively, since the input is a traditional event log, any other miner could also be used. Finally, the model is rendered by taking also the geographical position of labels into consideration.

5   The Analysis of Personal Processes

Self-tracking is a meaningful way to verify if certain requirements with respect to reference quantities are accomplished. Concerning a healthier life, many associations advise to do at least 30 min of moderate physical activity per day or eat fish at least twice a week. Those guidelines for a good lifestyle offer a rough description for individuals, mainly concerning about quantities and frequencies. However, some ways of satisfying these guidelines are probably less healthy than others, e.g., it may not be the best decision to eat fish while doing physical activity. Hence, a reference model that describes precisely how certain activities should be carried out in order to satisfy a guideline is required. If reference models are not available, simple rules can be used which should be satisfied by individuals on their daily routine. These rules may describe patterns that should satisfy an individual, e.g., `takingMedicines` should be followed by `EatingDrinking`. This can be formally specified with Linear Temporal Logic (LTL) formulas to be satisfied by the event log of activities [34]. Checking (temporal) rules on the event log may suffice in many situations. However, in this section we go one step further and try to use reference models for the analysis of personal processes, with the aim of providing a fine-grained analysis.

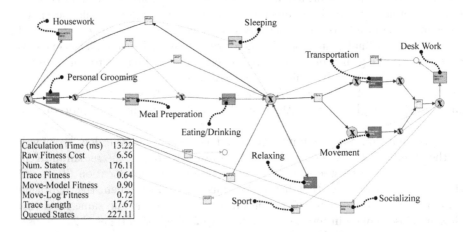

Fig. 4. Example of fitness analysis in ProM (http://www.promtools.org) of an individual with respect to a reference model (Petri net): places with yellow background (X) represent situations where the individual deviates from the process model. Transitions without a label denote silent events not appearing in the event log. (Color figure online)

The reference model has to provide the opportunity to describe certain actions in a specific *order* (e.g., `Sport` should be followed by `PersonalGrooming`), should allow explicit *choices* (e.g., after `DeskWork` only `EatingDrinking`, `Socializing`, or `Transportation` are expected actions) and should also consider *concurrency* actions. (e.g., `Transportation` and `Movement` may be overlapping activities). In general, reference models can be obtained in several ways.

One possibility would be to consult a domain expert for the creation of a desired reference model. A second option would be to collect event logs from successful individuals. These logs can be combined with the introduced techniques of the previous section to discover a reference model. Finally, a third option would be to translate the textual guidelines into process models, using recent techniques that apply *Natural Language Processing* to elicit process models [13].

The resulting reference model enables to apply *conformance checking* techniques to assess the adequacy of the reference process model in representing the traces of individuals [33]. Since the reference model describes the ideal behavior, it is meaningful to focus on analysis of the fitness of the reference model with respect to the traces of individuals. As already mentioned, a process model fits a given trace if it can reproduce it. An example of such analysis can be seen in Fig. 4 where an individual is analyzed with respect to an invented process model meant to represent a healthy behavior.

For the case of cost-based fitness analysis (see Sect. 3) of personal processes, an important part is the determination of costs for certain deviations. The selection influences the score that represents the deviation of model traces with respect to the observed behavior. In order to avoid to interfere the search for model traces that must be as much similar as possible to the observed ones, unitary cost will be assigned when computing an alignment. However, once the alignment is computed, the misalignment costs will be reassigned to detect important misalignments, if they exist. Thus, the majority of deviations from reference models may be not penalized. Instead, only certain deviations should be penalized by assigning a-posteriori high costs to particular misalignments. For instance, given the following partial alignment between a log trace (first row) and a reference model (second row):

≫	≫	EatingDrinking	≫	EatingDrinking	≫
Sport	MealPreparation	EatingDrinking	Movement	≫	Relaxing

Deviations like (≫, Sport) have high costs since the individual reached a situation where it was expected to do sport. Further, deviations that represent missing activities from the user perspective like (≫, MealPreparation) or (≫, Movement) are assigned with lower costs whereas deviations like (≫, Relaxing) have costs near to zero. Symmetrically, the cost of misalignments denoting activities observed in reality but not expected in the model must also be considered, e.g., (EatingDrinking, ≫). Groups of misalignments can be considered to improve or correct the costs of the whole alignment. For instance, looking at the misalignment of the example (≫, MealPreparation), which may have a low penalization since it does not represent a serious issue (denoting situations where the individual did not prepared a meal but the model requires this action), can be penalized only if it goes next to a synchronous step for the activity EatingDrinking.

There are techniques for deriving cost-based fitness analysis of imperative or declarative models [1,11]. These techniques can also be extended to consider other perspectives, i.e., costs or quantities for additional event data [12]. A typical advice on dietary guidelines is *to eat as many calories as one burn* [8]. These kinds of checks can be incorporated into the reference model by using the data conformance approach from van der Aalst et al. [12]. Therefore, deviations on quantities can also be verified with respect to the reference model.

6 Experiments

In this section, we present our own data set[1] as well as the experiments that address the introduced usage scenarios. Table 1 summarizes the considered data sets for the experiments and outlines the characteristics of them. In general, they describe the activities of daily living of individuals, e.g., at home and were manually created. Concerning the activity analysis, we focus on the distinction between working and weekend days. Further, we do not compare the results across the different data sets but expose that they support our introduced use cases.

Table 1. Overview of the considered data sets.

Reference	Scenario	Sensors	Name	Events	Description
Sztyler[a] [32]	daily routine	GPS, ACC, ORI	DailyR	1,386	data set that describes the daily routine of seven individuals
Cook [10]	smart apart-ment	Movement	hh102	736	daily routine of different people in an apartment for one month
			hh104	2,842	
			hh110	837	
Ordónez [25]	life at home	MAG, PRE, PIR, ELE	uniS	691	simple daily routine of two persons for several days at home
			uniD	870	detailed daily routine of two persons for several days at home

[a]http://sensor.informatik.uni-mannheim.de

6.1 Data Sets

Originally, the authors of these data sets created them for different purposes. Therefore, the data sets cover different aspects and provide also a different granularity concerning the considered labels. In the following, we describe these purposes and also present our own data set in more detail. Besides, these different purposes are also the reason that we created our own data set. Hence, the available data sets do not satisfy our entire introduced requirements.

---

[1] http://sensor.informatik.uni-mannheim.de.

Sztyler. Our data set (see footnote 1) covers seven subjects (age 23.1 ± 1.81) that recorded their daily routine for several days. In detail, the group covers five students, a worker, and a researcher which collected GPS data and recorded manually their current location, posture, and activity for the whole day. The subjects were not supervised but got an introduction and guidelines, e.g., we explained the meaning of the predefined labels to avoid that they choose different labels for the same situation. The data was collected using a regular smartphone and smart-watch combined with a self-developed sensor data collector and labeling framework (see Fig. 5). Besides, we also recorded the on-body device position and the acceleration and orientations sensor but do not consider this data during the experiments.

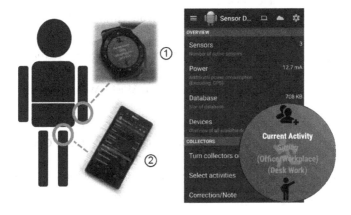

Fig. 5. Collector and labeling framework: Wear App (smart-watch, 1) and Hand App (smart-phone, 2). Our app is online available. (https://play.google.com/store/apps/details?id=de.unima.ar.collector&hl=en)

The framework consists of two parts, namely *Wear* and *Hand*. The *Wear* application allows to update the parameters (location, posture, and activity) immediately where the *Hand* application manages the settings and the storing of the data. The labels for the mentioned parameters were predefined and could not be changed or extended (see Table 2).

Concerning the activity labels, we focused on food intake, sport, different type of movements, but also (house) work so that we can compare the daily routine of several individuals to detect common activity patterns but also to analyze the different behaviors. The set of activity labels was minimized and structured to decrease the time which the individual needs to choose a suitable label. There are 12 activities and 33 sub-activities where an activity could be `EatingDrinking` and a corresponding sub-activity `Breakfast`[2]. It was possible to select several activity labels at the same time to record the current situation with a high accuracy (e.g., `Movement/gotoWork`, `Transportation/Train`, and

---

[2] So far, we do not consider the sub-activities in the presented use cases.

Table 2. Labeling parameters that have to be updated immediately when they had changed. The subjects had to select at least one of these activity labels to specify their current action. The selection of a sub-activity was optional.

Parameter	Labels
Device position	Chest, Hand, Head, Hip, Forearm, Shin, Thigh, Upper Arm, Waist
Environment	Building, Home, Office, Street, Transportation
Posture	Climbing, Jumping, Lay, Running, Sitting, Standing, Walking
Activity	Desk Work,
	Eating/Drinking – (Breakfast, Brunch, Coffee Break, Dinner, Lunch, Snack),
	Housework – (Cleaning, Tidying Up),
	Meal Preparation,
	Movement – (Go for a Walk, Go Home, Go to Work),
	Personal Grooming,
	Relaxing – (Playing, Listen to Music, Watching TV),
	Shopping,
	Socializing – (Bar/Disco, Cinema, at Home),
	Sport – (Basketball, Bicycling, Dancing, Gym, Gymnastics, Ice Hockey, Jogging, Soccer),
	Transportation – (Bicycle, Bus, Char, Motorcycle, Scooter, Skateboard, Train, Tram)

Sleeping). Thus, the individual could describe the current situation from several points of view. To keep the set of activity labels as small as possible, we provided some generic labels such as DeskWork. This label should be used if the individual works in an office (worker), attends a lecture or class room (student), or visits a school (pupil).

Summarizing, we recorded 74 cases which cover 1,386 events. A case is represented by one individual in one particular day and has an average duration of 12.1 h. Tables 3 and 4 illustrate the recorded data. The high standard deviation of the numbers of postures results from the different movement behavior.

Cook and Ordónez. Their data sets were recorded for different purpose. Cook et al. [10] created the data sets to evaluate a lightweight smart homes design to avoid customization and training. Originally, they considered primarily only movement sensors that record the movement pattern of one or several persons in an apartment. Afterwards, they labeled the record sensor data with the corresponding activity. In contrast, Ordónez et al. [25] investigated the possibility to derive activities of daily living from binary sensor streams in a home setting considering machine learning techniques.

Table 3. Annotated labels per day and individual.

Labels	Records (avg ± sd)
Activities	20 ± 7
Postures	80 ± 62
Environment	16 ± 4
Dev. position	8 ± 6

Table 4. Number of recorded values per day and individual.

Raw data	Records (avg.)
Acceleration	$2.7 * 10^6$
Orientation	$2.3 * 10^6$
Geo. location	70

Compared to our data set, Cook and Ordóñez only represent the home environment of the daily routine. However, they considered a broader set of activity labels which results in a more precise description of the behavior.

6.2 Results

In the following, we outline the results of our experiments based on the introduced data sets. The created personal process models from these data sets are available[3]. Based on the derived models, we just inspect them without additional tools. We distinguish between *Workdays* and the *Weekends* and focus on common activity patterns across several days and persons. In this context, we examined the differences between personal processes that consider more general activities (e.g., `grooming`) and such that breakdown the activities (e.g., `washing`, `showering`). As a result, we detected that the personal processes of several people that only describe the behavior at home are more similar than those that illustrates the whole day.

Table 5 illustrates the characteristics of the derived personal process models. The *Density* value represents the degree of connectedness, i.e., number of existing edges in proportion to number of possible edges. A lower value indicates that the personal process has fewer direct transitions between activities, i.e., it is simpler. Considering the models of the data sets *uniD*, *hh102*, *hh104*, and *hh110* it points out that they have the lowest density values but cover the largest set of activities (nodes). This shows that *zooming* into the daily routine of an individual does not lead to a complex structure but uncover common patterns and sequences of specific activities (e.g., `MealPrep.` → `EatingDrinking` → `Cleaning`). Besides, the density of the second model makes clear that the clustering of similar activities leads to a higher density (e.g., `grooming` vs. `toilet`, `wash`, and `shower`).

Further, we identified common patterns that occur in personal processes of different persons (see Patterns 1–4)[4]. For instance, for most people it is very

---

[3] http://sensor.informatik.uni-mannheim.de/#results.
[4] Sequence mining techniques may in principle extract similar patterns. One difference is the inability for these techniques to present process view of the extracted patterns.

Table 5. Characteristics of the derived imperative personal process models.

Data set	Weekday				Weekend			
	Nodes	Edges	Density	Duration	Nodes	Edges	Density	Duration
DailyR[1]	12	19	0.144	18.62	12	20	0.152	22.70
uniS[2]	10	15	0.167	25.23	10	15	0.167	24.33
uniD[3]	14	22	0.121	25.23	13	17	0.109	24.33
hh102[4]	16	24	0.100	28.73	16	27	0.110	19.70
hh104[5]	17	25	0.092	14.06	17	26	0.096	12.88
hh110[6]	15	20	0.095	30.44	14	17	0.093	18.68

Table 6. Characteristics of the derived declarative personal process models.

Data set	Weekday			Weekend		
	Nodes	Edges	Density	Nodes	Edges	Density
DailyR[1]	6/0	7/0	0.233/-	10/0	11/0	0.122/-
uniS[2]	12/4	81/3	0.614/0.250	12/5	100/4	0.758/0.200
uniD[3]	16/5	144/6	0.600/0.300	15/5	158/9	0.752/0.450
hh102[4]	18/4	160/6	0.523/0.500	18/5	197/12	0.644/0.600
hh104[5]	19/3	128/4	0.374/0.667	19/5	157/12	0.459/0.600
hh110[6]	17/4	158/5	0.581/0.417	14/10	156/18	0.857/0.200

common to go to the bathroom after the turn out. However, there are also patterns that depend on work or weekend days as it is the case for Pattern 3. The activity Outdoors has different meanings, i.e., during the week it represents working whereas in context of the weekend it is associated with free time activities. In this context, we detected that Relax is the usual activity which is performed after Outdoor for workdays. Considering the weekend, the behavior differs, i.e., also MealPreperation is a common activity.

$$(\text{Medication} \rightarrow) \text{ MealPrep.} \rightarrow \text{EatingDrinking} \rightarrow \text{Cleaning} \qquad (1)$$

$$\text{Sleep} \rightarrow \text{Toilet/Bath} \qquad (2)$$

$$\text{Outdoors} \rightarrow \text{Relax} \qquad (3)$$

$$\text{PersonalHygiene/Washing} \rightarrow (\text{Medication} \rightarrow) \text{ Sleep} \qquad (4)$$

We also noticed that the spend time on specific activities differs across different people but also different days and daytimes. The data sets which distinguish between breakfast, lunch, and dinner, showed that typically the used time for preparing the breakfast is significant lower than for lunch. Moreover, for activities such as sleeping, grooming (showering, toileting), and relaxing (spare time/TV), we observed that the spend time increased during the weekend.

Concerning declarative models, similar conclusions can be reached as it is illustrated in Table 6 where two experiments are reported: The models obtained with and without simplification. For simplification, we have filtered the process models obtained by using simple heuristics (e.g., removing negative constraints, or fake start/end nodes). For the DailyR benchmark, the obtained models are already simplified but only filtered constraints are derived, which implies to empty the model after manual simplification.

The results show that the personal process models lead to a better understanding of the personal activity data. Further, the resulting graphs, patterns, and features allow to verify certain requirements, e.g., regarding health care or a good lifestyle. As a result, the detected procedures and duration of certain activities can be used to determine the fitness of the derived model.

7 Future Work

So far, we only considered manually created event logs describing personal behavior. However, the automatic creation of them from personal data may enable full automation of the presented techniques. This entails a lot of unsolved problems such as the correct recognition of the activities as well as how granular they need to be. Hence, it may be easy to recognize that a person interacts with something in a living room, but it is more difficult to distinguish between *watching TV* and *reading a book*. In this context, the granularity of the recognized personal behavior may differ depending on the available indoor or outdoor activity recognition technology. Further, semi-supervised or unsupervised approaches may not allow to consider a predefined set of labels which may result in problems regarding the interpretation and evaluation.

When process mining is applied on personal data, different challenges and directions can be considered that will be explored in the future. First, the aggregation of collected data on different levels of abstraction (e.g., activities like Reading, WatchingTV, or Gaming into Entertainment) may enable the simplification of the derived process models. Another challenge is to deal with uncertain data. In particular, the data generated by classification-based methods for activity recognition will most probably be uncertain, since these methods are never a hundred percent accurate. However, provenance information such as explicit uncertain values will be available in most cases, and might serve as an additional input to process mining methods. Hence, process mining methods may need to be adapted in such new context.

With respect to future directions, we focus on two main aspects. On the one hand, the derived process models may be used for something more than just visualization or analysis, i.e., to support the activity of individuals on their daily routine. Notice that historical data of an individual is a rich source of information which may be crucial to influence the daily routine in order to reach a particular goal. In this context, process models can be enhanced and used at each decision point to assess the influence of the next step in satisfying the targeted goal. For instance, following the guideline of the previous section that

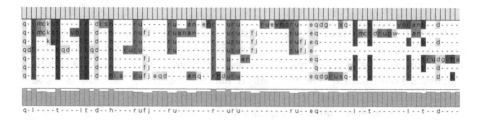

Fig. 6. Example of discovered trace cluster: letters in the bottom denote activities with high consensus. The Y-axis represents seven different traces where the X-axis illustrates the different events per traces.

advice to eat as many calories as one burn, activities can be annotated with respect to calorie levels (e.g., `EatingDrinking` produces an amount of calories while `Movement` takes an amount of calories). Then, historical activity data can be aggregated with this information to learn for all decision points the impact of the decision regarding the likelihood of satisfying the targeted goal, e.g., the balanced consumption of calories.

Thus, when an individual is about to start a new activity, recommendations can be provided based on the model's aggregated data corresponding to the current state. This deviates from current prediction and recommendation practices that do not consider the current state of the model explicitly.

Finally, another research line will be to preprocess the log with the goal of extracting patterns, and then transform the log accordingly, either by introducing hierarchy, or by ignoring outlier activities not following the learned patterns. For this purpose, *Trace alignment* techniques from van der Aalst et al. [7] can be applied. As an example, in Fig. 6 seven traces have been aligned resulting from one of our logs.

8   Conclusions

This paper discusses challenges and opportunities for process mining in the area of personalized health care. It represents the first step towards providing a fine-grained analysis and monitoring of personal processes, which may have very important applications in some domains (e.g., elderly care).

Acknowledgments. This work as been partially supported by funds from the Ministry for Economy and Competitiveness (MINECO) of Spain and the European Union (FEDER funds) under grant COMMAS (ref. TIN2013-46181-C2-1-R).

References

1. Adriansyah, A., Sidorova, N., van Dongen, B.F:. Cost-based fitness in conformance checking. In: Application of Concurrency to System Design Conference (ACSD 2011), Kanazawa, Japan, June 2011

2. Agrawal, R., Srikant, R.: Mining sequential patterns. In: Proceedings of the Eleventh International Conference on Data Engineering, pp. 3–14. IEEE (1995)
3. Aztiria, A., Izaguirre, A., Basagoiti, R., Augusto, J.C., Cook, D.J.: Automatic modeling of frequent user behaviours in intelligent environments. In: Sixth International Conference on Intelligent Environments (IE), pp. 7–12. IEEE (2010)
4. Bao, L., Intille, S.S.: Activity recognition from user-annotated acceleration data. In: Ferscha, A., Mattern, F. (eds.) PERVASIVE 2004. LNCS, vol. 3001, pp. 1–17. Springer, Heidelberg (2004)
5. Barkhuus, L., Polichar, V.E.: Empowerment through seamfulness: smartphones in everyday life. Pers. Ubiquit. Comput. **15**(6), 629–639 (2011)
6. Blair, S.N., Church, T.S.: The fitness, obesity, and health equation: is physical activity the common denominator? JAMA **292**(10), 1232–1234 (2004)
7. Bose, R.J.C., van der Aalst, W.M.P.: Process diagnostics using trace alignment: opportunities, issues, and challenges. Inf. Syst. **37**(2), 117–141 (2012)
8. Brown, N.: American heart association. http://www.heart.org. Accessed 29 Apr 2015
9. Joos, C.A.M.B., van Dongen, B.F., van der Aalst, W.M.P.: Quality dimensions in process discovery: the importance of fitness, precision, generalization and simplicity. Int. J. Coop. Inf. Syst. **23**(1), 1440001 (2014)
10. Cook, D.J., Crandall, A.S., Thomas, B.L., Krishnan, N.C.: CASAS: a smart home in a box. Computer **46**(7), 62–69 (2013)
11. de Leoni, M., Maggi, F.M., van der Aalst, W.M.P.: An alignment-based framework to check the conformance of declarative process models and to preprocess event-log data. Inf. Syst. **47**, 258–277 (2015)
12. de Leoni, M., van der Aalst, W.M.P.: Aligning event logs and process models for multi-perspective conformance checking: an approach based on integer linear programming. In: Daniel, F., Wang, J., Weber, B. (eds.) BPM 2013. LNCS, vol. 8094, pp. 113–129. Springer, Heidelberg (2013)
13. Friedrich, F., Mendling, J., Puhlmann, F.: Process model generation from natural language text. In: Mouratidis, H., Rolland, C. (eds.) CAiSE 2011. LNCS, vol. 6741, pp. 482–496. Springer, Heidelberg (2011)
14. Günther, C.W., van der Aalst, W.M.P.: Fuzzy mining – adaptive process simplification based on multi-perspective metrics. In: Alonso, G., Dadam, P., Rosemann, M. (eds.) BPM 2007. LNCS, vol. 4714, pp. 328–343. Springer, Heidelberg (2007)
15. Jensen, K., Kristensen, L.M., Wells, L.: Coloured Petrinets, CPN tools for modelling, validation of concurrent systems. STTT **9**(3–4), 213–254 (2007)
16. Jia, Y.: Diatetic and exercise therapy against diabetes mellitus. In: Second International Conference on Intelligent Networks and Intelligent Systems, ICINIS 2009, pp. 693–696. IEEE (2009)
17. Kim, E., Helal, S., Cook, D.: Human activity recognition and pattern discovery. IEEE Pervasive Comput. **9**(1), 48–53 (2010)
18. Lara, O.D., Labrador, M.A.: A survey on human activity recognition using wearable sensors. IEEE Commun. Surv. Tutorials **15**(3), 1192–1209 (2013)
19. Lara, Ó.D., Pérez, A.J., Labrador, M.A., Posada, J.D.: Centinela: a human activity recognition system based on acceleration and vital sign data. Pervasive Mob. Comput. **8**(5), 717–729 (2012)
20. Leotta, F.: Instrumenting and mining smart spaces. Ph.D. thesis, Universita di Roma - La Sapienza, March 2014
21. Li, Z.: Spatiotemporal pattern mining: algorithms and applications. In: Aggarwal, C.C., Han, J. (eds.) Frequent Pattern Mining, pp. 283–306. Springer, Cham (2014)

22. Liao, L.: Location-based activity recognition. Ph.D. thesis, University of Washington (2006)
23. Mans, R.S., van der Aalst, W.M., Vanwersch, R.J.: Process Mining in Healthcare: Evaluating and Exploiting Operational Healthcare Processes. Springer, Heidelberg (2015)
24. Giannotti, F., Nanni, M.: Efficient mining of temporally annotated sequences. In: Proceedings of the Sixth SIAM International Conference on Data Mining, vol. 124, pp. 348. SIAM (2006)
25. Ordónez, F.J., de Toledo, P., Sanchis, A.: Activity recognition using hybrid generative, discriminative models on home environments using binary sensors. Sensors 13(5), 5460–5477 (2013)
26. Pesic, M.: Systems, constraint-based workflow management : shifting control to users. Ph.D. thesis, Technische Universiteit Eindhoven (2008)
27. Riboni, D., Bettini, C., Civitarese, G., Janjua, Z.H., Helaoui, R.: Fine-grained recognition of abnormal behaviors for early detection of mild cognitive impairment. In: IEEE International Conference on Pervasive Computing and Communications (PerCom), pp. 149–154. IEEE (2015)
28. Rozinat, A., van der Aalst, W.M.P.: Conformance checking of processes based on monitoring real behavior. Inf. Syst. 33(1), 64–95 (2008)
29. Serral, E., De Smedt, J., Snoeck, M., Vanthienen, J.: Context-adaptive Petri Nets: Supporting adaptation for the execution context. Expert Syst. Appl. 42(23), 9307–9317 (2015)
30. Sun, H., De Florio, V., Gui, N., Blondia, C.: Promises, challenges of ambient assisted living systems. In: Sixth International Conference on Information Technology: New Generations, ITNG 2009, pp. 1201–1207. IEEE (2009)
31. Sztyler, T., Stuckenschmidt, H. On-body localization of wearable devices: an investigation of position-aware activity recognition. In: IEEE International Conference on Pervasive Computing and Communications (PerCom), pp. 1–9. IEEE (2016)
32. Sztyler, T., Völker, J., Carmona, J., Meier, O., Stuckenschmidt, H.: Discovery of personal processes from labeled sensor data-an application of process mining to personalized health care. In: Proceedings of the International Workshop on Algorithms & Theories for the Analysis of Event Data, ATAED, pp. 31–46 (2015)
33. van der Aalst, W.M.P.: Process Mining - Discovery, Conformance and Enhancement of Business Processes. Springer, Heidelberg (2011)
34. van der Aalst, W.M.P, de Beer, H.T., van Dongen, B.F.: Process mining, verification of properties: an approach based on temporal logic. In: CoopIS, Cyprus, pp. 130–147 (2005)
35. van der Aalst, W.M.P., Weijters, T., Maruster, L.: Workflow mining: discovering process models from event logs. IEEE Trans. Knowl. Data Eng. 16(9), 1128–1142 (2004)
36. Weijters, A.J.M.M., van der Aalst, W.M.P., de Medeiros, A.A.K.: Process mining with the heuristics miner-algorithm. Technical report WP 166, BETA Working Paper Series, Eindhoven University of Technology (2006)
37. Yin, J., Yang, Q., Pan, J.J.: Sensor-based abnormal human-activity detection. IEEE Trans. Knowl. Data Eng. 20(8), 1082–1090 (2008)
38. Zheng, Y.: Trajectory data mining: an overview. ACM Trans. Intell. Syst. Technol. (TIST) 6(3), 29 (2015)
39. Zhu, X., Zhu, G., vanden Broucke, S.K.L.M., Vanthienen, J., Baesens, B.: Towards location-aware process modeling and execution. In: Proceedings of the Workshop on Data and Artifact-Centric BPM (DAB 2014), Haifa (Israel), 7–1 September 2014

A Method for Assessing Parameter Impact on Control-Flow Discovery Algorithms

Joel Ribeiro$^{(\boxtimes)}$ and Josep Carmona

Universitat Politècnica de Catalunya, Barcelona, Spain
{jribeiro,jcarmona}@cs.upc.edu

Abstract. Given a log L, a control-flow discovery algorithm f, and a quality metric m, this paper faces the following problem: what are the parameters in f that mostly influence its application in terms of m when applied to L? This paper proposes a method to face this problem, based on *sensitivity analysis*, a theory which has been successfully applied in other areas. Clearly, a satisfactory solution to this problem will be crucial to bridge the gap between process discovery algorithms and final users. Additionally, recommendation techniques and meta-techniques like determining the *representational bias* of an algorithm may benefit from solutions to the problem considered in this paper. The method has been evaluated over a set of logs and two different miners: the inductive miner and the flexible heuristic miner, and the experimental results witness the applicability of the general framework described in this paper.

1 Introduction

Control-flow discovery is considered as one of the crucial features of Process Mining [16]. Intuitively, discovering the control-flow of a process requires to analyze its executions and extract the causality relations between activities which, taken together, illustrate the structure and ordering of the process under consideration.

There are many factors that may hamper the applicability of a control-flow discovery algorithm. On the one hand, the log characteristics may induce the use of particular algorithms, e.g., in the presence of *noise* it may be advisable to consider a noise-aware algorithm. On the other hand, the *representational bias* of an algorithm may hinder its applicability for eliciting the process underlying in a log [15].

Even in the ideal case where the most suitable control-flow discovery algorithm is used for tackling the discovery task, it may be the case that the default algorithm's parameters (designed to perform well over different scenarios) are not appropriate for the log at hand. In that case, the user is left alone in the task of configuring the best parameter values, a task which requires a knowledge of both the algorithm and the log at hand.

In this paper, a method to automatically assess the impact of parameters of control-flow discovery algorithms is presented. In our approach, we use an efficient technique from sensitivity analysis for exploring the parameter search space. In the next section, we characterize this sensitivity analysis technique and

© Springer-Verlag Berlin Heidelberg 2016
M. Koutny et al. (Eds.): ToPNoC XI, LNCS 9930, pp. 181–202, 2016.
DOI: 10.1007/978-3-662-53401-4_9

relate it with other approaches known in the literature that were used for similar purposes in other application areas.

We consider three direct applications of the method presented in this paper[1]:

(A) As an aid to users of control-flow discovery algorithms: given a log, an algorithm and a particular quality metric the user is interested in, a method like the one presented in this paper will indicate the parameters to consider. Then the user will be able to influence (by assigning meaningful values to these parameters) the discovery experiment.

(B) As an aid for recommending control-flow discovery algorithms: current recommendation systems for control-flow process discovery (e.g., [11]) do not consider the parameters of the algorithms. Using the methodology of this paper, one may determine classes of parameters whose impact refer to the same quality metric, and those can be offered as modes of the same algorithm tailored to specific metrics. Hence the recommendation task (i.e., the selection of a discovery algorithm) may then be guided towards a better use of a control-flow technique.

(C) As a new form of assessing the representational bias of an algorithm: given a log and an algorithm, it may well be the case that the impact of most of the algorithm's parameters is negligible. In that case, if the result obtained is not satisfactory, one may conclude that this is not the right algorithm for the log at hand.

The rest of the paper is organized as follows: Sect. 2 summarizes the contribution and discusses related work. Section 3 provides the necessary background and main definitions. Then Sect. 4 presents the main methodology of this paper, while Sect. 5 provides a general discussion on its complexity. Experimental results obtained through a prototype implementation are provided in Sect. 6. In Sect. 7 we provide further discussions on the positioning of the current contribution for its use in practice. Finally, Sect. 8 concludes the paper.

2   Related Work and Contribution

The selection of parameters for executing control-flow algorithms is usually a challenging issue. The uncertainty of the inputs, the lack of information about parameters, the diversity of outputs (i.e., the different process model types), and the difficulty of choosing a comprehensive quality measurement for assessing the output of a control-flow algorithm make the selection of parameters a difficult task.

The *parameter optimization* is one of the most effective approaches for parameter selection. In this approach, the parameter space is searched in order to find the best parameters setting with respect to a specific quality measure. Besides the aforementioned challenges, the main challenge of this approach is to select a robust strategy to search the parameter space. Grid (or exhaustive) search,

---

[1] This paper is an improved and extended version of [10].

random search [2], gradient descent based search [1] and evolutionary computation [8] are typical strategies, which have proven to be effective in optimization problems, but they are usually computationally costly. [3,7,19] are examples of parameter optimization applications on a control-flow algorithm. Besides the fact that only a single control-flow algorithm is considered in these approaches, all solutions rely on quality measurements that are designed to work with a specific type of process model.

A different approach, which may also be used to facilitate the parameter optimization, is known as *sensitivity analysis* [13] and consists of assessing the influence of the inputs of a mathematical model (or system) on the model's output. This information may help understanding the relationship between the inputs and the output of the model, or identifying redundant inputs in specific contexts. Sensitivity methods range from variance-based methods to screening techniques [13]. One of the advantages of screening is that it requires a relatively low number of evaluations when compared to other approaches. The *Elementary Effect* (EE) method [4,5,9] is a screening technique for sensitivity analysis that can be applied to identify non-influential parameters of computationally costly algorithms. In this paper, the EE method is applied to assess the impact of the parameters of control-flow algorithms.

3   Preliminaries

This section contains the main definitions used in this paper.

3.1   Event Log and Process Model

Process data describe the execution of the different process events of a business process over time. An *event log* organizes process data into a set of process instances, where a process instance represents a sequence of events describing the execution of activities (or tasks).

Definition 1 (Event Log). *Let T be a set of events, T^* the set of all sequences (i.e., process instances) that are composed of zero or more events of T, and $\delta \in T^*$ a process instance. An event log L is a set of process instances, i.e., $L \in \mathcal{P}(T^*)^2$.*

A *process model* is an activity-centric model that describes the business process in terms of activities and their dependency relations. Petri nets, Causal nets, BPMN, and EPCs are examples of notations for describing these models. For an overview of process notations see [16]. A process model can be seen as an abstraction of how work is done in a specific business. A process model can be discovered from process data by applying some control-flow algorithm.

---

^{2} $\mathcal{P}(X)$ denotes the powerset of some set X.

3.2 Control-Flow Algorithm

A control-flow algorithm is a process discovery technique that can be used for translating the process behavior given by an event log into a process model. These algorithms may be driven by different discovery strategies and provide different functionalities. Also, the execution of a control-flow algorithm may be constrained (controlled) by some parameters.

Definition 2 (Algorithm). *Let L be an event log, P a list of parameters, and R a process model. An (control-flow) algorithm A is defined as a function $f^A : (L, P) = R$ that represents in R the process behavior described in L and is constrained by P. The execution of f^A is designated as a* **discovery experiment.**

3.3 Quality Measure

A *measure* can be defined as a measurement that evaluates the quality of the result of an (control-flow) algorithm. A measure can be categorized as follows [16].

Simplicity measure: quantifies the results of an algorithm (i.e., a process model mined from a specific event log) in terms of readability and comprehension. The number of elements in the model is an example of a simplicity measure.

Fitness measure: quantifies how much behavior described in the log complies with the behavior represented in the process model. The fitness is 100 % if the model can describe every trace in the log.

Precision measure: quantifies how much behavior represented in the process model is described in the log. The precision is 100 % if the log contains every possible trace represented in the model.

Generalization measure: quantifies the degree of abstraction beyond observed behavior, i.e., a general model will accept not only traces in the log, but also some other traces that generalize them.

Definition 3 (Measure). *Let R be a process model and L an event log. A measure M is defined by*

- *a function $g^M(R) = x \in \mathbb{R}$ that quantifies the quality of R, or*
- *a function $g^M(R, L) = x \in \mathbb{R}$ that quantifies the quality of R according to L.*

The execution of g^M is designated as a **conformance experiment.**

3.4 Problem Definition

Given an event log L, a control-flow algorithm A constrained by the list of parameters $P = [p_1 = v_1, ..., p_k = v_k]$, and a quality measure M: *Assess the impact of each parameter* p_i $(i = 1, ..., k)$ *on the result of the execution of A over L, according to* M^3.

4   The Elementary Effect Method

The *Elementary Effect* (EE) method [4,5,9] is a technique for sensitivity analysis that can be applied to identify non-influential parameters of control-flow algorithms, which usually are computationally costly for estimating other sensitivity analysis measures (e.g., variance-based measures). Rather than quantifying the exact importance of parameters, the EE method provides insight into the contribution of parameters to the results quality.

One of the most efficient EE methods is based on Sobol quasi-random numbers [14] and a radial OAT strategy [5].[4] The main idea is to analyze the parameter space by performing experiments and assessing the impact of changing parameters with respect to the results quality. A Sobol quasi-random generator is used to determine a uniformly distributed set of points in the parameter space. Radial OAT experiments [5] are executed over the generated points to measure the impact of the parameters. This information can be used either (i) to guide on the parameters setup by prioritizing the parameters to be tuned, or (ii) as a first step towards parameter optimization. The different steps of the EE method are described in Algorithm 1.

4.1   Radial OAT Experiments

In this paper, an OAT experiment consists of a benchmark of some control-flow algorithm where the algorithm's parameters are assessed one at a time according to some quality measure. This means that $k + 1$ discovery and conformance experiments are conducted, the first one to set a reference and the next k to compare the impact of changing one of the k algorithm's parameters. The parameter settings for establishing the reference and changing the parameter's values are defined by a pair of points from the parameter space.[5] OAT experiments can use different strategies to explore these points. Figure 1 presents the most common strategies for performing OAT experiments. In the trajectory design, the parameter change compares the results for the point of the current experiment with the results for the point of the previous experiment. In the radial design, the parameter change compares the results for the point of the current experiment with the results for the initial point. From these two, the radial design has been proven to outperform the trajectory one [12].

Radial OAT experiments can be defined as follows (cf. Step 2 in Algorithm 1). First, a pair of points (α, β) is selected in the parameter space. Point α, the base point (point $(1, 1, 2)$ in Fig. 1), is used as the reference parameter setting

---

[3] Depending on the context, we will consider P either as a parameter list $[p_i, ..., p_k]$ or its concrete instantiation $[v_i, ..., v_k]$.

[4] OAT stands for One (factor) At a Time.

[5] A point in the parameter space is the result of assigning specific values to the parameters in the parameter list P: $p_1 = v_1, ..., p_k = v_k$.

Algorithm 1. The EE Method For Control-Flow Mining Algorithms

---

Input   : a control-flow algorithm A for which $P = [p_1 = v_1, ..., p_k = v_k]$ is its parameter list (cf. Definition 2), a measurement M (cf. Definition 3), and an event log L.

Output: The elementary effects of every parameter in P.

Init

   $k \Leftarrow$ number of parameters in P ;
   $r \Leftarrow 30$ (number of radial OAT experiments);

Step 1 – Generating Sobol points (cf. Sect. 4.2)

   $S \Leftarrow$ matrix of quasi-random Sobol numbers of dimensions $(r + 4, 2k)$;
   for *j=1* **to** *r* **do**
   | reference[j] $\Leftarrow (S[j, 1], S[j, 2], ..., S[j, k])$;
   | auxiliary[j] $\Leftarrow (S[j + 4, k + 1], S[j + 4, k + 2], ..., S[j + 4, 2k])$;
   end

Step 2 – Radial OAT Experiments (cf. Sect. 4.1)

   for *j=1* **to** *r* **do**
   | setting $\Leftarrow [p_1 = v_1, ..., p_k = v_k]$ (parameter setting of P);
   | **for** *i=1* **to** *k* **do** $v_i \Leftarrow$ normalize(reference[j], p_i);
   | $valueR \Leftarrow f^{\text{A·M}}(L, \text{setting})$ (cf. Eq. 1);
   | **for** *i=1* **to** *k* **do**
   | | $w \Leftarrow v_i$;
   | | $v_i \Leftarrow$ normalize(auxiliary[j], p_i);
   | | $valueA \Leftarrow f^{\text{A·M}}(L, \text{setting})$;
   | | $EE[i][j] \Leftarrow \frac{valueR - valueA}{w - v_i}$ (cf. Eq. 2);
   | | $v_i \Leftarrow w$;
   | **end**
   end

Step 3 – Computing the Elementary Effects (cf. Eq. 3)

   for *i=1* **to** *k* **do**
   | $\mu_i^\star = \frac{\sum_{j=1}^r |EE[i][j]|}{r}$;
   end
   return $\mu^\star$;

function normalize(Value $x \in [0, 1]$, Parameter p)
consists of a normalization process that maps x to a value of p;

---

of the experiment. A discovery and conformance experiment is executed with this parameters setting to set the reference quality value. Point β, the auxiliary point (point $(2, 2, 0)$ in Fig. 1), is used to compare the impact of changing the parameters, one at a time, from α to β. For each parameter p_i of P, a discovery and conformance experiment is executed using the parameter values defined by α for a parameter p_j of P $(j \neq i)$ and the parameter value defined by β for p_i (see the example in Fig. 1b). Insight into the impact of each parameter is provided by aggregating the results of the radial OAT experiments.

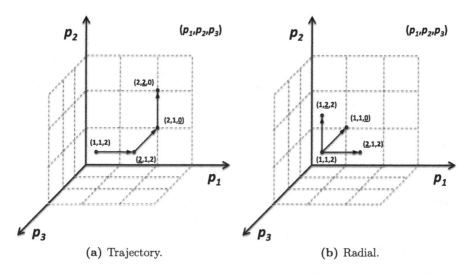

(a) Trajectory.   **(b)** Radial.

Fig. 1. Comparison between radial and trajectory samplings for OAT experiments over 3 parameters, using the points $(1,1,2)$ and $(2,2,0)$. The underlined values identify the parameter being assessed.

Let A be a control-flow algorithm, M a given measure, and L an event log. The function $f^{A \cdot M}(L, P)$ computes the quality of the result of A over L with respect to M, where $P = [p_1 = v_1, ..., p_k = v_k]$ is the list of parameters of A.

$$f^{A \cdot M}(L, P) = \begin{cases} g^M(f^A(L, P)) & \text{if } M \text{ does not depend on a log} \\ g^M(f^A(L, P), L) & \text{otherwise} \end{cases} \tag{1}$$

The elementary effect of a parameter p_i of P on a radial OAT experiment is defined by

$$EE_i = \frac{f^{A \cdot M}(L, \alpha) - f^{A \cdot M}(L, \alpha \hookleftarrow \alpha_i \cdot \beta_i)}{\alpha_i - \beta_i}, \tag{2}$$

where α, β are parameter settings of P (the base and auxiliary points), α_i and β_i are the ith elements of α and β, and $f^{A \cdot M}(L, \alpha \hookleftarrow \alpha_i \cdot \beta_i)$ is the value $f^{A \cdot M}(L, \alpha')$ where α' is α with β_i replacing α_i. The measure μ^* for p_i is defined by

$$\mu_i^* = \frac{\sum_{j=1}^{r} |EE_i^j|}{r}, \tag{3}$$

where EE_i^j is the elementary effect EE_i for j^{th} radial OAT experiment, and r the number of radial OAT experiments to be executed – typically between 10 and 50 [4]. In Algorithm 1, the measure μ^* is computed in Step 3. The total number of discovery and conformance experiments is $r(k + 1)$, where k is the number of parameters of A.

The impact of a parameter p_i of P is given as the relative value of $\mu_i^\star$ compared to that for the other parameters of P. A parameter p_j of P ($j \neq i$) is considered to have more impact on the results quality than p_i if $\mu_j^\star > \mu_i^\star$. The parameters p_j and p_i are considered to have equal impact on the results quality if $\mu_j^\star = \mu_i^\star$. The parameter p_i is considered to have no impact on the results quality if $\mu_i^\star = 0$. This measure is sufficient to provide a reliable ranking of the parameters [4,5].

4.2   Sobol Numbers

To apply the EE method as shown in the previous section, Sobol numbers are used in order to guarantee a good coverage of the parameter space. Sobol quasi-random numbers (or sequences) are low-discrepancy sequences that can be used to distribute uniformly a set of points over a multidimensional space. These sequences are defined by n points with m dimensions. Table 1 presents an example of a Sobol sequence containing ten points with ten dimensions.

Table 1. The first ten points of a ten-dimensional Sobol quasi-random sequence.

	d_1	d_2	d_3	d_4	d_5	d_6	d_7	d_8	d_9	d_{10}
x_1	0.5000	0.5000	0.5000	0.5000	0.5000	0.5000	0.5000	0.5000	0.5000	0.5000
x_2	0.7500	0.2500	0.2500	0.2500	0.7500	0.7500	0.2500	0.7500	0.7500	0.7500
x_3	0.2500	0.7500	0.7500	0.7500	0.2500	0.2500	0.7500	0.2500	0.2500	0.2500
x_4	0.3750	0.3750	0.6250	0.8750	0.3750	0.1250	0.3750	0.8750	0.8750	0.6250
x_5	0.8750	0.8750	0.1250	0.3750	0.8750	0.6250	0.8750	0.3750	0.3750	0.1250
x_6	0.6250	0.1250	0.8750	0.6250	0.6250	0.8750	0.1250	0.1250	0.1250	0.3750
x_7	0.1250	0.6250	0.3750	0.1250	0.1250	0.3750	0.6250	0.6250	0.6250	0.8750
x_8	0.1875	0.3125	0.9375	0.4375	0.5625	0.3125	0.4375	0.9375	0.9375	0.3125
x_9	0.6875	0.8125	0.4375	0.9375	0.0625	0.8125	0.9375	0.4375	0.4375	0.8125
x_{10}	0.9375	0.0625	0.6875	0.1875	0.3125	0.5625	0.1875	0.1875	0.1875	0.5625

Each element of a point of a Sobol sequence consists of a numerical value between zero and one (e.g., the element representing the second dimension (d_2) of point x_5 is 0.8750). A collection of these values (the entire point or part of it) may be used to identify a specific point in a parameter space. An element of a point of a Sobol sequence can be converted into a parameter value by some normalization process. For instance, a possible normalization process for an element $e \in [0, 1]$ to one of the n distinct values of some discrete parameter p can be defined by $\lfloor e \times n \rfloor$, which identifies the index of the parameter value in p corresponding to e. Notice that the parameter space must be uniformly mapped by the normalization process (e.g., each value of a Boolean parameter must be represented by 50 % of all possible elements).

Using the approach proposed in [5], a matrix of quasi-random Sobol numbers of dimensions $(r + 4, 2k)$ can be used to analyze the elementary effects of the k parameters of a control-flow algorithm by executing r radial OAT experiments (cf. Step 1 in Algorithm 1). The first k dimensions of the matrix's points define the base points, while the last k dimensions define the auxiliary points. Given that the first points of a Sobol sequence have the tendency to provide similar base and auxiliary points, it is identified in [5] the need of discarding the first four points of the sequence for the auxiliary points (i.e., the k rightmost columns should be shifted upward). Therefore, the base and auxiliary points can be computed from a Sobol sequence as follows. Let e_i^j be the element corresponding to the jth dimension (d_j) of the ith point (x_i) of the sequence. The ith base (α^i) and auxiliary (β^i) points are defined as follows.

$$\alpha^i = (e_i^1, e_i^2, ..., e_i^j) \ and \ \beta^i = (e_{i+4}^{j+1}, e_{i+4}^{j+2}, ..., e_{i+4}^{2j}). \tag{4}$$

4.3   Example: The FHM

The following example is used to illustrate the analysis of the parameter space of an algorithm in order to assess the impact of the algorithm's parameters on the results quality. Let us consider an event log that is characterized by two distinct traces: $ABDEG$ and $ACDFG$. The frequency of any of these traces is high enough to not be considered as noise. The behavior described by these traces does not contain any kind of loop or parallelism, but it does contain two long-distance dependencies: $B \Rightarrow E$ and $C \Rightarrow F$. Let us also consider the Flexible Heuristics Miner (FHM) [20] as the control-flow algorithm to explore the parameter space in order to assess the impact of the FHM's parameters on the results quality. The parameters of the FHM are summarized in Table 2. Notice that every parameter of the FHM is continuous, with a range between zero and one. The *relative-to-best* and the *long-distance* thresholds are optional. The former is only considered with the *all-tasks-connected* heuristic. The latter is only taken into account when the *long-distance dependencies* option is activated.

Table 2. The parameters of the Flexible Heuristics Miner [20]. The dependency and relative-to-best thresholds are used to select causal relations between process events. The loops thresholds are used to identify length-one and -two loops, while the long-distance threshold identify non-free-choice behavior.

Parameter	Domain	Optional?
Relative-to-best threshold	$[0, 1]$	Yes
Dependency threshold	$[0, 1]$	No
Length-one-loops threshold	$[0, 1]$	No
Length-two-loops threshold	$[0, 1]$	No
Long-distance threshold	$[0, 1]$	Yes

Figure 2 presents the two possible process models that can be mined with the FHM on the aforementioned event log, using all combinations of parameter values. Figure 2a shows the resulting Causal net where long-distance dependencies are not taken into account. Figure 2b shows the resulting Causal net with the long-distance dependencies. Notice that, depending on the quality measure, the quality of these process models may differ (e.g., the precision of the model with long-distance dependencies is higher than the other one). One may be interested in the exploration of the FHM's parameter space to get the process model that fulfills best some quality requirements.

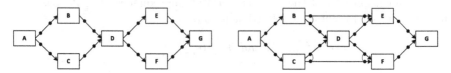

(a) The Causal net without long-distance dependency relations.

(b) The Causal net with long-distance dependency relations.

Fig. 2. The process models that can be mined with the FHM.

The analysis of the parameter space of the FHM starts with the generation of the Sobol numbers. Suppose that, for this analysis, one wants to execute $r = 30$ radial OAT experiments for assessing the elementary effects of the $k = 5$ FHM's parameters. So, a matrix of Sobol numbers of dimensions $(30 + 4; 2 \times 5)$ has to be generated (cf. Sect. 4.2). Table 1 shows the first ten points of this matrix. Table 3 presents the first five base and auxiliary points as well as the parameter values corresponding to these points. Notice that the parameters are represented in the points according to the ordering given in Table 2 (i.e., the first element of a point represents the first parameter and so on). The normalization process in this example is defined as follows. For the non-optional parameters (cf. Table 2), an element $e \in [0, 1]$ of a point of a Sobol sequence can be directly used to represent the value of the parameter. For the optional parameters, an element $e \in [0, 1]$ of a point of a Sobol sequence is normalized to a value $e' \in [0, 2]$, which maps the parameter space uniformly (i.e., the value of the parameter and whether or not the parameter is enabled). If $e' \le 1$ then e' is assigned as the value of the parameter; the parameter is disabled otherwise.

Table 4 presents the radial sampling for the first radial OAT experiment (first point in Table 3) as well as the result of the execution of $f^{A \cdot M}(L, P)$ and the elementary effect EE for each parameter. For executing $f^{A \cdot M}(L, P)$, A is the FHM, M the *Node Arc Degree* measure[6], and L the aforementioned event log.

---

[6] The *Node Arc Degree* measure consists of the average of incoming and outgoing arcs of every node of the process model.

Table 3. The first five points of the Sobol numbers.

Point	Base	Auxiliary
1	(.5000, .5000, .5000, .5000, .5000)	(.6250, .8750, .3750, .3750, .1250)
2	(.7500, .2500, .2500, .2500, .7500)	(.8750, .1250, .1250, .1250, .3750)
3	(.2500, .7500, .7500, .7500, .2500)	(.3750, .6250, .6250, .6250, .8750)
4	(.3750, .3750, .6250, .8750, .3750)	(.3125, .4375, .9375, .9375, .3125)
5	(.8750, .8750, .1250, .3750, .8750)	(.8125, .9375, .4375, .4375, .8125)
...	...	...

(a) The first five base and auxiliary points.

Point	Base	Auxiliary
1	(–, 0.50, 0.50, 0.50, –)	(–, 0.88, 0.38, 0.38, 0.25)
2	(–, 0.25, 0.25, 0.25, –)	(–, 0.13, 0.13, 0.13, 0.75)
3	(0.50, 0.75, 0.75, 0.75, 0.50)	(0.75, 0.63, 0.63, 0.63, –)
4	(0.75, 0.38, 0.63, 0.88, 0.75)	(0.63, 0.44, 0.94, 0.94, 0.63)
5	(–, 0.88, 0.13, 0.38, –)	(–, 0.94, 0.44, 0.44, –)
...	...	...

(b) The parameter values for the first five base and auxiliary points. The wildcard value '–' identifies that the parameter is disabled.

The elementary effects are computed as described in Sect. 4.1.[7] Notice that the elementary effect of a parameter can only be computed when the base and auxiliary points provide distinct parameter values (e.g., in Table 4, the first parameter is not assessed because it is disabled in both base and auxiliary points).

Table 4. Radial sampling for the first radial OAT experiment. The first line corresponds to the base point, while the others consist of the base point in which the element regarding a specific parameter is replaced by that from the auxiliary point; the underlined values identify the replaced element and the parameter being assessed.

Parameter values P	Result $f^{A \cdot M}(L, P)$	Elementary effect EE_i
(–, 0.50, 0.50, 0.50, –)	2.154	
(_, 0.50, 0.50, 0.50, –)		
(–, <u>0.88</u>, 0.50, 0.50, –)	2.154	0.0
(–, 0.50, <u>0.38</u>, 0.50, –)	2.154	0.0
(–, 0.50, 0.50, <u>0.38</u>, –)	2.154	0.0
(–, 0.50, 0.50, 0.50, <u>0.25</u>)	2.316	0.162

---

[7] For computing EE_i, $\alpha_i - \beta_i$ is considered to be 1 when the parameter is changed from a disabled to an enabled state, or the other way around (e.g., the last parameter in Table 4).

Table 5. The μ^* values of the FHM's parameters.

Parameter	μ^*
Dependency threshold	0.0
Relative-to-best threshold	0.0
Length-one-loops threshold	0.0
Length-two-loops threshold	0.0
Long-distance threshold	0.113

Table 5 presents the results of the analysis of the FHM's parameter space. The results identify the long-distance threshold as the only parameter to take into account for the parameter exploration. As expected, all other parameters have no impact on the results quality. This is explained by the fact that the log does not contain any kind of loop or noise. Notice that the μ^* absolute value does not provide any insight into how much a parameter influences the results quality. Instead, the μ^* measurement provides insight into the impact of a parameter on the results quality, compared to others.

5   Application

The EE method presented in the previous section can be applied to any control-flow algorithm constrained by many parameters, using some event log and a measure capable of quantifying the quality of the result of the algorithm. The presented method can be easily implemented on some framework capable of executing discovery and conformance experiments (e.g., ProM [18] or CoBeFra [17]). Several open-source generators of Sobol numbers are available on the web.

The computational cost of our approach can be defined as follows. Let L be an event log, A a control-flow algorithm constrained by the list of parameters $P = [p_1 = v_1, ..., p_k = v_k]$, and M a quality measure. The computational cost of a discovery experiment using A (with some parameter setting) over L is given by C_D. Considering R as the result of a discovery experiment, the computational cost of a conformance experiment over R and L (or just R) with regard to M is given by C_C. Therefore, the computational cost of a radial OAT experiment is given by $C_E = (k+1)(C_D + C_C)$, where k is the number of parameters of A. The computational cost of the EE method based on r radial OAT experiments is given by $C = r(k+1)(C_D + C_C)$. Assuming that, for the example given in Sect. 4.3, C_D is 0.1 s (i.e., the FHM takes 0.1 s on average to process the given log) and C_C is 0.025 s (i.e., it takes 0.025 s on average to compute the *Node Arc Degree* measure), the computational cost of the experiments is $C = 30(5+1)(0.1+0.025) = 22.5$ s.

5.1   Performance Optimization

Considering that both discovery and conformance experiments may be computationally costly, performance may become a critical issue for the application of this method. This issue can be partially addressed by identifying a set of potentially irrelevant parameters, and considering those parameters as a group. Then, by adjusting the $\mu^\star$ measurement to work with groups of two or more parameters [4], the group of parameters can be analyzed together using radial experiments that iterate over all elements of the same group simultaneously.

Suppose, for instance, that it is known that a given log does not have loops. So, for the FHM's parameters, the *length-one-loops* and *length-two-loops* thresholds may be grouped in order to avoid the execution of discovery and conformance experiments that are not relevant for the analysis. Recalling the example presented in Sect. 4.3, the radial experiments will iterate over one group of two parameters and three independent parameters (i.e., the *dependency*, the *relative-to-best*, and the *long-distance* thresholds). This means that, for the group of parameters, all elements of the same group are replaced simultaneously by the corresponding elements from the auxiliary point. Table 6 presents the adjusted radial sampling presented in Table 4. The first line corresponds to the base point, while the others consist of the base point in which the element(s) regarding a specific parameter (or group of parameters) is replaced by that from the auxiliary point; the underlined values identify the replaced element(s) and the parameter (or group of parameters) being assessed.

Table 6. Radial sampling for the first radial experiment considering a group of parameters.

Parameter values
$(-, 0.50, 0.50, 0.50, -)$
$(\underline{-}, 0.50, 0.50, 0.50, -)$
$(-, \underline{0.88}, 0.50, 0.50, -)$
$(-, 0.50, \underline{0.38}, \underline{0.38}, -)$
$(-, 0.50, 0.50, 0.50, \underline{0.25})$

The elementary effect of a group of parameters G from P on a radial experiment is defined by

$$EE_G = \frac{f^{A \cdot M}(L, \alpha) - f^{A \cdot M}(L, \alpha \leftharpoondown \alpha_G \cdot \beta_G)}{dist(\alpha_G, \beta_G)}, \tag{5}$$

where α, β are parameter settings of P (the base and auxiliary points), α_G and β_G are the elements of G in α and β, and $f^{A \cdot M}(L, \alpha \leftharpoondown \alpha_G \cdot \beta_G)$ is the value $f^{A \cdot M}(L, \alpha')$ where α' is α with β_G replacing α_G. The function $dist(A, B)$ computes the distance between A and B (e.g., the Euclidean distance). The measure $\mu^\star$ for G is defined by

$$\mu_G^\star = \frac{\sum_{j=1}^r |EE_G^j|}{r}, \tag{6}$$

where EE_G^j is the elementary effect EE_G for j^{th} radial OAT experiment, and r the number of radial experiments to be executed. The total number of discovery and conformance experiments depends on the number of groups.

6 Experiments and Tool Support

The theory of this paper has been implemented as a prototype tool. Source code and binaries can be accessed in the following link:

http://www.cs.upc.edu/~jcarmona/ee.zip

The tool is implemented in Java and, given an input log, provides the analysis of this paper for either the FHM or the Inductive Miner (IM) [6]. The tool is built on top of the CoBeFra framework [17].

A set of experiments using the FHM and the IM algorithms was conducted in order to evaluate the method proposed in this paper. The parameters of the FHM are summarized in Table 2, while the IM ones are in Table 7. It is important to mention that, for each parameter, we had to implement a function to map a point of a Sobol sequence to a point of the parameter space (e.g., see Table 3).

Table 7. The parameters of the Inductive Miner [6].

Parameter	Domain	Optional?
Noise threshold	$[0, 1]$	No
Incomplete threshold	$[0, 1]$	Yes

For these experiments, 5 reference models characterized by different behavior (i.e., containing both sequential and parallel activities, loops, and/or non-free choices) were selected for generating 11 synthetic event logs with different characteristics, including noise. A characterization of these generated logs is provided in Table 8. Besides the synthetic logs, 8 real-life logs were considered in the experiments as well. A characterization of the real-life logs is provided in Table 9, while Fig. 3 shows their underlying process models.

Figures 4 and 5 summarize the results of the impact analysis of the parameters of the FHM. The number of elements of the mined model, which can be considered as a simplicity measurement, is used to assess and compare the outcomes of the FHM. The results suggest that the Dependency Threshold and the Relative-to-Best Threshold are the parameters with more impact on the results; on average, these parameters together represent about 75 % of the impact of the FHM parameters. The Dependency and Relative-to-best thresholds have more influence in noisy or low structured processes. This observation is confirmed by the results described by Fig. 5a, with the Dependency Threshold playing a bigger role in noisier (or lower structured) processes. The results in Fig. 5b show the impact of the loop thresholds in processes with loops (length-one or -two), even

Table 8. Characterization of the synthetic logs used in the experiments. L1L, L2L and NFC stand for length-one loops, length-two loops and non-free choice constructs in the log, respectively.

Model	Log	Noise	L1L	L2L	NFC
M_1	L_1	0 %			
M_1	L_2	5 %			
M_1	L_3	10 %			
M_1	L_4	20 %			
M_2	L_5	0 %	✓	✓	
M_2	L_6	5 %	✓	✓	
M_2	L_7	10 %	✓	✓	
M_2	L_8	20 %	✓	✓	
M_3	L_9	0 %	✓		
M_4	L_{10}	0 %		✓	
M_5	L_{11}	0 %			✓

thought their impact is not significant. The results in Fig. 5c highlight the impact of the Long-distance Threshold in processes with non-free choice constructs.

Figures 6 and 7 summarize the results of the impact analysis of the parameters of the IM. As for the FHM, the number of elements of the mined model is used to assess and compare the outcomes of the IM. The absence of bars in the chart means that both Noise and Incomplete thresholds have no influence in the results. The absence of results for L_{17}, L_{18} and L_{19} is explained by the fact that, due to its highly unstructured nature, these logs require too much memory to be processed by the IM. The results suggest the Noise Threshold is the parameter with more impact on the results; on average, this parameter represents about 80 % of the impact of the IM parameters. As its name suggests,

Table 9. Characterization of the real-life logs used in the experiments.

Log	Process instances	Process events	Activities
L_{12}	10487	76899	21
L_{13}	6905	50884	8
L_{14}	23941	191536	8
L_{15}	956	11218	22
L_{16}	956	11218	22
L_{17}	17812	83286	42
L_{18}	12391	65653	70
L_{19}	12391	65653	70

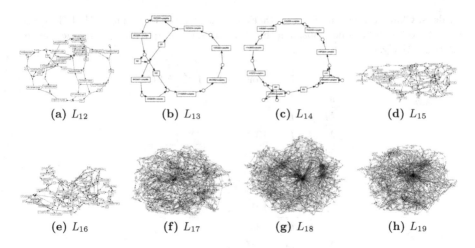

| (a) L_{12} | (b) L_{13} | (c) L_{14} | (d) L_{15} |

| (e) L_{16} | (f) L_{17} | (g) L_{18} | (h) L_{19} |

Fig. 3. The underlying process models of the real-life event logs.

the Noise Threshold have more influence in noisy or low structured processes. This observation is confirmed by the results provided in Fig. 7.

The main conclusion that can be drawn from this set of experiments is that the method proposed in this paper can be used to analyze the impact of parameters of control-flow discovery algorithms, on either synthetic or real-life event logs. With a few exceptions, the results obtained in these experiments are in line with our expectations. The execution of the method is constrained by the capability of the control-flow algorithm to handle the event log at hand, especially when using odd parameter settings. The results of the method can be used not only to identify influent parameters but also to get some insight into the characteristics of event logs. For example, if a loop-related parameter is identified as influent then one may assume that there is some kind of loop behavior in the log.

7   Discussion

The method's accuracy directly depends on how well the parameter space is explored and on how well this exploration reaches the different outcomes of the algorithm. Hence, it is crucial that all possible parameter settings[8] are represented in the parameter space, including dependencies among parameters. The premise is *if the user can choose some parameter setting then that setting must be taken it into account*, and the other way around. So, it is important to stress that there is the assumption that the control-flow algorithm will compute a valid result from any possible parameter setting, independently of the event log at hand.

In the following subsections we identify two issues that may arise in practice, even for well-defined parameter spaces. The occurrence of these issues may be

---

[8] All possible parameter settings the control-flow algorithm allows.

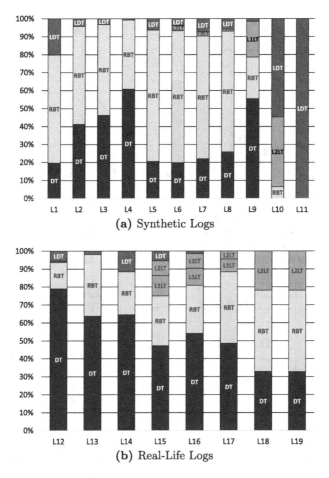

(a) Synthetic Logs

(b) Real-Life Logs

Fig. 4. The impact of the FHM parameters by event log. DT stands for Dependency Threshold, RBT for Relative-to-best Threshold, L1LT for Length-one-loops Threshold, L2LT for Length-two-loops Threshold, and LDT for Long-distance Threshold.

sporadic, and depends on either the characteristics of the event log or some implicit behavior of the control-flow algorithm. For both issues, we acknowledge that the methodology present in this paper is not suffice for detecting these cases, but the development of such functionalities goes beyond the scope of this work.

7.1 Dependencies Among Parameters

The method presented in this paper assesses the impact of each parameter of a control-flow discovery algorithm in the algorithm's execution on a given event log. In order to do so, the method executes a number of experiments and measures how parameters influenced the results, one by one. This means that every

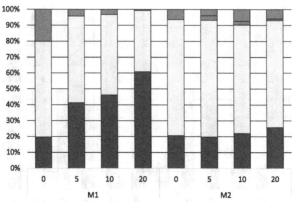

(a) Noise. The dark gray bar (bottom) represents the Dependency Threshold, the light gray bar (middle) represents the Relative-to-best Threshold, and the gray bars (top) represent the loops and the Long-distance thresholds.

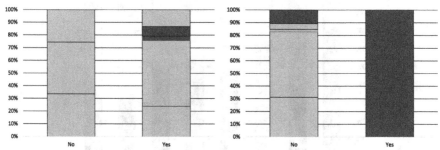

(b) Loops. The dark gray bars represent the loops thresholds, while the light gray bars represent the remaining thresholds.

(c) Non-free choice. The dark gray bar represents the Long-distance Threshold, while the light gray bars represent the remaining thresholds.

Fig. 5. The impact of the FHM parameters by noise, loops, and non-free choice.

parameter is considered as an independent parameter. Therefore, any dependency that may exist among parameters (i.e., parameters that influence the behavior of other parameters) has no influence in the parameter analysis, neither in exploration of the parameter space nor in the computation of the impact measurement. An obvious example of parameter dependency is when a boolean parameter X is used to enable a parameter Y, i.e., Y is an optional parameter. As mentioned before, X and Y should be considered as a single parameter with a domain that represents uniformly both X and Y. A more complex example is the dependency between the FHM's Dependency and Relative-to-best thresholds (DT and RBT). The RBT is not considered if the DT fulfilled some condition; low DT values tendentially disables the RBT. Unlike the optional parameters, this later case requires a deep understanding of the algorithm to be identified. The

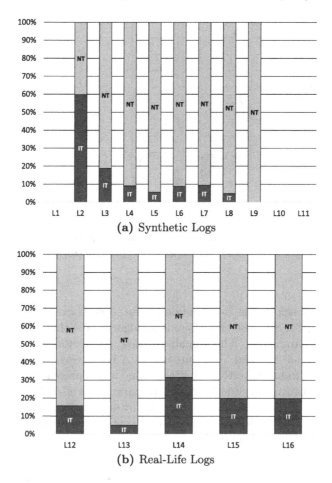

Fig. 6. The impact of the IM parameters by event log. NT stands for Noise Threshold, while IT is for Incomplete Threshold.

same can happen with other dependencies that may exist among parameters. We believe that, as long as the parameter space is well defined (i.e., the domain of all parameters is uniformly represented in the parameter space), any dependency that may exist among parameters will not affect negatively the results of our method. This should happen because the parameter space is explored uniformly, so most of the parameter values should be taken into account in the analysis, including dependency effects.

7.2   Unbalanced Parameter Domains

Due to unbalanced parameter domains or even to the nature of the event logs, it is not uncommon to find cases in which algorithms produce the same outcome in most of the parameter space, but having different outcomes in rather small

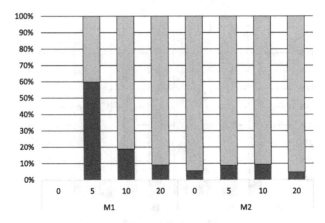

Fig. 7. The impact of the IM parameters by noise. The dark gray bar (bottom) represents the incomplete threshold, while the light gray bar (top) represents the noise threshold.

regions – usually next to the domain boundaries. A good example of this issue is provided in Fig. 8a. Suppose that there is an algorithm A that is constrained by two numerical parameters. The domain of these parameters is $[0, 1]$, and both parameters are not optional. The outcome of A is represented by regions with different colors (from white to dark gray). The dots represent the points to be assessed in order to analyze the impact of the parameters of A. As Fig. 8a depicts, the distribution of the points does not reach any gray region. So, as a result, the parameters of A will be identified as non-influential because no change can be detected by changing its values.

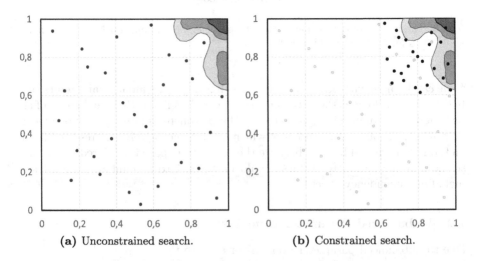

(a) Unconstrained search.   **(b)** Constrained search.

Fig. 8. Example of a two-dimensional parameter space.

A solution for this issue may be using a higher number of points for assessing the parameters at the expense of the method's performance. Another solution is constraining the parameter space, i.e., the exploration of the parameter space may be constrained to focus on specific areas. Using the same example of Fig. 8, the exploration can be constrained to parameter values from 0.6 to 1.0. Doing so, the distribution of the points would overlap with the gray regions (cf. Fig. 8b). As a result, the parameters of A would be identified as influential.

8   Conclusions and Future Work

To the best of our knowledge, this work is the first in presenting a methodology to assess the impact of parameters in control-flow discovery algorithms. The method relies on a modern sensitivity analysis technique that requires considerably less exploration than traditional ones such as techniques relying on genetic algorithms or variance-based methods.

In this work, we have applied the methodology on two of the most popular miners on a set of event logs. The results suggest the effectiveness of the method. We have noticed that simple conformance measures (and, thus, less computationally costly) are as good as any other complex measure for assessing the parameters influence. Nevertheless, we acknowledge that more experiments are necessary to get a better insight.

In the future, we plan to investigate the following four subjects by applying the method introduced in this paper to a wide range o control-flow algorithms. First, we would like to study the implication of having dependencies among parameters and unbalanced parameter domains on the quality of the method's results. Second, we are interested in the algorithmic perspective in order to study the most efficient form of assessing the impact of a parameter, with the method presented in this paper as a baseline. Third, we will try to incorporate the methodology described in this paper in the RS4PD, a recommender system for process discovery [11]. Finally, we are planning to explore the possibility of using the methodology presented in this paper to estimate the representation bias of control-flow algorithms.

Acknowledgments. This work as been partially supported by funds from the Spanish Ministry for Economy and Competitiveness (MINECO) and the European Union (FEDER funds) under grant COMMAS (ref. TIN2013-46181-C2-1-R).

References

1. Bengio, Y.: Gradient-based optimization of hyperparameters. Neural Comput. **12**(8), 1889–1900 (2000)
2. Bergstra, J., Bengio, Y.: Random search for hyper-parameter optimization. J. Mach. Learn. Res. **13**(1), 281–305 (2012)
3. Burattin, A., Sperduti, A.: Automatic determination of parameters' values for Heuristics Miner++. In: 2010 IEEE Congress on Evolutionary Computation (CEC), pp. 1–8, July 2010

4. Campolongo, F., Cariboni, J., Saltelli, A.: An effective screening design for sensitivity analysis of large models. Environ. Model. Softw. **22**(10), 1509–1518 (2007)
5. Campolongo, F., Saltelli, A., Cariboni, J.: From screening to quantitative sensitivity analysis. a unified approach. Comput. Phys. Commun. **182**(4), 978–988 (2011)
6. Leemans, S.J.J., Fahland, D., van der Aalst, W.M.P.: Discovering block-structured process models from event logs containing infrequent behaviour. In: Lohmann, N., Song, M., Wohed, P. (eds.) BPM 2013 Workshops. LNBIP, vol. 171, pp. 66–78. Springer, Heidelberg (2014)
7. Ma, L.: How to evaluate the performance of process discovery algorithms: a benchmark experiment to assess the performance of flexible heuristics miner. Master's thesis, Eindhoven University of Technology, Eindhoven (2012)
8. Michalewicz, Z., Schoenauer, M.: Evolutionary algorithms for constrained parameter optimization problems. Evol. Comput. **4**(1), 1–32 (1996)
9. Morris, M.D.: Factorial sampling plans for preliminary computational experiments. Technometrics **33**(2), 161–174 (1991)
10. Ribeiro, J., Carmona, J.: A method for assessing parameter impact on control-flow discovery algorithms. In: Proceedings of the International Workshop on Algorithms & Theories for the Analysis of Event Data, pp. 83–96 (2015)
11. Ribeiro, J., Carmona, J., Mısır, M., Sebag, M.: A recommender system for process discovery. In: Sadiq, S., Soffer, P., Völzer, H. (eds.) BPM 2014. LNCS, vol. 8659, pp. 67–83. Springer, Heidelberg (2014)
12. Saltelli, A., Annoni, P., Azzini, I., Campolongo, F., Ratto, M., Tarantola, S.: Variance based sensitivity analysis of model output. design and estimator for the total sensitivity index. Comput. Phys. Commun. **181**(2), 259–270 (2010)
13. Saltelli, A., Ratto, M., Andres, T., Campolongo, F., Cariboni, J., Gatelli, D., Saisana, M., Tarantola, S., Analysis, G.S.: Global Sensitivity Analysis: The Primer. Wiley, Hoboken (2008)
14. Sobol, I.M.: Uniformly distributed sequences with an additional uniform property. USSR Comput. Math. Math. Phys. **16**(5), 236–242 (1976)
15. van der Aalst, W.M.: On the representational bias in process mining. In: 20th Proceedings IEEE International Workshops on Enabling Technologies: Infrastructures for Collaborative Enterprises (WETICE 2011), Paris, France, 27–29 June 2011, pp. 2–7 (2011)
16. van der Aalst, W.M.P.: Process Mining: Discovery Conformance and Enhancement of Business Processes. Springer, Heidelberg (2011)
17. vanden Broucke, S., Weerdt, J.D., Baesens, B., Vanthienen, J.: A comprehensive benchmarking framework (CoBeFra) for conformance analysis between procedural process models and event logs in ProM. In: IEEE Symposium on Computational Intelligence and Data Mining, Grand Copthorne Hotel, Singapore. IEEE (2013)
18. Verbeek, H.M.W., Buijs, J., van Dongen, B.F., van der Aalst, W.M.P.: ProM 6: The process mining toolkit. In: Demo at the 8th International Conference on Business Process Management, vol. 615 of CEUR-WS, pp. 34–39 (2010)
19. Weijters, A.J.M.M.: An optimization framework for process discovery algorithms. In: Proceedings of the International Conference on Data Mining, Las Vegas, Nevada, USA (2011)
20. Weijters, A.J.M.M., Ribeiro, J.T.S.: Flexible heuristics miner (FHM). In: Proceedings of the IEEE Symposium on Computational Intelligence and Data Mining, CIDM, Paris, France. IEEE (2011)

Negotiations and Petri Nets

Jörg Desel[1(✉)] and Javier Esparza[2]

[1] Fakultät für Mathematik und Informatik,
FernUniversität in Hagen, Hagen, Germany
`joerg.desel@fernuni-hagen.de`
[2] Fakultät für Informatik, Technische Universität München, Munich, Germany
`esparza@in.tum.de`

Abstract. Negotiations have recently been introduced as a model of concurrency with multi-party negotiation atoms as primitive. This paper studies the relation between negotiations and Petri nets. In particular, we show that each negotiation can be translated into a 1-safe labelled Petri net with equivalent behaviour. In the general case, this Petri net is exponentially larger than the negotiation. For deterministic negotiations, however, the corresponding Petri has linear size compared to the negotiation, and it enjoys the free-choice property. We show that for this class the negotiation is sound if and only if the corresponding Petri net is sound. Finally, we have a look at the converse direction: given a Petri net, can we find a corresponding negotiation?

Keywords: Negotiations · Petri nets · Soundness · Free-choice nets

1 Introduction

Distributed negotiations have been identified as a paradigm for process interaction since some decades, in particular in the context of multi-agent systems [5]. This paradigm has been applied to various problems (see e.g. [2,17]), and it has also been studied in its own [13].

A distributed negotiation is based on a set of agents that communicate with each other to eventually reach a common decision. It can be viewed as a protocol with atomic negotiations as smallest elements. Multiparty negotiations can employ more than two agents, both in the entire negotiation and in its atoms. A natural way to formally model distributed multiparty negotiations is to model the behaviour of the agents separately and then to model the communication between agents by composition of these agent models. Petri nets and related process languages have been used with this aim, see e.g. [4,16,18].

In [8,9] we have introduced a novel approach to formally model negotiations. We argue that this model is sometimes more intuitive than Petri nets for negotiations, but it can also be applied to other application areas which are based

This work was partially funded by the DFG Project "Negotiations: A Model for Tractable Concurrency".

© Springer-Verlag Berlin Heidelberg 2016
M. Koutny et al. (Eds.): ToPNoC XI, LNCS 9930, pp. 203–225, 2016.
DOI: 10.1007/978-3-662-53401-4_10

on the same communication principles. Like Petri nets, our formalism has a graphical representation. *Atomic negotiations* are represented as nodes, with a specific representation of the participating agents. Roughly speaking, the semantics of an atomic negotiation is that these agents come together (and are thus not distributed and do not need any communication means during the atomic negotiation) to agree on one of some possible *outcomes*. Given an outcome, the model specifies, for each participating agent, the next possible atomic negotiations in which it can participate. Agents have *local states* which are only changed when an agent participates in an atomic negotiation.

Atomic negotiations are combined into *distributed negotiations*. The state of a distributed negotiation is determined by the atomic negotiations which the agents can participate in next and by all local states. As in Petri nets, these two aspects are carefully distinguished; the current next possible atomic negotiations are represented as *markings* of negotiations. A distributed negotiation is *deterministic* if, in each state, no agent is ready to engage in more than one atomic negotiation.

In [8, 9] we introduced negotiations and concentrated on their analysis. In particular, we studied the efficient analysis of *soundness*, a kind of well-behavedness, of negotiations by means of structural reduction rules. Our work was inspired by known reduction rules of Petri nets, but we did not show how to translate distributed negotiations to Petri nets. The present paper makes the relation to Petri nets explicit, providing a translation rule from distributed negotiations to Petri nets. In the general case, the Petri net associated with a negotiation by this translation can be exponentially larger than the negotiation; therefore analysis of negotiations via translation to Petri nets is not a feasible option (unless a more efficient translation exists). For restricted classes of negotiations, however, the corresponding Petri nets are smaller and enjoy nice properties, and in this case the converse direction is possible, too. Therefore, for these negotiations, translation to Petri nets opens additional feasible analysis options, beyond soundness.

The translation to Petri nets is implicitly used in a recent paper on the analysis of Coloured Workflow Nets [11]. The paper presents a reduction procedure for free-choice Coloured Workflow Nets, obtained by "translating" the reduction procedure of [8] for deterministic negotiations. The translation is non-trivial, because Petri nets lack the notion of "agent" at the core of the negotiation model. It is possible because of the intimate connection between the two models explained in this paper. The reduction procedure has been implemented and benchmarked on industrial examples [11].

Connection to Other Models. Negotiations are also related to other models of concurrency, like choreographies (see e.g. [3, 14, 15]) or message sequence charts and message sequence graphs (see e.g. [12]). The essential difference is the choice of the communication primitive: atomic negotiations in our model, multiparty rendez-vous for Petri nets, message-passing for choreographies. While these primitives can simulate each other, they exhibit different trade-offs between implementability (how difficult is it to realize them in hardware or software?) and analyzability. For example, the message-passing model is easy to implement, but the so-called realizability problem (does a global specification of the behaviour of a system admit an implementation in terms of sequential machines communicating through message passing?) has a high complexity. The negotiation primitive is, like rendezvous, more difficult to implement reliably[1], but our work in [10] shows that, at least for the special class of deterministic negotiations, the realizability problem can be solved in a more efficient way. Indeed, in [10] we introduce negotiation programs, a programming language for the global and structured description of negotiations. Our results show that every negotiation program admits a distributed implementation as a negotiation.

Organization. The paper is organised as follows. Section 2 repeats the syntax and semantics of negotiations. Section 3 provides the translation to Petri nets with the same behaviour. Section 4 discusses properties of these Petri nets. In Section 5 we show that Petri nets enjoying these properties can be translated back to negotiations, this way characterizing a class of Petri nets representable by negotiations. Section 6 is the conclusion.

2   Negotiations: Syntax and Semantics

We recall the main definitions of [8,9] for syntax and semantics of negotiations. Let A be a finite set of *agents*, representing potential participants of a negotiation. Each agent $a \in A$ has a (possibly infinite) nonempty set Q_a of *internal states* with a distinguished subset $Q_{0a} \subseteq Q_a$ of *initial states*. We denote by Q_A the cartesian product $\prod_{a \in A} Q_a$; a state is represented by a tuple $(q_{a_1}, \ldots, q_{a_{|A|}}) \in Q_A$. A *transformer* is a left-total relation $\tau \subseteq Q_A \times Q_A$, representing a nondeterministic state transforming function. Given $S \subseteq A$, we say that a transformer τ is an *S-transformer* if, for each $a_i \notin S$,

$$((q_{a_1}, \ldots, q_{a_i}, \ldots, q_{a_{|A|}}), (q'_{a_1}, \ldots, q'_{a_i}, \ldots, q'_{a_{|A|}})) \in \tau$$

implies $q_{a_i} = q'_{a_i}$. So an S-transformer only transforms internal states of agents in S or in a subset of S.

Internal states of agents and their transformers won't play an important role in this contribution. As will become clear later, states do not influence behaviour in negotiations, i.e., we can consider the control flow and data aspects separately. For the Petri net translation to be defined, local states and their transformers can be modelled by means of token colours and transition modes, respectively, i.e. by means of Coloured Petri nets. These Coloured Petri nets are without guards, because guards restrict transition occurrences by regarding data values.

2.1   Atomic Negotiations

Definition 1. *An* atomic negotiation, *or just an* atom, *over a set of agents A is a triple $n = (P, R, \delta)$, where $P \subseteq A$ is a nonempty set of* participants *of n, R*

---

[1] But by no means impossible. The literature also uses far stronger primitives, like reliable broadcasts [7].

is a finite, nonempty set of results, and δ is a mapping assigning to each result
$r \in R$ *a P-transformer* $\delta(r)$.

In the sequel, P_n, R_n and δ_n will denote the components of an atom n. For each result $r \in R_n$, the pair (n, r) is called an *outcome*. The difference between results and outcomes is that the same result can belong to different atoms whereas the sets of outcomes are pairwise disjoint. If we choose disjoint sets of results then we do not have to distinguish results and outcomes.

If the states of the agents before an atomic negotiation n are given by a tuple q and the result of the negotiation is r, then the agents change their states to q' for some $(q, q') \in \delta_n(r)$. Only the participants of n can change their internal states. However, it is not required that a P_n-transformer $\delta_n(r)$ actually changes the states of all agents in P_n. Each result $r \in R_n$ is possible, independent of the previous internal states of the participants of n.

As a simple example, consider an atomic negotiation n_{FD} with participants F (Father) and D (teenage Daughter). The goal of the negotiation is to determine whether D can go to a party, and, if she can go, the time at which she must return home. This time is a number between 8 and 12, thus avoiding that a smaller number, such as 1 am, represents a later point in time than, e.g., 12 pm.

The possible results are {yes, no, ask_mother}, whereas the agreed time is encoded in the internal states of the two participants: Both sets Q_F and Q_D contain a state *angry* plus a state t for every time $T_1 \leq t \leq T_2$ in a given interval $[T_1, T_2]$. The transformer $\delta_{n_{FD}}$ includes

$$\delta_{n_{FD}}(\text{yes}) = \{ ((t_f, t_d), (t, t)) \mid t_f \leq t \leq t_d \vee t_d \leq t \leq t_f \}$$
$$\delta_{n_{FD}}(\text{no}) = \{ ((t_f, t_d), (angry, angry)) \}$$
$$\delta_{n_{FD}}(\text{ask\_mother}) = \{ ((t_f, t_d), (t_f, t_d)) \}$$

where t_f and t_d are variables used to denote that F is in state $t_f \neq angry$ and D in state $t_d \neq angry$ before engaging in the negotiation atom n_{FD}. That is, if both participants are not *angry* and the result is yes, then F and D agree on a time t which is not earlier and not later than both suggested times; if it is no, then there is a quarrel and both participants get angry; if it is ask_mother, then the participants keep their previous times.

If one of the local states before the negotiation atom was *angry*, then the transformer $\delta_{n_{FD}}$ determines for each result that both agents will be *angry* after executing the atom.

2.2   Combining Atomic Negotiations

If the result of the atomic negotiation above is ask_mother, then n_{FD} is followed by a second atomic negotiation n_{DM} between D and M (Mother). The combined negotiation is the composition of n_{FD} and n_{DM}, where the possible internal states of M are the same as those of F and D, and n_{DM} is a "copy" of n_{FD}, but without the ask_mother result. In order to compose atomic negotiations, we add a *transition function* X that assigns to every triple (n, a, r) consisting of an atom n,

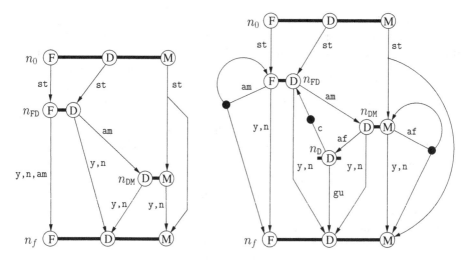

Fig. 1. An acyclic negotiation and the ping-pong negotiation.

a participant a of n, and a result r of n a set $\mathfrak{X}(n,a,r)$ of atoms. Intuitively, this is the set of atomic negotiations agent a is ready to engage in after the atom n, if the result of n is r.

Definition 2. *Given a finite set of agents A and a finite set of atoms N over A, let $T(N)$ denote the set of triples (n,a,r) such that $n \in N$, $a \in P_n$, and $r \in R_n$. A (distributed) negotiation is a tuple $\mathcal{N} = (N, n_0, n_f, \mathfrak{X})$, where $n_0, n_f \in N$ are the initial and final atoms, and*

$$\mathfrak{X}\colon T(N) \to 2^{(N \setminus \{n_0\})}$$

is the transition function.
Further, we demand that $\mathcal{N}$ satisfies the following properties:

(1) every agent of A participates in both n_0 and n_f;
(2) for every $(n,a,r) \in T(N)$: $\mathfrak{X}(n,a,r) = \emptyset$ iff $n = n_f$.

The graph associated with $\mathcal{N}$ has vertices N and edges

$$\{(n,n') \in N \times N \mid \exists\,(n,a,r) \in T(N)\colon n' \in \mathfrak{X}(n,a,r)\}.$$

The initial and final atoms mark the beginning and the end of the negotiation (and sometimes this is their only role). We may have $n_0 = n_f$. By definition of the transition function $\mathfrak{X}$, the initial atom n_0 does not belong to any $\mathfrak{X}(n,a,r)$. Notice that n_f has, as all other atoms, at least one result $\mathsf{end} \in R_{n_f}$.

2.3   Graphical Representation of Negotiations

Negotiations are graphically represented as shown in Fig. 1. For each atom $n \in N$ we draw a bar; for each participant a of P_n we draw a circle on the bar, called a *port*. For each $(n, a, r) \in T(N)$ with $n \neq n_f$, a hyperarc labelled by the result r leads from the port of a in n to all the ports of a in the atoms of $X(n, a, r)$. If $X(n, a, r)$ contains only one atom, this hyperarc is actually an arc. Instead of multiple (hyper)arcs connecting the same input port to the same output ports we draw a single (hyper)arc with multiple labels.

Figure 1 shows on the left the graphical representation of a negotiation where Father (F), Daughter (D) and Mother (M) are the involved agents. After the initial atom n_0, which has only one possible result st (start), the negotiation atoms described above take place. Notice that possibly Father and Daughter come to an agreement without involving Mother. So each agent of a distributed negotiation can be viewed as a potential participant, which necessarily participates only in the initial atom and in the final atom. In the figure, we write y for yes, n for no, and am for ask mother. Since n_f has no outgoing arc, the results of n_f do not appear in the graphical representation.

The negotiation on the right of Fig. 1 (ignore the black dots on the arcs for the moment) is the ping-pong negotiation, well-known in many families. The n_{DM} atom has now an extra result ask father (af), and Daughter can be sent back and forth between Mother and Father. After each round, D "negotiates with herself" (atom n_{D}) with possible results continue (c) and give up (gu).

2.4 Semantics

A *marking* of a negotiation $N = (N, n_0, n_f, X)$ is a mapping $x \colon A \to 2^N$. Intuitively, $x(a)$ is the set of atoms that agent a is currently ready to engage in next. The *initial* and *final* markings, denoted by x_0 and x_f, are given by $x_0(a) = \{n_0\}$ and $x_f(a) = \emptyset$ for every $a \in A$. By definition, the set of markings is finite.

A marking x *enables* an atom n if $n \in x(a)$ for every $a \in P_n$, i.e., if every agent that participates in n is currently ready to engage in n. If x enables n, then n can take place and its participants eventually agree on a result r; we say that the outcome (n, r) *occurs*. The occurrence of (n, r) produces a next marking x' given by $x'(a) = X(n, a, r)$ for every $a \in P_n$, and $x'(a) = x(a)$ for every $a \in A \setminus P_n$. We write $x \xrightarrow{(n,r)} x'$ to denote this, and call it a *small step*.

We write $x_1 \xrightarrow{\sigma}$ to denote that there is a sequence

$$x_1 \xrightarrow{(n_1, r_1)} x_2 \xrightarrow{(n_2, r_2)} \cdots \xrightarrow{(n_{k-1}, r_{k-1})} x_k \xrightarrow{(n_k, r_k)} x_{k+1} \cdots$$

of small steps such that $\sigma = (n_1, r_1) \ldots (n_k, r_k) \ldots$. If $x_1 \xrightarrow{\sigma}$, then σ is an *occurrence sequence* from the marking x_1, and x_1 enables σ. If σ is finite, then we write $x_1 \xrightarrow{\sigma} x_{k+1}$ and say that x_{k+1} is *reachable* from x_1. If x_1 is the initial marking then we call σ *initial occurrence sequence*. If moreover x_{k+1} is the final marking x_f, then σ is a *large step*.

As a consequence of this definition, for each agent a, $x(a)$ is always either $\{n_0\}$ or equals $X(n, a, r)$ for some outcome (n, r). The marking x_f can only be reached by the occurrence of (n_f, end) (end being a possible result of n_f), and it does not enable any atom.

Reachable markings can be graphically represented by placing tokens (black dots) on the forking points of the hyperarcs (or in the middle of an arc). Thus, both the initial marking and the final marking are represented by no tokens, and all other reachable markings are represented by exactly one token per agent.

Figure 1 shows on the right the marking in which Father is ready to engage in the atomic negotiations n_{FD} and n_f, Daughter is only ready to engage in n_{FD}, and Mother is ready to engage in both n_{DM} and n_f.

As mentioned before, the enabledness of an atom does not depend on the internal states of the agents involved; it suffices that all agents are ready to engage in this atom, no matter which internal states they have. Moreover, each result of the atom is possible, independent of the internal states. A given result then determines a state transformer and thus possible next states.

2.5   Reachability Graphs

An occurrence sequence of a negotiation can be arbitrarily long (see the ping-pong negotiation above). Therefore, the set of possible occurrence sequences can be infinite. Since we have markings and steps, an obvious way to describe behaviour with finite means is by reachability graphs:

Definition 3. *The* reachability graph *of a negotiation* N *has all markings reachable from* x_0 *as vertices, and an arc leading from* x *to* x' *and annotated by* (n, r) *whenever* $x \xrightarrow{(n,r)} x'$. *The initial marking* x_0 *is the distinguished* initial vertex.

Generally, enabled atoms with disjoint sets of participants can proceed concurrently, whereas atoms sharing a participating agent cannot. Formally, if two outcomes (n_1, r_1) and (n_2, r_2) are enabled by a reachable marking x and $P_{n_1} \cap P_{n_2} = \emptyset$ then the two outcomes can occur concurrently. The condition $P_{n_1} \cap P_{n_2} = \emptyset$ is also necessary for concurrent occurrences of outcomes because, in our model, a single agent cannot be engaged concurrently in two different atoms, and because two state transformers cannot operate concurrently on the local state of an agent. Thus concurrency between outcomes depends only on the involved atoms (and their participants) and not on the results.

Concurrency is formally captured by the *concurrent step reachability graph*, defined next. A *concurrent step* enabled at a reachable marking x is a nonempty set of pairwise concurrent outcomes, each of them enabled by x. It is immediate to see that all the outcomes of a concurrent step can be executed subsequently in arbitrary order and that the marking finally reached does not depend on the chosen order. We call this marking *reached by the concurrent step*.

Definition 4. *The* concurrent step reachability graph *of a negotiation* N *has all markings reachable from* x_0 *as vertices. An arc, annotated by a nonempty set of outcomes, leads from* x *to* x' *whenever any two distinct outcomes of this set are concurrent and the concurrent step leads from* x *to* x'. *Again,* x_0 *is the distinguished* initial vertex.

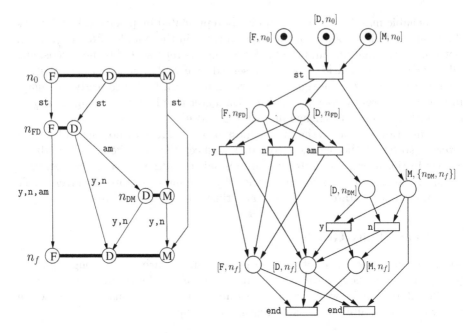

Fig. 2. Petri net semantics of the negotiation of Fig. 1.

3   From Negotiations to Petri Nets

We assume that the reader is acquainted with (low-level) initially marked Petri nets, the occurrence rule, reachable markings, liveness, and the graphical representation of Petri nets as directed graphs. For each place, there are directed arcs from all *input transitions* to the place and directed arcs from the place to all *output transitions*. *Input places* and *output places* of transitions are defined analogously. A *labelled* Petri net is a Petri net with a labelling function λ, mapping the transitions to some set of labels. Graphically, the label $\lambda(t)$ of a transition t is depicted as an annotation of t.

The semantics of negotiations uses many notions from Petri net theory. In this section, we provide a translation and begin with examples.

3.1   Examples

Figure 2 shows on the right the Petri net for the negotiation shown on the left (which was already shown in Fig. 1). Since the number of places of the Petri net equals the number of ports of the atoms of the negotiation, one might assume that the relation between ports and places is a simple one-to-one mapping. Moreover, the transitions of the Petri net have an obvious relation to the outcomes of the negotiations, if the two **end**-transitions are ignored.

Now we have a look at the two **end**-transitions of the Petri net. The left transition refers to the last result of the negotiation's occurrence sequence

$$(n_0, \mathtt{st}), (n_{\mathtt{FD}}, \mathtt{am}), (n_{\mathtt{DM}}, \mathtt{y}), (n_f, \mathtt{end}),$$

where **end** is a result of n_f. The right transition refers to the last result of the occurrence sequence

$$(n_0, \mathtt{st}), (n_{\mathtt{FD}}, \mathtt{y}), (n_f, \mathtt{end}) .$$

Hence, roughly speaking, the left transition refers to the left branch of the (only) proper hyperarc of the graphical representation of the negotiation, and the right transition refers to the right branch.

For a negotiation with more than one proper hyperarc, each occurrence sequence can involve a particular branching of a hyperarc (moreover, an atom can occur more than once, leading to different branches of the same hyperarc). For k hyperarcs with binary branching, this results in 2^k possible patterns. As can be seen in the following example, this can result in exponentially many transitions of the associated Petri net.

Figure 3 shows a class of negotiations with parameter k, involving agents $a_1, \dots, a_k$. These negotiations represent a distributed voting process. Each agent votes with possible outcome **yes** (y) or **no** (n) (one-participant-negotiations). For each **yes**-outcome there are two possible next atoms, $n_{\mathtt{accept}}$ and $n_{\mathtt{reject}}$, whereas for each **no**-outcome $n_{\mathtt{reject}}$ is the only possibility. So the atom $n_{\mathtt{accept}}$ is only enabled if all agents vote **yes**, while the atom $n_{\mathtt{reject}}$ is always enabled when all agents have voted.

A Petri net representing this behaviour necessarily has to distinguish the k possible **yes**-outcomes and **no**-outcomes, because final acceptance is only possible if all agents have accepted. So we need $2 \cdot k$ corresponding places, k for acceptance and k for rejection. When all agents came to a result, one of 2^k possible markings is reached. Only for one of these markings (all agents accepted), final acceptance is possible, and this will be represented by one transition. For the same constellation and for each of the $2^k - 1$ alternative constellations, we need a separate transition to remove the tokens and come to final rejection. So we end up with $2^k + 1$ transitions.

3.2   Formal Translation of Negotiations

We associate with a negotiation $\mathcal{N} = (N, n_0, n_f, \mathcal{X})$ over a set of agents A a labelled Petri net. The places of this net are, for each atom n except n_f, the pairs $[a, S]$ such that $a \in P_n$, $r \in R_n$, and $\mathcal{X}(n, a, r) = S$, plus, for each $a \in A$, the pair $[a, \{n_0\}]$. Observe that the number of places is linear in the size of $\mathcal{N}$ (which might exceed $|N|$ significantly, because, for each n in N, for each a in P_n and for each result $r \in R_n$ we have a set of possible successor negotiations in $\mathcal{X}$). In the sequel (and in the figures) we write $[a, n]$ instead of $[a, \{n\}]$. The *initial marking* assigns one token to each place $[a, n_0]$ and no token to all other places.

The net has a set of transitions $T(n, r)$ for each outcome (n, r). An input place of a transition in $T(n, r)$ reflects that a participant of negotiation n is

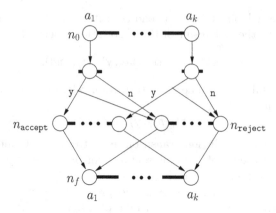

Fig. 3. A (not yet completely correct) negotiation for unanimous vote.

actually ready to engage in n (and possibly in other atoms as well). For a single agent, there might be more than one such place, resulting in several transitions. Each transition in $T(n, r)$ has input places referring to all involved participants, which results in a transition for each combination of respective input places.

Formally, let $P_n = \{a_1, \ldots, a_k\}$. $T(n, r)$ contains a transition $[n, r, L]$ for every tuple $L = ([a_1, S_1], \ldots, [a_k, S_k])$ such that $n \in S_1 \cap \ldots \cap S_k$. The set of input places of $[n, r, L]$ is $\{[a_1, S_1], \ldots, [a_k, S_k]\}$, and its set of output places is $\{[a_1, \mathcal{X}(n, a_1, r)], \ldots, [a_k, \mathcal{X}(n, a_k, r)]\}$. All transitions of the set $T(n, r)$ are labelled by the outcome (n, r). They all have the same output places. Moreover, they have the same number of input and output places, both of them equal to the number of participants of n.

For the negotiation on the left of Fig. 2, we get seven sets of transitions: $T(n_0, \mathtt{st})$, $T(n_{\mathrm{FD}}, \mathtt{y})$, $T(n_{\mathrm{FD}}, \mathtt{n})$, $T(n_{\mathrm{FD}}, \mathtt{am})$, $T(n_{\mathrm{DM}}, \mathtt{y})$, $T(n_{\mathrm{DM}}, \mathtt{n})$, and $T(n_f, \mathtt{end})$. All of them are singletons, with the exception of $T(n_f, \mathtt{end})$, which contains the two transitions shown at the bottom of the figure. We annotate transitions only by results r instead of outcomes (n, r) in the figure. Notice that here we assume a unique result $\mathtt{end}$ of n_f.

Proposition 1. *For each atom $n \neq n_f$, each transition labelled by (n, r) has exactly one input place $[a, X]$ for each agent $a \in P_n$, and exactly one output place $[a, Y]$ for each agent $a \in P_n$. Transitions labelled by $(n_f, \mathtt{end})$ have no output places.*

Proof. Follows immediately from the construction of the Petri net.   □

Corollary 1. *For each agent a, the number of tokens on places $[a, X]$ never increases. Since this number is one initially, it is at most one for each reachable marking.*   □

Corollary 2. *The Petri net associated with a negotiation is 1-safe, i.e., no reachable marking assigns more than one token to a place.*   □

Lemma 1. *The Petri net associated with a negotiation is deterministic, i.e., no reachable marking enables two distinct transitions with the same label.*

Proof. A transition labelled by (n, r) has an input place for each participant of n. Two equally labelled transitions cannot have identical sets of input places by construction. Hence, for at least one agent a there is a place $[a, X]$ which is input place of one of the transitions and a distinct place $[a, Y]$ which is input place of the other transition. Since, by Corollary 1, each reachable marking marks at most one of these two places, each reachable marking enables at most one of the transitions. □

The (sequential) behaviour of a labelled Petri net is represented by its reachability graph:

Definition 5. *The* reachability graph *of a Petri net has all reachable markings m as vertices, an arc annotated by t leading from m to m' when m enables transition t and the occurrence of t leads to m', and a distinguished initial marking m_0. The* label reachability graph *of a labelled Petri net is obtained from its reachability graph by replacing each transition by its label.*

In terms of reachability graphs, a labelled Petri net is deterministic if and only if its label reachability graph has no vertex with two outgoing edges which carry the same label. An occurrence sequence of a deterministic labelled Petri net is fully determined by the sequence of transition labels, as shown in the following proposition, and so is the sequence of markings reached.

For a labelling function λ and an occurrence sequence $\sigma = t_1 \, t_2 \, t_3 \ldots$, we write $\lambda(\sigma)$ for the sequence of labels $\lambda(t_1) \, \lambda(t_2) \, \lambda(t_3) \ldots$ in the sequel.

Proposition 2. *Let σ_1 and σ_2 be two finite, initially enabled occurrence sequences of a deterministic labelled Petri net with labelling function λ. Let m_1 be the marking reached by σ_1, and let m_2 be the marking reached by σ_2. If $\lambda(\sigma_1) = \lambda(\sigma_2)$ then $m_1 = m_2$.*

Proof. Since the labelled Petri net is deterministic, $\lambda(\sigma_1) = \lambda(\sigma_2)$ implies $\sigma_1 = \sigma_2$ □

3.3 Behavioural Equivalence Between Negotiations and Nets

In this subsection, we will employ the usual notion of isomorphism between reachability graphs:

Definition 6. *Two reachability graphs are isomorphic if there exists a bijective mapping φ between their sets of vertices, mapping the initial vertex of the first graph to the initial vertex of the second graph, such that there is an edge from u to v labelled by some t in the first graph if and only if there is an edge from $\lambda(u)$ to $\lambda(v)$ labelled by t in the second graph.*

Reachability graph isomorphism is a very strong behavioural equivalence notion for sequential behaviour. If moreover the concurrent step reachability graphs of two models are isomorphic, then also the concurrent behaviour of the systems coincide. We will show the existence of both isomorphisms between negotiations and associated Petri nets.

Proposition 3. *The reachability graph of a negotiation and the label reachability graph of the associated labelled Petri net are isomorphic.*

Proof. We interpret a token on a place $[a, \{n_1, \ldots, n_k\}]$ on the negotiation side as "agent a is ready to engage in the atoms of the set $\{n_1, \ldots, n_k\}$". It is immediate to see that this holds initially. By construction of the Petri net, a small step (n, r) of the negotiation is mimicked by an occurrence of a transition of the set $T(n, r)$, and hence by a transition labelled by (n, r). Moreover, the marking of the negotiation reached by the occurrence of the outcome corresponds to the marking of the net reached by the occurrence of the transition.   □

For comparing the concurrent behaviour of negotiations and associated labelled Petri nets, we have to define concurrent enabledness of transitions. This is easy in our setting, because the considered nets are 1-safe.

Definition 7. *Two transitions t and t' of a 1-safe Petri net are concurrently enabled at a reachable marking m if m enables both t and t' and if moreover t and t' have no common input place.*

Concurrent behaviour is captured by the concurrent step reachability graph and, for labelled Petri nets, by its label version. In the following definition, a set of transitions is said to be *concurrently enabled* if any two distinct transitions in this set are concurrently enabled.

Definition 8. *The* concurrent step reachability graph *of a Petri net has all reachable markings m as vertices, with a distinguished initial marking m_0. An arc, labelled by U, leads from m to m' if m concurrently enables a nonempty set U of transitions and the occurrence of all transitions of U (in any order) leads from m to m'.*

The label concurrent step reachability graph *of a labelled Petri net is obtained from its concurrent step reachability graph by replacing each set of transitions by the multiset of its labels.*

Fortunately, in our setting two equally labelled transitions are never enabled concurrently. Therefore the labels of concurrent steps will never be proper multisets, but just sets.

Lemma 2. *If two outcomes (n, r) and (n', r') of a negotiation are concurrently enabled at a marking reached by an initial occurrence sequence σ, then there is an initially enabled occurrence sequence μ of the associated labelled Petri net such that $\lambda(\mu) = \sigma$ and the marking reached by μ concurrently enables two transitions labelled by (n, r) and (n', r') respectively.*

Conversely, if a marking of the (λ-) labelled Petri net reached by an occurrence sequence μ concurrently enables two transitions t and t', then the marking of the negotiation reached by λ(μ) concurrently enables the two outcomes λ(t) and λ(t').

Proof. By construction of the Petri net, a transition t has an input place $[a, X]$ only if $\lambda(t) = (n, r)$ for an agent $a \in P_n$. Assume that two enabled transitions are not concurrent. Then they share an input place $[a, X]$ only if their labels refer to two outcomes (n, r) and (n', r') such that $a \in P_n$ and $a \in P_{n'}$. So $P_n \cap P_{n'} \neq \emptyset$, and thus the two outcomes are not concurrent.

Conversely, if two outcomes (n, r) and (n', r') are enabled but not concurrent, then some agent a belongs to both P_n and $P_{n'}$. In the Petri net, each transition labelled by (n, r) or by (n', r') has an input place $[a, X]$. Since each reachable marking marks only one place $[a, X]$ by Corollary 1, two distinct enabled transitions labelled by (n, r) or by (n', r') share this marked input place, whence they are not concurrent.   □

Corollary 3. *The concurrent step reachability graph of a negotiation and the label concurrent step reachability graph of its associated Petri net are isomorphic.*   □

3.4   Excursion: On the Voting Example

The reader possibly finds unsatisfactory that the negotiation given in Fig. 3 can reject even when all parties vote yes. This results in 2^k respective rejecting transitions of the Petri net. If we want to avoid this possibility in the Petri net, we just remove the single transition that removes tokens from all accept-places and enables overall rejection.

There also exists a negotiation with corresponding behaviour: we replace the atom $n_{\texttt{reject}}$ by k rejecting atoms $\texttt{reject}_i$, for $1 \leq i \leq k$. If agent a_i votes yes, then this agent is ready to engage in accept and in all $\texttt{reject}_j$ such that $j \neq i$. Any of the $\texttt{reject}_j$-atoms have a single result that leads to final rejection. When all agents vote yes then none of the $\texttt{reject}_i$-atoms are enabled, whence only overall acceptance can take place. Notice that this construction is a bit clumsy (see Fig. 4), but still does not require exponentially many elements, as the associated Petri net does.

As mentioned before, the Petri net obtained by translating the voting negotiation of Fig. 3 has exponentially many transitions. This does, however, not imply that every Petri net exhibiting the same behaviour as the voting example grows exponentially with the number of agents.

Consider e.g. the Petri net with an acceptance transition and a rejection transition for each agent, as before. Instead of $2 \cdot k$ places for acceptance and rejection, we define a single acceptance place such that each of the k accepting transitions adds a token to this place. Similarly, all rejecting transitions add a token to a single rejection place. After all agents have finished their voting, there are k tokens on the two places for acceptance and rejection. A final acceptance

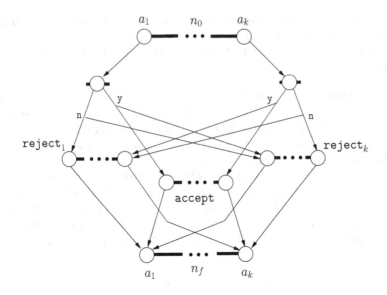

Fig. 4. A corrected negotiation for unanimous vote.

transition is enabled if the acceptance place carries all k tokens, whereas for each possible distribution of k tokens on the two places we define a separate rejecting transition. As above, we might exclude the rejecting transition consuming k tokens from the acceptance place. Formally, we define a place/transition Petri net with arc weights. Apparently this net has linear size with respect to k, the number of agents. The net is k-bounded, i.e., no reachable marking assigns more than k tokens to a place.

Another possibility of modelling the same behaviour is to provide k places for acceptance, one for each agent, and k places for rejection, as in our first Petri net. Now we add, for each agent, a transition moving a token from the corresponding acceptance place to the rejection place. This transition is labelled by the *empty word* τ. No matter how the agents voted, we can reach the marking with all tokens on the reject places by firing these τ-labelled transitions. Therefore, it suffices to have one acceptance transition that removes tokens from all acceptance places and one rejection transition that removes tokens from all rejection places. Firing a τ-labelled transition does not contribute to the observed behaviour of the Petri net. So this net is at least language equivalent to the negotiation of Fig. 3.

Summarizing, we have provided a systematic way to construct a 1-safe Petri net corresponding to a negotiation, which can be exponentially larger than the negotiation. For the voting example, this Petri net has exponentially many transitions. For this example we also provided a linear-sized Petri net with the same behaviour, which is, however, not 1-safe but k-bounded. Another Petri net with this behaviour is 1-safe, but has τ-labelled transitions. We actually do not know if, for negotiations in general, there always exist polynomial-sized Petri nets with the same behaviour which are 1-safe, which are bounded, which have no

τ-labelled transitions etc., i.e. all these problems are open. For the voting example, we did not find a polynomial-sized equivalent 1-safe Petri net without τ-labelled transitions.

4   Properties of the Net Associated with a Negotiation

4.1   S-components

An *S-component* of a Petri net is a subnet such that, for each place of the subnet, all input- and output-transitions belong to the subnet as well, and such that each transition of the subnet has exactly one input- and exactly one output-place of the subnet [6]. It is immediate to see that the number of tokens in an S-component never changes. A net is covered by S-components if each place and each transition belongs to an S-component. Nets covered by S-components carrying exactly one token are necessarily 1-safe. For example, every live and 1-safe free-choice net enjoys this nice property [6].

Petri nets associated with negotiations are not covered by S-components, only because the **end**-transitions have no output places. However, if we add an arc from each **end**-transition to each initially marked place, then the resulting net is covered by S-components:

Proposition 4. *The Petri net associated with a negotiation, with additional arcs from each **end**-transition to each initially marked place, is covered by S-components.*

Proof. We consider the Petri net with the additional arcs. For each agent a, the subnet generated by all places $[a, X]$ and all transitions labelled by (n, r) where $a \in P_n$, is an S-component (being generated implies that the arcs of the subnet are all arcs of the original net connecting nodes of the subnet). An arbitrary place of the net belongs to one such subnet, because it corresponds to an agent. Each transition has a label (n, r), and each atom n has a nonempty set of participants, whence the transition belongs to the subnet of some agent.   □

4.2   Soundness

The following notion of sound negotiations was inspired by van der Aalst's soundness of workflow nets [1]. It was first defined in [8].

Definition 9. *A negotiation is* sound *if each outcome occurs in some initial occurrence sequence and if, moreover, each finite occurrence sequence is a large step or can be extended to a large step.*

All the negotiations shown in the figures of this paper are sound. For an example of an unsound negotiation, consider again the ping-pong negotiation shown in Fig. 1 on the right hand side. Imagine that Daughter could choose to start negotiating with Father or with Mother. This would formally be expressed by replacing the arc from port D of n_0 to port D of n_{FD} by a hyperarc from port D of n_0 to ports D of both n_{FD} and n_{DM}. If, in this modified distributed negotiation, Daughter first negotiates successfully with Mother, a marking is reached where both Daughter and Mother can only engage in the final atom n_f, whereas Father is still only able to participate in n_{FD}. So the distributed negotiation has reached a marking which is neither final nor enables any outcome. We call such a marking a *deadlock*. Clearly, sound negotiations have no reachable deadlocks.

Since the Petri nets associated with negotiations are not workflow nets, we cannot immediately compare the soundness notions of workflow nets and of negotiations. Instead we define additionally *in/out-nets* associated with negotiations, which are obtained by a minor transformation from the originally constructed Petri nets. These in/out-nets are a generalisation of workflow nets, as defined in [1]. Soundness, as defined for workflow nets in [1], is generalized to in/out-nets in the following definitions.

Definition 10. *An in/out-net is a Petri net with two distinguished places p_{in} and p_{out} such that p_{in} has no input transition and p_{out} has no output transition.*

The initial marking of an in/out-net assigns one token to the place p_{in} and no token to all other places. In/out-nets also have a final marking, *assigning one token to p_{out} and no token to all other places.*

An in/out-net net is sound *if it has no dead transitions (i.e., each transition belongs to an initially enabled occurrence sequence) and, moreover, each initially enabled occurrence sequence is a prefix of an occurrence sequence leading to the final marking.*

A workflow net *is an in/out-net such that, for each place or transition x, there are directed paths from p_{in} to x and from x to p_{out}.*

Now we associate in/out-nets with negotiations.

Definition 11. *The in/out-net associated with a negotiation is obtained from the Petri net associated with the negotiation by the following transformations:*

1. *The Petri net associated with the negotiation has, for each participating agent, an initially marked place. We delete all except one of these places and adjacent arcs and rename the remaining initially marked place to p_{in}.*
2. *We add an initially unmarked place p_{out} and arcs from all transitions labelled by outcomes of the final atom n_f (which we called* **end** *before) to this place.*

In/out-nets associated with negotiations are not necessarily workflow nets because not every element is necessarily on a path from the initial place to the final place. However, this condition holds if the negotiation is sound, as the following proposition shows.

Proposition 5. *The in/out-net associated with a sound negotiation is a workflow net.*

Proof. By construction, the in/out-net has distinguished places p_{in} and p_{out}.

By definition of a distributed negotiation, the initial atom is not a possible next atom for any atom and any agent, i.e., it does not belong to any $X(n, a, r)$.

Hence, by construction, the initially marked places of the Petri net associated with the negotiation have no ingoing arcs. Since p_{in} is one of these places, it has no ingoing arc.

The new place p_{out} has no outgoing arc.

Since, by soundness of the negotiation, every atom (and therefore every outcome) can be enabled, a token can be moved from the initial atom to any other atom. Therefore, there is a directed path from the initial atom to any other atom (more precisely, there is a path in the graph of the negotiation). By the construction of the Petri net (and of the in/out-net), there are according paths from the place p_{in} to arbitrary places and transitions of the net.

Again by soundness of the negotiation, every occurrence sequence can be extended to a large step, i.e., the final atom can eventually be enabled and the final marking reached. So every token can be led to the final atom, and therefore there are paths in the graph of the negotiation from every atom to the final atom. By construction of the Petri net (and of the in/out-net), there are thus paths from any element to an **end**-transition, where **end** is an outcome of n_f, and – in the in/out-net – to the place p_{out}.   □

Next we show that, for sound negotiations, the associated Petri net and the associated in/out-net are behaviourally equivalent. To this end, we formally introduce an equivalence relation on the set of Petri nets:

Definition 12. *Two Petri nets N and N' are in the relation $\mathcal{R}$ if*

- *N' is obtained from N by the deletion of a place p and adjacent arcs and*
- *the reachability graphs of N and N' are isomorphic.*

The symmetrical, reflexive and transitive closure of $\mathcal{R}$ is called place equivalence.

Places p satisfying the condition of this definition are often called *implicit*. Clearly, by construction place equivalence is an equivalence relation.

Lemma 3.

(a) *Let N be a Petri net with two places p and p' with identical sets of input transitions, identical sets of output transitions and identical initial marking. Then deletion of p' together with adjacent arcs leads to a place-equivalent net.*

(b) *Let N be a Petri net with a place p with no output transition. Assume that there are no two distinct reachable markings m and m' that disagree only with respect to p, i.e., that satisfy*

$$m(p) \neq m'(p) \text{ and } m(p') = m'(p') \text{ for } p \neq p' .$$

Then deletion of p and adjacent arcs leads to a place-equivalent net.[2]

---

[2] Without the second condition, i.e., assuming only that p has no output transitions, the derived net is a *bisimular net*. It has in particular identical occurrence sequences as the original one, but it can have a smaller reachability graph because distinct reachable markings might differ only with respect to the place p.

Proof.

(a) The nets N and N' are obviously in the relation $\mathcal{R}$ as defined in Definition 12.
(b) Clearly, removing p does not change the behaviour in terms of occurrence sequences because a place can only restrict the enabledness of its output transitions, but p has no output transitions. The second assumption implies moreover that, for each reachable marking m, the number $m(p)$ follows uniquely from all $m(p')$, $p \neq p'$. So we have a bijective mapping from reachable markings of the Petri net N to reachable markings of the reduced net, which is formally given by the projection of markings to the set of places without p. It is easy to see that this bijection actually induces an isomorphism between the two reachability graphs.   □

Using this lemma we now show that, at least for sound negotiations, the associated Petri net and the associated in/out-net have the same behaviour.

Proposition 6. *Let $\mathcal{N}$ be a sound negotiation. The reachability graph of its associated Petri net is isomorphic to the reachability graph of its associated in/out-net.*

Proof. As argued in the proof of Proposition 5, the initially marked places of the Petri net associated with the negotiation have no ingoing arcs. Since the initial atom of the negotiation has all agents as participants, the transitions corresponding to its outcomes consume the tokens from all initially marked places. Therefore, all these places have the same (empty) set of input transitions and the same set of output transitions. So Lemma 3(a) applies and proves that the transformation leads to a net with identical reachability graph.

Next we show that adding the place p_{out} also does not change behaviour. We argue considering the in/out-net with the place p_{out} and show that removing this place leads to a net with isomorphic reachability graph. We aim at applying Lemma 3(b), and thus have to show that no two distinct reachable markings of the in/out-net differ only with respect to the marking of p_{out}.

By construction of the Petri net and of the corresponding in/out-net associated to the negotiation, firing a transition labelled with an outcome of the final atom removes all tokens from the net. This is because all agents participate in the final atom. Conversely, these transitions are the only transitions which do not produce tokens on some places. Therefore, there are tokens in the Petri net before one of these transitions occurs and there are no tokens in the Petri net afterwords. In particular, there can only be one occurrence of such a transition. In the in/out-net, occurrences of transitions representing final outcomes add a token to the place p_{out} and no other transition changes the marking of this place. Therefore, before the occurrence of a transition labelled by a final outcome there are marked places (one for each participant) and p_{out} is unmarked. After the occurrence of a transition labelled by a final outcome, p_{out} is the only marked place. So no two reachable markings differ only with respect to p_{out}, and Lemma 3(b) applies.   □

Unfortunately, soundness of a negotiation does not necessarily imply soundness of the associated in/out-net (which is, by Proposition 5, a workflow net). The reason is that soundness requires that every atom can occur but not that every branch of a hyperarc is actually used. If, for example, there was an additional hyperarc in Fig. 1 from the port F in n_0 to the ports F in n_{FD} and n_f instead of the arc from n_0 to n_{FD}, then the resulting negotiation would still be sound; actually, the behaviour does not change at all. The associated in/out-net, however, would have an additional transition **end** with new input place $[F, \{n_{FD}, n_f\}]$ (and other input places) which is never enabled. This net is therefore not sound.

4.3   Deterministic Negotiations

In [9], we concentrate on *deterministic negotiations*, which are negotiations without proper hyperarcs.

Definition 13. *A negotiation is* deterministic *if, for each atom n, agent $a \in P_n$ and result $r \in R_n$, $\mathfrak{X}(n, a, r)$ contains at most one atom (and no atom only if $n = n_f$).*

The term deterministic is justified because there is no choice for an agent with respect to the next possible atoms.

Since both, the exponential blow-up and the problem of useless arcs (branches of hyperarcs) stem from proper hyperarcs, we can expect that deterministic negotiations allow for better results. Actually, the Petri net associated with a deterministic negotiation is in fact much smaller, because all its places have the form $[a, X]$, where a is an agent and X is a singleton set of atoms. So the set of places is linear in agents and in atoms.

Before discussing soundness of deterministic negotiations, we make a structural observation. For the definition of free-choice nets used here, see [6].

Proposition 7. *The Petri net associated with a deterministic negotiation is a free-choice net, i.e., every two places either share no output transitions, or they share all their output transitions. The same holds for the in/out-net associated with a deterministic negotiation.*

Proof. Since, in a net associated with a deterministic negotiation, each place has the form $[a, X]$, where X is a singleton set $\{n\}$, all its output transitions are labelled by (n, r), r being a possible result of n. By construction, every other place $[b, \{n\}]$ has exactly the same output transitions as $[a, \{n\}]$ whereas all other places have no common output transition with $[a, \{n\}]$.

The transformations of Definition 11 do not destroy the free-choice property. $\qquad\square$

Proposition 8. *A deterministic negotiation is sound if and only if its associated in/out-net is sound.*

Proof. The translation from a negotiation to its associated Petri net can be rephrased in a much simpler way if the negotiation is deterministic, as follows:

- For each atom n and each a in P_n, we add a place $[a, n]$.
- For each atom n and result $r \in R_n$, we add a transition (n, r) (no two transitions correspond to the same outcome (n, r), so transitions can be identified with their previously used labels).
- Arcs connect all places $[a, n]$ with all transitions (n, r).
- For each transition (n, r) with $n \neq n_f$ and each $a \in P_n$ there is an arc from (n, r) to $[a, n']$, where n' is the unique atom in $\mathcal{X}(n, a, r)$.
- All places $[a, n_0]$ carry one token initially; all other places are initially unmarked.

It is immediate that to see that the behaviour of the negotiation is precisely mimicked by this Petri net. So the negotiation is sound if and only if the net has no dead transitions and moreover can reach the final (empty) marking from any reachable marking.

The result follows since the Petri net can, as above, be transformed into a behaviourally equivalent in/out-net. □

Combining Propositions 5 and 8 yields:

Corollary 4. *If a negotiation is deterministic and sound then its associated in/out-net is a sound workflow net.* □

5　From Petri Nets to Negotiations

In this section we study the converse direction: Given a labelled Petri net, is there a negotiation such that the net is associated with the negotiation? Obviously, for a positive answer the net has to enjoy all the properties derived before. In particular, it must have disjoint S-components and initially marked input places. However, in the general case it appears to be difficult to characterise nets that have corresponding negotiations.

We will provide an answer for the case of sound deterministic negotiations and sound free-choice workflow nets.

Proposition 9. *Every sound free-choice workflow net is place equivalent to a net which is associated with a sound deterministic negotiation.*

Proof. A workflow net is sound if and only if the net with an additional feedback transition moving the token from p_{out} back to p_{in} is live and 1-safe [1]. Live and 1-safe free-choice nets are covered by S-components [6]. Therefore a sound free-choice workflow net is covered by S-components as well. However, these S-components have not necessarily disjoint sets of places. Consequently, we cannot easily find candidates for agents involved in the negotiation to be constructed.

Instead we proceed as follows: We choose a minimal set of S-components that cover the net. Since each S-component of a live net has to carry a token, all these S-components contain the place p_{in}. Each S-component corresponds to an agent of the net to be constructed. Each conflict cluster, i.e., each set of places sharing the same output transitions, corresponds a negotiation atom (remember that the net is free-choice and therefore any two places either share all output transitions or do not share any).

Each place p of the net is contained in at least one S-component of the cover. Let C_p be the set of all S-components of the derived minimal cover containing p. If C_p contains more than one S-component, we duplicate the place p, getting a new place p' with input and output transitions like p.

The new net still has a cover by S-components, where one of the S-components containing p now contains p' instead. Repetition of this procedure eventually leads to a net where each place p belongs to exactly one S-component C_p of the cover. Finally we delete the place p_{out}. Both operations, duplication of places and deletion of p_{out}, lead to place-equivalent nets by Lemma 3.

The resulting net is associated with the following negotiation: The set of agents is the set of S-components of the minimal cover. The atoms are the conflict clusters of the net. The results of an atom are the transitions of the corresponding conflict cluster. The $\mathcal{X}$-function can be derived from the arcs of the Petri net leading from transitions to places.   □

6   Conclusions

This contribution presented a translation from a distributed negotiation to a behaviourally equivalent Petri net. The chosen notion of behavioural equivalence is very strong, namely isomorphism of the reachability graphs.

In the worst case, the translation yields a Petri net exponentially larger than the negotiation. We conjecture that this exponential blow-up is unavoidable, but currently we do not have a proof. The problem of the succinctness of negotiations with respect to weaker equivalence notions like bisimulation or language equivalence is also open. On the other hand, we have shown that for deterministic negotiations the translation only causes a linear growth. Further, for deterministic negotiations soundness and non-soundness is respected by the transformation to workflow-like Petri nets, whence in this case the reverse translation is possible as well.

The translation to Petri nets is implicitly used in [8,9], and in a recent paper on the analysis of Coloured Workflow Nets [11]. On the one hand, the fact that deterministic negotiations are so closed to workflow free-choice nets guided our efforts to obtain a reduction algorithm for the analysis of soundness and the input/output relation of negotiations. On the other hand, in [11] we transferred the reduction procedure back to Petri nets. The resulting reduction procedure has been successfully applied to a collection of industrial workflows.

Since we do not currently have a large suite of negotiation models, while such suites exist for workflow Petri nets, we have used negotiations mostly as a theoretical formalism to design new analysis techniques that can be later translated to workflow nets. In future work we plan to analyze the connection between negotiations and languages for the description of business processes. Negotiations could become an intermediate language between business processes and

Petri nets, offering more compact descriptions and cleaner analysis procedures and the possibility to apply the highly developed tool support for Petri net analysis. This includes in particular model checking tools that can verify properties formulated in an appropriate Temporal Logic. Application of such tools to negotiations requires not only prior transformation of the model but also of the formula. So we are interested in appropriate languages for formalizing relevant behavioural properties of negotiations.

References

1. van der Aalst, W.M.P.: The application of Petri nets to workflow management. J. Circ. Syst. Comput. **08**(01), 21–66 (1998)
2. Abdelzaher, T., Atkins, E.M., Shin, K.G.: QoS negotiation in real-time systems and its application to automated flight control. IEEE Trans. Comput. **49**(11), 1170–1183 (2000)
3. Basu, S., Bultan, T., Ouederni, M.: SIGPLAN notices. POPL 2012, **47**(1) (2012). issn = 0362-1340. ACM, New York
4. Chen, Y., Peng, Y., Finin, T., Labrou, Y., Chu, B., Yao, J., Sun, R., Willhelm, B., Cost, S.: A negotiation-based multi-agent system for supply chain management. In: Proceedings of Agents 99 - Workshop on Agent Based Decision-Support for Managing the Internet-Enabled Supply-Chain, pp. 15–20 (1999)
5. Davis, R., Smith, R.G.: Negotiation as a metaphor for distributed problem solving. Artif. Intell. **20**(1), 63–109 (1983)
6. Desel, J., Esparza, J.: Free Choice Petri Nets. Cambridge University Press, New York (1995)
7. Emerson, E.A., Kahlon, V.: Rapid parameterized model checking of snoopy cache coherence protocols. In: Garavel, H., Hatcliff, J. (eds.) TACAS 2003. LNCS, vol. 2619, pp. 144–159. Springer, Heidelberg (2003)
8. Esparza, J., Desel, J.: On negotiation as concurrency primitive. In: D'Argenio, P.R., Melgratti, H. (eds.) CONCUR 2013 – Concurrency Theory. LNCS, vol. 8052, pp. 440–454. Springer, Heidelberg (2013). Extended version in CoRR, abs/1307.2145, http://arxiv.org/abs/1307.2145
9. Esparza, J., Desel, J.: On negotiation as concurrency primitive II: deterministic cyclic negotiations. In: Muscholl, A. (ed.) FOSSACS 2014 (ETAPS). LNCS, vol. 8412, pp. 258–273. Springer, Heidelberg (2014). Extended version in CoRR, abs/1403.4958, http://arxiv.org/abs/1403.4958
10. Esparza, J., Desel, J.: Negotiation programs. In: Devillers, R., Valmari, A. (eds.) PETRI NETS 2015. LNCS, vol. 9115, pp. 157–178. Springer, Heidelberg (2015)
11. Esparza, J., Hoffmann, P.: Reduction rules for colored workflow nets. In: Stevens, P., Wasowski, A. (eds.) FASE 2016. LNCS, vol. 9633, pp. 342–358. Springer, Heidelberg (2016). doi:10.1007/978-3-662-49665-7_20
12. Genest, B., Muscholl, A., Peled, D.A.: Message sequence charts. In: Desel, J., Reisig, W., Rozenberg, G. (eds.) Lectures on Concurrency and Petri Nets. LNCS, vol. 3098, pp. 537–558. Springer, Heidelberg (2004)
13. Jennings, N.R., Faratin, P., Lomuscio, A.R., Parsons, S., Wooldridge, M.J., Sierra, C.: Automated negotiation: prospects, methods and challenges. Group Decis. Negot. **10**(2), 199–215 (2001)
14. Peltz, C.: Web services orchestration and choreography. IEEE Comput. **36**(10), 46–52 (2003). doi:10.1109/MC.2003.1236471

15. Salaün, G., Bultan, T., Roohi, N.: Realizability of choreographies using process algebra encodings. IEEE Trans. Serv. Comput. **5**(3), 290–304 (2012)
16. Simon, C.: Negotiation Processes - The Semantic Process Language and Applications. Shaker, Aachen (2008)
17. Winsborough, W.H., Seamons, K.E., Jones, V.E.: Automated trust negotiation. In: DARPA Information Survivability Conference and Exposition, DISCEX 2000 Proceedings, vol. 1, pp. 88–102. IEEE (2000)
18. Xu, H., Shatz, S.M.: An agent-based Petri net model with application to seller/buyer design in electronic commerce. In: Fifth International Symposium on Autonomous Decentralized Systems, ISADS 2001, Dallas, Texas, USA, 26–28 March 2001, pp. 11–18. IEEE Computer Society (2001)

A Formal Framework for Diagnostic Analysis for Errors of Business Processes

Suman Roy[1]([✉]) and A.S.M. Sajeev[2]

[1] Infosys Ltd., #44 Electronics City, Hosur Road, Bangalore 560 100, India
Suman_Roy@infosys.com
[2] Melbourne Institute of Technology, Sydney, NSW 2000, Australia
asmsajeev2@gmail.com

Abstract. Business process models expressed in languages such as BPMN (Business Process Model and Notation), play a critical role in implementing the workflows in modern enterprises. However, control flow errors such as deadlocks and lack of synchronization, and syntactic errors arising out of poor modeling practices often occur in industrial process models. A major challenge is to provide the means and methods to detect such errors and more importantly, to identify the location of each error. In this work, we develop a formal framework of diagnosing errors by locating their occurrence nodes in business process models at the level of sub-processes and swim-lanes. We use graph-theoretic techniques and Petri net-based analyses to detect syntactic and control flow-related errors respectively. While syntactic errors can be easily located on the processes themselves, we project control-related errors on processes using a mapping from Petri nets to processes. We use this framework to analyze a sample of 174 industrial BPMN process models having 1262 sub-processes in which we identify more than 2000 errors. We are further able to discover how error frequencies change with error depth, how they correlate with the size of the sub-processes and swim-lane interactions in the models, and how they can be predicted in terms of process metrics like sub-process size, coefficient of connectivity, sequentiality and structuredness.

Keywords: Verification · Formal methods · Processes · BPM Notation · Errors · Soundness · Petri nets · Workflow nets · Woflan · Diagnosis · Metrics

1 Introduction

Modern-day enterprises rely on streamlined business processes for implementing the workflows in the operation. This is particularly important for internet-based businesses where on-line processes such as accepting orders need to be seamlessly integrated with physical processes like delivery of products. Correct implementation of process models can result in significant cost savings in industry. For example, Hammer [Ham10] reports a computer manufacturer reducing time to

© Springer-Verlag Berlin Heidelberg 2016
M. Koutny et al. (Eds.): ToPNoC XI, LNCS 9930, pp. 226–261, 2016.
DOI: 10.1007/978-3-662-53401-4_11

market by 75 % and a consumer goods manufacturer eliminating out of stock scenarios by 50 % through properly managing their business processes. Specification and verification of such business processes have assumed importance as ISO 9000 certification and compliance force companies to create extensive documentation of business processes and to meet self-imposed goals [IC96].

Among the languages that have been developed for specifying business processes, BPMN (Business Process Model and Notation) [Obj11] seems to be quite popular. Its standardization body, the Object Management Group, lists a large number of vendors that provide tool support for BPMN (www.bpmn. org). BPMN also provides mappings to executable languages such as WS-BPEL (Web Services Business Process Execution Language) from the OASIS consortium [Aosftis07]; this particularly assists on-line businesses since almost every aspect of their processes are software enabled.

A major challenge in implementing business processes, however, is providing the means and methods to detect errors in process models and be able to locate the nodes where an errors occurs. In our previous work [RSBR14], we analyzed the occurrence of errors by considering process models as a whole. From a modeler's point of view, it is not sufficient to know if a model as a whole is erroneous; it is equally important to learn the locations in the model where errors occur, or which parts of a model have higher probabilities of being prone to errors in comparison to other parts. This knowledge will assist the modeler to spot errors at a finer granularity and make changes to the model accordingly. Further, in the absence of general modeling guidelines, poor modeling practices can lead to the use of erroneous constructs irrespective of the complexity of the problem. In programming, compilation is a necessary step that detects syntactic errors; on the other hand, modeling does not have such a mandatory error-checking phase. Therefore, diagnosing models to identify the locations of errors is critical for the validation of process models.

In this paper we develop a formal model for detecting and diagnosing errors for business processes. Our diagnosis method is largely automated as it requires almost no user intervention. Our data set originates from commercial business process models made available in a repository of Infosys Ltd., one of the largest IT enterprises of India with a global footprint. The models come from a number of business domains including banking, retail and healthcare. For business requirements modelling, Infosys uses BPMN through an in-house tool called InFlux. Thus, our method of diagnosing errors in commercial BPM processes and the results of our empirical analysis will be useful for an increasing number of organizations that use BPMN for their modelling.

In particular, we have formally verified and analyzed 174 industry models containing 1262 sub-processes (which exhibited 2428 errors) to develop a statistical model of error probabilities at sub-process levels. These errors are syntactic and control flow related. Syntactic errors can be detected using simple graph search algorithms. Control flow errors occur due to lack of soundness in the process model. Our diagnostic method hinges on soundness checking of processes using Petri net-based techniques. Towards that we force our process model to be in a well-formed form (after removing syntactic errors). Subsequently, we convert it to a free-choice Petri net preserving the soundness of the process. This Petri net can be reduced to a simplified version, *viz.* free-choice WorkFlow net (WF-net) for which polynomial time algorithm for soundness checking exists. Next, we use the Woflan tool [VBvdA01] for checking soundness of generated WF-nets. Woflan produces necessary diagnostic information for the nets from which the location of errors can be identified. These locations can be mapped back to processes so that we can locate the errors in them at the level of sub-processes and swim-lanes, thus providing microscopic diagnostic information through our analysis. Finally we report our experience on the diagnostic information of these commercial models to illustrate the usefulness of our method. This paper is a significantly extended version of our preliminary work reported in [RSS14] where we initially proposed the framework for diagnosing errors based on formal verification; here we expand the work with rigorous proof of the results and extensive empirical analysis of diagnosis of errors including logistic regression.

The rest of the paper is organized as follows. A discussion on related work is undertaken in Sect. 2. In Sect. 3 we discuss preliminaries of business processes including a graph-based definition of syntax and semantics of a process. In Sect. 4 we show how a process model can be converted to a Petri net, preserving soundness properties in two formalisms. WF-nets are introduced as a sub-class of Petri nets in Sect. 5 and their connection to processes in terms of soundness checking is established through results mentioned in Sect. 4. We describe Woflan, the tool for checking soundness of workflow models in Sect. 6 and briefly sketch its diagnostic functionalities. In Sect. 7 we discuss our method for checking and diagnosing errors, thus locating their position in the process through the use of Woflan tool. We provide an experience report of our diagnostic framework for real-life industry models in Sect. 8. We provide remarks on expressive power of our proposed framework, and more explicit evaluation of the originality of the results in Sect. 9. Finally, we provide concluding remarks in Sect. 10.

2   Related Work

Even though there is considerable literature on error modeling of business process models (which are reviewed below), not much work has been reported on diagnostic analyses of business processes. However, checking for soundness during the modeling phase of processes can lead to useful diagnostic information. Vanhatalo *et al.* have proposed a technique for control flow analysis of a process by modeling it as a workflow graph [VVL07]. In this technique, a process model is decomposed into single-entry-single-exit fragments [VVK08] in linear time, which are of much smaller size than the original process. As each error is contained in a fragment it can be reflected in a small context, thus making the job of error fixing easier. Each such fragment is separately checked for control-flow related errors using a fast heuristic. The authors have provided such heuristics for both sound and unsound fragments. The heuristics are proposed by observing that many of these fragments in real-life processes have a simple structure that can be quickly recognized. A drawback of this work, as pointed out by the authors, is that the rest of the fragments which could not be covered by the heuristic have to be analyzed by other techniques. Moreover, employing the appropriate heuristic for complex fragments may be beyond the realm of practitioners and thus can be an obstacle for automating the diagnosis analysis. In contrast, in our work, the aim is to provide an automated way of detecting diagnostic errors with very little user intervention so that a common practitioner can easily use it.

Fahland *et al.* [FFJ+11] carry out a major work on soundness checking of industrial business process models, - the authors show that modeling can be tightly coupled with control flow analysis. They use Petri net-based tool LoLA, Worflow analyzer Woflan and IBM Web-Sphere Business Modeler to detect errors in the processes. The authors talk about three challenges of soundness checking for making it acceptable to verification engineers, - coverage, immediacy and consumability. Under consumability they mention the importance of developing a user interface that should be capable of producing diagnostic information to users. As a part of this, they provide a visualization editor, which allows the user to click on an error message in the view and then locate the error in the model. In the process, the fragment containing the error would get highlighted along with the node causing the error. However, they do not formalize this diagnostic framework, nor do they perform statistical analysis of their sample data.

Researchers have worked on diagnosing workflow processes using Woflan tool [vdA97,VBvdA01]. Woflan was built to verify the correctness of process definitions of a Workflow Management System [vdA97]. It checks whether a process definition conforms to a workflow process definition and whether it is free of control flow-related errors such as deadlock and lack of synchronization (corresponding to a sound workflow definition). Woflan also produces useful diagnostic information for workflow processes [VBvdA01]. Specifically, the tool analyzes workflow process definitions incorporated from commercial products using Petri net-based analysis techniques and locates the source of a design error. This analysis can help the developer in finding and correcting the errors by providing to-the-point diagnostic information. However, Woflan cannot directly accept business processes as input models, hence one needs to convert such processes into WF-nets before they can be used as input to the Woflan tool, and the diagnostic information on nets have to be suitably mapped back onto the processes for highlighting the location of errors. With this in mind, we use a mapping algorithm to convert well-formed processes to free-choice WF-nets and identify the location of errors on these nets. The location of errors are mapped back to the process models using the inverse mapping (as the original mapping was bijective) so that we can pinpoint the location of errors in the original process models.

Although there is not much literature on empirical studies of errors for processes using diagnostic information, as mentioned before, there is considerable amount of work on error modeling for different kinds of process models, *viz.* BPM processes, EPC models, SAP models etc. Mendling *et al.* judge the quality aspects of models by studying the connection between errors such as deadlock and a set of metrics capturing various structural and behavioral aspects of process models [MNA07]. In another piece of work [MVvD+08], Mendling *et al.* consider a set of 604 sample EPC business process models from the SAP reference to check if the errors introduced due to the non-soundness of the models can be statistically explained by complexity metrics. These results are analyzed in detail in the thesis report of Mendling [Men07]. Cardoso *et al.* [CMNR06] survey complexities of metrics in various fields ranging from software engineering to cognitive science, and to graph theory, and later relate them to business process modeling. They use metrics which are analogous to the Line-of-Code, McCabe's Cyclomatic Complexity (called Control-Flow Complexity), Halstead Complexity Metric, and Information Flow Complexity. A connection between metrics and understanding of personal factors is established in [MRC07, MS08]. We refer the reader to [Men08] for an overview on the study of bottom-up metrics related to quality aspects. In another survey work [LG06], Gruhn and Laue explain how existing research results on the complexity of software can be extended to facilitate the analysis of the complexity of business process models by considering metrics such as size, control flow complexity, structure, comprehensiveness and modularization of the model. The authors conclude that most of the metrics related to business process models are mere adaptations of software complexity metrics.

Contributions of this Paper

In this paper we provide a rigorous and formal framework for analysis of soundness checking of business processes. In particular, we consider a specification formalism for processes using BPMN, *viz.* well-formed processes. We adopt a (soundness preserving) mapping which always produces free-choice Petri nets corresponding to these well-formed processes. Then we investigate the properties for a free-choice Petri net corresponding to soundness of the original process. Further, we propose a method for soundness checking of processes based on analyses of free-choice Workflow nets which is exploited by the Woflan tool as it produces useful diagnostic information for Workflow nets. Using the above results we show that the soundness of processes can be decided in polynomial time although such a result was already known in view of the work on decomposition of processes in [VVL07] and workflow-related analysis in [VVK08]. A significant work on soundness of business processes was carried out in [FFJ+11]. Although the authors therein stated equivalent characterizations of soundness of free-choice Petri nets and Workflow graphs (processes) they did not supply any proof. We supply rigorous arguments in developing our framework for error detection of processes thus unifying the notions of soundness in all the three formalisms – processes, Petri nets and Workflow nets. Our comprehensive analysis can be seen as a one-step improvement in rigorous analysis of soundness checking of processes.

Supplementing our earlier work on error detection for business processes [RSBR14] we provide a *diagnostic analysis* of errors occurring in processes in this work. Our diagnostic analysis is based on the in-depth analysis of soundness checking of business processes mentioned above and the useful diagnostic information provided by the Woflan tool. The tool verifies soundness for Workflow nets and pinpoints the occurrence location of such an error. As Woflan cannot accept business processes as input models the processes are required to be translated to WF-nets before they can be passed onto Woflan tool. Subsequently, we translate the diagnostic information back to the processes from WF-nets using a suitable mapping algorithm. This knowledge can aid the developer in locating the errors and taking appropriate remedial actions. Such a theoretical analysis is complemented by an experience report, in which we carry out an empirical analysis on diagnosis of errors for a sample of commercial process models at the sub-process level. Our analysis throws interesting highlights on the occurrence of errors at sub-process and swim-lane levels in business process models which will be useful to business houses dealing with process modeling. As there are very few work on diagnostic analysis of errors on business processes our work can certainly aid in future diagnostic initiatives for business processes.

Finally, we highlight our contribution in regard to the challenges listed in [FFJ+11] for adopting soundness checking techniques into mainstream industry. Three challenges were mentioned, coverage, immediacy and consumability. By coverage one has to ensure the error checker can handle all or most of the models. Immediacy poses the challenge of returning the results instantly. To meet the challenge of consumability one must develop a user interface for conveying the diagnostic information about the errors that could be easily consumed by verification engineers. In this work we have addressed all these challenges. For example, our tool is able to detect errors on all the industrial process models that we consider, it can also detect errors almost instantly and further, the tool provide useful diagnostic information to the practitioners by highlighting errors on the models on which they can take remedial actions.

3   Preliminaries on Business Processes

In this section we briefly describe how business processes are captured using Business Process Modeling Notation (BPMN), and discuss its syntax and semantics. Subsequently, we define the notion of soundness of a business process.

BPMN defines a Business Process Diagram (BPD) (also called a BPM process) which is based on flowchart related ideas, and provides a graphical notation for business process modeling using objects like nodes and edges. A *node* can be a task (also called an activity), an event or a split/join gateway (also called *control node*). By an *activity/task* we mean the work required to achieve an objective. In a BPD, we consider two types of events: start and end events. *Start events* denote the beginning of a process, and *end events* the end of a process. In a flow graph, the control flow relation linking two nodes is represented by a *directed edge* capturing the execution order between tasks of a BPD. A sequence is made of a collection of nodes connected serially through directed edges, each such node has an incoming and an outgoing arc. A gateway is meant for separating flows (called *split*), and combining flows (called *join*);

there are two kinds of gateways: AND-gateways (represented by a diamond with a "+" sign inside) and XOR-gateways (represented with a diamond having a "×" sign inside). An AND-split gateway (also called a *fork*) separates two concurrent paths and allows independent execution between them within a BPD. For synchronizing concurrent paths, an AND-join (also called a *synchronizer*) is used, it links all the incoming edges to it. A synchronizer delays its completion until all flows leading into the gateway complete their executions. From a XOR-split gateway (also called a *choice*), two or more outgoing control flow relations diverge resulting in mutually exclusive paths. A XOR-join gateway (also called a *merge*) is the counterpart of the XOR-split node and connects incoming mutually exclusive alternative paths into one path. A process can be decomposed into a (or more) child diagram(s), and each child diagram can be further decomposed into one or more child diagrams, and so forth. Each such child diagram is called a *sub-process*. The lowest-level process, which cannot be further decomposed, is labeled as a task. A sub-process acts like an independent process which can be invoked by a sub-process invocation activity. It is possible to define swim-lanes/roles for these processes just like partitions for activity diagrams; swim-lanes reflect those actors/agents that are responsible for execution of particular tasks/gateways assigned to them. The above elements constitute the basic set of constructs of BPMN. BPMN has additional advanced constructs such as exception event (which includes intermediate message, timer and error event) and message flow for denoting transmission of messages between two interacting processes (through send/receive task or message event), data-based decision or XOR gateways, OR-joins, priorities or cancellations etc., but we shall not consider them for our work, the reason being the industrial process models (in possession of Infosys Ltd.) that we consider can be modeled by this basic set of constructs. From now on, *by a process we shall mean a BPM process with the set of basic constructs discussed above.*

The lack of an unambiguous definition of the notation are hindrance to semantic analysis of BPM process models. This necessitates a proper formal modeling of BPM processes. There are many formalizations of BPM processes available. We use one which bears a close resemblance to those described in [ADW08,DDO08] and that of work-flows [LK05].

3.1 Syntax of BPM Process

A *BPM process* is a graph (also called a process model graph) $\mathbf{P} = (\mathcal{N}, \mathcal{F})$ where

- $\mathcal{N}$ is a finite set of nodes which is partitioned into the set of tasks $\mathcal{T}$, the set of gateways $\mathcal{G}$, and the set of events $\mathcal{E}$, *i.e.,*

$$\mathcal{N} \cong \mathcal{T} \uplus \mathcal{G} \uplus \mathcal{E}$$

- $\mathcal{G}$ can be further partitioned into disjoint sets of decision merges, $\mathcal{G}_M$ ($\mathcal{G}_M^{and}$ (synchronizer) and $\mathcal{G}_M^{xor}$ (merge)) and decision splits, $\mathcal{G}_S$ ($\mathcal{G}_S^{and}$ (fork) and $\mathcal{G}_S^{xor}$ (choice)),

- A set $\mathcal{E}$ of events which is a disjoint union of two sets of events $\mathcal{E}_s$ and $\mathcal{E}_f$, where
  - $\mathcal{E}_s$ is the set of start events (also called start nodes) with no incoming edges.
  - $\mathcal{E}_f$ is the set of end events (also called end/final nodes) with no outgoing edges.
- $\mathcal{F} \subseteq (\mathcal{N} \setminus \mathcal{E} \times \mathcal{N} \setminus \mathcal{E}) \bigcup (\mathcal{E}_s \times \mathcal{N} \setminus \mathcal{E}) \bigcup (\mathcal{N} \setminus \mathcal{E} \times \mathcal{E}_f)$ corresponds to sequence flows connecting tasks with tasks, tasks with gateways, gateways with tasks, start nodes with other nodes and other nodes with end nodes.

Further we can add swim-lanes to a BPM process. A BPM Process with swim-lanes is $\mathbf{P}_S = (\mathcal{N}, \mathcal{F}, \mathcal{S}, f)$, where additionally, $\mathcal{S}$ is a set of swim-lanes which is finite, and $f : (\mathcal{E} \cup \mathcal{A}) \rightarrow \mathcal{S}$ is a mapping from the set of events and activities to the set of swim-lanes $\mathcal{S}$. A process $\mathbf{Q}_P = (\mathcal{N}', \mathcal{F}')$ is said to be a sub-process of process $\mathbf{P} = (\mathcal{N}, \mathcal{F})$, if $\mathcal{N}' \subseteq \mathcal{N}$ and $\mathcal{F}' \subseteq \mathcal{F} \cap (\mathcal{N} \times \mathcal{N})$.

The size of a process is simply $|\mathcal{N}|$. Using graph-theoretic notion, we can define a path ρ as a finite sequence of nodes, $n_0, n_1, \ldots$, where $(n_i, n_{i+1}) \in \mathcal{F}, i = 0, 1, \ldots$. A path ρ begins at a start event n_0 if $n_0 = e_0 \in \mathcal{E}_s$.

We can define the pre-set and post-set of a node $n \in \mathcal{N}$ respectively as $\bullet n = \{n' \mid (n', n) \in \mathcal{F}\}$ and $n\bullet = \{n'' \mid (n, n'') \in \mathcal{F}\}$. Let $in(n)$ $(out(n))$ be the set of incoming (outgoing) edges to (out of) node $n \in \mathcal{N}$. A BPM process is *well-formed* [HFKV06] if and only if it has the following properties.

1. Start nodes have no incoming edges, however only one outgoing edge emanates from them. That is $\forall n_s \in \mathcal{E}_s, |in(n_s)| = 0$, and $|out(n_s)| = 1$.
2. Similarly, end nodes have no outgoing edges, however only one incoming edge leads into them. Again, $\forall n_f \in \mathcal{E}_f, |in(n_f)| = 1$, and $|out(n_f)| = 0$.
3. There is only one incoming edge to a task and exactly one outgoing edge from a task. That is, for every $n \in \mathcal{T}, |in(n)| = |out(n)| = 1$.
4. Each fork and choice has exactly one incoming edge and at least two outgoing edges. That is, for every $n \in \mathcal{G}_S, |in(n)| = 1$ and $|out(n)| > 1$.
5. Each synchronizer and merge has at least two incoming edges and exactly one outgoing edge. That is, for every $n \in \mathcal{G}_M, |in(n)| > 1$ and $|out(n)| = 1$.
6. Every node is on a path from some start node to some end node.

Let us now introduce a fragment of a process, known as a SESE fragment which will be required for subsequent discussions. Given a process model graph $\mathbf{P} = (\mathcal{N}, \mathcal{F})$ a *Single Entry Single Exit fragment (SESE fragment, in short)* [VVL07] $\mathbf{P}' = (\mathcal{N}', \mathcal{F}')$ is a non-empty subgraph of $\mathbf{P}$ such that $\mathcal{N}' \subseteq \mathcal{N}$ and $\mathcal{F}' = \mathcal{F} \cap (\mathcal{N}' \times \mathcal{N}')$ and there exist flow edges $e, e' \in \mathcal{F}$ with $\{e\} = \mathcal{F} \cap (\mathcal{N} \setminus \mathcal{N}' \times \mathcal{N}')$ and $\{e'\} = \mathcal{F} \cap (\mathcal{N}' \times \mathcal{N} \setminus \mathcal{N}')$; e and e' are called the *entry* and the *exit* edges respectively. A SESE fragment is called a *SESE block* if there are two disjoint paths from the node from which the source edge originates to the node to which the sink edge leads to (source and sink edges to be defined later).

3.2   Semantics of BPM Process

Let us now specify the semantics of control elements of a BPM process, which is similar to that of Petri nets. We follow the definition from [VVL07, WHM10], where a state of a process is represented by tokens on the edges of the control flow graph. Given a process $\mathbf{P} = (\mathcal{N}, \mathcal{F})$, a *state* of $\mathbf{P}$ is a mapping $\mu : \mathcal{F} \to \mathbb{N}$, also called a *token mapping*. At any time an edge contains zero or more tokens. The number of tokens may change during the execution of the process, when the transitions are taken. A *source edge* e_s connects a start event with some other node. If the latter node is an activity then it is called an *initial activity*. Similarly, a *sink edge* e_f is an edge which connects a node with an end event. Again, if the former node is an activity then it is called a *final activity*. A state μ' is reached from state μ via node n, written as $\mu \xrightarrow{n} \mu'$, if and only if one of the following is true.

1. Tasks, AND-splits and AND-joins: if $n \in \mathcal{T} \cup \mathcal{G}_S^{and} \cup \mathcal{G}_M^{and}$ then, $\mu'(e) = \mu(e) - 1$ when $e \in in(n)$, and $\mu'(e) = \mu(e) + 1$ when $e \in out(n)$, otherwise $\mu'(e) = \mu(e)$.
2. Choices/XOR-splits: if $n \in \mathcal{G}_S^{xor}$ then there exists $e' \in out(n)$ such that the following is true: $\mu'(e) = \mu(e) - 1$ when $in(n) = \{e\}$, and $\mu'(e) = \mu(e) + 1$ when $e = e'$, otherwise $\mu'(e) = \mu(e)$.
3. Merges/XOR joins: if $n \in \mathcal{G}_M^{xor}$ then there exists $e' \in in(n)$ such that the following is true: $\mu'(e) = \mu(e) - 1$ when $e = e'$, and $\mu'(e) = \mu(e) + 1$ when $out(n) = \{e\}$, otherwise $\mu'(e) = \mu(e)$.

The initial state is given by a marking μ_0 where $\mu_0(e_s) = 1$, for all $e_s \in \mathcal{E}_s$, and $\mu_0(e) = 0$ for all other edges e. A node n is said to be *activated* in a state μ if there exists state μ' such that $\mu \xrightarrow{n} \mu'$. A state μ' is *reachable* from a state μ, denoted as $\mu \xrightarrow{*} \mu'$, if there exists a (possibly finite) path, $\rho : n_s, n_1, \ldots, n_f (\in \mathcal{N})$ and a finite sequence of markings $\mu_1, \ldots \mu_k$ such that $\mu \xrightarrow{n_s} \mu_1 \xrightarrow{n_1} \cdots \xrightarrow{n_f} \mu_k$ and $\mu' = \mu_k$. The notion also includes the empty sequence ϵ, *i.e.*, we have $\mu \xrightarrow{\epsilon} \mu$ for every marking μ. A *state* is reachable in the process $\mathbf{P}$ if it is reachable from the initial state μ_0. A marking/state μ is called *unsafe* if there is an edge $e \in \mathcal{F}$ such that $\mu(e) > 1$.

3.3   Soundness of BPM Processes

van der Aalst first introduced the criteria for checking correctness of business processes, called soundness in [vdA97]. Subsequently, other researchers have provided different definitions of soundness for business processes. Our definition is close to the one adopted by Fahland *et al.* [FFJ+11].

A *terminated marking* is a reachable marking where no node can be activated. A *deadlock* is a terminated marking in which at least one non-sink edge is marked. For instance, a deadlock occurs when two edges out of a choice split are merged by a synchronizer (see Fig. 6(c)), or if a synchronizer node occurs as an entry to a cycle. A BPM process contains a *lack of synchronization (multiple instances of the same activity)* if an edge can have multiple tokens in any reachable state. A lack of synchronization arises, for example, if two parallel paths emanating from of a fork are joined by a merge (see Fig. 6(d)) or if the exit of a cycle corresponds to an fork. A BPM process is *sound* if it does not contain a lack of synchronization and it is deadlock-free.

4 Soundness Checking of Process Using Petri Nets-Based Techniques

There have been a number of formal models proposed for BPM processes: Petri net, automaton, process calculus, to name a few. These formal models can be used for proving the correctness of processes through powerful techniques like model checking. We shall use Petri nets (PN) and its subclass Workflow nets (WF-nets) as the underlying formal models of BPM processes for they are easily amenable to soundness analysis through model checking.

4.1 Syntax and Semantics of Petri Nets

We briefly introduce some basic notions of Petri nets. For a more elaborate description the reader is referred to [Rei85, RT86, vdA98, AAH98]. A Petri net is a directed bipartite graph with two kinds of nodes: *places* and *transitions*. Formally, a Petri net (or simply, a net) is a tuple $N = (P, T, F)$, where

- P is a finite non-empty set of places,
- T is a finite non-empty set of transitions such that $P \cap T = \emptyset$, and
- $F \subseteq (P \times T) \cup (T \times P)$ is a set of directed arcs, called the flow relation.

A *bag* over some alphabet Σ is a function from Σ to the natural numbers that assigns only a finite number of elements from Σ a positive value. If X is a bag over an alphabet Σ and $a \in \Sigma$, then $X(a)$ denotes the number of occurrences of a in X. A bag X is a sub-bag of bag Y, denoted by $X \leq Y$, if $X(a) \leq Y(a)$ for all $a \in \Sigma$. The set of all bags over Σ is denoted as $\mathcal{B}(\Sigma)$. A bag $M \in \mathcal{B}(P)$ is called a *marking* or *configuration* or *state* of net $N = (P, T, F)$. Moreover, there is a designated marking $M_N : P \rightarrow \mathbb{N}$, called the *initial marking* which is associated with the net. The associated Petri net is denoted as (N, M_N).

An input place of a transition t is a place p iff there exists a directed arc from p to t, whereas an output place of a transition t is a place p iff there is a directed arc from t to p. $\bullet t$ and $t \bullet$ denote the input and output places of a transition t respectively (they can be as well referred to as bags over the alphabet Σ). We use dual notations $\bullet p$ and $p \bullet$ for place p. A place is called *final* (also called *sink*) if $p \bullet = \emptyset$. Denote the set of final places as Γ. Similarly, a place p is called a *source/start* place if $\bullet p = \emptyset$. The set of all start places is denoted as Λ.

At any time a place contains zero, or more tokens. A marking M of N *enables a transition* t in T iff $\bullet t \leq M$. An enabled transition can fire. When a transition t fires, it consumes one token from each of its input place p and produces one token for each of its output place p. By $M \xrightarrow{t} M'$ we mean that marking M' is reached from marking M by firing t. For a finite sequence of transitions $\sigma \in T^*$, we say $M_1 \xrightarrow{\sigma} M_k$, if there is a transition sequence $\sigma = t_1 t_2 \ldots t_{k-1}$ and a firing sequence as follows: $M_1 \xrightarrow{t_1} M_2 \xrightarrow{t_2} \cdots \xrightarrow{t_{k-1}} M_k$. A state M_k is said to be *reachable* from state M_1 iff there is a transition sequence $\sigma = t_1 t_2 \ldots t_{k-1}$ such that $M_1 \xrightarrow{\sigma} M_k$. As before, one can talk about an empty transition sequence also. A state M is said to be *reachable* if M is reachable from the initial marking M_N. A Transition $t \in T$ is dead iff there is no marking reachable from M_N enabling t.

A Petri net is *live* if and only if for every reachable state M_1 from M_N and every transition t one can find a state M_2 reachable from M_1 that enables t. A place p is called *unbounded* if for any $\rho \in \mathbb{N}$ there is a marking M reachable from an initial marking M_N such that $M(p) > \rho$. A net is *unbounded* if it has an unbounded place. Otherwise, it is *bounded*. It is possible to detect the unbounded places of a Petri net, and thus decide whether the net is bounded or not, *i.e.*, it exhibits a finite behavior or not. A Petri net is strongly connected if and only if for every pair of nodes n_1 and n_2 there is a directed path from n_1 to n_2. Normally, a restricted class of Petri nets is used for modeling and analyzing workflow procedures; they are called free-choice. A Petri net is *free-choice* if and only if, for every two transitions t_1 and t_2, if $\bullet t_1 \cap \bullet t_2 \neq \emptyset$, then $\bullet t_1 = \bullet t_2$.

A Petri net is a *state machine* if and only if all transitions have exactly one input and output place, formally, $\forall t \in T : |\bullet t| = |t \bullet| = 1$. A Petri net $N' = (P', T', F')$ is a *subnet* of Petri net $N = (P, T, F)$ if and only if $P' \subseteq P$, $T' \subseteq T$, and $F' = F \cap ((P' \times T') \cup (T' \times P'))$. Further, a subnet N' is an *S-component* of N if and only if N' is a strongly connected state machine such that $\forall p \in P', \bullet p \cup p \bullet \subseteq T'$. A Petri net N is S-coverable if and only $\forall p \in P$ there exists an S-component $N' = (P', T', F')$ of N such that $p \in P'$.

Given a Petri net $N = (P, T, F)$ we define a *PT-handle* as a place-transition pair $(p, t) \in P \times T$ iff there exist two elementary (without repetition of nodes) directed paths from p to t sharing only two nodes p and t. Similarly, a transition-place pair $(t, p) \in T \times P$ is called a *TP-handle* iff there exist two elementary directed paths from t to p sharing only nodes p and t.

Let us now provide a definition of a p-sound Petri net. A Petri net is *1-safe* if for each place $p \in P$ and for any reachable marking M, $M(p) \leq 1$. A marking is called *final* if only final places contain tokens and all the other places are empty. A Petri net is *free of deadlock* if from any reachable marking, a final marking can be reached. This can be expressed as an "ALMOST EVERYWHERE" CTL formula [CGP99] $AGEF (\bigwedge_{p \notin \Gamma} (M(p) = 0) \wedge \bigvee_{p \in \Gamma} (M(p) > 0))$. A Petri net is *p-sound* if it is free of deadlock and is safe.

4.2   Mapping BPM Processes to Petri Nets

There are a few techniques available [DDO08, KtHvdA03] for mapping BPMN process models to Petri nets, preserving behaviors. We discuss one such mapping originally proposed in [vdAHV02]. Let us call this mapping "pertriconvert", which is shown in Fig. 1. A task in the process is mapped to a corresponding transition, for example, a task A is mapped to transition t_A (see Fig. 1(b)). This mapping creates many new places and transition nodes, including dummy places (drawn in dashed borders in Fig. 1(b)), which act like dummy nodes and used for composing two patterns and silent transitions (without labels)[1]. There are

---

[1] We mark a silent transition as t_{AB}, which connects place A to place B, for notational convenience.

two kinds of transitions used in the mapping. One of them is a *regular transition* which corresponds to an activity in the original process. The other one is called a *silent transition* and is generated during the mapping of start/end nodes and forks and synchronizers (see Fig. 1). Each pattern in a BPM process is mapped to a corresponding Petri net module preserving behavior. During conversion a (well-formed) business process is decomposed into patterns shown in the figure, and the corresponding Petri net module is generated for each of the patterns. Then using the connectivity information of the BPM patterns, these Petri net modules are connected (by identifying the adjacent dummy places) and finally, the whole Petri net is created. In the figure, dummy places are not specific to one particular module; they are basically used for connecting two modules. Below are the rules for mapping.

1. A start node is mapped to a pattern with two places and one silent transition in between.
2. An end node is mapped to a similar pattern with two places and one silent transition in between.
3. An activity node is mapped to a regular transition with one input place and one output place.
4. A fork (`AND-split`) node is mapped to a silent transition with one input place and two output places.
5. A synchronizer (`AND-join`) node is mapped to a silent transition with two input places and one output place.
6. A choice (`XOR-split`) is mapped to a place with two output (silent) transitions.
7. A merge (`XOR-join`) is mapped to a place with two input (silent) transitions.

The sub-process invocation activities are treated as simple activity nodes and these nodes are mapped likewise. In this work as mentioned before we do not consider message passing in the BPM process models, so we choose to ignore this aspect. Thus, given a BPM process $\mathbf{P} = (\mathcal{N}, \mathcal{F})$ the *corresponding Petri net* is $N_{\mathbf{P}} = (P, T, F)$, generated by the mapping "pertriconvert" for a well-formed process. With this correspondence one can establish the connection between a BPM process and the mapped Petri net.

Proposition 1. *This mapping "petriconvert" always produces a free-choice Petri net.*

Proof. Notice that only transitions with multiple inputs correspond to AND-join and their inputs can only be other merges or tasks and the only place where a place can feed two transitions is at an XOR-split. Let us consider one such situation in a BPM process where an XOR-split forces one outgoing edge to an AND-join and another edge to an arbitrary activity as shown in Fig. 2(a). However, using the mapping petriconvert this fragment of BPM process will be mapped to a fragment of Petri net as shown in Fig. 1 which cannot be non-free-choice. Hence. □

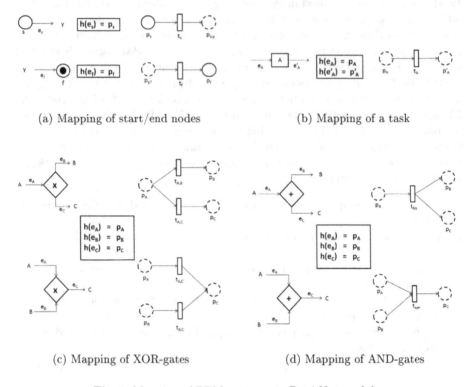

(a) Mapping of start/end nodes

(b) Mapping of a task

(c) Mapping of XOR-gates

(d) Mapping of AND-gates

Fig. 1. Mapping of BPM patterns to Petri Net modules

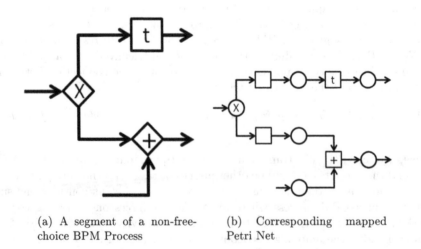

(a) A segment of a non-free-choice BPM Process

(b) Corresponding mapped Petri Net

Fig. 2. Fragment of free-choice Petri net and the corresponding BPM process

Theorem 1. *A BPM process* $\mathbf{P} = (\mathcal{N}, \mathcal{F})$ *is sound if and only if the corresponding Petri net* $N_{\mathbf{P}} = (P, T, F)$ *is p-sound. Further, the Petri net is at most linear in size of the original BPM process.*

Proof. We shall set up a bijection 'h' between the edges $\mathcal{F}$ of the process $\mathbf{P}$ and the places P of the mapped Petri net $N_{\mathbf{P}}$. A source edge in $\mathbf{P}$ is mapped to a start place in $N_{\mathbf{P}}$. Similarly, a sink edge is mapped to a final place. In $\mathbf{P}$ any edge (other than sink or source edge) can either lead into an activity or a gateway. In the former case the edge is mapped to a place leading to the appropriate transition in the mapped Petri net, in the later case the edge is mapped to a place which leads to an appropriate transition. Further when an edge leads to a gateway in the process, it is mapped to a place leading to transition/s in the Petri net depending on the type of gateway. Similar argument holds good for an outgoing edge from an activity or a gateway node. So, we have seen that for every edge $e \in \mathcal{F}$ in $\mathbf{P}$ there is a mapped place $h(e)$ in $N_{\mathbf{P}}$ and vice-versa, see Fig. 1. Define for any state μ in $\mathbf{P}$ a marking $g(\cdot)$ in $N_{\mathbf{P}}$ such that $\mu(e) = g(\mu)(h(e))$ for any $e \in \mathcal{F}$. Now we establish a connection between a state μ in $\mathbf{P}$ and the mapped marking $g(\mu)$ in $N_{\mathbf{P}}$. We claim $\mu \xrightarrow{n} \mu'$ if and only if $g(\mu) \xrightarrow{t} g(\mu')$ for some node n in $\mathbf{P}$ and some transition t in $N_{\mathbf{P}}$.   †

We consider the following three cases of a node n being activated in $\mathbf{P}$. For n being tasks, AND-splits and AND-joins, $\mu'(e) = \mu(e) - 1$ when $e \in in(n)$. As this edge e is mapped to a corresponding place leading to an appropriate transition t in Petri net, $g(\mu')(h(e)) = g(\mu)(h(e)) - 1$. In case when $e \in out(n)$, $\mu'(e) = \mu(e) + 1$. Hence $g(\mu')(h(e)) = g(\mu)(h(e)) + 1$. Therefore, $g(\mu) \xrightarrow{t} g(\mu')$.

If n is a choice (XOR-split), then there exists $e' \in out(n)$ such that $\mu'(e) = \mu(e) - 1$ when $in(n) = \{e\}$, which implies $g(\mu')(h(e)) = g(\mu)(h(e)) - 1$. And $\mu'(e) = \mu(e) + 1$ when $e = e'$, that is, $g(\mu')(h(e)) = g(\mu)(h(e)) + 1$. Otherwise $\mu'(e) = \mu(e)$, implying $g(\mu')(h(e)) = g(\mu)(h(e))$. As n will be mapped to an appropriate transition t in the mapped Petri net $g(\mu) \xrightarrow{t} g(\mu')$.

If n is a merge (XOR-join) we can handle the situation similarly.

Next we prove the claim in the other direction. Now it is given $g(\mu) \xrightarrow{t} g(\mu')$ for some t. We consider the following cases utilizing the free-choice property of nets. Suppose p is the place that feeds to a single transition t which again leads to another place p'. Then, $h^{-1}(p)$ leads to an activity and this activity feeds into $h^{-1}(p')$. Let this activity node be n. If transition t is fired under the marking $g(\mu)$ then $g(\mu')(p) = g(\mu)(p) - 1$ which implies $\mu'(h^{-1}(p)) = \mu(h^{-1}(p)) - 1$. That is $\mu \xrightarrow{n} \mu'$.

If t is a transition which is fed from only the place p and leads to two places p_1 and p_2 (wlog), then it is like an AND-split. If t is fired then $g(\mu')(p) = g(\mu)(p) - 1, g(\mu')(p_i) = g(\mu)(p_i) + 1, i = 1, 2$. This implies $\mu'(h^{-1}(p)) = \mu(h^{-1}(p)) - 1, \mu'(h^{-1}(p_i)) = \mu(h^{-1}(p_i)) + 1$, for $i = 1, 2$. That is $\mu \xrightarrow{n} \mu'$, where n is the parallel split node coming out of the edge $h^{-1}(p)$. An AND-join in the mapped Petri net can be handled in a similar fashion.

If p feeds into two transitions t_1 and t_2 which leads to two places p_1 and p_2 respectively (wlog), then it is like a XOR-split. If t_i is fired then

$g(\mu')(p) = g(\mu)(p) - 1, g(\mu')(p_i) = g(\mu)(p_i) + 1, g(\mu')(p_j) = g(\mu)(p_j), j \neq i$. This implies $\mu'(h^{-1}(p)) = \mu(h^{-1}(p)) - 1, \mu'(h^{-1}(p_i)) = \mu(h^{-1}(p_i)) + 1, \mu'(h^{-1}(p_j)) = \mu(h^{-1}(p_j)), j \neq i$. That is $\mu \xrightarrow{n} \mu'$, where n is the choice node outgoing from the edge $h^{-1}(p)$. A XOR-join in the mapped Petri net can be handled in a similar fashion.

Thus we showed $\mu \xrightarrow{n} \mu'$ if and only if $g(\mu) \xrightarrow{t} g(\mu')$. Using this, $\mu \xrightarrow{*} \mu'$ if and only $g(\mu) \xrightarrow{\sigma} g(\mu')$, for some transition sequence σ.

Now we prove that $\mathbf{P} = (\mathcal{N}, \mathcal{F})$ is sound if and only if the mapped Petri net $N_{\mathbf{P}} = (P, T, F)$ is p-sound. Suppose $\mathbf{P}$ contains a lack of synchronization. Then there is a reachable marking μ and an edge e in $\mathbf{P}$ which will contain $k\,(k > 1)$ tokens under μ. By the claim (†) there will be a reachable marking $g(\mu)$ in $N_{\mathbf{P}}$ which will assign k tokens to the place $h(e)$. That is, the Petri net $N_{\mathbf{P}}$ is not safe. Now suppose the Petri net $N_{\mathbf{P}}$ is not safe. Then there will be a reachable marking M from an initial marking M_N and a place p such that $M(p) = k\ (> 1)$. By the result proven above, there will be a reachable marking μ from an initial marking in $\mathbf{P}$ and an edge e such that $\mu(e) = k, M = g(\mu)$ and $e = h^{-1}(p)$. Hence e will be executed k number of times. That is, $\mathbf{P}$ contains a lack of synchronization.

Suppose $\mathbf{P}$ contains a deadlock. That is, it contains a terminated marking μ which assigns some token on a non-sink edge e. Using the claim (†), $N_{\mathbf{P}}$ also contains a reachable making M such that it assigns the same number of tokens on the place $h(e)$ and $M = g(\mu)$. As μ cannot proceed to any other marking (through reachability) in $\mathbf{P}$ no other marking can be reached from M in $N_{\mathbf{P}}$. Hence $N_{\mathbf{P}}$ is not free of deadlock.

Now to prove in the other direction, assume that $\mathbf{P}$ does not contain a deadlock. To show that $N_{\mathbf{P}}$ is free of deadlock. Consider an arbitrary reachable marking M in $N_{\mathbf{P}}$. Let P_m be the set of all places for which there is a path of length m to a final place. Pick a place with at least one token that can be moved (the corresponding transition has tokens in all its incoming positions), and which is also the least distant away the final place. Fire the corresponding transition. Suppose this sequence terminates after a finite number of steps. Then there are two possibilities:

1. the resulting configuration has only tokens at only the final places and no other places,
2. the resulting configuration has tokens in other places. A deadlock is found, but using our mapping with process (claim (†)) we would have found a deadlock in the process, a contradiction.

Otherwise, the sequence is infinite. But as our process (and the mapped Petri net) is free of lack of synchronization (1-safe), it follows that the set of configurations visited is finite. So, there must be a cycle. The infinite sequence will look like

$$M = M_1, M_2, \ldots, M_j, M_{j+1}, \ldots, M_k = M_j$$

Consider the tuples associated with $M_j, M_{j+1}, \ldots, M_k$. Let κ be the lowest index among $j, \ldots, k$ for which a transition with a token on its pre-set was fired.

If this number is 1, then we have a put a token in a final place and hence found a deadlock in the Petri net as well as in the process. Otherwise, suppose $\kappa > 1$. Note that when a transition is fired corresponding to a token with index j, a new token is inserted into a place whose index is $j - 1$ as we always fire a transition to reduce the distance of the token to the final place. Then a count at place $\kappa - 1$ is increased as we fire the cycle, but the count at position $\kappa - 1$ is never decreased. Therefore this cannot be a cycle, a contradiction.

From the mapping shown in Fig. 1, it can be seen there is only the addition of constant number of places for each of the patterns of the BPM process. Hence the generated Petri Net is at most linear in the size of the original BPM process. □

Corollary 1. *The mapping "petriconvert" maps a SESE block to either a TP-handle or a PT-handle. Conversely, for a handle which is guaranteed to have been created out of a well-formed process, an inverse mapping of "petriconvert" will ensure the creation of a SESE block of the original process.*

Proof. Let $\mathbf{P}_S = (\mathcal{N}', \mathcal{F}')$ be a SESE fragment of a process with e_1 and e_2 being the entry and exit edges respectively. The mapping petriconvert will produce a net $N_{\mathbf{P}_S} = (P', T', F')$. Consider bijection '$h$' between the edges $\mathcal{F}'$ of the process $\mathbf{P}_S$ and the places P' of the mapped Petri net $N_{\mathbf{P}}$, which will yield: $h(e_1) = p_{in}, h(e_2) = p_{out}$. As e_1 does not come out of any node in $\mathbf{P}_S$, pre-set of p_{in} will have nothing in common with T', and post-set of p_{in} will not be contained in T'. Hence p_{in} is the entry place for $N_{\mathbf{P}_S}$. Similar argument says that p_{out} is the exit place for $N_{\mathbf{P}_S}$.

Moreover, for a SESE net which is guaranteed to have been created out of well-formed process, a converse mapping of "petriconvert" will ensure the creation of SESE fragment of the original process. This is because the mapping h, between the edges of the process $\mathbf{P}$ and the places of the mapped Petri net is bijective, and an inverse mapping h^{-1} can be employed to produce the SESE block. □

Although LoLA [Wol07] can be employed to verify soundness of processes there are a couple of reasons for not using this tool in our work. LoLA produces a counter-example in case of violation of properties and further analysis has to be carried out to retrieve diagnostic information on processes. Also LoLA is mainly used in the Linux environment and we are looking for windows-based tool for soundness checking in order to integrate the analysis with our in-house process modeling tool InFlux. Woflan, the Workflow net analyzer [VBvdA01] offers this option. Woflan is mainly used for verifying properties of Workflow nets which is introduced next.

5   Workflow Net

In this section we discuss how soundness checking of processes can be performed through soundness checking of Workflow nets.

5.1   Soundness of WF-nets

In practice we often use Workflow nets (WF-nets) [vdA97,KtHvdA03] which are a subclass of Petri nets. Formally, a Petri net is a *WorkFlow net* (or *WF-net*) if and only if, there is only one source place i with $\bullet i = \emptyset$, there is only one sink place o with $o\bullet = \emptyset$ and if a transition t^* is added to the net connecting the place o with the place i then the resulting Petri net becomes strongly connected.

Let us consider the usual notion of soundness of WF-nets. For any place i, state $[i]$ denotes a marking which assigns a token to place i and no token to other places. A WF-net $PN = (P, T, F)$ is *sound* if and only if a state M is reachable from the state $[i]$, then the state $[o]$ can be reached from M, state $[o]$ is the only state reachable from state $[i]$ with at least one token in place o and no other token in other places, and there is no dead transition in $(PN, [i])$.

For a complex WF-net it is not easy to check the soundness property using this definition. An alternate way to check soundness of a WF-net is by extending the notion of WF-net and linking it to liveness and boundedness. An extended WF-net $\overline{PN}$ is obtained by short-circuiting o to i with a new transition t^*. For a WF-net PN it is natural to have $[i]$ as the initial marking as it corresponds to the creation of a new case, so much so, we restrict our attention to WF-net $(PN, [i])$. The following result holds [vdA97, VBvdA01] (Fig. 4 depicts such an equivalence).

Theorem 2. *A WF-net PN is sound if and only if $(\overline{PN}, [i])$ is live and bounded.*

Soundness checking is intractable for arbitrary WF-nets. However, soundness checking for free choice WF-nets can be decided in polynomial time [vdAHV02]. It can be indeed shown that the soundness of a BPM process would actually coincide with the usual notion of soundness of WF-nets, and it can be performed in polynomial time.

Theorem 3. *Suppose $PN = (P, T, F)$ is a free-choice WF-net. Then the following are equivalent.*

1. $(PN, [i])$ *is 1-safe and free of deadlock (satisfies the CTL formula).*
2. $(\overline{PN}, [i])$ *is live and 1-bounded.*

Proof. (1) $\Rightarrow$ (2): As $(PN, [i])$ is free of deadlock and 1-safe, it is possible to reach a marking M which assigns a single token only to place o and no token to any other place. Now fire the transition t^* from this marking. In the new marking place i contains a single token, from where the original net can be simulated, which generates only safe markings as $(PN, [i])$ is 1-safe. Hence $(\overline{PN}, [i])$ is 1-bounded. Now to prove $(\overline{PN}, [i])$ is live. Let t be the first transition (traversing the underlying graph in a breadth-first manner) which cannot be fired under a marking M' reachable from $[i]$. Without loss of generality, suppose there are two places (not final) $p_1, p_2 \in \bullet t$ where $M'(p_1) > 0, M'(p_2) = 0$. As the net is free-choice both these places cannot simultaneously feed tokens into any other transition. We can still reach other configurations from this marking, specifically a marking M which assigns a single token only to place o as before. However, p_1

will continue to hold tokens under M also, which is a contradiction. Therefore, $(\overline{PN}, [i])$ is live.

Now to prove (2) $\Rightarrow$ (1): If $(\overline{PN}, [i])$ is 1-bounded then the original net is safe. Suppose $(\overline{PN}, [i])$ is live. It implies that for every reachable state M from $[i]$ there is a reachable state in which t^* will be enabled. In particular, from any state M which is reachable from state $[i]$, one can reach a state $M_f + o^2$ where $\bullet t^* = \{o\}$. In this state t^* can be enabled. If t^* is fired, a new state, say $M_f + i$ is reached. As $(\overline{PN}, [i])$ is 1-bounded, M_f has to be equal to the empty state. It is easy to see that $M_f + o$ is the desired final state, hence $(PN, [i])$ is free of deadlock, that is, it satisfies the CTL formula.   □

Now we establish the connection between p-soundness and soundness of free-choice WF-nets.

Theorem 4. *Let PN be a sound free-choice WF-net. Then the short-circuited $\overline{PN}$ is S-coverable.*

Proof. By hypothesis $\overline{PN}$ is free-choice, live and bounded. By a result (Theorem 5.6 in [DE95]) every Petri net which is free-choice, live and bounded must be S-coverable.   □

The following theorem says that S-coverability of a short-circuited WF-net is a sufficient condition for 1-boundedness of the net.

Theorem 5 *(Theorem 4.4 of [VBvdA01]). Let PN be a WF-net and its short-circuited WF-net $\overline{PN}$ S-coverable. Then $(\overline{PN}, [i])$ is 1-bounded.*

Theorem 6. *Let PN be a free-choice WF-net. Then PN is sound if and only if PN is p-sound.*

Proof. Suppose PN is sound. Then $(\overline{PN}, [i])$ is live and bounded. By Theorem 4 $\overline{PN}$ is S-coverable. So, by Theorem 5, $(\overline{PN}, [i])$ is 1-bounded. Hence PN is p-sound by Theorem 3. The other side also follows from Theorem 3.   □

Theorem 7. *Let $\mathbf{P}$ is a well-formed process model having a unique start node and a unique final node. Assume pertriconvert($\mathbf{P}$) = PN, then*

1. *PN is a free-choice WF-net.*
2. *PN is sound if and only if $\mathbf{P}$ is sound.*

Proof. Use Theorems 1 and 6.   □

5.2   Multi-terminal Petri Nets to WF-nets

We have seen that soundness of processes can be checked using the results on soundness of WF-nets, the crux of the proof lies in mapping processes to Petri nets preserving soundness/p-soundness. However, one needs to check whether all

---

[2] The notation $M + p$ stands for a marking which assigns exactly one token to place p.

the Petri nets which are created through the mapping are WF-nets. If a process has multiple start nodes then we put a fork (AND-split) to connect them which results in a process having one single start node, which in turn, gets mapped into a Petri net with a unique start place. For Petri nets having multiple final places, we adopt an algorithm due to Kiepuszewski et al. [KtHvdA03]) in which a p-sound Petri net with multiple end/final places can be converted into a net with a single final place. New edges are added to the net so that every end node is marked in every run. Finally, all the end nodes of the original node are joined with a dummy end node by using a synchronizer. This algorithm preserves the p-soundness of the original multi-terminal Petri net. We call this mapping "extend".

Let the original Petri Net be a tuple $N = (P, T, F)$ and the Petri net obtained after applying the construction be $N' = \text{extend}(N) = (P', T', F')$. We formally describe the construction along the lines described in [FFJ+11].

- $\Gamma \subseteq P$ is defined as the set of final places of N
- For each $p \in \Gamma$ let $Back(p) \subseteq P \cup T$ be the set of all nodes having a path to p.
- For each place $q \in Back(p)$, T_q is defined as the set of transitions connected from q but not belonging to T_q, i.e., $T_q = \{t \in T \mid q \in Back(p) \wedge q \in P \text{ s.t. } (q, t) \in F, \text{ for } t \in T, \text{ but } t \notin Back(p)\}$.

The extended Petri net $N' = (P', T', F')$ is defined as:

- $P' = P \cup \{p_f\}$, where p_f is the new unique final place.
- $T' = T \cup \{t_f\}$, where t_f is a new transition.
- $F' = F \cup \{(t, p) \mid p \in \Gamma \wedge t \in T_p\} \cup \{(p, t_f) \mid p \in \Gamma\} \cup \{(t_f, p_f)\}$

Let us now take an example of a Petri net N (originally from [KtHvdA03]) shown in Fig. 3(a) to illustrate the construction above. In N, we have

$$\Gamma = \{p_8, p_9, p_{10}\},$$
$$Back(p_8) = \{p_1, t_1, p_2, t_2, p_3, t_3, p_8\},$$
$$Back(p_9) = \{p_1, t_1, p_2, t_4, p_4, t_5, p_5, t_6, p_6, t_8, p_9\},$$
$$Back(p_{10}) = \{p_1, t_1, p_2, t_4, p_4, t_5, p_5, t_7, p_7, t_9, p_{10}\},$$
$$T_{p_8} = \{t_4\}, T_{p_9} = \{t_2, t_7\}, T_{p_{10}} = \{t_2, t_6\}.$$

The extended net N' is shown in Fig. 3(b) which has a unique final place. The following theorem holds.

Theorem 8 [KtHvdA03]. *Let N be a p-sound free-choice Petri Net. Let N' be the Petri net obtained by using the construction above, i.e., $N' = \text{extend}(N)$. Then N' is also free choice and the nets N and N' are bi-similar. Also N' is p-sound. Moreover, N' is linear in the size of N.*

Proof. The first part of the theorem follows from Theorem 5.1 in [KtHvdA03]. As p-soundness checking implies verification of CTL properties (see Sect. 4) and bi-similarity preserves CTL formulas, N' is also p-sound.

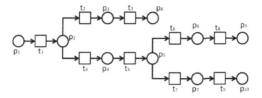

(a) A Petri net N with multiple final places

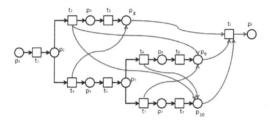

(b) Extended Petri Net $Extend(N)$

Fig. 3. Illustration of the construction Extend

In the constructed Petri net extend(N) only a new transition t_f and a place p_f are introduced. Hence the size of N' is linear in size of the N.   □

In fact, bi-similarity also preserves p-soundness in the other direction, *i.e.*, if *extend*(N) is p-sound then so is N. In fact, as a by-product we arrive at the result that the soundness checking of a BPM process can be decided in polynomial time in the size of the process. For that we use the equivalent conditions of soundness for the three formalisms in Fig. 4.

Corollary 2. *The soundness checking of a BPM process can be decided in polynomial time.*

Proof. Suppose the BPM process **P** contains only one start event and a final event. Then mapping petriconvert will produce a WF-net $N_{\mathbf{P}}$ preserving the soundness, which is linear in size of **P** (Theorem 7 and Proposition 1). The soundness of $N_{\mathbf{P}}$ can be decided in polynomial time, this uses time that is cubic in the size of the process model, by using the rank theorem for Petri nets [DE95]. Hence the claim follows. If **P** contains multiple start events then we can add a new start event which would connect all the old start events through a AND-split. In case of **P** having multiple end events, it is converted to extend(**P**) which is linear in size of **P** (Theorem 8). Then repeat the step as before to conclude that soundness of **P** can be checked in polynomial time.   □

Notice that such a result was already known in view of the work on decomposition of processes in [VVL07] and workflow related analysis in [vdAHV02].

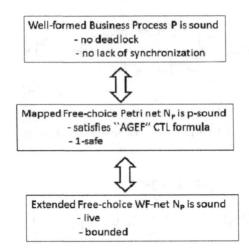

Fig. 4. Equivalent conditions for soundness for three models

However, we emphasize that we can also arrive at this result through our analysis.

We remark that the construction involving the extension of the Petri net (referred to in Theorem 8) may generate spurious errors, as illustrated by the example in Fig. 5. While the original net with multiple end nodes shown in Fig. 5(a) contains only a deadlock error (a marking under which t_2 is enabled, and places p_2 and p_3 contain tokens), and is 1-safe, $extend(N)$ contains the same deadlock and is not 1-safe (a marking which puts 2 tokens in places p_4 and p_7).

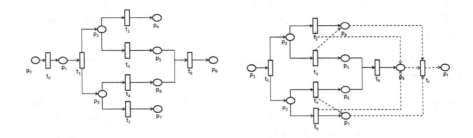

(a) Original Petri Net N with multiple end nodes with a deadlock

(b) Extended Petri Net $extend(N)$ with single end node with deadlock which is unsafe

Fig. 5. An example of extended Petri Net with spurious error

6   Checking Soundness of WF-nets with Woflan

A process is verified for soundness by looking for the absence of control-flow related errors such as, deadlock and lack of synchronization. As observed before, in this work, we convert processes to Petri nets (preserving behaviors due to soundness) and use the tools available for the analysis of Petri nets for soundness checking. There has been some work on soundness checking of industrial process models in [FFJ+11] where the authors chose to work with both LoLA and Woflan tools. These tools are robust and produce reliable results with useful diagnostic information. However for reasons mentioned earlier, we choose to work only with Woflan for checking soundness, thus obtaining useful diagnostic information, and further integrate these results with our in-house modeling tool InFlux under windows environment.

Woflan (WOrkFLow ANalyzer) [VBvdA01], is a tool used for checking the soundness of work flow models. This tool uses a combination of Petri net analysis techniques such as structural Petri net reduction and S-coverability, and a form of state space exploration. It analyzes the process model specified in terms of WF-net for syntactic correctness and qualitative properties like soundness. Woflan takes an input a model in the form of a WF-net. It reports an error if the input is not in the specified form of a WF-net. Then it checks if the short-circuited net (with an additional transition connecting the sink place with the source place) is bounded (also called proper Workflow). It also verifies whether the short-circuited net is live, thus verifying if the original net is sound. It can generate diagnostic report on unsound processes indicating the exact nature of the errors and location of their occurrences.

The diagnosis analysis of Woflan is carried out by detecting errors at different stages (executed in a step-by-step manner) [VvdA00, VBvdA01]. The diagnosis process is started by importing the WF-net from some modeling tool. As mentioned above, Woflan checks whether the imported net corresponds to the definition of a WF-net. If it does not, the tool supplies the diagnostic information such as, the list of tasks that are not connected to the source place, and/or absence of a sink place etc. At this stage the diagnosis process should stop, and the designer must make the necessary modifications to the WF-net. In the next step, Woflan checks if any thread of control cover exists. A thread of control cover is reflected by an S-component in the short-circuited WF-net. The tool returns the list of S-components in the short-circuited WF-net, as well the list of places not contained in any of these S-components. A place that does not belong to a thread of control (*i.e.* a S-component) is a suspicious place which can potentially lead to un-soundness. Nevertheless, it is possible to construct an unsound net which becomes S-coverable on short-circuiting. If there are no uncovered places then the net is 1-bounded. Moreover, if the WF-net is free-choice then the net is sound. Woflan provides another diagnostic information on the free-choice property in terms of the set of so-called confusions. A *confusion* corresponds to a non-free-choice cluster, where a cluster is a connected component of a net obtained by removing all arcs from transitions to places. A non-free choice cluster normally is a combination of XOR-split and

AND-join (see Fig. 2(b)). Woflan also searches for mismatches along with confusions. There are two kinds of *mismatches*, AND-OR mismatch and OR-AND
mismatch which correspond to TP-handle and PT-handle respectively. A mismatch occurs, for example, when two parallel flows created by an AND-split
are joined by a XOR-join (AND-OR mismatch), or two alternate flows created a
XOR-split are synchronized by an AND-join (OR-AND mistmatch). Woflan provides the diagnostic information by reporting all the TP-handles and PT-handles
in the short-circuited net. The subset of these handles in the non-circuited nets
(*i.e.*, both the paths between two nodes of the pair do not contain the short-
circuited transition) produce the useful information, they often reflect AND-OR
and OR-AND mismatches. These information will be exploited for soundness
checking method that we would employ. The tool further detects uniform invariant cover, weighted invariant cover, improper conditions etc [VBvdA01] which
will not be of much relevance to our work. The tool also looks for absence of
dead tasks and live tasks even if each place belongs to a thread of control cover
as the WF-net may still be unsound (*e.g.* when it is non-free-choice). If there
are none, it can be concluded that the net is sound.

The diagnosis view exhibits all properties of the WF-net in a tree-like manner. The root corresponds to the name of WF-net. It has two child nodes: the
top one shows the diagnosis results, and the other one captures the diagnostic
properties as depicted in Fig. 8. The diagnosis result reflects the results generated because of main properties (workflow properness, thread of control cover,
confusion, mismatches etc.). Each of these results is captured by a dialog box
supplied by the tool (see Figs. 8(b) and (c)). Again the node for diagnostic properties puts together all the diagnostic information provided by all dialogs (see
Fig. 8(d)).

7   Error Detection and Diagnosis Report for Process Models

In this section we discuss the steps we follow for checking and diagnosing errors
for BPM processes. First, we discuss different kinds of errors that occur in
processes.

7.1   Errors Occurring in Processes

As described in [RSBR14], we associate two kinds of errors associated with
process models: syntactic errors and control-flow related errors. Syntactic errors
are often caused by poor modeling practices leading to non-conformance to well-
formedness of processes [RSBR14]). The syntactic errors are listed in the first
part of Table 1. Note that the list is complete with respect to the definition of
a well-formed process and as such a well formed process does not contain any
syntactic error. Figure 6(a) gives an example of a process with no error and
Fig. 6(b) an example of a process with syntactic errors. There are two typical

Table 1. Errors in processes

Nature of error	Accumulation node
Syntactic error	
1. Start node with multiple outgoing edges [Multi_start]	Start node
2. End node with multiple incoming edges [Multi_end]	End node
3. Task node with multiple incoming/ outgoing edges [Multi_task]	Task node
4. Hanging node [Hanging]	Hanging node itself
5. Gateway with multiple incoming/ outgoing edges [Multi_gateway]	Gateway node itself
Control flow-related errors	
6. Deadlock [Deadlock]	The gateway in the associated SESE fragment where token gets stuck
7. Lack of synchronization [Lack_of_synch]	The gateway in the associated SESE fragment where multiple tokens can pass

control flow related errors that can take place in processes as mentioned in Sect. 3: deadlock (Fig. 6(c)) and lack of synchronization (Fig. 6(d)).

With each error ϵ we associate an accumulation node ϵ_α, which indicates the exact location of error occurrence; this will be needed later to calculate the depth of an error. For example, for the error Multi_start (in Table 1) the accumulation node is the corresponding start node, while for Multi_end it is the appropriate end node. The accumulation points for other syntactic errors are listed in Table 1. Finding out the accumulation point for control flow related errors is somewhat tricky. Recall that a deadlock occurs when a token gets stuck on a non-sink edge which would be an incoming edge of gateway node, an AND-join. This node is the accumulation node for this deadlock error, (*e.g.*, the gateway G2 in Fig. 6(c)). A lack of synchronization occurs when an edge has got multiple tokens in a reachable state. The node from which this edge emanates is a gateway node. (*e.g.*, the gateway XOR-join G2 in Fig. 6(d)). This join node is the accumulation point for this lack of synchronization error. The method of identification of these accumulation points through our diganostic analysis is discussed later.

7.2   Preprocessing to Find Syntactic Errors

For error detection purposes, we abstract out the control flow graph of the process and carry out a depth-first search of this graph. The reason for detecting syntactic errors in the beginning is many-fold. Although an off-the-shelf model checking tool such as Woflan [VBvdA01, VvdA00] can detect syntactic errors like hanging nodes or dead tasks (tasks that do not lead to a final place) there is no need to feed models with syntactic errors to these verification tools, when

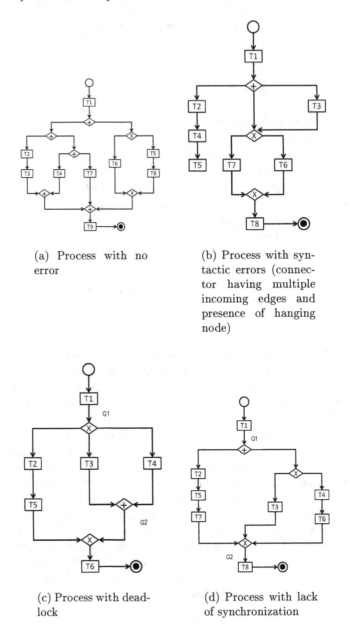

(a) Process with no error

(b) Process with syntactic errors (connector having multiple incoming edges and presence of hanging node)

(c) Process with deadlock

(d) Process with lack of synchronization

Fig. 6. Different kinds of errors occurring in InFlux Processes

they can be filtered using a pre-processor. These errors can create various problems. A start node with multiple outgoing edges causes ambiguity, whereas an end event with multiple incoming edges can cause the process to terminate more than once. An activity with multiple incoming edges can be executed twice while

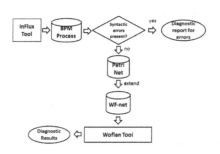

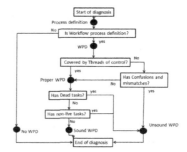

(a) Different steps for error checking for processes

(b) A schematic diagram for diagnosis of errors for processes

Fig. 7. Detection and Diagnosis of errors: schematic view

it is difficult to provide semantics for an activity with multiple outgoing edges. A hanging node does not lead to a successful termination of the process. A gateway with multiple incoming and outgoing edges can behave simultaneously as a split and merge node. If a BPM process does not contain any such error we move to the second level of error checking by performing soundness analysis with the aid of formal verification. The different steps taken for detecting errors for processes are shown in Fig. 7(a).

7.3   Verifying Soundness with Woflan

As the mapped WF-net is provided as an input to Woflan tool it checks if this net corresponds to the definition of a WF-net, which is always the case because of the preprocessing steps. Next we verify the soundness of a WF-net by exploiting its free-choice property. The tool checks for the presence of any thread of control cover of the input WF-net, which boils down to checking if the short-circuited net is S-coverable. If each of the places belongs to some thread of control cover, then the net is S-coverable and hence 1-bounded by Theorem 5, and the original process does not contain any lack of synchronization. However, the net might still not be sound. In the next step, the tool searches for non-live or dead transition in the short-circuited net by exploring state space, which would correspond to deadlock in the original process. If it fails to find one such transition it decides that the net is sound (from Theorem 6) and so is the original process (by Theorem 7). In case a dead transition or a non-live transition is found we choose the one which appears first in the list, then we look for the pre-set or post set of this transition. As we have the original process at our disposal we use the inverse of mapping petriconvert shown in Fig. 1 to find out the corresponding edge in the process and subsequently, the gateway that is causing the deadlock.

If the short-circuited net is not S-coverable, that is, there are some places which are not covered by some threads of control, then the (free-chioce) WF-net is not sound and hence the original BPM process is not sound. This follows from

Theorem 4. The places detected thus are suspicious places and possible sources of unsound behavior. However, we get the useful diagnostic information in the next step where the tool catches mismatches (confusions are non-existent as the net is free-choice). A *mismatch* is actually a TP-handle or a PT-handle. The tool clearly marks out two disjoint paths in the handle detected with source place/transition and sink transition/place properly identified. By Corollary 1 we can find out the corresponding SESE block which contains the relevant error. Further the inverse of mapping "petriconvert" will map the pre-set of sink transition/sink place to the appropriate edge on the process, from which the accumulation node of the error (that will correspond to pre-set/post-set of this edge as the case may be) can be found. A schematic view of our diagnostic analysis is shown in Fig. 7(b).

There are situations when spurious (control flow related) errors will be generated for the mapped WF-nets as observed in Sect. 5 and shown in Fig. 5. However, these errors are eliminated at the net level itself and are not reflected on the original process. Let $N = (P, T, F)$ be the original net and $N' = extend(N) = (P', T', F')$ be the net obtained after applying the construction discussed in Sect. 5. Let ϵ be an error detected on N' and $N'_\epsilon = (P'_\epsilon, T'_\epsilon, F'_\epsilon)$ be the mismatch generated by Woflan tool corresponding to this error. If $P'_\epsilon \cap (P' \setminus P) = \emptyset$ and $T'_\epsilon \cap (T' \setminus T) = \emptyset$ then ϵ is not a spurious error, otherwise it is spurious and is not reported.

7.4   Diagnostic Information

In the end, our tool will print diagnostic information on the process under consideration. In the case of syntactic errors it highlights the accumulation node for each of the errors along with incident edges. For control-flow related errors we can identify the SESE block containing the error as discussed before and highlight the block along with the corresponding accumulation node on the process. In the end, we generate a text report for all the errors detected through our tool. Our method seems to scale well as we have been able to detect and report all the errors of a process model having 1154 nodes and 102 sub-processes. This model contains 254 errors, one such error (Multi_task) is nested as deep as the 7th sub-process level.

As an example let us consider a process shown in Fig. 8(a). Its corresponding mapped Petri net is also shown. The diagnosis views due to lack of thread of control cover and PT-handle (OR-AND mismatch) are shown in Figs. 8(b) and (c) respectively. The diagnosis report appears in Fig. 8(d) and the errors are highlighted in Fig. 8(e).

8   An Experience with Diagnosis of Industrial Models

In this section we use our diagnostic framework to locate errors in industrial process models and report our experience to analyse the efficacy of this framework on industrial BPM models. One hundred and seventy four models were

Original Process

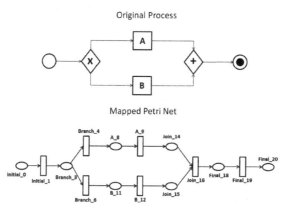

Mapped Petri Net

(a) An example process and the mapped WF-net

Thread Of Control

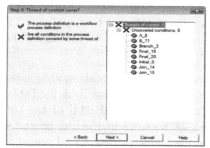

OR-AND Mismatch

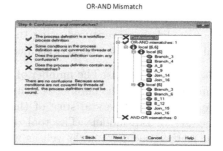

(b) A dialog box for thread of control cover

(c) A dialog box for OR-AND mismatch

Diagnosis

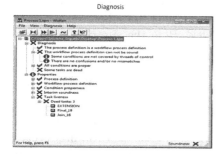

Errors in Mapped Petrinet

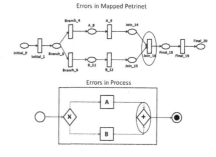

Errors in Process

(d) A diagnosis view for example process

(e) Error highlighted on WF-net and process

Fig. 8. An example process and Diagnostic information provided by Woflan

Table 2. Sub-processes and swim-lanes statistics (total no. of processes = 174)

	Minimum	Maximum	Mean	Std. Dev.
Sub-processes in a process model	0	124	6.59	20.23
Swim-lanes in a process model	0	202	11.75	26.86

Table 3. Descriptive statistics of sub-processes (total no. of 1262 sub-processes)

	Minimum	Maximum	Mean	Std. Dev.
Sub-process size	0	118	11.6	10.38
Swim-lane interactions	0	57	2.27	4.72
Coefficient of connectivity	0	2.5	0.99	0.28
Sequentiality	0	1	0.58	0.33

made available to us from a repository of Infosys. They were from seven different business domains ranging from banking to communication, to healthcare and energy. The models are checked for syntactic errors, followed by soundness. The input models were captured using the graphical editor built within the InFlux tool. The steps in the diagnostics analysis are shown in Fig. 7(b)[3].

Descriptive Statistics. The number of sub-processes in the sample models varied from 0 to 124, and the number of swim-lanes from 0 to 202 (See Table 2). Table 3 gives the descriptive statistics of the different metrics [RSBR14] of the sub-processes in the models. The tool detected 2428 errors in the sub-processes. Our method seems to scale well as we have been able to detect and report all the errors of a process model having 1154 nodes, 102 subprocesses; this model contained 254 errors with one of the errors nested as deep as 7th subprocess level. Table 4 captures the proportion of different types of errors found (See Sect. 7.1 for an explanation of each error type).

We analyzed the errors further to understand at what depth the errors frequently occur and how they correlate with the size of the subprocesses and the interaction between swim-lanes in the models. Here the size of a subprocess denotes the number of nodes appearing in it and the interaction between swim-lanes is the total number of flow-edges which pass from one swim-lane to another. Finally, the depth of an error is the shortest distance between the start node of the process and the accumulation node of the error.

Error Depth versus Error Frequency. We study the shape of the curve of error frequency vs error depth in process models. As more than one error may occur in a process model we consider the error depth of a process as the depth of the error which is maximum of all depths of errors in that process. The original hypothesis is that there is a non-linear relation between these two variables in process models

---

[3] WPD stands for Worflow Process Definition [VBvdA01], it is actually a proper WF-net.

Table 4. Error percentages

Error type	Number	Percent
Multi_start	20	0.8
Multi_end	300	12.4
Multi_task	1211	49.9
Hanging	499	20.5
Multi_gateway	389	16
Deadlock	9	0.4
Lack of Synchronization	0	0
Total	2428	100

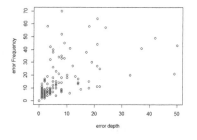

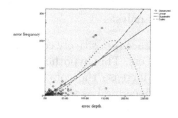

(a) Error Frequncy vs Error Depth

(b) Fitting curve for Error Frequncy vs Error Depth

Fig. 9. Relation between Error Frequency and Error Depth

across all the domains. The scatter diagram (Fig. 9(a)) supports this hypothesis. The correlation co-efficient between these two variables is $\rho = 0.585$ and in the hypothesis testing p-value is turns out to be less than 0.001 which again reconfirms the hypothesis. Further investigation is needed to understand why this behavior is observed.

Further we fit the data into some regression model by the method of curve fitting. It is impossible to build regression model of exponential and logarithmic fitting. We produce the curve fitting of error frequency with error depth excluding the models with zero errors in Fig. 9(b). The goodness of fitting can be measured by R^2 values depicted in the Table 5, in which logarithmic and power models cannot be computed. It shows the highest R^2-value is attained for quadratic curve fitting.

Correlation of Errors with Subprocess Structures. We performed correlation analyses to test the following hypotheses. For a sub-process its error occurrence is defined as the number of errors occurring within the sub-process divided by the total number of errors in the process, while error occurrence for a process

Table 5. Parameter estimates for fitting curve between error depth (indep variable) and error frequency (dep variable)

	Model summary					Parameter estimates		
	R^2	F	df1	df2	Sig	Const	b1	b2
Linear	0.473	117.664	1	131	0.000	−4.980	1.000	-
Logarithmic	-	-	-	-	-	-	-	-
Quadratic	0.486	61.495	2	130	0.000	0.448	0.572	0.003
Compound	0.468	115.470	1	131	0.000	2.772	1.029	-
Exponential	0.468	115.470	1	131	0.000	2.772	0.028	-

with no sub-process is always 1. We do not consider sound processes (with no error) for this analysis.

- Error occurrence is positively correlated with number of swim-line interactions of a sub process. This hypothesis is based on the observation that swim-lane interactions increase the coupling between sub-processes. Prior research in software engineering has shown that coupling increases error occurrences (for example, see [SB91]). This hypothesis is supported by a statistically significant correlation ($p < 0.001$) for the total number of errors and also the fact that the higher value of the correlation (measured as Pearson $\rho = 0.579$) indicates that there is strong influence of swim-line interactions on sub-process errors.
- Error occurrence is positively correlated with the size of sub-processes. The reason is that as size increases, the chances of modelers committing design errors increase. This hypothesis is also supported by a moderate and positive correlation ($\rho = 0.497, p < 0.001$) for total number of errors. Thus the size of sub-processes and swim-line interactions could be better determinants of error probability.

The correlation is significant and strong for syntactic errors with Interaction between swim-lanes and size of sub-processes ($\rho = 0.82, 0.98$ respectively). This is statistically significant by hypothesis also ($p < 0.001$).

Table 6 shows the correlations (Spearman's ρ) and their statistical significance. We used Cohen's criteria to test the strength of correlations whereby a value of ρ being 0.5 or above is considered to be strong, between 0.3 and 0.5 moderate and between 0.1 and 0.3 weak. We do not consider deadlock errors as there is no significant correlation between error occurrence and deadlock errors.

Logistic Regression Analysis. In our previous work [RSBR14], we looked at the relationship between error occurrence in a process and several associated metrics. In addition to size, three metrics were used to derive a predictive statistical model for error probability; coefficient of connectivity, sequentiality and structuredness. Here we repeat the analysis to see how these metrics would relate to error probability at the sub-process level. The dependent variable is a boolean variable 'hasError', which assumes a value of 1 if the sub-process has an error, otherwise it is 0. The independent variables considered are sub-process Size, Coefficient of Connectivity, Sequentiality and Structuredness (for definitions see [RSBR14]). All variables make statistically significant contributions to the model.

The model fit is very good with $\chi^2(4, N = 1261) = 720.68$ $(p < 0.001)$, indicating that the model is able to distinguish between cases those have errors and those have not. The Cox & Snell R Squared and Nagelkerke R squared values show that variations between 43.5 % and 58.8 % in the dependent variable are explained by the model.

The following equation predicts the presence of an error if $p(e_s) > 0.5$ where: $p(e_s) = e^x/(1 + e^x)$ and

$$x(\mathbf{Q_P}) = 0.268 * S_{\mathcal{N}}(\mathbf{Q_P}) + 1.191 * CNC(\mathbf{Q_P})$$
$$- 4.601 * \Xi(\mathbf{Q_P}) - 1.05 * \Phi(\mathbf{Q_P})$$

which is parameterized by the sub-process $\mathbf{Q_P}$ occurring in a process $\mathbf{P}$. As the Size and Coefficient of Connectivity of the sub-process increase, the probability of the sub-process having error(s) increase, whereas sub-processes with higher Sequentiality and Structuredness have lower probability of error occurrence.

Sensitivity (i.e., the percentage of cases with errors that are correctly predicted) and specificity (i.e., the percentage of cases without errors that are correctly predicted) of the regression model are 90.6 % and 77 % respectively.

9   Discussion

The aim of the work is to bring forth a cleaner representation of soundness properties of (a subset of) business processes and soundness properties of Workflow nets (WF-nets), and a connection between them. We start by defining the syntax and semantics of business processes and go on to define the soundness of them. We also introduce WF-nets, and define their syntax and semantics. Then we define soundness of WF-nets. We establish that the soundness of business processes coincide with that of WF-nets that are obtained from business processes through a (previously introduced) mapping. We have shown the equivalence between soundness of two formalisms through some intermediate results for which we provide rigorous proofs. We admit that in the process we borrow some results which were proven elsewhere (for example Theorems 2, 4 and 5 etc.), the other theorems may have used them. Some of these results were not explicitly stated before, e.g., Theorems 3 and 6, we provided proof for them

Table 6. Results related to correlations for error occurrence

	No of errors		Syntactic error	
	ρ	p	ρ	p
Interaction between Swim-lanes	0.579	<0.0001	0.832	<0.0001
Size of Sub-processes	0.497	<0.0001	0.981	<0.0001

also. Also we have stated and proved a direct result - Theorem 7, which links the soundness of a process and a WF-net as depicted in Fig. 4. Theorem 1 is stated differently in a different context in [vdAHV02]. We have chalked out a clean proof of it in our setting which is one of the major contributions of our work. Also we make use of the correspondence between a SESE fragment of a process and a TP-handle or a PT-handle of the mapped WF-net (as captured by Corollary 1) in our diagnostic framework, which is a novelty of our approach.

The equivalence result stated above (e.g., see Fig. 4) helps us to use the efficient algorithm available for soundness checking of WF-nets for verification of the soundness of business processes. As we are considering only well-formed processes that can be mapped to free-choice Petri nets (Proposition 1) our framework is capable of handling only a subset of free-choice Petri nets, though can be extended to deal with non free-choice nets with some modifications. We have shown that (proved elsewhere also [VVL07] using a different technique) the soundness of this subset of Petri nets can be decided in polynomial time in their sizes. However we use Woflan for supplying diagnostic information on WF-nets which can be mapped onto the processes, and this tool uses state space search for which the soundness checking can take up exponential time for the industrial process models that we consider for our experiment.

10   Conclusion

In this paper we have provided a formal framework for a cleaner representation of results on soundness of processes and its connection to Petri nets and WF-nets with formal proofs (using some previously known results). These results nicely tie the soundness of processes with that of WF-nets which can be verified with the Woflan tool. Based on this analysis we propose a diagnostic procedure for errors occurring in business processes using the relevant diagnostic information provided by Woflan tools for WF-nets. We acknowledge that the Woflan tool adopts state space search which can take exponential time, whereas the authors in [VVL07] claim that they can perform soundness checking of business processes (and provide some diagnostic information) in linear time using a decomposition technique in which the processes are broken down into smaller Single-entry-single-exit components [VVK08]. Each such component is then checked for soundness by employing heuristics. However, heuristics for some complex fragments might be difficult to figure out and would need expert intervention. This can be a major hindrance to automate diagnosis of processes. On the other hand, our method is automated, and our experimentation with 174 commercial BPMN models having 2428 errors has discovered that error detection in practical commercial situations are not affected by the algorithmic complexity.

Further we have conducted an empirical analysis of diagnosis of errors in BPMN-based business process models and their relationships with metrics. In particular, this work has helped enhance the understanding of occurrence of error at the sub-process and swimlane level which would be of help to modelers for modifying the processes based on this information. Moreover, this will aid in predicting error probability based on the structural characteristics at the sub-process level too.

The results of our study add to the knowledge of BPMN modeling community in the following ways: (a) it provides a method to locate errors at exact locations of the business process models, (b) it assists developers to make appropriate changes to models once the errors are detected in any business process and (c) it makes available a predictive model that the community can use to assess error probability based on easy to measure metrics such as size, coefficient of connectivity and structuredness computed at the level of sub-processes.

Acknowledgements. The authors are grateful to Prof. K. Narayan Kumar of CMI, Chennai for help on the technical content of the paper. They also thank Sidharth Bihary (a former Infosys employee) for contributing to different ideas of the paper from time to time. Thanks are due to Srivibha S., an ex-Infosys employee for helping with the implementation of the diagnostic framework. Finally the authors are indebted to anonymous referees for helpful comments which have improved the quality of the paper.

References

[AAH98] Adam, N.R., Atluri, V., Huang, W.-K.: Modeling and analysis of work-flows using Petri nets. J. Intell. Inf. Syst. **10**(2), 131–158 (1998)

[ADW08] Awad, A., Decker, G., Weske, M.: Efficient compliance checking using BPMN-Q and temporal logic. In: Dumas, M., Reichert, M., Shan, M.-C. (eds.) BPM 2008. LNCS, vol. 5240, pp. 326–341. Springer, Heidelberg (2008)

[Aosftis07] OASIS Advancing open standards for the information society. OASIS Web Services Business Process Execution Language (WSBPEL) (2007). https://www.oasis-open.org/committees/tc_home.php?wg_abbrev=wsbpel

[CGP99] Clarke, E.M., Grumberg, O., Peled, D.: Model Checking. The MIT Press, Cambridge (1999)

[CMNR06] Cardoso, J., Mendling, J., Neumann, G., Reijers, H.A.: A discourse on complexity of process models. In: Eder, J., Dustdar, S. (eds.) BPM Workshops 2006. LNCS, vol. 4103, pp. 117–128. Springer, Heidelberg (2006)

[DDO08] Dijkman, R.M., Dumas, M., Ouyang, C.: Semantics and analysis of business process models in BPMN. Inf. Softw. Technol. **50**(12), 1281–1294 (2008)

[DE95] Desel, J., Esparza, J.: Free Choice Petri Nets. Cambridge University Press, New York (1995)

[FFJ+11] Fahland, D., Favre, C., Jobstmann, B., Koehler, J., Lohmann, N., Völzer, H., Wolf, K.: Instantaneous soundness checking of industrial business process models. In: Dayal, U., Eder, J., Koehler, J., Reijers, H.A. (eds.) BPM 2009. LNCS, vol. 5701, pp. 278–293. Springer, Heidelberg (2009)

[Ham10] Hammer, M.: What is business process management? Hand. Bus. Process Manage. **1**, 3–16 (2010)

[HFKV06] Hauser, R., Friess, M., Küster, J.M., Vanhatalo, J.: Combining analysis of unstructured workflows with transformation to structured workflows. In: 10th IEEE International Enterprise Distributed Object Computing Conference (EDOC 2006) (2006)

[IC96] Issa, R.R.A., Cox, R.F.: Using process modeling and workflow integration to gain (ISO 9000) certification in construction. In: CIB W89 Beijing International Conference on Construction, Modernization, and Education, Beijing, China (1996)

[KtHvdA03] Kiepuszewski, B., ter Hofstede, A.H.M., van der Aalst, W.M.P.: Fundamentals of control flow in workflows. Acta Informatica **39**, 143–209 (2003)

[LG06] Laue, R., Gruhn, V.: Complexity metrics for business process models. In: Business Information Systems, 9th International Conference on Business Information Systems (BIS 2006), vol. 85 of LNI, pp. 1–12. GI, (2006)

[LK05] Liu, R., Kumar, A.: An analysis and taxonomy of unstructured workflows. In: van der Aalst, W.M.P., Benatallah, B., Casati, F., Curbera, F. (eds.) BPM 2005. LNCS, vol. 3649, pp. 268–284. Springer, Heidelberg (2005)

[Men07] Mendling, J.: Detection and prediction of errors in EPC business process models. Ph.D. thesis, Vienna University of Economics and Business Administration (2007)

[Men08] Mendling, J.: Metrics for Process Models: Empirical Foundations of Verification, Error Prediction, and Guidelines for Correctness. LNBIP, vol. 6. Springer, Heidelberg (2008)

[MNA07] Mendling, J., Neumann, G., van der Aalst, W.M.P.: Understanding the occurrence of errors in process models based on metrics. In: Meersman, R., Tari, Z. (eds.) OTM 2007, Part I. LNCS, vol. 4803, pp. 113–130. Springer, Heidelberg (2007)

[MRC07] Mendling, J., Reijers, H.A., Cardoso, J.: What makes process models understandable? In: Alonso, G., Dadam, P., Rosemann, M. (eds.) BPM 2007. LNCS, vol. 4714, pp. 48–63. Springer, Heidelberg (2007)

[MS08] Mendling, J., Strembeck, M.: Influence factors of understanding business process models. In: Abramowicz, W., Fensel, D. (eds.) BIS 2008. LNBIP, vol. 7, pp. 142–153. Springer, Heidelberg (2008)

[MVvD+08] Mendling, J., Verbeek, H.M.W., van Dongen, B.F., van der Aalst, W.M.P., Neumann, G.: Detection and prediction of errors in EPCs of the SAP reference model. Data Knowl. Eng. **64**(1), 312–329 (2008)

[Obj11] Object Management Group. Business process modeling notation (BPMN) version 2.0. OMG Final Adopted Specification (2011). http://www.omg.org/spec/BPMN/2.0/

[Rei85] Reisig, W.: Petri Nets: An Introduction. Springer, Berlin (1985)

[RSBR14] Roy, S., Sajeev, A.S.M., Bihary, S., Ranjan, A.: An empirical study of error patterns in industrial business process models. IEEE Trans. Serv. Comput. **7**(2), 140–153 (2014)

[RSS14] Roy, S., Sajeev, A.S.M., Sripathy, S.: Diagnosing industrial business processes: early experiences. In: Jones, C., Pihlajasaari, P., Sun, J. (eds.) FM 2014. LNCS, vol. 8442, pp. 703–717. Springer, Heidelberg (2014)

[RT86] Rozenberg, G., Thiagarajan, P.S.: Petri nets: basic notions, structure, behavior. In: Rozenberg, G., de Bakker, J.W., de Roever, W.-P. (eds.) Current Trends in Concurrency. LNCS, vol. 224, pp. 585–668. Springer, Heidelberg (1986)

[SB91] Selby, R.W., Basili, V.R.: Analyzing error-prone system structure. IEEE Trans. Softw. Engi. **17**(2), 141–152 (1991)

[VBvdA01] Verbeek, H.M.W., Basten, T., der Aalst, W.M.P.: Diagnosing workflow processes using Woflan. Comput. J. **44**, 246–279 (2001)

[vdA97] van der Aalst, W.M.P.: Verification of workflow nets. In: Azéma, P., Balbo, G. (eds.) ICATPN 1997. LNCS, vol. 1248, pp. 407–426. Springer, Heidelberg (1997)

[vdA98] van der Aalst, W.M.P.: The application of Petri nets to workflow management. J. Circuits Syst. Comput. **8**(1), 21–66 (1998)

[vdAHV02] van der Aalst, W.M.P., Hirnschall, A., Verbeek, H.M.W.E.: An alternative way to analyze workflow graphs. In: Pidduck, A.B., Mylopoulos, J., Woo, C.C., Ozsu, M.T. (eds.) CAiSE 2002. LNCS, vol. 2348, pp. 535–552. Springer, Heidelberg (2002)

[VvdA00] Verbeek, H.M.W.E., van der Aalst, W.M.P.: Woflan 2.0 a Petri-net-based workflow diagnosis tool. In: Nielsen, M., Simpson, D. (eds.) ICATPN 2000. LNCS, vol. 1825, pp. 475–484. Springer, Heidelberg (2000)

[VVK08] Vanhatalo, J., Völzer, H., Koehler, J.: The refined process structure tree. In: Dumas, M., Reichert, M., Shan, M.-C. (eds.) BPM 2008. LNCS, vol. 5240, pp. 100–115. Springer, Heidelberg (2008)

[VVL07] Vanhatalo, J., Völzer, H., Leymann, F.: Faster and more focused control-flow analysis for business process models through SESE decomposition. In: Krämer, B.J., Lin, K.-J., Narasimhan, P. (eds.) ICSOC 2007. LNCS, vol. 4749, pp. 43–55. Springer, Heidelberg (2007)

[WHM10] Weber, I., Hoffman, J., Mendling, J.: Beyond soundness: on the verification of semantic business process models. Distrib. Parallel Databases **27**, 271–343 (2010)

[Wol07] Wolf, K.: Generating petri net state spaces. In: Kleijn, J., Yakovlev, A. (eds.) ICATPN 2007. LNCS, vol. 4546, pp. 29–42. Springer, Heidelberg (2007)

MCC'2015 – The Fifth Model Checking Contest

Fabrice Kordon[1][✉], Hubert Garavel[2], Lom Messan Hillah[3],
Emmanuel Paviot-Adet[1], Loïg Jezequel[4], César Rodríguez[5],
and Francis Hulin-Hubard[6]

[1] Sorbonne Universités UPMC Univ. Paris 06, LIP6 CNRS UMR 7606,
75005 Paris, France
Fabrice.Kordon@lip6.fr
[2] Inria, Univ. Grenoble Alpes, LIG, 38000 Grenoble, France
[3] Univ. Paris Ouest Nanterre La Défense, LIP6 CNRS UMR 7606,
75005 Paris, France
[4] Univ. Nantes, IRCCyN UMR CNRS 6597, 44321 Nantes, France
[5] Univ. Paris 13, Sorbonne Paris Cité, CNRS, LIPN, 93430 Villetaneuse, France
[6] CNRS, LSV, Ecole Normale Supérieure de Cachan, 94235 Cachan, France

Abstract. The Model Checking Contest (MCC) is an annual competition between software tools that verify concurrent systems using state-space exploration techniques, either explicit-state or symbolic. The present article provides a comprehensive account of the 2015 edition of the MCC. The principles of the contest are described, together with its underlying software infrastructure. The tools that competed in 2015 are listed and the results of the contest are summarized.

1 Goals and Scope of the Model Checking Contest

For more than a decade, one has seen the emergence of software contests that assess the capabilities of verification tools on complex benchmarks, so as to identify which theoretical approaches are the most fruitful ones in practice, when applied to realistic examples. Notable events that have significant impact on the involved communities include: the SAT competition (nine editions since 2002), the Satisfiability Modulo Theories Competition (ten editions since 2005), the Hardware Model Checking Contest (eight editions since 2007), the Verified Software Competition (four editions since 2010), the Rigorous Examination of Reactive Systems Challenge (five editions since 2010), the Timing Analysis Contest (one edition in 2011), and the Competition on Software Verification (four editions since 2012). The existence of long-lasting events is a clear indication of interest and usefulness.

The *Model Checking Contest* (MCC for short — five editions since 2011) belongs to this family of scientific contests. It aims at evaluating model-checking tools that analyze formal descriptions of concurrent systems, i.e., systems in which several processes run simultaneously, communicating and synchronizing together. Examples of such systems include hardware, software, communication protocols, and biological models. So far, all editions of the MCC used Petri nets

© Springer-Verlag Berlin Heidelberg 2016
M. Koutny et al. (Eds.): ToPNoC XI, LNCS 9930, pp. 262–273, 2016.
DOI: 10.1007/978-3-662-53401-4_12

to describe such systems, but there is a long-term goal to open the contest to other model-checking tools not primarily based on Petri nets.

Since the first edition MCC'2011 within the context of a workshop associated to the Petri Nets conference, the contest team has attracted key people with diverse knowledge, who are actively contributing to the selection of benchmark models, the automated generation of temporal-logic formulas, and all technical aspects related to performance measurements and tool assessment. Today, the MCC team gathers scientists from CNRS, Inria, Université Pierre & Marie Curie, Université Paris Ouest Nanterre La Défense, Université Paris 13, and Université de Nantes.

The present paper reports about the fifth edition MCC'2015, which was organized in Brussels as a satellite event of the 36th International Conference on Application and Theory of Petri Nets and Concurrency. This is the first publication devoted to the MCC since its origins, and it will be followed by detailed presentations of the tools that reached the top-three podiums in June 2015. The paper is organized as follows. Section 2 presents the collection of benchmarks on which the participating tools are assessed. Section 3 explains how temporal-logic formulas are automatically generated for the contest examinations. Section 4 details how tools are executed and how information is retrieved from their execution. Section 5 lists the participating tools, and Sect. 6 summarizes the results of the contest. Finally, Sect. 7 gives some concluding remarks and suggests desirable enhancements for future MCC editions.

2   Collected Benchmarks

All tools participating in a given edition of the MCC are evaluated on the same benchmark suite, which is updated every year. The yearly edition of the MCC starts with a *call for models* inviting the scientific community at large (i.e., beyond the developers of the participating tools) to propose novel benchmarks that will be used for the MCC. The benchmarks obtained this way are merged with those of the former years to form a growing collection (continuously expanded since 2011) that gathers systems from diverse academic and industrial fields: software, hardware, networking, biology, etc. This collection of benchmarks[1] is a perennial result of the MCC organization work — should the contest halt, the collection would remain available to the scientific community. The usefulness of this collection is already witnessed by over thirty scientific publications[2].

Models and Instances. The collection of MCC benchmarks consists of *models*, each corresponding to a particular academic or industrial problem, e.g., a distributed algorithm, a hardware protocol in a circuit, a biological process, etc. Models may be *parameterized* by one or a few variables representing quantities such as the number of agents in a concurrent system, the number of message

---

[1] The collection of benchmarks is available from http://mcc.lip6.fr/models.php.
[2] The list of publications is available from http://mcc.lip6.fr.

Table 1. Accumulation of models and instances over the years (supplemented with the 2016 data)

Year	2011	2012	2013	2014	2015	2016
New models	7	12	9	15	13	*11*
All models	7	19	28	43	56	*67*
New instances, among which:	95	101	70	138	121	*139*
– *new colored nets*	43	37	24	33	27	*9*
– *new P/T nets*	52	64	46	105	94	*130*
– *new NUPNs (among P/T nets)*	0	0	1	5	15	*62*
All instances	95	196	266	404	525	*664*

exchanged and the like. To each parameterized model are associated as many *instances* (typically, between 2 and 30) as there are different combinations of values considered for the parameters of this model; each non-parameterized model has a single associated instance. Each instance corresponds to a Petri net that will actually be submitted to all participating tools.

Models come from diverse sources: 34 % of the models originate from high-level colored Petri nets, which are then automatically unfolded to P/T nets; 14 % of the models have been produced from formal descriptions written in LOTOS [18] or more recent process-calculi languages that translate to LOTOS, from which Petri nets can be automatically generated using the CADP toolbox [17]; the remaining 52 % have been manually specified as genuine P/T nets, e.g., using a graphical editor. Table 1 illustrates the growth of the collection since the first edition of the MCC; the notion of NUPN (*Nested-Unit Petri Net*) is discussed below.

All instances in the MCC benchmark collection are provided as PNML files [19]. After each annual call for models, the MCC model team examines all the files received to check their conformance to the PNML standard and, if needed, normalize their contents to avoid some known ambiguities of PNML — for instance, to give the same value to the id and **name** attributes of each place and each transition (thus ensuring unique naming conventions across all the participating tools), and to replace multiple occurrences of arcs between the same place and the same transition by a unique arc with multiplicity greater than one.

Forms and Properties. Each MCC model is described in a *form*, which is a two- or three-page PDF document giving a high-level description of the model: origin, functionality, bibliographic references, and graphical representation (if available). The form defines the model parameters, if any, and their corresponding values, as well as the size (number of places, transitions, and arcs) of each instance of the model. The form also lists essential *properties* of the model, both *structural* (e.g., strongly connected, loop free, etc.) and *behavioural* ones (e.g., safeness, liveness, reversibility, etc.) — the truth value of a property being unknown for those instances too complex to be analyzed. Finally, the form gives information about the size of the reachable marking graph of each instance (number of markings, number of transition firings, maximal number of tokens per place and per marking) — possibly with unknown or approximate answers. The contents of the model forms evolve regularly, as new information and properties are added every year.

Basically, each form is a LaTeX file to be manually written by the person who submitted the model. This approach raises practical issues, as the numerical and Boolean answers provided for sizes and properties are sometimes incomplete or erroneous. Moreover, the annual addition of new models in the collection and of new properties in the forms makes manual handling cumbersome and error-prone. To address this issue, an automated tool chain has been progressively developed by the MCC model team: each P/T net instance is processed in sequence by two tools, PNML2NUPN [10] and CÆSAR.BDD [1], to produce a LaTeX file containing numerical and Boolean answers that help checking and completing manually-written model forms. This tool chain works satisfactorily, although with three limitations: *(i)* it does not handle colored-net instances — but their structural and behavioural properties, as well as the size of their marking graphs, are expected to be the same as for the corresponding unfolded P/T-net instances; *(ii)* for P/T nets that are not one-safe, answers given for behavioural properties may be approximate; *(iii)* for large and/or complex instances, behavioural properties also get approximate answers, as the symbolic (BDD-based) marking-graph exploration (done using the CUDD library [2]) is halted by a timeout after a few minutes.

Nested-Unit Petri Nets. A large proportion (43 %) of the MCC models are one-safe P/T nets (also called elementary nets or condition-event systems). Even if such nets are simpler than colored nets or general P/T nets, most related verification problems are computationally hard, namely PSPACE-complete [15]; indeed, there are many one-safe P/T-net instances that no participating tool has been able to entirely analyze so far.

A plausible explanation for such difficulties is that verification is made harder because relevant information about the real systems to be modelled has been lost when formalizing these systems as low-level Petri nets: preserving such information all along the modelling and analysis steps would hopefully make verification easier. This is the motivation behind *Nested-Unit Petri Nets* (NUPN for short) [16], a P/T-net extension that retains structural and hierarchical information by recursively expressing a net in terms of parallel and sequential compositions.

In 2015, the NUPN paradigm was adopted by the MCC team to foster progress in the analysis of large models. A PNML tool-specific extension[3] has been defined to incorporate NUPN information in PNML files, and 8 models (totalling 21 instances) have been enriched with NUPN information. At present, 4 model checkers (CÆSAR.BDD, ITS-Tools, LTSmin, and pnmc) are already able to exploit the NUPN information.

---

[3] See http://mcc.lip6.fr/nupn.php.

3   Formulas

Tools competing in the MCC are evaluated over four categories of verification tasks: state-space generation, reachability analysis, LTL analysis, and CTL analysis. To maximize tool participation, we further divided the three latter categories into subcategories containing only formulas with a restricted syntax. In 2015, we progressed in the consolidation of these formula languages and provided simplified BNF grammars for each (sub)category, still preserving backward compatibility with previous MCC editions.

Each tool developer may choose in which categories/sub-categories the tool participates. For each model instance and each subcategory, 16 formulas are automatically generated and stored into a single XML file (of which a textual version is also provided for the convenience of tool developers). Each tool participating in the corresponding subcategory is requested to evaluate, on the corresponding instance, all or part of the formulas contained in the XML file.

One of the main criticisms about the formulas generated for MCC'2014 was that many of these formulas were trivially true or false, or could be decided immediately by examining only the initial state or a small fragment of the state space. Generating formulas that are "harder" to model check (not to say realistic verification goals) is a difficult problem, at least because: *(i)* we need a large amount of formulas (in 2014, we used about 40 000 formulas), and *(ii)* we usually have little knowledge about the expected properties of the MCC models gathered over the years (namely, only a few models come with associated "meaningful" properties).

To improve the quality of formulas, in 2015 we adopted a new strategy for their generation. Using the grammar of each category, we generated random formulas of up to certain depth (7 operators). We subsequently filtered all generated formulas, in two steps. First, we used SAT solving to filter out formulas being equivalent to true or false independently of the model. Each formula passing the SAT filter was then submitted to SMC [12], a CTL bounded model checker that we developed ad-hoc for the competition. If SMC was able to decide the satisfiability of the formula by examining only the first 1000 reachable states (computed using BFS exploration), then we discarded the formula. Otherwise, we considered the formula to be *hard* enough and included it in the XML file. The process continued until either we found 16 hard formulas or we had examined 320 (= 20 × 16) random formulas. In the latter case, we completed the file with (up to 16) random formulas, which might be fairly easy to solve; such a situation mainly happened for small nets having less than 1000 reachable states, or when the formula syntax in a given category made it difficult to find hard formulas — the particular grammar chosen for formula has an impact in this respect, and this is indeed something to work on for the next editions of the MCC.

Among the formulas submitted to SMC, 33.0 % were declared satisfiable, 57.4 % unsatisfiable, and 9.6 % hard. In other words, less than 10 % of the generated random formulas were actually retained. About 11.3 % of the XML files had to be completed with at least one random formula, leading to a proportion of 8.7 % non-hard formulas.

The generation-and-filtering strategy took about two days of CPU to produce the 65 490 formulas used in the 2015 edition. The higher quality of this generation process is confirmed by the increase of CPU time required to process all examinations on all models for all tools. Compared to MCC'2014 (157 days of CPU time), we observed a ten-time increase for MCC'2015 (1541 days of CPU time) where only a two-time increase was expected, based on the new models and larger set of formulas introduced in 2015. Such a larger increase, which actually matches the aforementioned filtering rate (9.6 %), clearly indicates that the new strategy produces more demanding formulas that better exercise the capabilities of model checkers.

4   Monitoring Environment and Experimental Conditions

Due to, at least, the growth of the MCC collection of benchmarks, the number of required executions to evaluate tools is increasing every year. From 54 293 in 2013, it grew to 83 308 in 2014, and to 169 078 in 2015. Such a number of executions thus requires a dedicated software environment that can take benefits from recent multi-core machines and powerful clusters. Moreover, we need to measure key aspects of computation, such as CPU or peak memory consumption, in the least intrusive way.

Since the second edition of the Model Checking Contest in 2012, we have been confident that relying on virtual machines to operate tools is a suitable solution. To achieve this in an automated way, we developed *BenchKit* [20], a software technology (based on QEMU) for measuring time and memory during tool execution. First used during MCC'2013, *BenchKit* was then enhanced for MCC'2014 with new management facilities to ease its operation and, for MCC'2015, with the possibility to assign several cores to virtual machines.

BenchKit is operated using configuration files that define consistent sets of runs. Each run represents an execution, i.e., one tool performing one examination on one (instance of a) model. To cope with the ever-increasing need for CPU, we used several machines in 2015, namely:

- *bluewhale03* (Univ. Geneva), a 40-core, 2.8-GHz machine with 512 GB of RAM,
- *ebro* (Univ. Rostock), a 64-core, 2.7-GHz machine with 1024 GB of RAM,
- *quadhexa-2* (Univ. Paris Ouest Nanterre), a 24-core, 2.66-GHz machine with 128 GB of RAM,
- *small* (Sorbonne Univ., UPMC), a portion of a cluster consisting of five 24-core, 2.4-GHz nodes with 64 GB of RAM each.

These powerful computing machinery (152 cores in total) enabled each tool to be run in a 64-bit virtual machine with 16 GB of memory and either one core (for sequential tools) or four cores (for parallel tools).

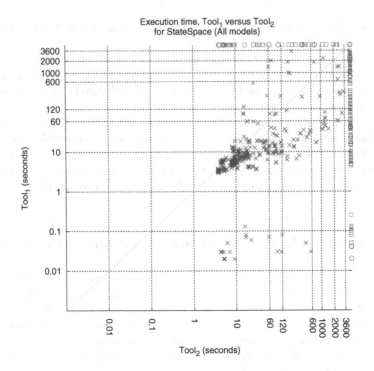

Fig. 1. Example of comparison chart between $Tool_1$ and $Tool_2$. Each point represents an execution and, if below (resp. above) the diagonal, indicates that $Tool_1$ (resp. $Tool_2$) has won. Faulty executions are displayed on the top and right lines. The grey color means the missing tool did not compete, and the red color means the tool was disagreeing with the majority of other tools. (Color figure online)

To enable relevant comparison of executions between tools, we divided the set of runs into several consistent subsets. Within each subset, all the examinations related to a given model have been executed on the same machine for all the tools. Then, from the raw data produced by *BenchKit* (execution time, total CPU, memory peak, sampling of memory and CPU usage), we automatically generated summary charts in HTML format. Figure 1 provides an example of such a chart comparing two tools in a given examination. Such charts are produced for all the possible tool comparisons and tell how well the verification techniques implemented in the tools scale with the benchmarks under study.

The post-analysis scripts that aggregate data, generate summary HTML pages, and compute scores for the contest are implemented using 15 kLOC of Ada and a bit of bash. *BenchKit* itself consists in approximatively 1 kLOC of bash.

5   Participating Tools

Ten tools were submitted in 2015: Cunf [3], GreatSPN-Meddly [4], ITS-Tools [5], LoLA 2.0 [6], LTSmin [7], Marcie [8], pnmc [9], PNXDD [11], StrataGEM 0.5.0 [13], and TAPAAL [14] (four variants, two of them using parallel computing).

Table 2. List of participating tools in 2015 and the techniques they implement.

Tool information		Verification techniques																
Name	Institution	P/T nets	Colored nets	Parallel comp.	CEGAR	Dec. Diag.	Explicit	Net Unfold	SAT/SMT	Stat. Compr.	State Eq.	Stat. Var. Re	Struct. Red	Stub. Sets	Symmetries	Topological	Unfold. to P/T	Use NUPN
Cunf	Univ. Paris 13 (FR)	✓						✓	✓									
GreatSPN-Meddly	Univ. Torino (IT)	✓	✓			✓									✓			
ITS-Tools	UPMC (FR)	✓	✓	✓	✓	✓			✓							✓		✓
LoLA 2.0	Univ. Rostock (DE)	✓					✓				✓			✓	✓	✓		
LTSmin	Univ. Twente (NL)	✓		✓		✓						✓						✓
Marcie	Univ. Cottbus (DE)	✓	✓			✓										✓		
pnmc	IRT St-Exupery (FR)	✓				✓												✓
PNXDD	UPMC (FR)	✓				✓										✓		
StrataGEM	Univ. Geneva (CH)	✓	✓			✓										✓		
TAPAAL	Univ. Aalborg (DK)	✓	✓				✓				✓		✓					

Table 2 lists the participating tools, and indicates which classes of Petri nets and which verification techniques are supported by each tool: parallel computing, CEGAR, use of decision diagrams (symbolic approaches), explicit model checking, unfolding, use of SAT/SMT solvers, use of state-compression techniques (other than decision diagrams), exploitation of state equations, static variable reordering, use of structural reductions, use of stubborn sets, exploitation of symmetries, use of topological or structural information, unfolding transformation into equivalent P/T nets (for colored nets), and use of Nested-Unit Petri Net (NUPN) information when available.

6   Results

All examinations on the models were processed in the following way. First, tools were invoked on the "known" models (i.e. those of past years). Then, they were confronted with the "scrambled" models that are the "known" ones but presented as new ones. Finally, they had to process the new "surprise" models (those submitted by the community in 2015). This led to 169 078 runs, from which we extracted a much larger number of computed values (e.g., size of the state space, maximum number of tokens per marking, result of a given formula) that were stored and compiled in order to: *(i)* evaluate the reliability of the tools, and then *(ii)* compute an overall score.

Computation of the Reliability of the Tools. Ensuring the reliability of a verification tool is important. We thus decided to use the Model Checking Contest for this purpose too. However, determining if the answers issued by tools are correct is a difficult question, due to the lack of a reference verified result. So, we compare the results of each tool to those of other tools, relying upon a majority-based approach to compute the scores. This is done in three steps: *(i)* identifying the set of values for which a majority of tools agree; we need at least three agreeing tools to select such a value, *(ii)* identifying, for each tool, the c computed values that are produced within this set, and *(iii)* checking, within these c values, the n ones that are correct by the identified majority.

Table 3 (central part) summarizes the reliability rate we computed for each tool. The four columns provide the following data: the computed rate, the number of correct values (C), the number of values in the selected set for the tool (S), and, as an indication, the number of examinations the tool participates in (i.e. provides at least an answer for one instance of a model). Then, the reliability is trivially the ratio C/S.

Some outcomes need an explanation. There are tools with a lower reliability rate such as GreatSPN-Meddly, ITS-Tools, LTSmin, or one of the TAPAAL variants. In fact, these tools exhibited bugs introduced in recent development (TAPAAL), or translation mistakes (in formulas for GreatSPN-Meddly and ITS-Tools, in the PNML import for LTSmin). Such bugs could not be identified by their developers before the full benchmark was passed and compared to other tools outputs. We believe this is a valuable information for tool developers, helping them to increase the confidence when implementing new algorithms.

In some cases, we also have tools for which the reliability rate was computed on a very small dataset. Usually, these tools only participate in one examination. For PNXDD, we discovered too late a configuration problem in the virtual machine that was only standing for scrambled and surprise models. We regret this problem was not detected during the qualification procedure. StrataGEM, and pnmc also participated in only one examination, which probably makes the tool simpler, and thus easier to be more reliable.

We think the procedure is fair, even if rare cases where the majority of tools might be wrong cannot be excluded. Some tool developers have reported that they included the outputs of the MCC in their own built system to increase the reliability of their tool, which will most probably lead, next year, to a better reliability rate.

Computation of the Overall Score for Each Tool. All computed values were then used to elaborate scores. Only correct values were considered and one

Table 3. Summary of results — grey cells mean that the tool was among the top-three winners. When there are several variants for a tool, only the best variant is considered for the podium.

Tool	Reliability informations				Examinations scores			
	Rate	Correct	Selected	Nb	State	Reach.	CTL	LTL
Cunf	96.96%	4728	4876	3	–	17894	–	–
GreatSPN-Meddly	62.30%	11966	19206	10	6434	43686	withdrawn	–
ITS-Tools	64.05%	10890	17003	4	10696 ^{3rd}	31279	–	–
LoLA 2.0	97.80%	25796	26378	6	–	111869 ^{1st}	–	–
LTSmin	79.13%	13995	17687	5	7806	45060	–	–
Marcie	92.52%	18443	19934	10	14714 ^{1st}	66579 ^{3rd}	33381 ^{1st}	–
pnmc	99.59%	741	744	1	12554 ^{2nd}	–	–	–
PNXDD	88.89%	56	63	1	562	–	–	–
STrataGEM	100.00%	243	243	1	5600	–	–	–
TAPAAL (SEQ)	99.88%	22880	22907	7	6132	79579 ^{2nd}	–	–
TAPAAL (MC)	99.75%	23247	23306	7	5966	76256	–	–
TAPAAL-OTF (SEQ)	96.19%	19001	19733	7	3872	66316	–	–
TAPAAL-OTF (PAR)	88.43%	15253	17248	7	3650	48129	–	–

wrong value disqualifies the tool for the considered examination on the instance of the model. When results were uncertain (i.e., only two distinct answers), the respective reliabilities of the tools were compared to decide which tool was right. We also discarded lonely answers from tools whose reliability was less than 0.9. Then, outputs were weighted: ×1 for "known" models, ×2 for "scrambled" ones and ×3 for "surprise" ones. Finally, points were summed up for each tool and for each examination category: state-space generation, reachability formulas, CTL formulas, and LTL formulas.

The right part of Table 3 summarizes this result. First, no tool did compete on the LTL formulas, which is unfortunate. Marcie won the state-space generation, followed by pnmc and ITS-Tools, which scaled well but exhibited low reliability in many cases. LoLA won the reachability examination, followed by TAPAAL (the "classical" sequential version), and Marcie. For CTL formulas, Marcie is the only participant (and winner) because a bug was signaled too late by the GreatSPN developers in the CTL translation; they preferred to withdraw the tool from this competition.

We are aware that a single table cannot express all details[4] found in the hundreds of thousands charts and tables generated automatically from execution runs. However, we believe such results are useful for the community to: (i) recognize the great effort of building prototype tools and use them for the verification of real systems, (ii) identify the forces and weaknesses of these tools, and (iii) participate in their improvement. In particular, we note that most of the winning tools share a particularity: they combine several techniques, as shown in Table 2.

---

[4] See http://mcc.lip6.fr/2015/results.php.

7   Conclusion — Future Evolutions

All in one, the fifth edition of the Model Checking Contest was successful and ran smoothly, despite the many novelties introduced in 2015: support of Nested-Unit Petri Nets (to open the contest to verification tools operating on concurrent state machines), new XML syntax for temporal-logic formulas, enhanced techniques to automatically generate non-trivial formulas, and virtual machines with multiple cores in *BenchK*it. The main disappointment for the MCC team was the absence of submitted tools participating in the LTL category: this could perhaps be interpreted as a sign of decreasing academic interest in linear-time formulas and, if confirmed over the coming years, a pragmatic answer to the longstanding linear-time vs branching-time dilemma.

The following developments are planned for the next editions of the Model Checking Contest:

- *Concerning the models:* future calls will enrich the collection with new models; the forms will be made more detailed by adding a few missing model properties (e.g., extended free choice); an online repository is being developed, which will offer easy access (using web browsing or programming interfaces) to the collection of models; the proportion of NUPN models is expected to grow, as work is going on to automatically synthesize a NUPN structure for "flat" 1-safe nets.
- *Concerning the formulas:* the community will be actively encouraged to submit properties together with the surprise models, so as to have more "semantically meaningful" formulas associated to each model; the grammar used to describing the syntax of certain categories of formulas will be improved; the generation algorithms will be improved to produce "higher-quality" formulas, even at the cost of discarding some contest categories if necessary.
- *Concerning the contest itself:* new procedures will be added for an early detection of issues similar to that discovered too late with the PNXDD tool (see Sect. 6); also, if tool developers agree, negative scores could be introduced to penalize tools giving incorrect verdicts.

Acknowledgments. The MCC team heartily thanks all scientists who proposed new models in 2015 and the tool developers for their participation effort. Acknowledgments are also due to the Universities of Rostock, Geneva, Paris Ouest Nanterre La Défense, and Pierre & Marie Curie for giving access to the powerful computers needed to operate the contest. We are grateful to Hugues Evrard for proof-reading the present paper.

References

1. CÆSAR.BDD. http://cadp.inria.fr/man/caesar.bdd.html
2. CUDD. http://vlsi.colorado.edu/~fabio/CUDD
3. Cunf. https://github.com/cesaro/cunf
4. GreatSPN-Meddly. http://www.di.unito.it/~greatspn/index.html
5. ITS-Tools. http://ddd.lip6.fr

6. LoLA 2.0. http://www.service-technology.org/lola
7. LTSmin. http://fmt.cs.utwente.nl/tools/ltsmin
8. Marcie. http://www-dssz.informatik.tu-cottbus.de/DSSZ/Software/Marcie
9. pnmc. http://ahamez.github.io/pnmc
10. PNML2NUPN. http://pnml.lip6.fr/pnml2nupn
11. pnxdd. https://projets-systeme.lip6.fr/trac/research/NEOPPOD/wiki/pnxdd
12. SMC. https://github.com/mcc-petrinets/formulas/tree/v1.0-mcc2015/smc
13. StrataGEM 0.5.0. http://sourceforge.net/projects/stratagem-mc
14. TAPAAL. http://www.tapaal.net/
15. Cheng, A., Esparza, J., Palsberg, J.: Complexity results for 1-safe nets. Theor. Comput. Sci. **147**(1–2), 117–136 (1995)
16. Garavel, H.: Nested-unit petri nets: a structural means to increase efficiency and scalability of verification on elementary nets. In: Devillers, R., Valmari, A. (eds.) Petri Nets 2015. LNCS, vol. 9115, pp. 179–199. Springer, Heidelberg (2015)
17. Garavel, H., Lang, F., Mateescu, R., Serwe, W.: CADP 2011: a toolbox for the construction and analysis of distributed processes. Int. J. Softw. Tools Technol. Transf. (STTT) **15**(2), 89–107 (2013)
18. ISO/IEC. LOTOS – A Formal Description Technique Based on the Temporal Ordering of Observational Behaviour. International Standard 8807, International Organization for Standardization – Information Processing Systems – Open Systems Interconnection, Geneva, September 1989
19. ISO/IEC. High-level Petri Nets - Part 2: Transfer Format. International Standard 15909–2:, International Organization for Standardization – Information Technology – Systems and Software Engineering, Geneva (2011)
20. Kordon, F., Hulin-Hubard, F.: BenchKit, a tool for massive concurrent benchmarking. In: 14th International Conference on Application of Concurrency to System Design (ACSD 2014), Tunis, Tunisia, pp. 159–165. IEEE Computer Society, June 2014

Running LoLA 2.0 in a Model Checking Competition

Karsten Wolf[✉]

Institut für Informatik, Universität Rostock, Rostock, Germany
karsten.wolf@uni-rostock.de

Abstract. We report on the performance of the tool LoLA 2.0 in the model checking contest (MCC) 2015. As in the years before, LoLA ranked first in the reachability category of the contest. We identify critical success factors and discuss the impact of the contest design. Conclusions include further improvements for the tool as well as suggestions concerning the setup of future contests.

1 Introduction

LoLA [27] (a Low Level Petri net Analyzer) is a tool for explicit traversal of the state space of a place/transition net. Development started in 1997. The original purpose was the validation of state-of-the-art state space reduction techniques which now serve as the core set of verification techniques. LoLA is implemented in the C++ programming language and available under an open-source licence at www.service-technology.org. In 2014, version 2.0 was released. It can evaluate arbitrary queries specified in temporal logic (LTL or CTL). Its particular strength, however, is checking reachability of deadlocks or reachability of states satisfying a given property. Several case studies [7,10,14,18,23,24] appreciate the capabilities of LoLA to check reachability.

Consequently, LoLA has participated with constant success in the reachability categories of the Petri net model checking contests (MCC) which have been organized since 2011 [9]. The last competition taken into consideration for this paper took place in 2015. Our main contribution here is the identification of major factors for the sustaining success of LoLA.

We shall proceed as follows. First, we briefly elaborate on the design of the MCC. This way, we can use data from the MCC for illustrating subsequent observations. Then we analyse the impact of the explicit state space traversal used by LoLA. Related to this topic, we go through available state space reduction techniques and their contribution to the overall performance. We continue with looking at selected implementation details of LoLA. Finally we report on design decisions that directly respond to challenges in the design of the MCC.

2 The Model Checking Contest

For a general introduction to the contest, we refer to the paper on MCC 2015 also in this volume. Here, we discuss only a few details that are relevant to our subsequent discussion and that have not been reported there.

© Springer-Verlag Berlin Heidelberg 2016
M. Koutny et al. (Eds.): ToPNoC XI, LNCS 9930, pp. 274–285, 2016.
DOI: 10.1007/978-3-662-53401-4_13

In all subsequent numerical analyses, we shall ignore the "scrambled" models, as the corresponding results are roughly the same as for "known" models. The only difference is that there is slightly less time available for scrambled models as their translation from the PNML [1] format into the input language of the tool may require some of the available time.

We only reflect on the reachability category as this is the only one where LoLA participated. This category was further divided into six *subcategories*: *deadlock, fireability, fireability-simple, cardinality, bounds,* and *compute-bounds.* In the deadlock subcategory, reachability of a deadlock (a marking that does not enable any transition) in a given net instance is investigated. In the compute-bounds subcategory, an arithmetic expression E referring to the number of tokens on places is given. The task is to determine $\max\{E(m) \mid m \text{ reachable}\}$. In all other categories, tools decide reachability or invariance of a given state predicate. A state predicate is a Boolean combination of propositions. The subcategories use different atomic propositions. The reachability competition comprised a total of 3150 examinations containing 42525 individual queries for each tool. 34125 queries (all but the compute-bounds subcategory) have a Boolean result and shall be the basis for subsequent analysis. This analysis considers only the number of completed queries. We ignore the "honour" points that were issued but had no significant impact on the ranking of tools.

In 2013, scores were calculated separately for each subcategory and each net class (coloured, place/transition). That is, there was a winner for, e.g., deadlocks in place/transition nets and another winner for fireability-simple in coloured nets. In 2014, all subcategories were aggregated but net classes were kept separate (that is, there was just one winner for the whole reachability category in place/transition nets, but a second one for reachability in coloured nets). In 2015, both subcategories and net classes were aggregated (that is, there was only a single winner for the whole reachability category). None of the changes was announced in the corresponding call for participation. Consequently, participants were in the very unfortunate situation that they could not anticipate the impact of their decisions (concerning participation in a category or subcategory) w.r.t. the final scoring.

Supporting coloured net input and all types of atomic propositions requires tremendous programming efforts and a deep understanding of semantic subtilities of the particular input language concerning the arc inscriptions. In the past, several tools attempted to support coloured nets but failed to integrate them correctly. In 2015, this was one of the reasons for LoLA to win the reachability competition despite rejection of any coloured net input. The substantial effort for supporting coloured nets is even more problematic for newcomers to the contest. Consequently, we would suggest to return to a separate scoring for the two net classes, or to let tools choose whether to read a net instance either in place/transition or in coloured net format, but to score the instance only once.

3 Explicit Versus Symbolic Model Checking

Some participants in the MCC use symbolic verification techniques. Others, including LoLA, do explicit state space verification.

An explicit model checker generates and evaluates states one by one. Its main strategy for alleviating state explosion is to apply state space reduction. That is, it traverses a subset of the reachable states that is as small as possible yet, by construction, sufficiently large for evaluating the given query. Different queries require different subsets to be traversed. Building a state space that preserves several queries at once is not recommendable since it easily grows beyond any limit. Consequently, LoLA processes a single examination (16 queries for the same net instance) by generating 16 separate reduced state spaces. It must carefully schedule the individual queries w.r.t. the available run time.

In symbolic model checking, an implicit representation of the set of reachable states, or the set of paths through the system is generated. Here, we focus on decision diagrams [3,4] for representing sets of states (other symbolic techniques such as SAT based model checking [6] have not been used in the MCC). A reachability check consists of generating a decision diagram that represents the set of all reachable states, and then evaluating all queries in an examination. The main strategy for alleviating state explosion consists of modifying the data structure such that the *representation* of the set of states becomes as small as possible. The representation depends on the net instance but not on the query. Hence, most time is spent on generating the decision diagram while subsequent evaluation of the queries is easy.

Reachability checkers based on decision diagrams and explicit reachability checkers respond very differently to the size of an examination. Increasing the size of an examination causes a proportional increase of run time for an explicit tool since additional (reduced) state spaces need to be traversed. For a symbolic model checker, the decision diagram still needs to be generated only once. Evaluation of additional queries requires only little additional time. In fact, the result sheets of MCC 2015 show that symbolic tools (e.g. Marcie [11]) return either all answers (decision diagram generated in time) or no answer (timeout at diagram generation) for a given examination in most of the cases. In contrast, explicit tools more frequently return incomplete lists of answers to an examination. Hence, the size of an examination may create a substantial bias for or against classes of participating tools and thus it should be chosen with care.

Call a query *positive* if it is a reachability query ($EF\phi$ in the temporal logic CTL) returning true (reachable) or an invariance query ($AG\phi$) returning false (not invariant). Dually, call a query *negative* if it is a reachability query returning false (unreachable) or an invariance query returning true (invariant). All these kinds of queries appeared in the reachability competition (excluding the compute-bounds subcategory where the result is an integer number).

An explicit tool, such as LoLA, typically applies on-the-fly verification. This means that, as soon as a witness or counterexample marking is found, state space generation for a positive query is stopped. In many cases, significantly less time and space is needed than for full state space generation. In principle,

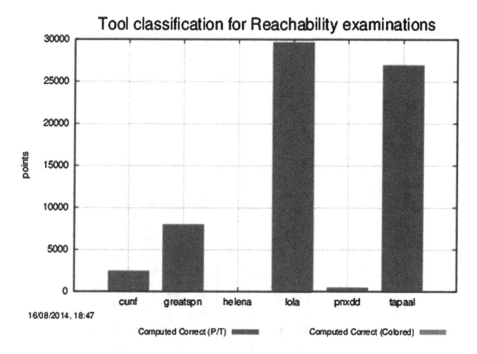

Fig. 1. Final scores in the reachability category of MCC 2014 [15]

on-the-fly verification can be applied to a symbolic model checker as well. The effect, however, is not as significant as for explicit state space tools. On negative queries, on-the-fly verification has to generate the whole (reduced) state space.

The difference between explicit and symbolic model checkers could be observed in MCC 2014 (see Fig. 1). Due to a less sophisticated procedure of generating queries, more than 90 % of the queries were positive. Consequently, LoLA and TAPAAL [8] (the other participant in 2014 that used explicit state space methods) ranked a long way ahead of the symbolic tools. We conclude that the proportion between positive and negative queries is another design parameter in the contest that needs to be chosen with care. Explicit tools benefit from a larger number of positive queries while symbolic tools will show better performance on negative queries. After MCC 2014, we reported this insight to the organizers. In response, the queries were balanced between positive and negative in MCC 2015. In effect, the gap between explicit and symbolic tools was much smaller in the reachability category.

The following numerical evaluation adds evidence to the thesis that explicit tools greatly benefit from positive queries. In 2015, LoLA solved 12284 positive

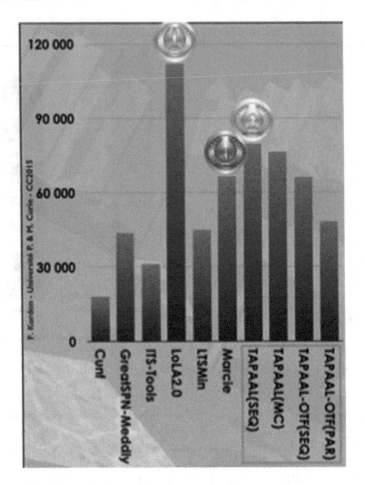

Fig. 2. Final scores in the reachability category of MCC 2015 [16].

queries and 6330 negative queries[1]. In comparison, the most successful symbolic tool in MCC 2015, Marcie, solved 6250 positive and 4460 negative queries. The numbers show that the performance of LoLA on positive queries, benefitting from the on-the-fly principle, is the decisive strength of LoLA. The silver medalist of the 2015 reachability competition, TAPAAL, solved 7720 positive and 5308 negative queries. Although TAPAAL does not benefit from the on-the-fly principle as broadly as LoLA, its performance on positive queries is clearly better than

---

[1] Based on the result sheets of the MCC 2015. Not included are 290 queries that LoLA found to be equivalent to a formula without temporal operators. Such formulas could be evaluated by just inspecting the initial marking. Also not included are 603 extremely long formulas where a time limit was reached while parsing the query. Also not included is the compute-bounds subcategory.

its performance on negative queries, and the gap between positive and negative ones is larger than for the symbolic tool Marcie (Fig. 2).

Another direct comparison between LoLA and Marcie underpins this finding: There were 6425 positive queries solved by LoLA but not by Marcie while there were only 191 positive queries that were solved by Marcie but not by LoLA. These include cases where, on some large net instances, the preprocessing of LoLA consumed all the available run time as well as cases where a witness state was reachable but could not be found early enough to benefit from the on-the-fly effect. Looking at the negative queries, there were 2544 solved by LoLA but not by Marcie and 1377 solved by Marcie but not by LoLA. Here, we cannot conclude that the techniques of LoLA are superior to the ones used by Marcie. There are net instances that are "explicit-friendly" and others that are "symbolic-friendly". In MCC 2015, the explicit-friendly queries just happened to outnumber the symbolic-friendly ones.

4   LoLA Versus Other Explicit Tools

For explicit state space tools, several reduction techniques are available for alleviating the state explosion problem. To our best knowledge, LoLA is the tool with the largest collection of such techniques (even beyond the participants of the MCC). In recent contests, we applied the stubborn set method [25] and the symmetry method [12].

The stubborn set method has an excellent cost/benefit ratio in the realm of distributed systems. That is, the overhead required for computing a stubborn set of transitions in every marking m (which are the transitions to be explored in m) is more than compensated by the much smaller number of markings to be explored at all. Thanks to the stubborn set method, we can manage many state spaces which originally have 10^{20} or even more reachable markings. Such state spaces can otherwise be handled only by symbolic tools or tools applying abstraction.

For reachability, there exist several different stubborn set approaches. They substantially differ in their performance on positive resp. negative queries. For the contest, we applied a version of goal-oriented stubborn sets [17] that performs extremely well on positive queries while its performance is not very impressive on negative queries. The way stubborn sets are computed in this version, implements a heuristics that steers the state space exploration directly to the witness state in many examples and produces very short witness paths (which has been observed by other users of LoLA as well [24]). The average witness path length using stubborn sets in LoLA is 7264. Repeating all experiments of the contest without using stubborn sets, LoLA produced witness paths of average length 567630 (numbers only concern those positive instances where both experiments succeeded). The explored state space often consists of little more than the states on the witness path. With this strategy, we can solve more positive queries than any other tool. Additionally, we spend less time on positive queries than other tools including explicit ones. Hence, we get the maximum effect out of the on-the-fly principle. This explains LoLA's lead of 12284 solved positive queries over TAPAAL with 7720 solved positive queries. There were 4963 positive queries solved by LoLA but not by TAPAAL compared to 399 queries solved by TAPAAL but not by LoLA.

The resulting penalty on negative queries is limited, for three reasons. First, the time saved on the positive queries generates additional time available on the negative queries in the same examination. Second, stubborn sets can be computed extremely quickly in the chosen version. That is, we can explore many more states in a certain time than using other versions of stubborn sets that show better reduction on negative queries. In fact, the most limiting resource in the contest is time, not space: The available time has to be shared out between the queries within an examination while each query can use all of the available memory. This is an artifact of the contest conditions as usually memory consumption is seen as the limiting factor for model checking. Third, at least those other explicit state space tools that do not use the partial order reduction will have trouble with negative queries as well. In 2013, we submitted several configurations of LoLA as individual participants. The configuration using goal-oriented stubborn sets clearly outperformed the other configurations. Hence, there is experimental evidence supporting the decision to use goal-oriented stubborn sets. For explaining the performance of LoLA on negative queries, however, another reduction technique needs to be investigated.

About half of the net instances of MCC 2015 exhibit a substantial amount of symmetry. The main source of symmetry is the fact that many net instances are created from high level net schemes. The regularities in the arc inscriptions translate into symmetry in the resulting place/transition nets. LoLA is able to apply the symmetry method based on graph automorphisms [20,21]. It computes a generating set for the set of graph automorphisms of the net and uses it to transform every computed marking into an approximation of its canonical representative w.r.t. symmetry. The resulting state space is not necessarily the smallest one obtainable by the symmetry method but the balance between run-time and reduction is better than for many other versions of the symmetry method [13]. In LoLA1, the symmetry method could only be applied for deadlock verification. With LoLA2, we are able to apply the method for arbitrary reachability queries. The reason is that an asymmetric query can break the symmetry present in the net. Hence, LoLA2 computes the automorphisms in a graph that joins the net and the formula tree of the property. This way, only automorphisms that preserve both the net structure and the query are computed.

Applying the symmetry method under contest conditions requires some pragmatism. First, computation of the generating set of the symmetries may be quite time-consuming. If we reach the time limit while still computing symmetries, we may miss quite some low hanging fruits concerning on-the-fly verification. For this reason, we implemented an optional time limit for symmetry calculation. When this limit is reached, we stop searching for further symmetries and use those symmetries for state space reduction that we have found so far. That is, we trade preprocessing time for reduction power but make sure that enough time is left for exploring significantly many states. Second, reduced graph generation slows down when the net has many symmetries. On the other hand, the use of the symmetry method significantly increases the number of solved negative queries as the state space obtained by applying both the symmetry and the stubborn set method is more likely to fit into the available memory. Hence, we are able to solve 6330 negative queries, that is, more than our strongest competitors. LoLA solved 1551 negative queries that were not solved by TAPAAL and TAPAAL solved 529 negative queries that were not solved by LoLA. These include instances with timeouts during pre-processing as well as instances where the overhead induced by the symmetry method slowed down calculation of an otherwise doable state space. We do not know whether these arguments fully explain the gap between LoLA and TAPAAL as we have only incomplete information about the reduction techniques implemented there.

In general, we observe that the numbers on negative queries do not vary as much as the numbers for positive queries. For negative queries, all tools need to explore the whole (reduced) state space. This state space grows with increasing scaling factors (size of color sets or number of tokens) in net instances that stem from the same net scheme. For several net schemes, the used scaling factors form a sequence like 2 - 5 - 10 - 20 - 50 - 100 and so on, that is a non-linearly growing sequence. The related state spaces may exponentially depend on the scaling factor. A list of net instances can be roughly partitioned into three categories: "easy enough for everybody", "making the difference", and "too hard for everybody". Clearly, the second category is the relevant one for ranking tools. We analysed that, for some nets, this category is quite small or even empty, especially for net schemes with the mentioned scaling sequence. In other words, a state space that is "easy enough for everybody" in one instance generated from a net scheme may be "too hard for everybody" in the next one. This observation is supported by additional experiments. After the contest, we repeated the examinations of the contest with much more generous time and space limits. We solved only very few additionally negative queries. Hence, the small difference between tools on negative queries may be well explained by the small number of net instances in the "making the difference" category.

5   Design Decisions in LoLA Related to the Contest

Besides the stubborn set method and the symmetry method, LoLA offers additional reduction techniques that we decided not to apply. First, we would like to mention the sweep-line method [5,22]. This method is useful when memory is the limiting resource as used memory can be freed to make room for new states, at the price of additional run-time. Due to the setup of the contest, especially the structure of examinations, we found time to be the limiting factor (as explained earlier). Hence, the sweep-line method is not useful in the MCC. A second interesting method is Bloom-filtering [2]. Here, only hash values of markings are recorded. In case of hash collisions, state space exploration may be incomplete. This means that we would need to return "unknown" to all negative queries, or to deliberately return a value that may be incorrect (with low probability). We found none of the alternatives to be satisfying.

Some features have been implemented in LoLA for MCC 2015 in response to our analysis of MCC 2014. In 2014, a single call of LoLA yielded a result to a single query. That is, for processing an examination of 10 queries, we would call LoLA 10 times, including 10 times parsing and preprocessing the net instance. Additionally, we were not able to process queries like "$EF\ \phi_1\ AND\ AG\ \phi_2$" that used to be offered as reachability problems in past contests. We did so for a good reason: releasing the memory for all data structures that internally represent the state space (for stepping from one state space to another) takes more time that quitting the program and re-starting it with a new query. For 2015, we found the following solution. We parse the net only once and perform all the pre-processing that we need for efficient state space exploration. As soon as we are ready to start the actual exploration, we apply the UNIX fork() command that creates a child process that is identical to its parent. State space exploration is done in the child process and its result communicated to the parent process. Then the child process is killed. This way, the whole process of releasing memory is delegated to the (much more efficient) process management of the operating system. The next query is applied by forking a new child, inheriting all data structures from the initial parsing and preprocessing. Hence, in MCC 2015 we processed a whole examination with just one call to LoLA that sequentially forked 16 children. Much more time for actual state space exploration was available than in 2014.

When processing an examination, our main problem is to organise the available run time w.r.t. the individual queries. Spending all time on a hard negative query, we would possibly miss some low hanging fruits, that is positive queries appearing in the end of the list of queries in an examination. Unfortunately, the classification into positive and negative queries can only be done *after* they have been processed. Hence, we have no strategy for solving first the positive queries (to earn points) and then the negative queries (to see whether additional points can be collected). Responding to this problem, we have introduced a time limit for each individual state space exploration. As positive queries may require much less run time, we set the individual time limit not to $\frac{1}{16}$ of the time limit for the whole examination of 16 qeuries, but to a much higher value. That is, we placed a bet that at least some of the queries require less than $\frac{1}{16}$ of the time given for processing the examination. The chosen value is not necessarily the optimal setting but quite easy to implement.

In 2014, LoLA could not participate in the compute-bounds subcategory. Such a query does not yield a Boolean value but a number. Such queries could not be translated into anything offered by LoLA. In MCC 2014 we learned that this subcategory was no longer scored separately. Additionally, LoLA ranked only few points ahead of TAPAAL (see above for explanations). Hence, we decided that we had to collect at least the low-hanging fruits in this sub-category. We implemented a procedure for evaluating bound expressions and were able to apply the symmetry method and a dedicated variant of the stubborn set method, both preserving the maximum value of the given expression. This way, we were able to solve 2571 queries and to rank fourth in the sub-category, less than 1000 solved queries short of the winner. For computing bounds, every query requires computation of the whole (reduced) state space. This way, there is no benefit at all from on-the-fly verification. Consequently, the thesis that the main advantage of LoLA is its performance on positive queries, is supported once more.

6   Further Development of LoLA

As far as the contest is concerned, not much room is left for improvements on positive queries. Hence, we are focussing on negative queries. We do not believe that minor improvements to our state space reduction methods will enable us to enlarge the "making the difference" category. Consequently, we are looking for completely different solutions. For deadlock checking, we plan to check the siphon/trap property (Commoner/Hack property). We have already implemented an evaluation of the property based on SAT-checking [19] but not yet used in the contest, for lack of stability of this feature. If the siphon/trap property holds (and is applicable to a net instance), the net is deadlock-free. Hence, we hope that this method will help us to answer some negative deadlock queries where state space calculation does not terminate.

A related method for reachability queries is the Petri net state equation. If it does not have a solution (with a constraint added to describe the target states), we can assert unreachability. With Sara [26], we have a tool where this method is augmented with abstraction refinement such that it is able to process both positive and negative queries. In several cases, Sara is able to outperform LoLA. Consequently, we aim at integrating Sara as part of the LoLA tool such that the state equation based algorithms of Sara run in parallel to the state space exploration of LoLA. In 2015, this would have made sense for the first time, as the organisers offered the possibility to use four cores by each tool. This means that running Sara would not slow down parallel execution of LoLA anymore.

As the organisers decided in 2015 that results for place/transition nets and coloured nets are aggregated to a single result, we shall work on a coloured net input for LoLA2. Nevertheless, we would suggest to return to a separate scoring just to make it easier for new participants to connect their tool to the contest environment.

Last but not least, we intend to add state space reduction to the general LTL and CTL model checking routines in LoLA, and to participate in the respective categories in MCC 2016.

7   Conclusion

The model checking contest is an interesting arena for comparing tools that use very different technologies. Through the competition, an enourmous amount of data is available for analysis. In this paper, we gave an example of such an analysis by evaluating the effect of on-the-fly verification. Additionally, as the previous sections show, the MCC is a beautiful incentive to add features to tools.

We argued that some design decisions in the structure of the contest necessarily create a bias, in particular between symbolic and explicit tools. We would thus suggest that such decisions should be carefully supervised by the contest committee. We further observed that aggregation of categories in the final scoring may create severe obstacles for new participants to enter the MCC.

Considering our plans for further improvements to LoLA, we are confident that our tool will remain a strong contestant in the reachability category of the MCC. At the same time, the additional power will pay off in even better applicability of LoLA in real-life case studies.

References

1. Billington, J., et al.: The Petri Net Markup Language: concepts, technology, and tools. In: Aalst, W.M.P., Best, E. (eds.) ICATPN 2003. LNCS, vol. 2679, pp. 483–505. Springer, Heidelberg (2003)
2. Bloom, B.H.: Space/time trade-offs in hash coding with allowable errors. Commun. ACM 13(7), 422–426 (1970)
3. Bryant, R.E.: Symbolic Boolean manipulation with ordered binary-decision diagrams. ACM Comput. Surv. 24(3), 293–318 (1992)
4. Burch, J.R., Clarke, E.M., McMillan, K.L., Dill, D.L., Hwang, L.J.: Symbolic model checking: 10^{20} states and beyond. Inf. Comput. 98(2), 142–170 (1992)
5. Christensen, S., Kristensen, L.M., Mailund, T.: A sweep-line method for state space exploration. In: Margaria, T., Yi, W. (eds.) TACAS 2001. LNCS, vol. 2031, pp. 450–464. Springer, Heidelberg (2001)
6. Clarke, E.M., Biere, A., Raimi, R., Zhu, Y.: Bounded model checking using satisfiability solving. Formal Methods Syst. Des. 19(1), 7–34 (2001)
7. Das, D., Chakrabarti, P.P., Kumar, R.: Functional verification of task partitioning for multiprocessor embedded systems. ACM Trans. Des. Autom. Electr. Syst., 12(4) (2007)
8. David, A., Jacobsen, L., Jacobsen, M., Jørgensen, K.Y., Møller, M.H., Srba, J.: TAPAAL 2.0: integrated development environment for timed-arc Petri nets. In: Flanagan, C., König, B. (eds.) TACAS 2012. LNCS, vol. 7214, pp. 492–497. Springer, Heidelberg (2012)
9. Kordon, F., et al.: The MCC web page. http://mcc.lip6.fr
10. Fahland, D., Favre, C., Koehler, J., Lohmann, N., Völzer, H., Wolf, K.: Analysis on demand: instantaneous soundness checking of industrial business process models. Data Knowl. Eng. 70(5), 448–466 (2011)
11. Heiner, M., Rohr, C., Schwarick, M.: MARCIE – model checking and reachability analysis done efficiently. In: Colom, J.-M., Desel, J. (eds.) PETRI NETS 2013. LNCS, vol. 7927, pp. 389–399. Springer, Heidelberg (2013)
12. Huber, P., Jensen, A.M., Jepsen, L.O., Jensen, K.: Reachability trees for high-level Petri nets. Theor. Comput. Sci. 45(3), 261–292 (1986)
13. Junttila, T.A.: Computational complexity of the place/transition-net symmetry reduction method. J. UCS 7(4), 307–326 (2001)
14. Kaiser, A., Kroening, D., Wahl, T.: Dynamic cutoff detection in parameterized concurrent programs. In: Touili, T., Cook, B., Jackson, P. (eds.) CAV 2010. LNCS, vol. 6174, pp. 645–659. Springer, Heidelberg (2010)
15. Kordon, F.: Report from MCC at PETRI NETS (2014)

16. Kordon, F.: Report from MCC at PETRI NETS (2015)
17. Kristensen, L.M., Schmidt, K., Valmari, A.: Question-guided stubborn set methods for state properties. Formal Methods Syst. Des. **29**(3), 215–251 (2006)
18. Lohmann, N., Kopp, O., Leymann, F., Reisig, W.: Analyzing BPEL4Chor: verification and participant synthesis. In: Dumas, M., Heckel, R. (eds.) WS-FM 2007. LNCS, vol. 4937, pp. 46–60. Springer, Heidelberg (2008)
19. Oanea, O., Wimmel, H., Wolf, K.: New algorithms for deciding the siphon-trap property. In: Lilius, J., Penczek, W. (eds.) PETRI NETS 2010. LNCS, vol. 6128, pp. 267–286. Springer, Heidelberg (2010)
20. Schmidt, K.: How to calculate symmetries of Petri nets. Acta Inf. **36**(7), 545–590 (2000)
21. Schmidt, K.: Integrating low level symmetries into reachability analysis. In: Graf, S. (ed.) TACAS 2000. LNCS, vol. 1785, pp. 315–330. Springer, Heidelberg (2000)
22. Schmidt, K.: Automated generation of a progress measure for the sweep-line method. STTT **8**(3), 195–203 (2006)
23. Stahl, C., Reisig, W., Krstic, M.: Hazard detection in a GALS wrapper: a case study. In: Proceedings of ACSD. IEEE (2005)
24. Talcott, C., Dill, D.L.: The pathway logic assistant. In: Proceedings of Computational Methods in Systems Biology (2005)
25. Valmari, A.: Stubborn sets for reduced state space generation. In: Rozenberg, G. (ed.) Advances in Petri Nets 1990. LNCS, vol. 483, pp. 491–515. Springer, Heidelberg (1989)
26. Wimmel, H., Wolf, K.: Applying CEGAR to the Petri net state equation. Logical Meth. Comput. Sci. **8**(3) (2012)
27. Wolf, K.: Generating Petri net state spaces. In: Kleijn, J., Yakovlev, A. (eds.) ICATPN 2007. LNCS, vol. 4546, pp. 29–42. Springer, Heidelberg (2007)

MARCIE's Secrets of Efficient Model Checking

Monika Heiner[✉], Christian Rohr[✉], Martin Schwarick,
and Alexey A. Tovchigrechko

Chair of Data Structures and Software Dependability,
Brandenburg University of Technology Cottbus-Senftenberg,
Postbox 10 13 44, 03013 Cottbus, Germany
marcie@informatik.tu-cottbus.de
http://www-dssz.informatik.tu-cottbus.de

Abstract. MARCIE is a Petri net analysis tool supporting qualitative and quantitative analyses including model checking facilities. Particular features are symbolic state space analysis including efficient saturation-based state space generation, evaluation of standard Petri net properties, and CTL model checking. Most of MARCIE's features build on Interval Decision Diagrams (IDDs) to efficiently encode interval logic functions representing marking sets of bounded Petri nets. This allows the efficient support of qualitative state space based analysis techniques. Among others, MARCIE applies heuristics for the computation of static variable orders to obtain concise IDD representations. In this paper we focus on those aspects which are crucial for MARCIE's regular success in the annual Model Checking Contest of the Petri net community.

Keywords: Petri nets · Interval decision diagrams · Reachability analysis · Model checking · CTL

1 Introduction

MARCIE is a tool for the analysis of Petri nets extended by special arcs (read, inhibitory, equal and reset arcs) and Generalised Stochastic Petri nets (GSPN). For qualitative analysis it supports the efficient symbolic generation of the state space, the symbolic analysis of general behavioural properties, and symbolic CTL model checking [19]. For quantitative analysis it offers symbolic CS(R)L model checking and the computation of reward expectations [16]. Additionally, MARCIE provides simulative and explicit approximative numerical analysis techniques [5].

MARCIE has proven its efficiency, performance and reliability for various qualitative analyses in the four Model Checking Contests (MCC) held so far in conjunction with the annual International Conference on Application and Theory of Petri Nets and Concurrency; since 2012 it regularly reached excellent and award-winning results [9–12]. In this paper we focus on the most important aspects crucial for MARCIE's accomplishments – symbolic encoding of marking sets by Interval Decision Diagrams (IDDs), saturation-based state space generation, and approved heuristics for the structure-based computation of static variable orders.

© Springer-Verlag Berlin Heidelberg 2016
M. Koutny et al. (Eds.): ToPNoC XI, LNCS 9930, pp. 286–296, 2016.
DOI: 10.1007/978-3-662-53401-4_14

2   Interval Decision Diagrams

In this section we recall Interval Decision Diagrams (IDDs) as defined in [19]. They can be seen as a generalisation of Binary Decision Diagrams (BDDs). An IDD is a Directed Acyclic Graph (DAG) with two terminal nodes labelled with 0 and 1. Non-terminal nodes have an arbitrary number of outgoing arcs labelled with intervals of natural numbers (including zero) partitioning the set of natural numbers. IDDs represent interval logic functions [13], and Reduced Ordered Interval Decision Diagrams (ROIDDs) provide a canonical representation of interval logic functions. Remarkably, ROIDD are often able to concisely describe huge sets of Petri net markings, and there are efficient algorithms for the manipulation of interval logic functions using ROIDDs.

From now on, when talking about IDDs, we actually refer to ROIDDs.

Definitions. An interval decision diagram for the variables $X = \{x_1, \ldots, x_n\}$ is a tuple $[V, E, v_0]$, where V is a finite set of nodes, $E \subseteq V \times \mathcal{I} \times V$ is a finite set of arcs labelled with intervals on $\mathbb{N}_0$, $[V, E]$ forms a DAG, and v_0 is the root of the IDD.

Furthermore, the following conditions must hold. V has to include two terminal nodes (leaves); i.e., nodes without outgoing arcs. One node is labelled with 0, the other one with 1. All other nodes v are called non-terminal nodes. Every non-terminal node v is labelled with a variable $\mathrm{var}(v)$, where $\mathrm{var} : V \to X$ is surjective, and v has $k_v > 0$ outgoing arcs with intervals $I_j \in \mathcal{I}$. The intervals form a partition over $\mathbb{N}_0$. A variable may appear only once as label of a node on every path from the root to a terminal node, and all variables appear always in the same order on all paths (as usual in Ordered Decision Diagrams).

Every interval logic function can be represented by an IDD by help of the Boole-Shannon expansion. The decomposition is applied recursively until leaves are reached.

Shared IDDs are an extension of IDDs: a single multi-rooted DAG permits to represent a collection of interval logic functions. All functions in the collection must be defined over the same set of variables using the same variable ordering. Thanks to the canonicity of IDDs, two functions in the collection are identical, if and only if the IDDs representing these functions have the same root in the Shared IDD. The following interval logic functions are encoded in the Shared IDD shown in Fig. 1:

- $f_0 = 0$,
- $f_1 = 1$,
- $f_2 = x_2 > 0$,
- $f_3 = (x_1 \in [4, 9) \land x_2 > 0) \lor (x_1 \geq 9)$,
- $f_4 = (x_1 = 0 \land x_2 > 0) \lor x_1 \geq 1$.

Notice that all nodes of the Shared IDD in Fig. 1 are numbered (the numbers given in parentheses next to the non-terminal nodes). The terminal nodes get the numbers 0 and 1. We use these numbers to address nodes, and in the given

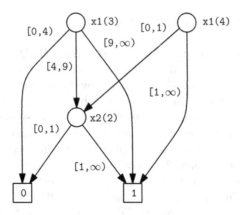

Fig. 1. A shared IDD example.

case, the node numbers correspond to the function indices. To simplify the IDD algorithms we assume that the function *var* labels terminal nodes with a special variable x such that $x >_\pi var(v)$ for all non-terminal nodes $v \in V$.

Operations. We use Shared IDDs in all algorithms for operations on IDDs. The following interval logic operations (given by their signatures) are implemented in MARCIE:

$$\text{Equivalence check} : \text{IDD} \times \text{IDD} \rightarrow \mathbb{B}$$
$$\text{Apply operation} : \text{IDD} \times \text{IDD} \rightarrow \text{IDD}$$
$$\text{Negation} : \text{IDD} \rightarrow \text{IDD}$$
$$\text{Cofactors} : \text{IDD} \times \mathbb{N}_0 \rightarrow \text{IDD}$$

Reasoning in terms of sets of markings is isomorphic to reasoning in terms of interval logic functions [19]. Thus, the logic operations we presented so far allow an efficient manipulation of sets of markings. Additionally, we introduce specific symbolic operators taking into account the Petri net dynamics, which are required for an efficient reachability analysis.

Petri net related operations (given by their signatures):

$$\text{Pick} : \text{IDD} \rightarrow M$$
$$\text{Fire} : \text{IDD} \times T \rightarrow \text{IDD}$$
$$\text{RevFire} : \text{IDD} \times T \rightarrow \text{IDD}$$
$$\text{Img} : \text{IDD} \rightarrow \text{IDD}$$
$$\text{PreImg} : \text{IDD} \rightarrow \text{IDD}$$

A detailed description of the implemented operations on IDDs is given in [17].

Implementation. MARCIE is implemented in C++, available for Linux and Mac OSX (Windows version on request), and is free of charge for non-commercial use. We take advantage of a couple of approved implementation techniques discussed in [3], and additionally address some IDD-specific problems.

We use a global hash table *UniqueTable* to find a node in a Shared IDD, and we merge the data structures of the hash table and IDDs forming a Shared IDD.

```
1 struct SharedIDD {
2   array<Node> nodes;
3   array<unsigned> uniqueTable;
4   list<RefCount> extRefs;
5   unsigned firstFree;
6 };
```

```
1 struct Node {
2   unsigned var;
3   list<unsigned> children;
4   list<unsigned> arcs;
5   unsigned nextFree;
6   unsigned nextInUTable;
7   bool mark;
8 };
```

All IDD nodes are saved in the array *nodes*. For every IDD node v we store an index of a variable var(v), a list of children, and a list of labels of outgoing arcs. *firstFree* is the index of the first free IDD node, free nodes are linked using the member *nextFree*. A node in the Shared IDD is located by help of a hash function. *uniqueTable*[k] contains the index of the first IDD node with the hash value k, all IDD nodes with the same hash key are linked using the member *nextInUTable*.

We denote the IDDs representing functions of a user of the IDD package as externally referenced. The member *extRefs* counts the references to the roots of externally referenced IDDs. The garbage collection is triggered automatically if all free nodes are exhausted during an IDD operation. The garbage collection first marks all nodes reachable from the roots of externally referenced IDDs using a simple recursive function and the member *mark*. Afterwards, all not marked nodes are linked in the free list, and the IDD operation is repeated, which triggered the garbage collection.

The hash table *ResultTable* stores the results of already calculated subproblems and thus prevents the IDD algorithms from being exponential. Because of the use of Shared IDDs, the results saved in the hash table remain valid even across top-level calls to IDD operations. Hence, the hash table has to be initialised only with the initialisation of the IDD package and after garbage collections, but not for each call of an IDD operation.

In [3], it was proposed to implement *ResultTable* as a hash-based cache. In hash-based caches, a more recent entry overwrites the previous one when a collision occurs. Obviously, a hash-based cache requires less memory and is faster, as no collision management is needed. Each hash-based cache entry stores the key and the result of an operation. The use of hash-based caches introduces the possibility of recalculating previous results and leads in the worst case to the exponential complexity of IDD operations. However, appropriate hash functions and cache sizes generally come along with a gain both in terms of average memory usage and runtime.

For further efficiency improvement we do not deploy the function *Apply* for the most frequently used operations, i.e. *intersection, union* and *difference*. Instead, these operations are implemented as dedicated IDD operations.

A specific IDD issue is the handling of intervals and lists of children. Obviously, every partition $P = \{[0, a_1), [a_1, a_2), \ldots, [a_n, \infty)\}$ of $\mathbb{N}_0$ can be uniquely represented by a sequence of natural numbers $a_1, a_2, \ldots, a_n$. Thus, we store an IDD node's children and the labels of its outgoing arcs as lists of unsigned integers. The list implementation must be, of course, memory efficient, and permit fast operations required by IDD algorithms. The most frequently used operations are:

- creation and deletion of lists,
- copying and comparison of lists,
- appending and removing list elements,
- functions like compute the intersection of partitions.

All IDD algorithms can be written without loss of efficiency in such a way that they access the list elements sequentially. We exploit this fact and use single linked lists. The data structure is sketched in the following listing.

```
1 struct ListNode {          1 struct UList {
2 unsigned data;             2 ListNode* first;
3 ListNode* next;            3 ListNode* last;
4 };                         4 };
```

Lists storing labels of outgoing arcs of a node are always sorted. Hence, the function to compute the intersection of partitions is implemented as a simple merge operation of two sorted lists. References to the first and last element of a list are stored in the next field of nodes referenced by the members *first* and *last*. This allows fast appending of elements at the beginning and at the end of the list. Moreover, *last.data* stores the length of the list, while *first.data* is used for the reference counting. We implement a lazy copy and shared list nodes. If a copy operation creates a list, then elements of the old list are not copied to the new one; instead, the new list shares all its nodes with the old list. Frequent allocations and deletions of small objects like list nodes lead to high memory fragmentation, its inefficient usage, and in the long run to very high memory requirements. To avoid this problem, we use a pool of list nodes. The pool allocates large chunks of memory and undertakes the management of free nodes. When a list operation needs a new node, it is requested from the pool. Nodes not needed anymore are returned back to the pool. The use of shared lists and a pool of nodes substantially decreased the memory requirements of the IDD package.

3   Variable Ordering

The variable ordering (i.e. place ordering in the Petri net terminology) is known to have a strong influence on a decision diagram's size and, thus, on the runtime.

A bad choice may even totally preclude the state space's constructability. In general, finding an optimal ordering is infeasible, even checking if a particular ordering is optimal is NP-complete.

Let $f = f(a_1, \ldots, a_n, b_1, \ldots, b_n)$ be an interval logic function defined as

$$f = \bigwedge_{1 \le i \le n} ((a_i = 0 \wedge b_i = 0) \vee (a_i > 0 \wedge b_i > 0)).$$

The number of nodes in the IDD representing f will be

- $3n + 2$, if we use the variable ordering π_1 defined as

$$a_1 <_{\pi_1} b_1 <_{\pi_1} a_2 <_{\pi_1} b_2 <_{\pi_1} \cdots <_{\pi_1} a_n <_{\pi_1} <_{\pi_1} b_n.$$

- $3 \cdot 2^n - 1$, if we use the variable ordering π_2 defined as

$$a_1 <_{\pi_2} a_2 <_{\pi_2} \cdots <_{\pi_2} a_n <_{\pi_2} b_1 <_{\pi_2} b_2 <_{\pi_2} \cdots <_{\pi_2} b_n.$$

Two IDDs representing f for $n = 2$ are shown in Fig. 2. The variable ordering π_1 is used for the left IDD, π_2 for the right.

We decided to use static variable ordering, because the analysis time can not be improved by dynamic variable ordering, if a good variable ordering is defined heuristically [20]. There is no general rule for the best method, but heuristics arranging related variables closely together in the ordering bring often good results. MARCIE incorporates two heuristics taking this into account.

Heuristic 1. It is certainly safe to assume that pre- and post-places of a transition depend on each other. Thus, our saturation algorithm suggests that variables corresponding to adjacent places of a transition should be close to each

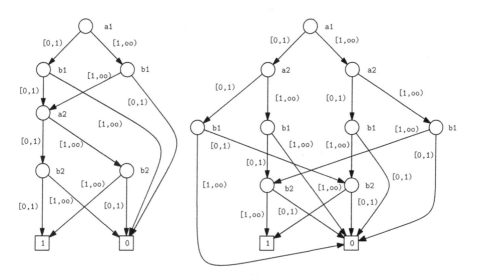

Fig. 2. Two IDDs for the same function with different variable orderings.

other in the applied ordering. The simple greedy algorithm proposed in [14] for the computation of a zero-suppressed BDD's variable ordering benefits from this idea. The ordering π is constructed in a bottom-up manner. Assuming $x_1 <_\pi x_2 <_\pi \ldots <_\pi x_{|P|}$, we assign places to the variables starting from the variable $x_{|P|}$. To select a place for a variable x_i, we compute weights $W(p)$ for all places $p \in P \setminus S$, where S denotes the set of places already assigned to some variable. Then, the place p with the highest weight $W(p)$ is assigned to the variable x_i. This is repeated until all places are assigned to some variable.

$$S = \bigcup_{i<j\leq|P|} Pl(x_j) \ , \ W(p) = \frac{f(p)}{|\bullet p \cup p\bullet|}$$

$$f(p) = \sum_{\substack{t \in \bullet p, \\ |\bullet t| > 0, \\ |t\bullet| > 0}} \left(\frac{g(t)}{|\bullet t|} + \frac{2 \cdot |t \bullet \cap S|}{|t\bullet|} \right) + \sum_{\substack{t \in p\bullet, \\ |\bullet t| > 0, \\ |t\bullet| > 0}} \left(\frac{h(t)}{|t\bullet|} + \frac{|\bullet t \cap S| + 1}{|\bullet t|} \right)$$

$$g(t) = \begin{cases} 0.1 & \text{if } |\bullet t \cap S| = \emptyset \\ |\bullet t \cap S| & \text{otherwise} \end{cases} , \ h(t) = \begin{cases} 0.2 & \text{if } |t \bullet \cap S| = \emptyset \\ 2 \cdot |t \bullet \cap S| & \text{otherwise.} \end{cases}$$

We notice also that moving those variables down in the ordering which have a large number of different values (token numbers on places) can decrease the breadth of an IDD and thus reduce its size. P-invariants and traps can help to find places that potentially induce such variables worth moving down. Moreover, it is safe to assume that places belonging to the same P-invariant depend on each other. These facts can be deployed to adjust the weight function W.

Heuristic 2. The second heuristic, introduced in [19], is an adaptation of the previous one. The two summands of $f(p)$ were split into two parts each. This increases $W(p)$ for pre-/post-places of transitions having many of its adjacent places already selected.

$$S = \bigcup_{i<j\leq|P|} Pl(x_j) \ , \ W(p) = \frac{f(p)}{|\bullet p \cup p\bullet|}$$

$$f(p) = \sum_{\substack{t \in \bullet p, \\ |\bullet t| > 0}} \left(\frac{g_1(t)}{|\bullet t|} \right) + \sum_{\substack{t \in \bullet p, \\ |t\bullet| > 0}} \left(\frac{g_2(t)}{|t\bullet|} \right) + \sum_{\substack{t \in p\bullet, \\ |\bullet t| > 0}} \left(\frac{|\bullet t \cap S| + 1}{|\bullet t|} \right) + \sum_{\substack{t \in p\bullet, \\ |t\bullet| > 0}} \left(\frac{h(t)}{|t\bullet|} \right)$$

$$g_1(t) = \begin{cases} 0.1 & \text{if } |\bullet t \cap S| = \emptyset \\ |\bullet t \cap S| & \text{otherwise} \end{cases} , \ g_2(t) = \begin{cases} 0.1 & \text{if } |t \bullet \cap S| = \emptyset \\ 2 \cdot |t \bullet \cap S| & \text{otherwise} \end{cases}$$

$$h(t) = \begin{cases} 0.2 & \text{if } |t \bullet \cap S| = \emptyset \\ 2 \cdot |t \bullet \cap S| & \text{otherwise .} \end{cases}$$

Both heuristics allow us to compute automatically reasonable good IDD variable orderings for most of the Petri nets, we encountered so far. For exceptional cases, MARCIE provides the option to manually fine-tune the computed ordering.

- plain order – in the order as read from the file,
- reverse order – in the reverse order as read from the file,
- random order – according to a discrete uniform distribution,
- read from file – read from a user-specified file,
- lexicographical order – according to the names in a lexicographical way.

Likewise, the transition ordering may have a crucial impact on the performance of the chaining and the saturation algorithms. There are several options to chose from: plain, random, read from file, and three heuristics derived from the net structure (one of those heuristics is the default).

The dramatic effect which different variable orderings may have on the state space construction is illustrated in [15].

4 Qualitative Analysis

State Space Generation. The traditional symbolic approach employing BDDs to encode transition relations builds on characteristic functions to represent binary relations between sets. The function *Img* (see Sect. 2) is then implemented using standard BDD operations. This technique is not very well suited for Petri nets. The transition relation becomes too large and firing becomes a prohibitively inefficient operation. Notice that we also would have to introduce an upper bound to keep the relation finite.

To avoid these problems, we use *action lists* which encode single transitions and implement the function *Fire* as a special IDD operation. Action lists naturally support enabling and firing rules of Petri nets with extended arcs. They allow a more flexible implementation of the function *Fire* compared to simple lists of places. This data structure is used in the function *RevFire*, too. Replacing the general purpose function *Img* by a special IDD operation *Fire* allows the application of different traversal techniques, all along with the in most cases well-suited variable orderings, the efficient hash-based cache, the use of shared lists and a memory pool, which can enormously speed up the construction and exploration of state spaces.

There are three categories of symbolic state space generation algorithms.

1. Breadth-First Search (BFS): an iteration fires sequentially all transitions (according to the transition ordering) before adding the new states to the state space.
2. Transitions chaining: like BFS, but the state space is updated after the firing of each single transition.
3. Saturation algorithm (SAT): Transitions are fired in conformance with the decision diagram, i.e. according to an ordering, which is defined by the variable ordering. A transition is saturated if its firing does not add new states

to the current state space. Transitions are bottom-up saturated (i.e. starting at the terminal nodes and going towards the root). Having fired a given transition, all preceding transitions have to be saturated again, either after a single firing (single) or the exhausted firing (fixpoint) of the current transition; see [7,19] for details.

It is worth mentioning that these strategies do not require a priori knowledge of the boundedness degree to construct the finite state space for a given bounded Petri net. The algorithm terminates if the state space is finite and the IDD fits into the available memory. Actually, IDDs permit also the encoding of infinite sets of states.

Reachability Analysis. The constructed state space can be efficiently evaluated by the following options, making use of Shared IDDs, the dedicated IDD operations *intersection*, *union* and *difference*, and the hash-based cache. The boundedness of each individual place as determined by the state space construction can be written to a file. Symbolic algorithms for the computation and enumeration of the terminal strongly connected components determine efficiently liveness and reversibility. Before checking reversibility or liveness, we first make a cheaper test for any reachable dead markings. If this is the case, the net can not be reversible and has no live transitions.

On request, all live/not live transitions are written to a file. The dead state analysis with trace generation determines all reachable dead states, which can be written to a file as an interval logic expression, i.e., as an expression containing only atomic propositions over integer variables combined by logic operators. All empty places do not appear in this expression. A transition sequence producing one of the reachable dead states can be written to a file as well (witness).

CTL Model Checking. The Computation Tree Logic (CTL) [4] is a widely used branching time logic. It permits to specify properties over states and paths of a labelled transition system (LTS), the Kripke structure. Path quantifiers specify whether path formulas, which can be written by means of temporal operators, should be fulfilled on all paths or at least on one path starting in some state. One can interpret the reachability graph of a Petri net as a Kripke structure and thus apply CTL model checking algorithms.

Conventional symbolic CTL algorithms build on a breath-first order exploration of the state space. Diverting from this strategy can improve significantly the efficiency of symbolic algorithms for Petri nets. We observed that the performance of the symbolic state space exploration depends strongly on the model structure. Sometimes, forward state traversals are quite efficient, whereas intermediate IDDs created during the backward state space exploration become too large and can not be handled efficiently. A CTL model checking algorithm based mainly on forward state traversals was suggested in [8]. This algorithm is implemented in MARCIE using the functions presented in Sect. 2. Thus, it benefits from the saturation technique, too.

An important feature of a model checker is the ability to generate counterexamples or witnesses. When this feature is enabled and the model checker determines that a formula with a universal path quantifier is not satisfied, it can find a computation which demonstrates why the negation of the formula is true. Likewise, when the model checker determines that a formula with an existential path quantifier is satisfied, it can find a computation that demonstrates why it is so. A counterexample for a universally quantified formula is a witness for the dual existentially quantified formula. Thus, it is enough to consider how to generate witnesses for the operators **EX**, **EU**, and **EG**. A single computation of **EX** can be considered as a cheap operation. Our saturation-based implementation allows to improve significantly the efficiency of **EU**. Unfortunately, we could not employ the saturation technique to improve the computation of **EG**.

A detailed description of the implemented algorithms is given in [19].

5   Conclusions

In this paper, we have presented selective implementation issues of MARCIE – a Petri net analysis tool that supports, among others, the efficient generation of the state space, the analysis of general behavioural and reachability properties, and CTL model checking. The models have to be bounded. However, no a priori knowledge of the boundedness degree is required. Crucial points for the tools performance are the data structures used for the symbolic state space representation, the ordering of places (DD variables) and the ordering of transitions (chaining and saturation algorithms), and the algorithms, which exploit strongly connected components and the saturation principle.

Additionally, but beyond the scope of this paper are MARCIE's skills of quantitative analysis techniques for Generalised Stochastic Petri nets based on the underlying continuous-time Markov chain (CTMC). Among others, it provides a multi-threaded on-the-fly computation of the CTMC [18]. It is thus less sensitive to the number of distinct rate values than approaches based on, e.g., Multi-Terminal Decision Diagrams. Further, it offers symbolic CS(R)L model checking and permits to compute reward expectations [16]. Finally, MARCIE provides simulative and explicit approximative numerical analysis techniques [5].

A couple of comparative performance studies can be found in [1,2,6].

References

1. Blätke, M., Heiner, M., Marwan, W.: BioModel Engineering with Petri Nets, pp. 141–193. Elsevier Inc. (2015)
2. Blätke, M., Rohr, C., Heiner, M., Marwan, W.: A Petri net based framework for biomodel engineering. In: Benner, P., Findeisen, R., Flockerzi, D., Reichl, U., Sundmacher, K. (eds.) Large-Scale Networks in Engineering and Life Sciences. MSSET, pp. 317–366. Springer, Heidelberg (2014)
3. Brace, K.S., Rudell, R.L., Bryant, R.E.: Efficient implementation of a BDD package. In: Proceedings of the 27th ACM/IEEE Design Automation Conference, pp. 40–45. ACM/IEEE, IEEE Computer Society Press (1990)

4. Clarke, E.M., Emerson, E.A., Sistla, A.P.: Automatic verification of finite state concurrent systems using temporal logic specifications. ACM TOPLAS **8**(2), 244–263 (1986)
5. Heiner, M., Rohr, C., Schwarick, M.: MARCIE – model checking and reachability analysis done efficiently. In: Colom, J.-M., Desel, J. (eds.) PETRI NETS 2013. LNCS, vol. 7927, pp. 389–399. Springer, Heidelberg (2013)
6. Heiner, M., Rohr, C., Schwarick, M., Streif, S.: A comparative study of stochastic analysis techniques. In: Proceedings of CMSB 2010, pp. 96–106. ACM digital library (2010)
7. Heiner, M., Schwarick, M., Tovchigrechko, A.: DSSZ-MC – a tool for symbolic analysis of extended Petri nets. In: Franceschinis, G., Wolf, K. (eds.) PETRI NETS 2009. LNCS, vol. 5606, pp. 323–332. Springer, Heidelberg (2009)
8. Iwashita, H., Nakata, T., Hirose, F.: CTL model checking based on forward state traversal. In: Proceedings of ICCAD 1996, pp. 82–87. IEEE Computer Society (1996)
9. Kordon, F., Garavel, H., Hillah, L.M., Hulin-Hubard, F., Linard, A., Beccuti, M., Evangelista, S., Hamez, A., Lohmann, N., Lopez, E., Paviot-Adet, E., Rodriguez, C., Rohr, C., Srba, J.: HTML results from the Model Checking Contest @ Petri Net (2014 edn.) (2014). http://mcc.lip6.fr/2014
10. Kordon, F., Garavel, H., Hillah, L.M., Hulin-Hubard, F., Linard, A., Beccuti, M., Hamez, A., Lopez-Bobeda, E., Jezequel, L., Meijer, J., Paviot-Adet, E., Rodriguez, C., Rohr, C., Srba, J., Thierry-Mieg, Y., Wolf, K.: Complete Results for the 2015 Edition of the Model Checking Contest (2015). http://mcc.lip6.fr/2015/results.php
11. Kordon, F., Linard, A., Becutti, M., Buchs, D., Fronc, L., Hulin-Hubard, F., Legond-Aubry, F., Lohmann, N., Marechal, A., Paviot-Adet, E., Pommereau, F., Rodrígues, C., Rohr, C., Thierry-Mieg, Y., Wimmel, H., Wolf, K.: Web Report on the Model Checking Contest @ Petri Net 2013 (2013). http://mcc.lip6.fr
12. Kordon, F., Linard, A., Buchs, D., Colange, M., Evangelista, S., Fronc, L., Hillah, L., Lohmann, N., Paviot-Adet, E., Pommereau, F., Rohr, C., Thierry-Mieg, Y., Wimmel, H., Wolf, K.: Raw Report on the Model Checking Contest at Petri Nets 2012. CoRR abs/1209.2382 (2012)
13. Lautenbach, K., Ridder, H.: A completion of the S-invariance technique by means of fixed point algorithms. Technical report, Universität Koblenz-Landau (1995)
14. Noack, A.: A ZBDD package for efficient model checking of Petri nets (in German). Technical report, BTU Cottbus, Department of CS (1999)
15. Schwarick, M., Heiner, M.: CSL model checking of biochemical networks with interval decision diagrams. In: Degano, P., Gorrieri, R. (eds.) CMSB 2009. LNCS, vol. 5688, pp. 296–312. Springer, Heidelberg (2009)
16. Schwarick, M., Rohr, C., Heiner, M.: MARCIE - model checking and reachability analysis done efficiently. In: Proceedings of QEST 2011, pp. 91–100. IEEE CS Press (2011)
17. Schwarick, M., Tovchigrechko, A.: IDD-based model validation of biochemical networks. Theor. Comput. Sci. **412**(26), 2884–2908 (2011)
18. Schwarick, M.: Symbolic on-the-fly analysis of stochastic Petri nets. Ph.D. thesis, BTU Cottbus, Department of CS (2014)
19. Tovchigrechko, A.: Model checking using interval decision diagrams. Ph.D. thesis, BTU Cottbus, Department of CS (2008)
20. Yang, B., Bryant, R.E., O'Hallaron, D.R., Biere, A., Coudert, O., Janssen, G., Ranjan, R.K., Somenzi, F.: A performance study of BDD-based model checking. In: Gopalakrishnan, G.C., Windley, P. (eds.) FMCAD 1998. LNCS, vol. 1522, pp. 255–289. Springer, Heidelberg (1998)

A Symbolic Model Checker for Petri Nets: pnmc

Alexandre Hamez[✉]

Steery.io, Donneville, France
alexandre.hamez@gmail.com

Abstract. Symbolic model checking with decision diagrams is a very efficient technique for handling large models. However, even when using advanced algorithms, model checking tools still need to be carefully written. Indeed, they are both CPU and memory bounded: in addition to the algorithms complexity, the limiting factors are the available memory and how fast computations are performed. Thus, each saved CPU cycle or byte can make the difference between a successful model checker and a failing one.

We present **pnmc**, a symbolic model checker for Petri Nets, and `libsdd`, its associated library which implements Hierarchical Set Decision Diagrams and automatic saturation. Reliability aside, choices were always made to favour performance.

The combination of advanced algorithms for symbolic model checking and advanced coding techniques offer very good results as shown in the Model Checking Contest 2015, which is used as a background to present **pnmc** and `libsdd`.

Keywords: Tool · Petri nets · Symbolic model checking · Decision diagrams

1 Introduction

Model checking [9] suffers from the well-known state space explosion problem: realistic (industrial-size) models often yield state spaces too large to be computed or stored in memory. Over the years, many techniques have been devised to tackle this problem.

The introduction of symbolic model checking [6], using Reduced Ordered Binary Decision Diagrams (BDDs) [5], made it possible to handle larger models. State spaces and transition relations are encoded using BDDs, which provides two benefits: (1) common parts of states are shared, using less memory; (2) the transition relation is applied symbolically, resulting in the computation of several states at a time, using less computation time. The combination of these benefits often allows improvements of several orders of magnitude.

Since the advent of BDDs, various kinds of decision diagrams have been devised. Data Decision Diagrams [10] and Hierarchical Set Decision Diagrams (SDDs) [11] are among the most successful versions since then. Using structural

© Springer-Verlag Berlin Heidelberg 2016
M. Koutny et al. (Eds.): ToPNoC XI, LNCS 9930, pp. 297–306, 2016.
DOI: 10.1007/978-3-662-53401-4_15

information [18] and automatization [13] of the saturation technique [8], they can provide another order of magnitude improvement.

libsdd is a C++ library that provides an implementation of SDDs and a framework to manipulate them, using automatic saturation. pnmc is a model checker for Petri nets, built on top of libsdd, implementing symbolic state space generation, as well as symbolic reachability analysis.

The Model Checking Contest [15] is a yearly event dedicated to the evaluation of model checkers. Its objective is to *compare the efficiency of techniques according to characteristics of models*. It offers a way to evaluate the performances and the reliability of pnmc and libsdd, providing a huge set of Petri nets models with various characteristics.

pnmc was quite successful as it ranked second out of 11 tools in the 2015 edition of MCC. We attribute this to the combination of a good theory (SDD and automatic saturation) and a carefully crafted implementation with no compromises when performance is concerned.

This paper is organized as follows. Section 2 offers a brief presentation of Hierarchical Set Decision Diagrams and Symbolic Model Checking, Sects. 3 and 4 present respectively libsdd and pnmc. Section 5 details the technical choices in libsdd optimization. Section 6 analyses the Model Checking Contest results, and Sect. 7 discusses future works.

2   Symbolic Model Checking with Hierarchical Set Decision Diagrams

Hierarchical Set Decision Diagrams. SDDs [11] are shared decision diagrams in which arcs are labelled by a set of values, instead of a single value. As ordinary decision diagrams, they have the same distinctive features: canonical node representation, dynamic programming and variable ordering issues.

As SDDs encode sets of values and support standard set operations ($\cup, \cap, \setminus$), they can be used as labels, making hierarchical encoding possible. This unique feature enables recursive encoding of regular models (e.g., a protocol using a ring architecture), potentially yielding an exponential reduction in state space size [18].

Symbolic Model Checking. Usually, when performing symbolic model checking, a system's next state function is encoded using one or more decision diagrams, with two variables per state signature variable.

In the case of SDDs, however, a mechanism called *inductive homomorphisms* makes the definition of user operations possible. These homomorphisms are mappings that transform SDDs into other SDDs. Basic homomorphisms (e.g. fixpoint, composition, etc.) are available enabling the construction of complex firing rules.

An important feature provided by these homomorphisms is a set of rewriting rules for homomorphisms [13] allowing to automatically make use of saturation algorithms (originally devised in [8]): when computing the least fixpoint of a transition relation over a set of states, this algorithm offers gains of one to three orders of magnitude over classical BFS fixpoint algorithms. These rewriting rules are transparent, thus users need only to express their firing rule, the homomorphism evaluation takes care of applying the saturation dynamically.

3   A Generic Library for SDD: libsdd

We briefly present in this section the salient features of the libsdd library, the backbone of pnmc.

Generic Design. The goal of libsdd is to provide a generic framework to create and manipulate SDDs. To do so, we use the C++ template facility: users can specify what type of set of values they wish to store on arcs.

The default type is a set of discrete integers, but any type that supports set union, intersection and difference can be used, including continuous domains. Even other decision diagrams, such as BDDs, could be used as they describe set of values.

Variable Order. Symbolic techniques based on decision diagrams can suffer from the variable order problem [4]. To mitigate this problem, libsdd offers three ways to specify variable ordering:

- Use model natural order: as naive as it may seem, models are often specified in such a way that related places are close to each other, which is a key point to ensure a good variable ordering;
- Use FORCE ordering heuristic [2], which often provides good results when nothing is known about models to analyse;
- Use a hand-crafted order: obviously, this must be performed by someone with insights on both decision diagrams and models.

Related Work. libDDD [1] is the first library that implemented SDDs (it also provides an implementation of Data Decision Diagrams).

Being older, libDDD provides more functionalities than libsdd, especially in regard to the number of rewriting rules used to perform automatic saturation. For instance, it is able to permute commutative operands, which in turns make grouping related operands more likely. This often has a very beneficial impact on performances.

libsdd provides fewer rewriting rules, but it has been written with an emphasis on performances from the ground up.

4   A Petri Net Symbolic Model Checker: pnmc

The pnmc model checker is built on top of libsdd. However it's more than a frontend for this library. SDDs and homomorphisms are just a framework to manipulate states in a symbolic way. The role of pnmc is to create and optimise the transition relation for Petri nets.

For instance, pnmc reorders operations using the variable order to optimize the firing rule. It can also use the fact that a Petri net is safe to optimize some operations (for Time Petri nets).

pnmc supports state space generation and verification of dead states and transitions for P/T Petri nets with a few extensions (inhibitors, reset and test arcs are supported). pnmc also supports the state space generation of Time Petri nets, using discrete time semantics.

File formats supported by pnmc are: Tina's .net and .ndr, NUPN and PNML (P/T Petri nets only). In the case of .net files, we added an extension to express modules[1], that is, how some places are related to each other. This information is used to create a hierarchical encoding.

Time Petri Nets. pnmc can symbolically generate the state space of Time Petri Nets, using discrete time semantics. It implements the same algorithm used by Tina [3], with the difference that pnmc uses a symbolic approach and Tina an enumerative one.

It has been found, comparing Tina and pnmc that symbolic generation performs often better for small time intervals. However, as soon as time intervals become larger, the enumerative approach is very often more competitive.

Comparable work is presented in [16], although with a few differences regarding the time discretisation.

NUPN. This particular Petri net format [12] has the advantage of clearly identifying components (*units*) by grouping related places. Hierarchy is also captured by describing how units contain each other, starting from a root unit. Moreover, the Petri net is guaranteed to be safe. Combined with this structural information, place invariants can be automatically deduced.

pnmc leverages these structural informations. First, this hierarchy can be directly mapped onto the SDD hierarchy. Second, the presence of invariants make it possible to use only one variable per unit (to describe which place is marked in the unit), rather than one variable per place as it's the case for standard Petri nets. This usually has a very beneficial impact on performances as the number of SDDs stored in memory is often much smaller.

However, the firing rule is completely different. This is why this particular case is handled by a different tool, caesar.sdd (also built on top of libsdd), which originally started as a fork of pnmc. Work is ongoing to merge it back.

---

[1] This extension remains backward compatible with Tina.

However, it shows that libsdd is versatile and can easily be used in different contexts. During the MCC, caesar.sdd was used for all models that were provided with a NUPN specification.

Related Work. The Smart model checker [7] is the first tool to implement saturation, using Multi-Valued Decision Diagrams. However, the firing rule had to be manually modified which is a tedious process.

ITS tools [17] and PNXDD, participated in the Model Checking Contest 2015, both use libddd as a backend, and as such, automatic saturation.

5 Technical Choices

In this section, we present technical choices that made libsdd, and, by extrapolation, pnmc (and caesar.sdd) efficient. These optimisation tips should prove useful for most model checking tools' authors.

The key property of an efficient model checker is obviously the algorithms and heuristics it uses. However, even the most efficient algorithm could be spoilt by a poorly and hastily written implementation.

The rationale for choosing what to optimise was as follows: we first used available libraries (e.g., for hash tables or memory management) to make a fast implementation of algorithms possible; and as soon as a performance bottleneck was identified when profiling, we rolled out a custom version tailored to our needs.

Language. Choosing the right language for the right job is a very important point that is often overlooked (and arguably controversial). On the one hand, using "easy" languages like Java and Python or "expressive" ones like OCaml let us write new algorithms quickly. On the other hand, languages like C or C++ offer all the tools to manage memory manually and to optimize algorithms, exactly the way we want, but at the cost of a much larger code base (and often harder to write and to test).

In this regard, we chose C++ 14 to implement libsdd and pnmc in order to be able to fine-tune all memory or CPU intensive parts, as well as to provide easily portable code.

For instance, the C++ template mechanism allows us to choose at compile time the best fitted algorithm when building a new SDD. Using the type of the values that an SDD stores on arcs, and if this type fulfills some requirements, we can switch from a $O(n^2)$ algorithm to a $O(n)$ one at compile-time, thus with no runtime overhead.

Memory. Model checking is a CPU and memory bound process. Obviously, optimizing algorithms should be done in a first step. But once this is done, optimizing memory access should not be overlooked as using memory is not cheap: not only allocating memory is costly, but also *how* to allocate it matters.

Furthermore, over the years, the main memory has been slower to access from the CPU (from up to a thousands of CPU cycles).

For instance, when inserting a new value in a sorted container, the complexity is logarithmic when using a binary tree and linear when using a sorted array. However on modern hardware, memory access is so slow compared to the CPU speed that, in practice, one should often use a contiguous array when storing up to thousands values. The key here is *contiguous memory*: a tool should be written in such a way that, when fetching memory to perform some computation, all data needed by this computation are in contiguous memory locations.

Unrolled SDD Nodes. A way to apply this idea to decision diagrams is to avoid memory indirection (accessing a value via a pointer). Let's take the case of an SDD node: it is basically just a variable associated to a set of labels leading to SDD successors. As this set's size is unknown at compile-time, we need to allocate the list of successors dynamically. Thus, each node contains a pointer to this list. This memory indirection causes several problems: the memory is fragmented and CPU cache misses occur more often.

A very simple optimisation is to remove this memory indirection by storing successors directly into the SDD node, very much like unrolled linked lists. This simple trick brought an improvement of 20 % in our benchmarks, for both memory and CPU[2].

Linear Allocation for Recursive Algorithms. Evaluation of homomorphisms on SDDs is a highly recursive process. However, each recursive call incurs dynamic memory allocations as the size of temporary memory placeholders cannot be predicted ahead of time.

To optimise this scheme, we rolled out our own memory allocator to simulate a stack on a pre-allocated buffer. So, allocating or deallocating memory is only a matter of moving a pointer up or down in said buffer, which is a constant-time operation, rather than a costly call to allocate memory (which possibly involves a system call).

Custom Reference Counting Garbage Collector. All decision diagrams implementations need some kind of garbage collector, whether it's provided by the language, like Java, or implemented in the decision diagram library.

To minimize memory footprint, we implemented a deterministic reference-counting garbage collector: as soon as a SDD node is no longer needed (by caches or ongoing computations), it's discarded.

Pre-allocation of Buffers. As dynamic allocations are unavoidable (new SDDs and homomorphism operations are created all the time), we chose to pre-allocate big buffers at startup for operations' caches. Thus, most of the time, pnmc won't need to request new memory chunks from the OS too frequently. It presents a

---

[2] Due to memory alignment requirements, this trick may not be used on some CPU or platforms. However, it's not a problem on "standard" configurations like Linux/x86.

minor drawback for the Model Checking Contest: pnmc always start with 2 GB of memory, whatever the model is. So, pnmc may seem to be a memory hog for small models, even though it's a strategy to make it faster.

Other Optimisations. Many other optimisation techniques were implemented. For instance: a custom algebraic data type to store SDDs for fast runtime dispatch and small memory footprint; an intrusive custom hash table; a continuation-based hash function; memory pools.

6   Model Checking Contest 2015

The Model Checking Contest [15] is a yearly event dedicated to the evaluation of model checkers. This contest is a great opportunity to evaluate performance. Indeed, it benchmarks different model checkers against a comprehensive set of models on the same hardware. There are 370 models with scaling parameters, totalling a number of 525 models. It is maintained by other people than the tools' authors, providing a fair and unbiased comparison.

More than comparing tools performances against each other, it's also an excellent opportunity to validate results, and thus to assess tools' reliability. Furthermore, it also permits to compare different techniques (symbolic, SAT, explicit, etc.) to identify which one performs better for which type of model (for instance, asynchronous vs. synchronous specifications).

The models are partitioned in 3 sets:

- *Known*. This set is known by model checker authors before the contest and thus can be optimized for ahead of time (for instance, for model checkers using decision diagrams, a variable order can be pre-computed);
- *Stripped*. This set is a subset of the first one, except that the models are given under a new name, making impossible to optimize them beforehand (reproducing the case where the user is not the tool's author, so with possibly less experience on how to use the tool with the optimal settings);
- *Surprise*. It regroups all models that are unknown to tools' authors, with the same limitations on possibly pre-computed optimizations.

Because some models are given twice (in *Known* and *Stripped* categories), model checkers are handed a total of 929 instances, 628 of them being P/T Petri nets.

pnmc only participated in the *StateSpace* category, as the parsing and processing of accessibility formulae wasn't ready in time. Furthermore, it only processed P/T Petri nets, as coloured nets are not handled. When a model was provided with a NUPN specification, pnmc handed over this model to `caesar.sdd` in order to use a dedicated firing rule.

Variable Order. For *Known* models, we chose to manually create variable orders for most models. The strategy was simply to identify and group places that seem to belong to the same component. For both *Stripped* and *Surprise* models, we used the FORCE heuristic.

Analysis of MCC 2015 Results. For its second appearance at MCC, pnmc finished second in the State Space category[3]. It processed correctly[4] 385 out of 628 instances (61.3 %). This makes pnmc the tool which processed the largest number of specifications in the *StateSpace* category for P/T Petri nets.

It should be noted that pnmc is reported having incorrect results for three models (Parking-PT-832, Raft-PT-03 and Raft-PT-05). This was, however, not a state space generation failure: it's an error due to a rounding issue by the MCC benchmark scripts[5]. Thus, pnmc should be considered 100 % reliable in this contest.

Finally, as explained in Sect. 5, pnmc may seem to use a lot of memory, even for small specifications. This is due to a pre-allocation scheme minimizing the amount of memory allocations, which makes the state space generation faster.

7   Future Work

The participation of pnmc in the Model Checking Contest showed that the variable order still remains a major problem for decision diagrams. Orders deduced manually often performed better than the ones produced by heuristics. This is a major problem as we can't expect users to produce good orders by themselves. Our future works will therefore mostly focus on this topic.

Producing manually orders, we observed that a trend often emerges: we always first looked for regular patterns, like state machines of processes or shared resources. Thus, we think that using Petri nets structural properties, like invariants, is a promising path for computing variable orders. We also plan to add the heuristics introduced in [14] which provide good orders for large models.

Also, we'll focus on providing the possibility to verify more reachability properties.

8   Conclusion

We presented both pnmc, a symbolic model checker for Petri nets, and libsdd, a library that implements Hierarchical Set Decision Diagrams.

We showed how carefully writing a model checker, using appropriate paradigms and technical choices, can produce a very efficient tool. However we cannot stress enough the fact that writing an optimized code is only second to designing efficient algorithms, which in the case of pnmc is *automatic saturation* associated to *Hierarchical Set Decision Diagrams*.

The results of the Model Checking Contest 2015 were used to assess the performances and reliability of pnmc, proving that it's an efficient tool that can be used with confidence for state space generation and simple reachability analysis.

---

[3] pnmc also ranked second on its first appearance at the 2014 edition.

[4] Which means that more than one tool agreed on the result.

[5] MCC organizers fixed this issue by requiring a normalized output and by using more significant digits when comparing results.

Availability. Both `libsdd` and `pnmc` are released under the BSD license and are freely available (respectively at https://github.com/ahamez/libsdd and https://ahamez.github.io/pnmc). They have been successfully compiled and tested on Linux and Mac OS X, with GCC $\geq$ 5.1 and Clang $\geq$ 3.4, on x86 64 bits architectures.

Both have been exhaustively tested: unit tests for `libsdd` cover more than 90 % of the code base; `pnmc` is tested against a set of Petri nets that represent all corner cases that have been encountered so far. It's also regularly tested against all models of the Model Checking Contest to ensure that new features and optimizations don't introduce any regressions.

Acknowledgments. Part of this work was done at the ISAE-SUPAERO institute.

We are very grateful to Bernard Berthomieu for his guidance in writing the transition relation for Time Petri Nets with discrete semantics.

Finally, none of this work would have been possible without the help of Alban Linard on the first version of the `libsdd` library, which laid out all the important concepts of the current version.

References

1. libDDD web site. http://ddd.lip6.fr
2. Aloul, F.A., Markov, I.L., Sakallah, K.A.: Force: a fast and easy-to-implement variable-ordering heuristic. In: Proceedings of the 13th ACM Great Lakes Symposium on VLSI, GLSVLSI 2003, pp. 116–119. ACM, New York (2003). http://doi.acm.org/10.1145/764808.764839
3. Berthomieu, B., Ribet, P.O., Vernadat, F.: The tool TINA - construction of abstract state spaces for petri nets and time petri nets. Int. J. Prod. Res. **42**(14), 2741–2756 (2004)
4. Bollig, B., Wegener, L.: Improving the variable ordering of OBDDs is NP-complete. IEEE Trans. Comput. **45**(9), 993–1002 (1996)
5. Bryant, R.: Graph-based algorithms for Boolean function manipulation. IEEE Trans. Comput. **35**(8), 677–691 (1986)
6. Burch, J., Clarke, E., McMillan, K.: Symbolic model checking: 10^{20} states and beyond. Inf. Comput. **98**(2), 153–181 (1992). Special issue for best papers from LICS90
7. Ciardo, G., Jones, R.L., Miner, A.S., Siminiceanu, R.I.: Logical and stochastic modeling with Smart. In: Kemper, P., Sanders, W.H. (eds.) TOOLS 2003. LNCS, vol. 2794, pp. 78–97. Springer, Heidelberg (2003). http://dx.doi.org/10.1007/978-3-540-45232-4_6
8. Ciardo, G., Lüttgen, G., Siminiceanu, R.I.: Saturation: an efficient iteration strategy for symbolic state-space generation. In: Margaria, T., Yi, W. (eds.) TACAS 2001. LNCS, vol. 2031, pp. 328–342. Springer, Heidelberg (2001). http://www.springerlink.com/content/mbff40ngvw3m8k2b
9. Clarke, E., Grumberg, O., Peled, D.: Model Checking. MIT Press, Cambridge (2000)
10. Couvreur, J.-M., Encrenaz, E., Paviot-Adet, E., Poitrenaud, D., Wacrenier, P.-A.: Data decision diagrams for petri net analysis. In: Esparza, J., Lakos, C.A. (eds.) ICATPN 2002. LNCS, vol. 2360, pp. 101–120. Springer, Heidelberg (2002). http://www.labri.fr/publications/mvtsi/2002/CEPPW02

11. Couvreur, J.-M., Thierry-Mieg, Y.: Hierarchical decision diagrams to exploit model structure. In: Wang, F. (ed.) FORTE 2005. LNCS, vol. 3731, pp. 443–457. Springer, Heidelberg (2005). http://dx.doi.org/10.1007/11562436_32

12. Garavel, H.: Nested-unit petri nets: a structural means to increase efficiency and scalability of verification on elementary nets. In: Devillers, R., Valmari, A. (eds.) PETRI NETS 2015. LNCS, vol. 9115, pp. 179–199. Springer, Heidelberg (2015). http://dx.doi.org/10.1007/978-3-319-19488-2_9

13. Hamez, A., Thierry-Mieg, Y., Kordon, F.: Building efficient model checkers using hierarchical set decision diagrams and automatic saturation. Fundam. Inf. **94**(3–4), 413–437 (2009). http://dx.doi.org/10.1007/978-3-319-19488-2_9

14. Hong, S., Kordon, F., Paviot-Adet, E., Evangelista, S.: Computing a hierarchical static order for decision diagram-based representation from P/T nets. In: Jensen, K., Donatelli, S., Kleijn, J. (eds.) Transactions on Petri Nets and Other Models of Concurrency V. LNCS, vol. 6900, pp. 121–140. Springer, Heidelberg (2012). http://dx.doi.org/10.1007/978-3-642-29072-5_5

15. Kordon, F., Garavel, H., Hillah, L.M., Hulin-Hubard, F., Linard, A., Beccuti, M., Evangelista, S., Hamez, A., Lohmann, N., Lopez, E., Paviot-Adet, E., Rodriguez, C., Rohr, C., Srba, J.: HTML Results from the Model Checking Contest @ Petri Net, 2014th edn. (2014). http://mcc.lip6.fr/2014

16. Thierry-Mieg, Y., Bérard, B., Kordon, F., Lime, D., Roux, O.H.: Compositional analysis of discrete time petri nets. In: Proceedings of the 1st Workshop on Petri Nets Compositions (CompoNet 2011), vol. 726, pp. 17–31. CEUR, Newcastle, June 2011

17. Thierry-Mieg, Y.: Symbolic model-checking using its-tools. In: Baier, C., Tinelli, C. (eds.) TACAS 2015. LNCS, vol. 9035, pp. 231–237. Springer, Heidelberg (2015). http://dx.doi.org/10.1007/978-3-662-46681-0_20

18. Thierry-Mieg, Y., Poitrenaud, D., Hamez, A., Kordon, F.: Hierarchical set decision diagrams and regular models. In: Kowalewski, S., Philippou, A. (eds.) TACAS 2009. LNCS, vol. 5505, pp. 1–15. Springer, Heidelberg (2009). http://dx.doi.org/10.1007/978-3-642-00768-2_1

TAPAAL and Reachability Analysis of P/T Nets

Jonas F. Jensen, Thomas Nielsen, Lars K. Oestergaard, and Jiří Srba[(✉)]

Department of Computer Science, Aalborg University,
Selma Lagerlöfs Vej 300, 9220 Aalborg East, Denmark
srba@cs.aau.dk

Abstract. We discuss selected model checking techniques used in the tool TAPAAL for the reachability analysis of weighted Petri nets with inhibitor arcs. We focus on techniques that had the most significant effect at the 2015 Model Checking Contest (MCC). While the techniques are mostly well known, our contribution lies in their adaptation to the MCC reachability queries, their efficient implementation and the evaluation of their performance on a large variety of nets from MCC'15.

1 Introduction

Petri nets [15] are a popular formalism for a high level modelling of distributed systems. Currently, there are more than 80 tools registered in the database of Petri net tools [8] and an annual model checking contest aiming at comparing the performance of the different tools has been running since 2011. In the last two editions of the contest, MCC'14 [10] and MCC'15 [11], our model checker TAPAAL [4] won a second place in the reachability category. In this paper, we report on the main verification techniques implemented in our tool and demonstrate their performance on the class of Petri nets from the latest edition of the model checking contest.

TAPAAL is a tool suite that apart from the verification engine for P/T nets supports also the modelling and analysis of a timed extension of the Petri net formalism called timed-arc Petri nets (for more details see [9]). The tool supports both continuous and discrete time verification and while the details about the continuous-time engine [5] and the discrete-time engine [1] were previously published, the untimed verification engine has not been presented yet.

We focus here solely on the TAPAAL verification techniques directly related to our participation in the model checking contest. The details about the other participating tools and a report on the competition results can be found in [11]. In what follows, we first describe an efficient heuristic search technique for explicit exploration of the Petri net state-space, then we discuss the adaptation of the state-equation approach to the case of cardinality queries and finally we demonstrate the applicability of the sequential and parallel structural reduction rules into the context of checking cardinality queries on weighted nets with inhibitor arcs.

TAPAAL is open-source and publicly available at www.tapaal.net. Citations to the related work connected to the techniques used in our tool are given at

© Springer-Verlag Berlin Heidelberg 2016
M. Koutny et al. (Eds.): ToPNoC XI, LNCS 9930, pp. 307–318, 2016.
DOI: 10.1007/978-3-662-53401-4_16

the respective sections of the paper. All experiments reported in this paper use the competition nets and queries from MCC'15 but the verification was rerun locally as we needed to compare the different options and techniques (the data for the different combinations of these parameters is not available at the MCC'15 web-page as we submitted there only the best working configuration of our tool).

2   Definitions

Let $\mathbb{N}_0$ denote the set of natural numbers including zero. A Petri net (PN) with inhibitor arcs is a tuple $N = (P, T, F, I)$ where

- P is a finite, nonempty set of *places*,
- T is a finite set of *transitions* such that $P \cap T = \emptyset$,
- $F : (P \times T) \cup (T \times P) \to \mathbb{N}_0$ is the *flow* function, and
- $I \subseteq P \times T$ is the set of inhibitor arcs such that $(p, t) \in I$ implies $F(p, t) = 0$.

Let $N = (P, T, F, I)$ be a PN. A *marking* is a mapping $M : P \to \mathbb{N}_0$ that assigns tokens to places. The set $\mathcal{M}(N)$ denotes the infinite set of all markings on N. A *marked PN* is a pair (N, M_0) where $M_0 \in \mathcal{M}(N)$ is an initial marking.

The *preset* of a place/transition y is defined as $^\bullet y \stackrel{def}{=} \{z \in P \cup T \mid F(z, y) > 0\}$. Likewise, the *postset* is $y^\bullet \stackrel{def}{=} \{z \in P \cup T \mid F(y, z) > 0\}$. We denote the set of inhibitor places of a transition t as $I(t) \stackrel{def}{=} \{p \in P \mid (p, t) \in I\}$ and transitions that a place p inhibits as $I(p) \stackrel{def}{=} \{t \in T \mid (p, t) \in I\}$.

A transition $t \in T$ is *enabled* in a marking M if for all $p \in {}^\bullet t$ we have $F(p, t) \leq M(p)$ and $M(p) = 0$ for all $p \in I(t)$. A transition t enabled in a marking M can *fire* and produce a marking M' such that $M'(p) = M(p) - F(p, t) + F(t, p)$ for all $p \in P$, written as $M \stackrel{t}{\to} M'$. This firing relation is in a natural way extended to a sequence of transitions $w \in T^*$ so that $M \stackrel{\epsilon}{\to} M$ and for $w = tw'$ we write $M \stackrel{w}{\to} M'$ if $M \stackrel{t}{\to} M''$ and $M'' \stackrel{w'}{\to} M'$. We also write $M \to M'$ if $M \stackrel{t}{\to} M'$ for some $t \in T$. The reflexive and transitive closure of $\to$ is denoted by $\to^*$. Finally, let $\mathcal{R}(M) = \{M' \mid M \to^* M'\}$ be the set of markings reachable from M.

As usual, Petri net places are denoted by circles and can contain dots representing tokens, transitions are drawn as rectangles, input and output arcs are depicted as arrows labelled with their weights (if a label is missing we assume the default weight 1) and inhibitor arcs are denoted by circle-headed arrows.

After having introduced the standard syntax and semantics of Petri nets, we shall now define the reachability problem for cardinality queries, as the main MCC'15 competition category in the reachability analysis.

A *cardinality formula* is given by the abstract syntax

$$\varphi ::= e \bowtie e \mid \varphi \wedge \varphi \mid \varphi \vee \varphi \mid \neg\varphi$$
$$e ::= n \mid p \mid e + e \mid e - e \mid n \cdot e$$

where $\bowtie \in \{\leq, <, =, \neq, >, \geq\}$, $n \in \mathbb{N}_0$ and $p \in P$.

The satisfaction relation $M \models \varphi$ for a given marking is defined in the natural way such that $M \models e_1 \bowtie e_2$ iff $eval(M, e_1) \bowtie eval(M, e_2)$ where $eval(M, e)$ is the evaluation of the arithmetical expression e into a number, assuming that $eval(M, p) = M(p)$ for $p \in P$ (in other words, a place p evaluates to the number of tokens currently present in it).

For a marked Petri net (N, M_0), we write $(N, M_0) \models EF\,\varphi$ if there is a marking M such that $M_0 \rightarrow^* M$ and $M \models \varphi$. As an example, the query $EF\,p \geq 5 \wedge q \neq 3$ asks whether we can reach a marking where the place p contains at least 5 tokens and the number of tokens in the place q is different from 3.

Note that the MCC'15 verification queries [11] also contain other types of reachability questions: (i) *reachability firability* where we consider the atomic proposition $fire(t)$ that is true in a given marking iff the transition t is fireable, (ii) *reachability compute bounds* where the expression $bounds(X)$ for $X \subseteq P$ is added as an atomic expression of e and it reports the maximum number of tokens in the places from X in any reachable marking and (iii) *reachability deadlock* where we ask if there is a reachable marking M such that there is no $t \in T$ and no M' where $M \xrightarrow{t} M'$.

We notice that firability can be encoded as a cardinality query

$$fire(t) \equiv \bigwedge_{p \in {}^\bullet t} p \geq F(p, t) \wedge \bigwedge_{p \in I(t)} p = 0$$

and deadlock can be encoded as the cardinality query

$$deadlock \equiv \bigwedge_{t \in T} \neg fire(t) \ .$$

In TAPAAL, we indeed encode reachability firability queries into the cardinality queries but we use a dedicated deadlock proposition in order to be able to apply structural reductions (see Sect. 5). The computation of bounds for a given set of places X is done by exploring the whole state-space while still being able to apply some structural reduction rules. Details are discussed in Sect. 5.

3 Explicit Search Algorithm with Heuristic Distance

We shall now describe the explicit search algorithm used in TAPAAL for answering reachability cardinality queries. The search is based on the standard search algorithm using passed/waiting sets (see e.g. [3]) as given in Algorithm 1 but with the important addition of exploring first the markings with the shortest distance to a given cardinality query φ. The distance $\text{DISTANCE}(M, \varphi)$ is computed in Algorithm 2 and it returns a nonnegative integer. If $M \models \varphi$ then the distance function returns 0, otherwise the distance tries to estimate how far away is the marking M from satisfying the query φ.

This is achieved by first estimating the distance between two integer values w.r.t. a given comparison operator $\bowtie$, as defined by the Δ function in Algorithm 2. Intuitively, the function $\Delta(v_1, \bowtie, v_2)$ returns the smallest number

---

Algorithm 1. Best-First Reachability Search

1: **function** BEST-FIRST-REACHABILITY-SEARCH(N, M_0, φ)
2:     **if** $M_0 \models \varphi$ **then**
3:         **return** *true*
4:     **end if**
5:     $Waiting := \{M_0\}$ ▷ Priority queue
6:     $Passed := \{M_0\}$ ▷ Set of passed markings
7:     **while** $Waiting \neq \emptyset$ **do**
8:         $M := \underset{M \in Waiting}{\arg\min} \text{ DISTANCE}(M, \varphi)$ ▷ A shortest distance marking
9:         $Waiting := Waiting \setminus \{M\}$
10:         **for** M' such that $M \overset{t}{\to} M'$ where $t \in T$ **do**   ▷ For each successor marking
11:             **if** $M' \notin Passed$ **then**
12:                 $Passed := Passed \cup \{M'\}$
13:                 **if** $M' \models \varphi$ **then**
14:                     **return** *true*   ▷ Output true and terminate
15:                 **end if**
16:                 $Waiting := Waiting \cup \{M'\}$ ▷ Marking M' should be explored
17:             **end if**
18:         **end for**
19:     **end while**
20:     **return** *false*   ▷ No reachable marking satisfying φ was found
21: **end function**

---

by which either v_1 or v_2 must be changed in order to make the predicate $v_1 \bowtie v_2$ valid. The basic distance Δ is then extended to the logical connectives: for conjunction both conjuncts have to hold and hence we add the distances of the conjuncts together, and for disjunction where only one of the disjuncts needs to hold, we take the minimum. The negation is simply propagated down to the atomic predicates using De Morgan's laws.

The heuristics operates very satisfactory in many scenarios as it relies on the assumption that similar markings are likely to be just a few firings away from each other. Nevertheless, in some scenarios the heuristic estimate may degrade the search performance.

We performed a number of experiments comparing the heuristic search strategy against breadth-first-search (BFS) and depth-first-search (DFS) on the competition nets and queries from MCC'15 [11]. We selected a number of hard border-line instances of problems where we still expected to get a reasonable number of conclusive answers for positive reachability queries, resulting in 1296 executions (432 executions for each search strategy). Out of those, we selected models and queries where at least one search strategy found a reachable marking satisfying the given cardinality query and where at least one search strategy took more than 3 s (in order to filter out the trivial instances). This resulted in 492 executions (164 for each search strategy) and the results are presented in Fig. 1.

The table shows that the heuristic search was the fastest one in 89 instances, which is more than the sum of cases where BFS or DFS won (75 instances

---

Algorithm 2. Distance Heuristics

1: **function** DISTANCE(M, φ)
2:     **if** $\varphi = e_1 \bowtie e_2$ **then**
3:         **return** $\Delta(eval(M, e_1), \bowtie, eval(M, e_2))$
4:     **else if** $\varphi = \varphi_1 \wedge \varphi_2$ **then**
5:         **return** DISTANCE(M, φ_1) + DISTANCE(M, φ_2)
6:     **else if** $\varphi = \varphi_1 \vee \varphi_2$ **then**
7:         **return** min{DISTANCE(M, φ_1), DISTANCE(M, φ_2)}
8:     **else if** $\varphi = \neg(e_1 \bowtie e_2)$ **then**
9:         **return** $\Delta(eval(M, e_1), \overline{\bowtie}, eval(M, e_2))$
10:     **else if** $\varphi = \neg(\varphi_1 \wedge \varphi_2)$ **then**
11:         **return** min{DISTANCE($M, \neg\varphi_1$), DISTANCE($M, \neg\varphi_2$)}
12:     **else if** $\varphi = \neg(\varphi_1 \vee \varphi_2)$ **then**
13:         **return** DISTANCE($M, \neg\varphi_1$) + DISTANCE($M, \neg\varphi_2$)
14:     **else if** $\varphi = \neg(\neg\varphi_1)$ **then**
15:         **return** DISTANCE(M, φ_1)
16:     **end if**
17: **end function**

where $\overline{\bowtie}$ is the dual arithmetical operation of $\bowtie$ (for example $\overline{<}$ is the notation for $\geq$) and where

$$\Delta(v_1, =, v_2) = |v_1 - v_2|$$

$$\Delta(v_1, \neq, v_2) = \begin{cases} 1 & \text{if } v_1 = v_2 \\ 0 & \text{otherwise} \end{cases}$$

$$\Delta(v_1, <, v_2) = \max\{v_1 - v_2 + 1, 0\} \quad \Delta(v_1, >, v_2) = \Delta(v_2, <, v_1)$$

$$\Delta(v_1, \leq, v_2) = \max\{v_1 - v_2, 0\} \quad \quad \Delta(v_1, \geq, v_2) = \Delta(v_2, \leq, v_1)$$

---

in total). The heuristic strategy timed out in only 19 cases (where either BFS or DFS provided an answer) compared to the large number of runs where BFS and DFS did not find the answer. Finally, the heuristic strategy was in 17 cases the only one that found a marking satisfying the given cardinality query, whereas BFS provided a solo answer in 9 cases and DFS in only 2 cases.

In conclusion, if we use only a single-core for the verification, the heuristic search is preferable, however, in case of more available cores, it may be a good idea to run all three different search strategies independently.

4   State Equations for Cardinality Queries

In this section we present an adaptation of the technique based on integer programming (state-equations [12,13]) which can be in some cases used to efficiently disprove reachability by over-approximating the state-space, hence avoiding the full state-space exploration. Let $N = (P, T, F, I)$ be a PN and let $M_0, M \in \mathcal{M}(N)$ be markings on N. If there is a sequence of transitions w such that $M_0 \xrightarrow{w} M$ then a well-known fact (see e.g. [13]) says that there is a nonnegative solution to the following system of equations over the variables $\{x_t \mid t \in T\}$:

Search Strategy	Winner	No. of Timeouts	Solo Answer
Heuristic	89	19	17
BFS	26	70	9
DFS	49	53	2

Fig. 1. Heuristic, BFS and DFS search strategies (timeout at 5 min)

$$M_0(p) + \sum_{t \in T} (F(t,p) - F(p,t)) \cdot x_t = M(p) \quad \text{for all } p \in P .$$

Clearly, if we set x_t to be the number of times t was fired in the sequence w, then this gives us the requested solution. Conversely, if there is no solution to the state-equations then M is not reachable from M_0. On the other hand, a solution to the state-equations does not in general imply that M is reachable from the marking M_0.

Esparza and Melzer [7] proposed to use integer linear programming in order to solve the state-equations, ensuring that $x_t \in \mathbb{N}_0$ for all $t \in T$ and thus providing a more accurate approximation. We shall generalize this approach to cardinality queries which may require several calls to a linear program solver. A *restriction* is a function $r : P \to \mathbb{N}_0 \times (\mathbb{N}_0 \cup \{\infty\})$ from places to right-open intervals representing the allowed number of tokens in each of the places (if $r(p) = [0, \infty]$ then there is no restriction on the number of tokens in p). Given two restrictions r_1 and r_2, we introduce the combined restriction $combine(r_1, r_2)$ defined as $combine(r_1, r_2)(p) = r_1(p) \cap r_2(p)$ where we assume here the standard interval intersection operator. We use the notation $\langle p_1 \mapsto [a_1, b_1], \dots p_n \mapsto [a_n, b_n] \rangle$ to represent a restriction r such that $r(p_1) = [a_1, b_1], \dots, r(p_n) = [a_n, b_n]$ and $r(p) = [0, \infty]$ for all $p \in P \setminus \{p_1, \dots, p_n\}$. For example, $combine(\langle p \mapsto [2, \infty], q \mapsto [2, 10] \rangle, \langle p \mapsto [0, 7] \rangle) = \langle p \mapsto [2, 7], q \mapsto [2, 10] \rangle$.

Let us now define the function *constraints* that for a given cardinality query φ returns a set of restrictions. For simplicity, we assume that the negation has already been pushed (using De Morgan rules) all the way to the atomic propositions where the negation can be replaced by the dual atomic propositions.

$$
\begin{aligned}
constr(p = n) &= \{\langle p \mapsto [n, n] \rangle\} \\
constr(p \neq n) &= \{\langle p \mapsto [0, n-1] \rangle, \langle p \mapsto [n+1, \infty] \rangle\} \\
constr(p \leq n) &= \{\langle p \mapsto [0, n] \rangle\} \\
constr(p \geq n) &= \{\langle p \mapsto [n, \infty] \rangle\} \\
constr(p < n) &= \{\langle p \mapsto [0, n-1] \rangle\} \\
constr(p > n) &= \{\langle p \mapsto [n+1, \infty] \rangle\}
\end{aligned}
$$

$$
\begin{aligned}
constr(\varphi_1 \vee \varphi_2) &= constr(\varphi_1) \cup constr(\varphi_2) \\
constr(\varphi_1 \wedge \varphi_2) &= \{combine(r_1, r_2) \mid r_1 \in constr(\varphi_1), r_2 \in constr(\varphi_2)\}
\end{aligned}
$$

The actual use of state-equations in the setting of cardinality queries is now described in Algorithm 3.

Algorithm 3. Disproving Reachability Using Integer Programming

1: **function** DISPROVE-REACHABILITY(N, M_0, φ)
2:   Let $N = (P, T, F, I)$.
3:   **for all** $r \in constr(\varphi)$ **do**
4:     $LP := \emptyset$ ▷ Let LP be an empty system of inequations
5:     **for all** $p \in P$ **do**
6:       Let $[min, max] = r(p)$.
7:       $LP := LP \cup \{M_0(p) + \sum_{t \in T} (F(t,p) - F(p,t)) \cdot x_t \geq min\}$
8:       $LP := LP \cup \{M_0(p) + \sum_{t \in T} (F(t,p) - F(p,t)) \cdot x_t \leq max\}$
9:     **end for**
10:     **if** LP has an integer solution **then**
11:       **return** "Inconclusive"
12:     **end if**
13:   **end for**
14:   **return** "$M \not\models EF\,\varphi$"
15: **end function**

Our implementation of the algorithm uses lpsolve [2] for the linear programming part and performs fast on most of the competition nets. We have selected two smallest instances of each scalable model from the known models used in MCC'15 in order to be able to make a full state-space search on most of these models for the purpose of our analysis. Then we ran the state-equation test for all cardinality queries, resulting in the total number of 1024 executions. If the over-approximation using state-equations succeeded (disproved reachability), we report this and terminate, otherwise we continue with the state-space search using the heuristic strategy with 5 min timeout. In 125 runs we did not get a conclusive answer and reached the timeout, in 405 runs the answer was negative (cardinality query was not reachable) and in the remaining 494 cases the query was reachable. Out of the 405 runs where the cardinality query was disproved, the state-equation technique succeeded in 118 cases (and hence the expensive state-space search was completely avoided). Moreover, it took on average only 0.15 s to perform the state-equation check, with only four tests exceeding 2 s. The most expensive over-approximation test was for the model PolyORBNT-S05J30 where it took 4.25 s.

The over-approximation using state-equations is a fast and efficient method to disprove the reachability of cardinality queries and it manages in almost 30 % of cases to provide a conclusive answer. In order to further increase the percentage of cases with conclusive answers, we plan to experiment with trap reduction [7] and other techniques in order to make the technique applicable to even more cardinality queries.

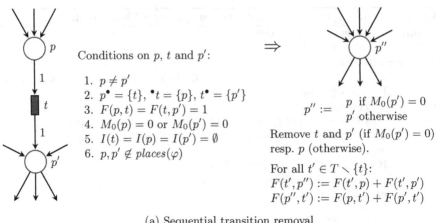

Conditions on p, t and p':

1. $p \neq p'$
2. $p^{\bullet} = \{t\}$, $^{\bullet}t = \{p\}$, $t^{\bullet} = \{p'\}$
3. $F(p,t) = F(t,p') = 1$
4. $M_0(p) = 0$ or $M_0(p') = 0$
5. $I(t) = I(p) = I(p') = \emptyset$
6. $p, p' \notin places(\varphi)$

$p'' := \begin{cases} p & \text{if } M_0(p') = 0 \\ p' & \text{otherwise} \end{cases}$

Remove t and p' (if $M_0(p') = 0$) resp. p (otherwise).

For all $t' \in T \setminus \{t\}$:
$F(t', p'') := F(t', p) + F(t', p')$
$F(p'', t') := F(p, t') + F(p', t')$

(a) Sequential transition removal

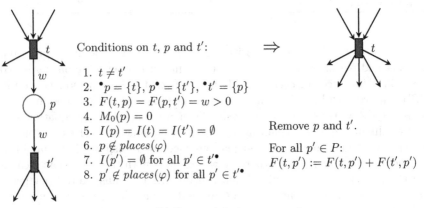

Conditions on t, p and t':

1. $t \neq t'$
2. $^{\bullet}p = \{t\}$, $p^{\bullet} = \{t'\}$, $^{\bullet}t' = \{p\}$
3. $F(t,p) = F(p,t') = w > 0$
4. $M_0(p) = 0$
5. $I(p) = I(t) = I(t') = \emptyset$
6. $p \notin places(\varphi)$
7. $I(p') = \emptyset$ for all $p' \in t'^{\bullet}$
8. $p' \notin places(\varphi)$ for all $p' \in t'^{\bullet}$

Remove p and t'.

For all $p' \in P$:
$F(t, p') := F(t, p') + F(t', p')$

(b) Sequential place removal

Fig. 2. Sequential rules for a cardinality formula φ and initial marking M_0

5   Structural Reductions

We shall now present a set of structural reduction rules that allow us to reduce the net structure and decrease the size of the state-space, while preserving the answers to cardinality queries. The classical reduction rules for preserving liveness, safeness and boundedness were introduced in [13, 14]. We extend them to weighted nets with inhibitor arcs and specialize to the use for cardinality queries. The extension is not completely straightforward as a number of side conditions must be satisfied in order to preserve correctness—in fact TAPAAL was the only tool at MCC'15 that used structural reduction techniques. The rules are presented in Figs. 2 and 3 and they are relative to a given initial marking M_0 and a cardinality query φ, where $places(\varphi)$ is the set of all places that occur in the query φ.

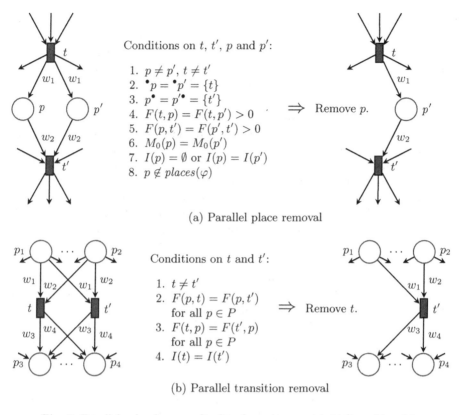

Conditions on t, t', p and p':

1. $p \neq p'$, $t \neq t'$
2. ${}^\bullet p = {}^\bullet p' = \{t\}$
3. $p^\bullet = p'^\bullet = \{t'\}$
4. $F(t, p) = F(t, p') > 0$
5. $F(p, t') = F(p', t') > 0$
6. $M_0(p) = M_0(p')$
7. $I(p) = \emptyset$ or $I(p) = I(p')$
8. $p \notin places(\varphi)$

$\Rightarrow$ Remove p.

(a) Parallel place removal

Conditions on t and t':

1. $t \neq t'$
2. $F(p, t) = F(p, t')$
   for all $p \in P$
3. $F(t, p) = F(t', p)$
   for all $p \in P$
4. $I(t) = I(t')$

$\Rightarrow$ Remove t.

(b) Parallel transition removal

Fig. 3. Parallel rules for a cardinality formula φ and initial marking M_0

Theorem 1. *Let (N, M_0) be a marked Petri net and let φ be a cardinality query. Let N' be the net N after the application of some reduction rules from Figs. 2 and 3. Then $(N, M_0) \models EF \varphi$ if and only if $(N', M_0) \models EF \varphi$.*

Proof. As cardinality queries are only concerned about the number of tokens in places, it is easy to see that the parallel transition rule in Fig. 3b is harmless as the transitions t and t' are enabled at the same time and they have the same firing effect, so we can easily remove one of them without affecting the reachable markings. Similarly, the parallel places rule in Fig. 3a ensures that the number of tokens in p and p' remain the same in any reachable marking (ensured by the assumption that p and p' contain the same number of tokens already in the initial marking). Now we can remove the place p, provided that p is not used in the cardinality query φ and either there are no inhibitor arcs connected to p or the places p and p' inhibit exactly the same set of transitions.

For a given net N, let N' be a net after one application of the sequential transition rule in Fig. 2a that removed the transition t. We shall first argue that if $(N, M_0) \models EF \varphi$, meaning that $M_0 \xrightarrow{w} M$ for some sequence of transitions w such that $M \models \varphi$, then also $(N', M_0) \models EF \varphi$. To show this, let w' be the transition sequence obtained from w by removing all occurrences of the transition t. Observe now that due to the fact that no inhibitor arcs are connected to p and p' (condition 5), we can execute from M_0 in N' the sequence w' (M_0 is a valid marking also in N' due to condition 4 requiring that the place we removed in N' has no tokens in M_0) and obtain a marking M' such that $M'(\overline{p}) = M(\overline{p})$ for all $\overline{p} \in P \smallsetminus \{p, p'\}$ and $M'(p'') = M(p) + M(p')$. As the query φ does not contain the places p and p' (condition 6), we can conclude that also $M' \models \varphi$ and hence $(N', M_0) \models EF\,\varphi$. For the opposite direction, assume that $M_0 \overset{w}{\to} M'$ in the net N' such that $M' \models \varphi$. We shall now fire this transition sequence w in the original net N such that whenever the transition t that was removed in N' is enabled, we insert its firing into the sequence w as long as it is enabled. This will guarantee that all tokens from p are moved to p' due to the requirement that the single input and output arcs of t have weight 1 (conditions 2 and 3) and that t is not connected with any inhibitor arcs (condition 5). As p is not an input place for any other transition than t (condition 2), moving the tokens from p to p' does not influence the firing of other transitions in N. Similarly, the configuration of tokens in p and p' cannot influence the firing of other transitions in N' due to the absence of inhibitor arcs connected to p and p' (condition 5). Now, let M be the marking reached in N after firing the sequence of transitions described above. Clearly, $M(\overline{p}) = M'(\overline{p})$ for all $\overline{p} \in P \smallsetminus \{p, p'\}$ and as φ is not referring to the places p and p' (condition 6), we get $M \models \varphi$ implying that $(N, M_0) \models EF\,\varphi$.

The arguments for the rule in Fig. 2b, omitted due to space limitations, are analogous to the sequential transition removal rule discussed above.   □

Note that the more places occur in the query φ, the fewer reduction rules are in general applicable. The reachability of a deadlock can be expressed using a cardinality query but then all places connected to some transition will be mentioned in the query and hence the structural reduction rules will not be applicable. However, for deadlock we can reduce the net w.r.t. some trivial query that does not contain any places (e.g. $EF\,2 < 1$) and now (N, M_0) is deadlock-free if and only if (N', M_0) is deadlock-free.

Theorem 2. *Let (N, M_0) be a marked Petri net. Let N' be the net N after the application of some reduction rules from Figs. 2 and 3 for a query $\varphi = 2 < 1$. Then (N, M_0) has a deadlock if and only if (N', M_0) has a deadlock.*

Proof. The proof is very similar to the proof of Theorem 1 but some of the additional conditions like the requirement $p \neq p'$ in the rule from Fig. 2a (condition 1) are important as removing the transition t in case of $p = p'$ can create a new deadlock in N' that is not present in N.   □

For the competition queries that ask to compute the maximum number of tokens in the net, we may only use reduction rules from Figs. 2b and 3b as the other two rules possibly decrease the maximum number of reachable tokens.

We have conducted experiments on the same nets as in Sect. 4 in order to see how many nets can be reduced and to what degree. The reductions were performed relative to a query that does not contain any places (as e.g. deadlock) in order to see the maximal possible reduction. If a query contains many places, the number of applications of the reduction rules may be possibly lower. The data show that out of the 261 nets, 118 of them were reducible, with an average reduction of 35 % of the net size (measured as the number of places plus the number of transitions). Some nets are reducible by only a few percent while others allow a reduction of up to 95 % (e.g. the house construction net). As reducing the size of a net can imply up to an exponential decrease in the size of the state-space, the effect of the reductions significantly contributes to the performance of our verification engine.

6   Tool Implementation

The verification engine for P/T nets, employing the techniques described in earlier sections, has been efficiently implemented in C++ and made publicly available as a part of the tool suite TAPAAL [4]. It includes a GUI for drawing the nets, graphical query creation dialog and advanced debugging (simulation) options. The tool allows us to import the MCC competition nets in PNML format as well as the cardinality and deadlock queries, and process them either individually or in a batch processing mode.

Regarding the implementation details, our experiments showed that the incidence matrix representation of a Petri net is preferred over the linked list representation as even though on larger nets the linked list representation preserves some space, it is remarkably slower [6] (likely due to the cache coherence issues). Finally, it is important to remark that for larger nets with several hundreds of places and transitions, an efficient implementation of the structural reduction rules is of great importance as a naive coding of the rules using up to four nested loops (like the rule in Fig. 3a) will use too much of the preprocessing time.

7   Conclusion

We described the most essential verification techniques used in the P/T net engine of TAPAAL. Each of the techniques has a significant performance effect, as documented by a number of experiments run on the nets and queries from MCC'15. We believe that it is the combination of these techniques and a relatively simple explicit search engine that contributed to the second place of our tool in the years 2014 and 2015. We are currently working on optimizing the performance of the successor generator, space optimizations and extending the reachability analysis to the full CTL model checking.

Acknowledgments. The fourth author is partially affiliated with FI MU, Brno, Czech Republic.

References

1. Andersen, M., Gatten Larsen, H., Srba, J., Grund Sørensen, M., Haahr Taankvist, J.: Verification of liveness properties on closed timed-arc Petri nets. In: Kučera, A., Henzinger, T.A., Nešetřil, J., Vojnar, T., Antoš, D. (eds.) MEMICS 2012. LNCS, vol. 7721, pp. 69–81. Springer, Heidelberg (2013)
2. Berkelaar, M., Eikland, K., Notebaert, P.: lp_solve 5.5, open source (mixed-integer) linear programming system. Software, 1 May 2004. http://lpsolve.sourceforge.net/5.5
3. David, A., Behrmann, G., Larsen, K.G., Yi, W.: A tool architecture for the next generation of UPPAAL. In: Aichernig, B.K. (ed.) Formal Methods at the Crossroads. From Panacea to Foundational Support. LNCS, vol. 2757, pp. 352–366. Springer, Heidelberg (2003)
4. David, A., Jacobsen, L., Jacobsen, M., Jørgensen, K.Y., Møller, M.H., Srba, J.: TAPAAL 2.0: integrated development environment for timed-arc Petri nets. In: Flanagan, C., König, B. (eds.) TACAS 2012. LNCS, vol. 7214, pp. 492–497. Springer, Heidelberg (2012)
5. David, A., Jacobsen, L., Jacobsen, M., Srba, J.: A forward reachability algorithm for bounded timed-arc Petri nets. In: SSV 2012, vol. 102, EPTCS, pp. 125–140. Open Publishing Association (2012)
6. Dyhr, J., Johannsen, M., Kaufmann, I., Nielsen, S.M. Multi-core model checking of Petri nets with precompiled successor generation. Bacherol thesis. Department of Computer Science, Aalborg University, Denmark (2015)
7. Esparza, J., Melzer, S.: Verification of safety properties using integer programming: beyond the state equation. Form. Meth. Syst. Design **16**, 159–189 (2000)
8. Heitmann, F., Moldt, D.: Petri nets tool database (2015). http://www.informatik.uni-hamburg.de/TGI/PetriNets/tools/db.html
9. Jacobsen, L., Jacobsen, M., Møller, M.H., Srba, J.: Verification of timed-arc Petri nets. In: Černá, I., Gyimóthy, T., Hromkovič, J., Jefferey, K., Králović, R., Vukolić, M., Wolf, S. (eds.) SOFSEM 2011. LNCS, vol. 6543, pp. 46–72. Springer, Heidelberg (2011)
10. Kordon, F., Garavel, H., Hillah, L.-M., Hulin-Hubard, F., Linard, A., Beccuti, M., Evangelista, S., Hamez, A., Lohmann, N., Lopez, E., Paviot-Adet, E., Rodriguez, C., Rohr, C., Srba, J.: HTML results from the Model Checking Contest @ Petri Net (2014 edn.) (2014). http://mcc.lip6.fr/2014
11. Kordon, F., Garavel, H., Hillah, L.M., Hulin-Hubard, F., Linard, A., Beccuti, M., Hamez, A., Lopez-Bobeda, E., Jezequel, L., Meijer, J., Paviot-Adet, E., Rodriguez, C., Rohr, C., Srba, J., Thierry-Mieg, Y., Wolf, K.: Complete Results for the 2015 Edition of the Model Checking Contest (2015). http://mcc.lip6.fr/2015/
12. Murata, T.: State equation, controllability, and maximal matching of Petri nets. IEEE Trans. Autom. Contr. **22**(3), 412–416 (1977)
13. Murata, T.: Petri nets: properties, analysis and applications. Proc. IEEE **77**(4), 541–580 (1989)
14. Murata, T., Koh, J.Y.: Reduction and expansion of live and safe marked graphs. IEEE Trans. Circ. Syst. **27**(1), 68–70 (1980)
15. Petri, C.A.: Kommunikation mit Automaten. Ph.D. thesis, Darmstadt (1962)

Author Index

Printed in the United States
By Bookmasters